Global Perspectives on the Rule of Law

Global Perspectives on the Rule of Law is a collection of original research on the rule-of-law from a panel of leading economists, political scientists, legal scholars, sociologists, and historians. The chapters critically analyze the meaning and foundations of the rule-of-law and its relationship to economic and democratic development, challenging many of the underlying assumptions guiding the burgeoning field of rule-of-law development. The combination of jurisprudential, quantitative, historical/comparative, and theoretical analyzes seeks to chart a new course in scholarship on the rule-of-law: the volume as a whole takes seriously the role of law in pursuing global justice, while confronting the complexity of instituting the rule-of-law and delivering its promised benefits.

Written for scholars, practitioners, and policymakers, *Global Perspectives* offers a unique combination of jurisprudential and empirical research that will be provocative and relevant to those who are attempting to understand and advance the rule-of-law globally. The chapters progress from broad questions regarding current rule of development efforts and the concept of rule-of-law to more specific issues pertaining to economic and democratic development. Specific countries, such as China, India, and seventeenth-century England and the Netherlands, serve as case studies in some chapters, while broad global surveys feature in other chapters. Indeed, this impressive scope of research ushers in the next generation of scholarship in this area.

James J. Heckman shared the Nobel Prize in Economics in 2000. He is the Henry Schultz Distinguished Service Professor of Economics at the University of Chicago and a Research Professor at the American Bar Foundation.

Robert L. Nelson is the Director of the American Bar Foundation, the MacCrate Research Chair in the Legal Profession at the ABF, and Professor of Sociology and Law at Northwestern University.

Lee Cabatingan is a Research Associate at the American Bar Foundation and a graduate student in the department of Anthropology at the University of Chicago.

Law, development and globalization

Series Editor: Julio Faundez
University of Warwick

During the past decades, a substantial transformation of law and legal institutions in developing countries has taken place. Whether prompted by market-based policies or the international human rights movement, by the relentless advance of the process of globalization or the successive waves of democratization, no area of law has been left untouched. The aim of this series is to promote cross-disciplinary dialogue and cooperation among scholars and development practitioners interested in understanding the theoretical and practical implications of the momentous legal changes taking place in developing countries.

Other titles in the series:

State Violence and Human Rights: State Officials in the South
Andrew M. Jefferson and Steffen Jensen (eds)

The Political Economy of Government Auditing: Financial Governance and the Rule of Law in Latin America and Beyond
Carlos Santiso

Forthcoming titles in the series:

Marginalized Communities and Access to Justice
Yash Ghai and Jill Cottrell (eds) (2009)

Law in the Pursuit of Development: Principles into Practice?
Amanda Perry-Kesaris (ed.) (2010)

Social Movements, Law and the Politics of Land Reform
George Meszaros (2010)

Governance through Development: Poverty Reduction Strategies and the Disciplining of Third World States
Celine Tan (2010)

Global Perspectives on the Rule of Law

Edited by James J. Heckman,
Robert L. Nelson, and Lee Cabatingan

Routledge
Taylor & Francis Group
LONDON AND NEW YORK

First published 2010
by Routledge
2 Park Square, Milton Park, Abingdon, Oxon, OX14 4RN

Simultaneously published in the USA and Canada
by Routledge
270 Madison Avenue, New York, NY 10016

A GlassHouse book

Routledge is an imprint of the Taylor & Francis Group, an informa business

Typeset in Sabon by
Taylor & Francis Books
Printed and bound in Great Britain by
CPI Antony Rowe, Chippenham, Wiltshire

British Library Cataloguing in Publication Data
A catalogue record for this book is available from the British Library

Library of Congress Cataloging in Publication Data
Global perspectives on the rule-of-law / edited by James J. Heckman, Robert L. Nelson, and Lee Cabatingan.
p. cm.
"A GlassHouse book."

ISBN-13: 978-0-415-49955-2 (hbk)
ISBN-10: 0-415-49955-0 (hbk)
ISBN-13: 978-0-203-87059-4 (ebk)
ISBN-10: 0-203-87059-X (ebk)

1. Rule of law. I. Heckman, James J. (James Joseph) II. Nelson, Robert L., 1952–
III. Cabatingan, Lee.
K3171.G58 2009
340'.11 – dc22

2009010624

ISBN10: 0-415-49955-0 (hbk)
ISBN10: 0-203-87059-X (ebk)

ISBN13: 978-0-415-49955-2 (hbk)
ISBN13: 978-0-203-87059-4 (ebk)

We dedicate this book to the memory of Thomas S. Amorde
(1981 to 2008)
First year law student, University of Chicago

His intellectual intensity and dedication to creating knowledge about law shaped the origins of this project

Contents

Illustrations

Figures

Tables

Notes on contributors

Franklin Allen is the Nippon Life Professor of Finance and Economics and Co-Director of the Financial Institutions Center at the Wharton School of the University of Pennsylvania. He has published extensively on the topics of financial crises, comparative financial systems, and other related issues.

Amrit Amirapu is a doctoral student of Economics at Boston University. He holds a Master Degree in Quantitative Methods in the Social Sciences from Columbia University and conducts research as part of the Millennium Villages Project of the Earth Institute at Columbia University. He studies the intersection of development with institutions, agricultural productivity, and empirical microeconomics.

Lee Cabatingan is a Research Associate at the American Bar Foundation, a former attorney, and a current graduate student in the Department of Anthropology at the University of Chicago. She studies legal anthropology of socialist states.

Thomas Carothers is Vice President for Studies at the Carnegie Endowment for International Peace. He is author or editor of many books and articles on democracy promotion and rule-of-law assistance.

Brad Epperly is a doctoral candidate in the Department of Political Science at the University of Washington, Seattle, studying comparative politics and political economy. His primary research interest is the development of effective institutions in transitioning societies, especially Eastern Europe and the former Soviet Union.

Yash Ghai, Emeritus Professor at the University of Hong Kong, is the head of the Constitution Advisory Support Group of the United Nations Development Program in Nepal. He has also served as a Special Representative of the UN Secretary-General in Cambodia on human rights.

Tom Ginsburg is a Professor of Law at the University of Chicago, a Co-Director of the Comparative Constitutions Project, and a Co-Director of the Center on Law and Globalization. His work focuses on comparative and international law from an interdisciplinary perspective.

Antara Haldar is a doctoral student of law at Trinity College at the University of Cambridge and a Research Fellow at Columbia University. Her research interests extend to law and development, legal theory, women and the law, and international law.

Terence C. Halliday is Co-Director of the Center on Law and Globalization, a joint collaboration of the American Bar Foundation and the University of Illinois College of Law, and Research Professor at the American Bar Foundation. He specializes in the globalization of law, markets, and political liberalism.

Ron Harris is a Professor of Law and Legal History at Tel-Aviv University. A leading economic historian of the Industrial Revolution in England, his current research focuses on the early history of the English and Dutch East India Companies.

James J. Heckman, a Nobel Laureate, is the Henry Schultz Distinguished Service Professor of Economics at the University of Chicago. His recent research includes evaluation of social programs, econometric models of discrete choice and longitudinal data, the economics of the labor market, and alternative models of the distribution of income.

Timur Kuran is a Professor of Economics and Political Science and the Gorter Family Professor of Islamic Studies at Duke University. His recent publications focus on the economic history of the Middle East, the economic and political effects of Islam, and contemporary Islamization movements.

Margaret Levi is the Jere L. Bacharach Professor of International Studies in the Department of Political Science at the University of Washington, Seattle, and a Professor of Politics at the US Studies Centre at the University of Sydney.

Robert L. Nelson is the Director of the American Bar Foundation, the MacCrate Research Chair in the Legal Profession at the ABF, and Professor of Sociology and Law at Northwestern University. His research focuses on the practice of law and the relationship between law and social inequality.

Katharina Pistor is the Michael I. Sovern Professor of Law at Columbia Law School and researches issues related to comparative law and institutional development. She has conducted several studies on the legal framework for the evolving corporate governance regime in transitional economies.

Jun "QJ" Qian is a Professor in the Finance Department at the Carroll School of Management at Boston College and a Research Fellow at the Wharton Financial Institutions Center. His recent research addresses how financial contracts connect law and institutions with economic and financial outcomes.

Amartya Sen is a Nobel Laureate economist at Harvard University and recognized authority on development and social justice. Amongst his substantial contributions to these fields is his theory of social justice based on human capabilities.

Barry R. Weingast is a Senior Fellow at the Hoover Institution and the Ward C. Krebs Family Professor in the Department of Political Science at Stanford University. He is an expert in political economy and public policy, the political foundation of markets and economic reform, US politics, and regulation.

Acknowledgments

This volume would not have been written if not for the vision and leadership of William Neukom, President of the American Bar Association in 2007–8, who created the World Justice Project and included original scholarship as one of the pillars of that effort. Bill had the wisdom and courage to charge James Heckman and myself with assembling the best minds in the fields of law, economics, international relations, politics, and sociology to examine fundamental questions about the forces that lead to the rule-of-law and the consequences that flow from rule-of-law systems.

Once we were given the resources to proceed, we were ably assisted by Thomas S. Amorde, in whose memory this volume is dedicated. Thomas passed away while completing his first year of law school at the University of Chicago. Other key contributors were Steve Hoffman, Eileen Gallagher, and others at the American Bar Foundation; Claudia Dumas, the extraordinary Executive Director of the World Justice Project, who arranged funding for our efforts and was a constant intellectual sounding board; the staff of the World Justice Project, including Susanna Brown, Rose Murray, and others; the professional staff of the American Bar Association, who are too numerous to mention but who include Karl Camillucci and Katy Englehart; and the very talented and committed members of the planning committee of the World Justice Project, which was chaired by William Hubbard, and included Larry Bailey, Thomas Hayward, James Silkenat, R. William Ide III, Robert Grey, Deborah Enix-Ross, Carolyn Lamm, Mark Agrast, J. Anthony Patterson, William Allen, Stephen Zack, Llewellyn Pritchard, Roderick Matthews, and many others. We are very thankful to the William and Flora Hewlett Foundation, the Ford Foundation, and the Bill & Melinda Gates Foundation, who supported specific components of the scholarship program.

Despite the strong support from the American Bar Association and the World Justice Project for the scholarly efforts included here and in the companion volume on access to justice, the views expressed in these chapters are those only of the authors themselves and do not reflect the positions of our sponsors or funding agencies.

Finally we want to thank the authors who came together to take seriously questions about the rule-of-law, who quickly produced a set of original research papers, and who have been wonderfully responsive to the suggestions of the editors. It has been enormously exciting intellectually to work with scholars of such stature in law and social science. We hope the relationships we have forged in this collaboration may lay the basis for future endeavors to advance objective and rigorous analyses of the origins and consequences of the rule of law.

Robert L. Nelson
James J. Heckman
Lee Cabatingan
Chicago, Illinois
December 2008

A preface and an introduction

Robert L. Nelson and Lee Cabatingan

The genesis of Global Perspectives on the Rule of Law

Initially and broadly referred to as "rule-of-law scholarship," the research in this volume was catalyzed by the equally broadly titled "World Justice Project," a "multinational, multidisciplinary initiative to strengthen the rule-of-law worldwide" (American Bar Association 2008). As part of its mission, the World Justice Project sought to generate new scholarship on the rule-of-law that would (again, stated broadly) (1) advance the understanding of the processes that lead to and impede the development of the rule-of-law in different national contexts, and (2) advance the understanding of the contributions that the rule of law can make to reducing poverty, violence, and corruption, and increasing education and health. Given the complexity and variety of issues falling within this directive, the Project quickly settled on a strategy of organizing groups of scholars to examine specific aspects of the rule of law, rather than attempt a single research statement.

The resulting two volumes of conference papers prepared for the World Justice Forum held in Vienna in July 2008 are key elements of this scholarly effort. The first volume, which, as noted above, was informally called "rule-of-law scholarship," has evolved into *Global Perspectives on the Rule of Law*. It explores foundational questions and debates on the rule of law, with special emphasis on the relationship between the rule-of-law and economic and political development. The second volume, *Marginalized Communities and Access to Justice* (Ghai and Cottrell forthcoming), focuses on access to justice and the particular challenges that traditionally marginalized social groups face in attempting to achieve justice through formal and informal justice systems. Born from the same origins, these volumes have been published concurrently and, together, offer a wide expanse of new research on the rule of law that will hopefully stimulate and encourage the next generation of scholarship in this area.

In the introduction to this volume we hope to provide a rough outline of the concept of the rule-of-law, allowing the following chapters to fill out this sketch through the authors' research and differing perspectives. We also endeavor to identify some of the themes that have brought together this group of authors and have guided the organization of this book. Indeed, while the breadth of issues, regions, and academic fields covered in this volume are impressive, significant overarching messages can be extracted from this body of work. In this way, we view this project as an important contribution to both micro-level and macro-level analyses of rule-of-law. The "global" of *Global Perspectives*, therefore, should be taken to represent two aspects of this project: the diverse, multifaceted research reflective of the diverse, multifaceted world community, as well as the universality of the themes that arise from the totality of this work.

Defining the rule-of-law

From the outset it is important to recognize that the rule-of-law can be defined in many different ways for different purposes. Judith Sklar, the noted jurisprudential scholar, has observed that the term has been used by everyone from social democrats to conservatives to authoritarian rulers, and is therefore in danger of becoming meaningless (Sklar 1987). Despite this, the use of the term is unavoidable in policy and scholarly circles. Indeed, the various ways in which the rule-of-law is defined have been the subject of ongoing discussions amongst the contributors to this book.

Offering a broad framework, Thomas Carothers notes in Chapter 1 that there are at least two concepts of the rule of law circulating: one that emphasizes the procedural aspects of a rule-of-law system (such as independent courts), and one that insists that the rule-of-law provides elements of substantive justice. History contains many examples of legal systems that offered procedural elements of the rule-of-law but denied substantive justice: the slave era in the United States, apartheid in South Africa, to name but two. If the rule-of-law must guarantee substantive justice, how far should that principle go? Does it mandate more than equality of opportunity?

The divergence between these two versions of the rule-of-law is sometimes referred to as "thin" versus "thick" rule-of-law. Brian Tamanaha has suggested that this simple dichotomy is not quite so clear and can better be understood as a progression along which both formal and substantive aspects of the rule-of-law can be "thinner" or "thicker" (Tamanaha 2004: 91). Beginning at the "thinner" end, formal law may take the shape of "rule-by-law," wherein law articulates state power. Moving along the continuum, formal law may progress to "formal legality" and, eventually, to the "thicker" end of the spectrum by constituting "democracy and legality" (ibid.). Similarly, substantive justice may provide a thin version of "individual rights" in property, contract, and so forth, develop into an intermediate form of "rights to human dignity," and progress finally to the thick version of "social welfare rights," which would entail substantive equality, preservation of community, and so on (ibid.).

A related concern is whether the terminology of the rule-of-law contains an effort to impose a Western or perhaps even a United States perspective of law on the rest of the world. Obviously, different cultures and different legal traditions define law and its place in society differently. It would be wrongheaded to equate the rule of law with a particular legal tradition's prescriptions for the character and role of legal institutions. Nonetheless, it may be possible to build a definition of the rule of law around a central tenet of Western and non-Western traditions, namely that law imposes limits on the exercise of power by government and private interests (Tamanaha 2004: 137 et seq.). Moreover, as one reads the chapters in this volume and those collected in *Marginalized Communities and Access to Justice* (Ghai and Cottrell forthcoming), one finds marginalized groups in many non-Western contexts invoking the rule of law. For these groups, law is seen as a mechanism for delivering justice within their local situation. At a pragmatic level, then, despite a lack of consensus on all the components of the rule of law, there is some set of core principles in the concept that is not solely a Western creation (see, e.g., Sen, Chapter 3 in this volume).

As will be evident, the following chapters do not attempt to utilize, create, or agree upon a single definition of the rule-of-law. Rather, different authors define rule-of-law in their own terms, in a way that makes sense for their own research projects. From a tool for comparison (e.g. Kuran, Chapter 4), to an end goal (e.g. Weingast, Chapter 2), to a means to another end (e.g. Pistor *et al.*, Chapter 11), the broad spectrum of what may be meant when the concept of "rule-of-law" is invoked is well represented here. In part, it is this flexibility – even ambiguity – of rule-of-law that makes it a fascinating topic of research.

Assessing current rule-of-law development efforts

Part I of this volume examines the celebrity status that rule-of-law has recently achieved – where it is simultaneously viewed as the key to democracy, the road to development, and the formidable opponent to authoritarianism. Amidst this fervor, Thomas Carothers offers a staid analysis of the trends in rule-of-law development. His contribution sets the tone of the book by highlighting the frenzied pace of rule-of-law reform projects and providing a much-needed critical eye. Carothers argues that the pervasive lack of an analytical stance in rule-of-law development projects frequently leads to "temptations to believe certain things about the rule-of-law and its place on the international stage that are misleading and sometimes unhelpful" (p. 19). It is to these temptations, four in particular, that Carothers devotes his chapter. And it is to localized renditions of these temptations that many of the other authors direct their attention.

In this way, Carothers' words are particularly instructive as one reads the chapters included in Parts III and IV of this volume. The temptations identified by Carothers – consensus, reductionism, sequencing, and ease – can be identified in many of the case studies featured in these chapters. Thomas Ginsburg, in Chapter 8, for example, draws into question the tendency towards a belief in sequencing, something Carothers describes as a (misguided) idea that transitional countries must build the rule of law before taking steps toward democratization. As Ginsburg illustrates, quite often the exact opposite occurs; a transition to democracy precedes the development of an independent court system, an institution classically associated with the rule-of-law.

Similar to Carothers, Barry Weingast provides a sobering assessment of rule-of-law development efforts and wholly dispels the possibility of belief that rule of law is somehow easy – another of the temptations identified by Carothers. Weingast asks the question, "Why do developing countries prove so resistant to the rule-of-law[?]" (p. 28).

Indeed, as Weingast progresses through his analysis of the difficulties faced in achieving rule-of-law in developing nations, the challenges seem nearly insurmountable. Adopting an approach that he developed with Douglass C. North and John Joseph Wallis (the NWW approach), Weingast provides a novel explanation for why it has been so difficult to successfully transplant various rule-of-law institutions from developed nations to developing nations. Unfortunately, Weingast concludes, this new understanding does not bring with it an easy solution. Under the NWW approach, which divides the world's societies into two broad social orders based on their means for controlling violence, a society must transition from one social order to the other in order to achieve rule of law. This transition, Weingast argues, is incredibly difficult, highly unlikely, and historically remarkable. He points out that very few, mostly European, states have successfully navigated this transformation, a success rate that, no doubt, suggests a bleak future for rule-of-law development projects.

Global justice and the world community

Part II also focuses on larger issues concerning the rule-of-law and includes contributions by Amartya Sen (Chapter 3) and Timur Kuran (Chapter 4). Though neither author makes it his explicit project, both chapters whittle away at the idea that the rule of law is a Western creation by identifying concepts in other cultures that share many of the same or similar ideals. Both authors also highlight the necessity of being able to assess or compare the realized justness in a given society, with Sen and Kuran each arguing that true justice may not be achieved through the mere provision of tangible things – whether legal institutions, increased incomes, or written laws and constitutions. For *nyaya*, in Sen's words, or rule of law, in Kuran's chapter, to be achieved, there must be something more. In many ways, it is this "something more" that several of the contributors to this volume seek to identify and explore. Weingast (Chapter 2), for example, argues that total social transformation is what is missing, while Levi and Epperly (Chapter 9) identify principled principals as the necessary ingredient for establishing rule-of-law. Sen and Kuran do an excellent job at introducing this inquiry.

Sen is perhaps best known for his work on the capability approach, a concept he first introduced in a lecture delivered at Stanford University in 1979 (1980). The novelty and the strength of the capability approach is the shift of attention onto "'basic capabilities': a person being able to do certain things" (Sen 1980: 218). Indeed, capability theory is primarily and ultimately concerned with the *actual* freedom that a person can exercise in choosing between different ways of living valued by that particular individual (Sen 1990b: 114). The focus is not on the specific bundle of life functionings, with "functionings" defined as "parts of the state of a person – in particular the various things that he or she manages to do or be in leading a life" (Sen 1993: 31), that a person ultimately achieves, but on the freedom that that individual had to choose a certain assemblage of functionings (Sen 2004a: 334–35; 1993: 38–39; 1990b: 116). In other words, it is not the achievement of a certain life, but the freedom to choose a life composed of personally valuable functionings. "It is this actual freedom that is represented by the person's 'capability' to achieve various alternative combinations of functionings, or doings and beings" (Sen 1990b: 114).

In the decades that followed Sen's introduction of the capability approach, it has developed into a significant theory used to analyze issues of human development, human rights, equality, justice, and other social and economic concerns. In his contribution to this volume, Sen integrates the capability approach into his argument for a new theory of global justice. He frames his chapter with a discussion of the classical Sanskrit words *niti* and *nyaya*. *Niti*, he explains, is often used by Indian legal theorists to designate institutional propriety, something Sen acknowledges is important to a conception of justice. It is *nyaya*, however, that is viewed as the critical objective of justice; it represents "a more comprehensive concept of realized justice" (p. 55). While *niti* and *nyaya* may complement each other, Sen argues that *nyaya* and the comprehensive notion of justice that it encompasses must be central to discussions of world justice and the rule-of-law.

In formulating a theory of global justice, Sen critically engages John Rawls's theory of justice as fairness. Sen has previously used Rawls's work as a springboard for his own arguments (see, e.g., Sen 1990a and 2002). Here, Sen poses four broad questions as an outline to his argument that Rawls's theory of justice as fairness is deeply problematic and fundamentally flawed in that it seeks *niti*, rather than *nyaya*.

Critical to Sen's theory of global justice and his critique of Rawls is that a theory of global justice must be practically useful and grounded in reality. Through it, for example, one must be able to compare two imperfectly just societies and still be able to determine which is more just (albeit not *perfectly* just). And, explicitly invoking the capability approach, Sen argues that a theory of global justice must take into account "*actual opportunities* of living" (p. 68). The use of capability theory, he argues, extends "the reach of the evaluative exercise, especially for world justice" and the pursuit of *nyaya* (p. 68).

Kuran, in his contribution, also emphasizes the necessity of comparison when assessing issues of law and justice. Kuran, however, does not compare one society to another, as Sen suggests might be possible, but explores the comparative potential of rule-of-law itself. Specifically, he evaluates Islamic law – as it existed in centuries past and as it exists now – with regard to its compatibility with the rule-of-law. He identifies four primary features of rule-of-law (government accountability, equal access to justice and the political process, efficient judicial and political systems, and the protection of fundamental human rights) and systematically addresses the existence, disappearance, or absence of these principles in Islamic law. His chapter serves as both a historical exposition on the foundations of Islamic law and a revelatory piece of research on contemporary Islamic law and politics.

Through this project, Kuran illustrates the historic existence of rule-of-law principles in a non-Western culture. At the same time, he shows how these principles have been buried under the weight of time, have been lost through antiquated institutions, and have been, for many years, divorced from actual practice. Kuran's research thus carries with it an important message: in the quest to establish rule-of-law, not only is it problematic to transplant a legal system from one state to another, but it is equally difficult to introduce a legal system from one time period to another. As Kuran puts it, "The imposition of Islamic law on a society in any one of its pre-modern formulations would result in massive failures, at least as measured by the extent to which the rule-of-law principles are satisfied" (p. 87).

Rule of law and economic development

The role of the rule of law in economic development has become a subject of central importance in modern economics (see, e.g., Haggard *et al.* 2008; Dam 2006; Glaeser *et al.* 2004; Glaeser and Shleifer 2002; Weingast 1995; North 1990). Daniel Kaufmann, the former chief economist at the World Bank Institute and a participant in our scholars group, has measured several aspects of governance, including rule-of-law, over time and across more than 200 countries. Based on these indicators, Kaufmann and colleagues assert that by moving one standard deviation ahead on the rule-of-law index, a nation's GDP increases by 300 percent (Kaufmann *et al.* 2007a; *Economist* 2008). Bolstered by such studies, there is a consensus that levels of economic development are positively correlated with more robust legal systems.

But there have been active debates about the effects of legal origins (whether common-law systems offer comparative advantages to civil-law systems) and the direction of causation between economic and legal development. Historical and cross-national comparisons loom large in this literature, as scholars have sought to explain seeming anomalies of nations that have achieved rapid rates of economic growth while not developing all aspects of a rule-of-law system.

The chapters in Part III of this volume represent different perspectives within these debates. Using different methods, examining different empirical cases, and reaching different conclusions, there is agreement that to some degree "institutions matter" to economic development. However, how much they matter, in what ways they matter, and in which direction – economic growth or economic regression – they matter, differs dramatically, based on the specific circumstances of specific countries and cultures. Institutions and their alternatives are at the heart of these analyses.

Perhaps the most important set of institutions relating to equity and opportunity within developed nations are those associated with the welfare state. Like other topics covered in this book, the welfare state, complete with its institutions and policies, has become a concept that is tightly intertwined with the notion of the rule-of-law, but exists on a foundation of misleading or missing data and analyses. James Heckman, in Chapter 5, notes that the promises of the welfare state, such as the right to economic security, are often perceived to be integrally related to and even conflated with the promises of the rule-of-law. Thus, as states seek to establish one, they often also expect to benefit from the other. These assumptions, however, are made without a full understanding of what constitutes a successfully functioning welfare state.

Addressing this void, Heckman examines variations among modern welfare states and their effects on economic performance from the 1980s through 2006. The overly generalized "welfare state" – so closely associated with the rule-of-law – does not necessarily lead to steady economic growth, decreased inequality, or increased social inclusion, leading Heckman to caution against an uncritical embrace of the welfare policies of European states. Instead, in the spirit of Carothers' call for an analytical stance, Heckman looks at individual features of specific welfare states. He argues that those systems and features of systems "that respect the basic incentives of economic life are the most successful" (p. 116).

Heckman's chapter adds several innovations to discussions of the relationship between rule-of-law, modern welfare-state systems, and economic development. He notes that there is considerable variation in types of welfare systems and describes the major features of four types (Nordic/corporatist; Continental; Mediterranean; and Anglo-Saxon). Second, he argues that it is critical to use appropriate indicators of economic performance that can show the impact of incentives. He criticizes the existing literature which points to the superior performance of Nordic/corporatist systems. Heckman insists that when employment rates are corrected for public employment programs, the Nordic advantage disappears. He concludes that in a global economy, the nation states that will best succeed are those which invest in educational systems (such as Ireland, Japan, and the United States) and which provide incentives for economic participation. He warns that efforts to preserve some aspects of the welfare state will benefit some segments of society at the expense of others.

Moving away from the relative sophistication of welfare policy and its relationship to economic growth, come even more fundamental questions regarding rule-of-law and economic development. Do China and India, for example, with their surging economies, illustrate a strong positive correlation between rule-of-law and economic vitality? Franklin Allen and Jun Qian (Chapter 6) argue that they do not – even more, Allen and Qian argue that it is *because of* the lack of a pervasive legal culture, legal institutions, and written laws that China and India have experienced such tremendous growth. This environment allows businesses to utilize "nonlegal" avenues of contract enforcement, dispute resolution, and property protection, such as age-old mechanisms based on trust and reputation. According to the authors, for these states, where technological advances and economic changes occur rapidly and frequently, these nonlegal mechanisms allow for quick adaptation to changing circumstances and avoid the rent-seeking behavior and barriers to competition that sometimes accompany more fully developed legal systems. Thus, while a rule-of-law culture may promote sustained and steady economic growth in developed, stable countries, it may not necessarily do so for more volatile states in economic flux.

Allen and Qian's argument will certainly provoke further debate about the role of law in China and India. Traditional law and society scholars will suggest that Allen and Qian may exaggerate the role of formal law in business in the United States (Macaulay 1963). We might also question whether Allen and Qian have given adequate attention to other factors driving growth in China and India, such as relatively low labor costs, powerful state actors in China, and vibrant market institutions in India. Pierre Landry's work, which was presented at an earlier World Justice Project meeting on the rule-of-law, directly examines the quite dramatic growth of intellectual-property law in China (Landry 2008). Landry suggests that the Chinese intellectual-property system has become much more effective in the last 15 years, in part due to a strategy of devoting greater resources to a smaller number of actors who generate large numbers of patent applications. Eva Pils' work on the property rights of Chinese peasants, which was presented as part of the scholarship on access to justice, offers a very different view of the need for law in the Chinese context (Pils 2008). Without legal protection, peasants will suffer serious harm to their livelihood. And China may experience more widespread civil unrest. Thus, what may be good for the economy may not be so for other aspects of the nation-state – something, undoubtedly, that must be considered in developing rule-of-law projects and measuring their success.

Ron Harris contributes to the discussion regarding when, where, why, and which legal institutions can make a difference in the economic growth of a state. His theoretically significant and historically rich case study in Chapter 7 elaborates on the complexity of the relationship between law, finance, and economic growth. By comparing two of history's most notable corporations, the Dutch East India Company and the English East India Company of the seventeenth and early eighteenth centuries, Harris provides an important test of prominent theories about law and development and illustrates how difficult it has been to pinpoint the reason or reasons for economic development. While law and legal institutions certainly played a role in the historic emergence of a secondary market in company shares – the focus of Harris' study – so too did various historical contingencies, the strength of the state, the source of the law, and many other factors. Contrary to the predictions of the legal origins theory, which holds that common-law legal systems facilitated economic development, Harris establishes that the Dutch, working in a continental legal system, successfully established a large private corporation almost a century before the English did the same. Moreover, both the Dutch and the English markets grew up on the margins of the legal system, in merchant and maritime law, not within the core province of judge-made law. Harris also uses his historical comparison to add proof to the North and Weingast thesis that for private markets to succeed there must be credible commitments that the state will have limited powers to confiscate wealth. Both the Dutch and English cases achieved these credible commitments, albeit in a different fashion. And the relative weakness of the English state, compared to the Dutch state, forced the development of a more innovative and cooperative market that proved more effective at long-term growth.

In suggesting the contemporary policy implications of his analysis, Harris provides a message that has run throughout this volume. While he cautions that the political and economic environment of the seventeenth century is very different from the challenges that lesser-developed countries face today, he suggests that law matters to the development of business organizations and stock markets. But law reform is contingent on other social and political conditions. When designing business institutions there often are tradeoffs between long-term and short-term growth, smaller-scale voluntary cooperation and large-scale coerced investment, and so forth.

> Because political and social environments and institutional baselines are often different in different LDCs and emerging economies, the same size cannot fit all. It is wise to recognize that conditions are different and that preferences in tradeoffs are different in different localities, and accordingly there should be plurality in policy recommendations.
>
> (Harris, this volume: 169)

The chapters included in Part III suggest the importance of ongoing research on the relationship between legal institutions and economic growth – a relationship that many simply assume is invariably positive. While research does suggest that stronger rule-of-law institutions will promote economic growth in most contexts, these authors caution against the wholesale export of legal institutions. It is critical to appreciate that variations in legal forms, many of which fall within a definition of rule-of-law systems, can affect economic development. The challenge for scholarship is not just to note the positive relationship between rule-of-law and economic growth, but to develop better theories of what kinds of rule-of-law systems better promote development for specific states.

Rule of law and political development

Part IV concludes this volume with an analytical look at the relationship between the rule-of-law and political development. Much of the scholarship relies on historical and comparative analysis to test theories about the conditions under which the rule of law can develop and the conditions that will tend to undermine the rule of law. Institutions are, again, a primary feature in this discussion and play a central role in the analyses of Ginsburg (Chapter 8) and Pistor *et al.* (Chapter 11). The actors – specifically those individuals or groups of individuals who effect the development of rule of law – also garner attention here. Levi and Epperly (Chapter 9), as well as Halliday (Chapter 10), investigate the actual human beings involved in the progression or regression of rule-of-law. On the flip side, those who are acted upon, i.e. the intended recipients of the benefits of rule-of-law, are equally important in the exploration of the relationship between rule-of-law and political development. Pistor *et al.* and Ghai (Chapter 12) turn their attention to these populations.

Thomas Ginsburg opens Part IV with a discussion of the role of courts – an institution frequently viewed as the centerpiece of rule-of-law – in the development of the democracy. The operating assumption, and, therefore, common practice, of many rule-of-law development projects is that it is necessary to establish rule-of-law institutions, such as courts, laws, and constitutions, which can assist in the fostering of a new democracy. This is precisely the temptation of "sequencing" that Carothers addresses. Ginsburg takes a closer look at this relationship – do institutions like courts *really* lead to the development of democracy?

He finds that while they can serve as "upstream triggers for democratization," there are also three other possible roles that courts can play in relation to democracy: "downstream guarantors of authoritarian position;" "downstream democratic consolidators;" or even irrelevant institutions to democratization projects (p. 179). In fact, in contrast to the sequencing temptation, Ginsburg argues that courts are far more likely to play a secondary role in democratic transitions – helping to strengthen democratic consolidation only *after* a transition has been secured. On this point, Ginsburg is careful to recognize the circumstantial and even personal factors that affect the role of courts, noting, "Which role they play, and at what times, depends ultimately on the decisions of individual judges" (p. 191).

Not only must the relationship between institutions and democracy be questioned, but also the relationship between institutions and equality, where a similar temptation of sequencing exists. Framing their research question much like the one asked by Ginsburg, Katharina Pistor, Antara Haldar, and Amrit Amirapu ask: do the institutions associated with rule-of-law necessarily lead to the equality associated with democracy? Their research explores how, within a country, different groups are affected differently by rule-of-law projects. Specifically, they assess whether the laws passed in the name of rule-of-law are directly correlated to the improved status of women, something many quickly (or, as the authors show, *too* quickly) accept as a given.

In approaching this problem, the authors systematically analyze the relation between already existing indices measuring rule-of-law and those measuring gender equality. Their most general, and perhaps most startling, conclusion is that there is "hardly any meaningful correlation" between gender equality and rule-of-law (p. 257). In a world populated by social norms, law, they argue, may simply not be the universally accepted legitimate authority that many have assumed. Similar to Kuran's discussion of Islamic law, the great divide separating law on the books and law in practice challenges the very foundations of many rule-of-law development projects.

Margaret Levi and Brad Epperly (Chapter 9) agree that "[i]nstitutions are not sufficient on their own" to bring about rule-of-law (p. 208). In a sense, too, they agree that social norms underlie the existence of a deeply rooted belief in and commitment to the rule-of-law, and it is the creation and composition of these social norms that is truly important. In order for rule-of-law to develop, something must have instilled in society a legitimating belief in the state, such that public compliance with the law is voluntary and reliable. Levi and Epperly identify "principled principals" acting at the time of the founding or refounding of the state as the critical element in the establishment of the legitimating beliefs that foster rule-of-law.

The principled leader is faced with the daunting task of leading by example in order to encourage the principled behavior of lower-level officials and establish a "common set of values" (p. 208) for the whole population to follow. Thus, while Levi and Epperly see rule-of-law as initially resting on the shoulders of an individual actor, the principled principal must quickly garner the support of the bureaucracy and, ultimately, the commitment of the nation. Institutions, while still important, play only a secondary role by constraining the power of a government that is already at least partially willing to have its power constrained. This analysis should offer fairly straightforward (re)direction to rule-of-law development projects. Specifically, to focus *not* on institutional development in new states, but on the identification, ascension, and success of a principled principal.

Terence Halliday also focuses on the role of various actors in the development, maintenance, or loss of basic legal freedoms associated with political liberalism. Basic legal freedoms, he explains, such as freedom from arbitrary state power, freedom of speech, and property rights, are fundamentally intertwined with notions of rule-of-law. His chapter, thus, directly examines how legal actors, including private lawyers, public lawyers, judges, prosecutors, and legal academics – an array of actors he dubs the "legal complex" – can impact the institutionalization of basic legal freedoms and the development of rule-of-law. Through his analysis and drawing from an impressive volume of historical data (succinctly represented in Table 10.1), Halliday identifies factors that are integral to the creation of a cohesive and comprehensive theory of the mobilization of the legal complex on behalf of political liberalism, basic legal freedoms, and the rule-of-law.

Like that of many of the scholars contributing to this book, Halliday's research confirms that the development of rule-of-law within a state is a complex process about which we are only beginning to theorize. His methodical study contributes to the understanding of the rule-of-law by providing concrete factors that must be considered in discussions of rule-of-law development. His work also highlights the breadth of factors – who, when, where, etc. – that interact to produce varying results with regard to the institutionalization of basic legal freedoms and rule-of-law. Not only must we understand each factor individually, but, as Halliday begins to give shape to an overarching theory, we see that we must also understand the complicated relationships between these factors.

Yash Ghai (Chapter 12) closes the discussion regarding rule-of-law and political development and the volume as a whole by calling attention once more to the human element of these debates. His remarks on the challenges that rule-of-law projects and constitution-building efforts encounter with the rise of ethnic consciousness around the world highlight the changing landscapes that must be successfully navigated. Foundational concepts in the constitutions of liberal states, such as a public/private distinction, citizenship, equality, and human rights, have been wholly reconfigured as claims of ethnicity have come to the fore. Equality, for example, has come to mean a recognition of difference, rather than equality among individuals – a radical departure from the nameless, faceless equality sought after by liberal states. In a multi-ethnic state, citizenship, too, consists of far more than an individual's relationship with the state. Instead, it has come to represent a complex set of relationships.

Because the old models of constitution-making can provide little guidance in this uncharted territory, Ghai explores not only the difference between old and new foundational terms, but also the direction that the constitutions of multi-ethnic states have taken to accommodate these new understandings. Ghai argues that constitutions have had to become works of multi-ethnic negotiation with power vested in communities, rather than individuals. There is no one way to accomplish this and, using examples from around the globe, Ghai illustrates the many variations of multi-ethnic constitutions. As if the rule-of-law and the role of constitutions were not complicated enough, Ghai's work illuminates an even more convoluted road ahead which must take into account the rise in ethnic consciousness.

Conclusion

The World Justice Project scholars program was intended to engage at the highest academic level serious questions about the meaning, sources, impediments to, and consequences of the rule of law. As the complexity of the contributions to this volume show, we have made progress in advancing these inquiries, but the debates about these issues should and will continue.

By no means is the relationship between rule of law and economic development or rule-of-law and political development certain, unidirectional, complete, or fully understood. And the roles of institutions, individual actors, and development agencies within these relationships – topics that are taken up in this volume – are similarly vague. While courts, constitutions, written laws, and other institutions may have the potential to contribute to the building of a rule-of-law society and the development of the economy and democracy, there is some agreement that these institutions cannot succeed without careful forethought, precise tailoring, and a certain degree of luck. Principled leaders must exist and persist, social norms must bend or break, and legal actors must display a level of activism; constitutions must be crafted to address multi-ethnic concerns; and formal legal systems must consider traditional ones. How, when, whether, and to what extent outside development groups should take part in such processes is, at best, barely understood.

Even with a better understanding of all of these elements, Weingast suggests, rule-of-law may still prove to be elusive without an entire social transformation.

It would, however, be contrary to the goals of this project and the hopes of its contributors to allow this body of work to stymie progress in the field of rule-of-law. While anyone who promotes an agenda of social change through the rule-of-law must be sensitive to the great variety of meanings that have been attached to the phrase, we continue to see value in pursuing a rule-of-law framework. It is, as Sen suggests, an expansive concept closely linked to global justice, and one, as Kuran, Pistor, and others illustrate, useful to understanding and comparing societies and legal systems. Indeed, much of the research presented here also acknowledges the positive contributions that law, and more broadly institutions and actors, can make to the creation of societies that are less violent, better educated, healthier, more free, and more prosperous.

Yet, as academic research and practical applications of rule-of-law continue, it is important to keep in mind both the pitfalls – or "temptations" – identified by Carothers and, as the chapters collected here exemplify, our still limited understanding of the rule-of-law and all that it entails. It is this critical stance, one that is too often missing in rule-of-law development projects, which this volume advocates.

Part I

Assessing rule-of-law development

Chapter 1

Rule-of-law temptations

Thomas Carothers

In an article I published in *Foreign Affairs* ten years ago, entitled "The Rule of Law Revival," I called attention to a striking trend – the rise in international policy circles of attention to and concern over strengthening the rule-of-law in countries around the world (Carothers 1998). Suddenly, I wrote, it seemed that talk of the rule-of-law was everywhere and that rule-of-law development was being held out as the answer to a multitude of diverse policy challenges, whether it was how Russia could consolidate its shaky transition away from communism, how China could solidify its meteoric economic growth, or how Mexico could resist the capture of its state institutions by narcotraffickers.

I attributed this noteworthy rise to the fact that the rule-of-law appeared to be crucial to moving forward with both halves of the dual economic and political transition that in the 1990s had become the defining framework for changes in much of the developing world and the post-communist world. That is to say, on the one hand rule-of-law development would facilitate economic transitions to the market model, by helping achieve legal and institutional predictability and efficiency in a variety of areas crucial to the operation of a market economy. And on the other hand, it would help bolster fledgling democratic experiments by undergirding new constitutions, electoral systems, and political and civil rights. Moreover, progress on the rule-of-law would help alleviate the two serious problems – corruption and ordinary crime – whose growing severity in many countries appeared to be the major negative side effects of the many attempted economic and political transitions. In short, I argued, rule-of-law development owed its new prominence in international policy circles to its apparent promise of being what could be called "an elixir of transitions" (ibid.: 99).

In the intervening ten years, international attention to rule-of-law development has only continued and in fact even increased. Political leaders all over assert a commitment to building the rule-of-law. Officials in donor countries express a determination to help support rule-of-law development worldwide and the number of organizations and initiatives dedicated to rule-of-law assistance keeps multiplying. The rule-of-law field continues to radiate an almost constant sense of discovery. Policy actors and aid practitioners keep discovering it and becoming seized with enthusiasm for the rule-of-law. They are often surprised to learn that what seems to them a vital discovery is in fact a relatively late arrival to a revival that has been going on for quite some time.

This continued rise of the rule-of-law star reflects the fact that the connections between the rule-of-law to economic and political development, although perhaps not as straightforward as some early enthusiasts presumed, are real. In the economic domain, the simplistic idea that the rule-of-law automatically helps foster economic growth has come under useful critical scrutiny (see, e.g., Haggard *et al.* 2008). Yet at least some positive link appears plausible and is enough to animate many aid practitioners.

In the political domain, the problems encountered by many countries with regard to democratization have only strengthened the view of many Western policy experts that the rule-of-law is a necessary focus. Faced, for example, with the disappointing slide in Russia toward soft authoritarianism, some Western observers conclude that the West's (and Russia's) mistake was insufficient focus on the rule-of-law early on after the collapse of the Soviet Union. The catastrophic problems in Iraq after the ouster of Saddam Hussein prompted a similar conclusion on the part of some US observers who argued that a greater rule-of-law aid effort should have preceded the democracy-building project. When in Egypt the Muslim Brotherhood made a surprisingly strong showing in the 2005 parliamentary elections, some analysts cautioned that Egypt should not move ahead with a political opening until it first consolidates the rule-of-law.

Moreover, the rule-of-law has also gained further impetus in this decade from the continued advance of globalization. Already by the late 1990s it was becoming clear that globalization tends to increase incentives and even pressures for rule-of-law development both within countries and among countries. Countries seeking a share of the increasing flow of capital and goods across borders find that weak rule-of-law can be an obstacle. Weak legal protection for foreign investors, for example, can discourage foreign direct investment. High levels of crime and corruption may have similar effects. The increasing flow of goods and capital create a need for regulating and managing them, which stimulates rule-of-law development.

Globalization has proven in this decade to be less benign and much less a process of spreading Western norms than many US observers believed or hoped it would be ten years ago. Nevertheless, its continued intensification continues to bolster the need for rule-of-law development in many countries. For many Americans, globalization has come in this decade to be associated with challenges or even threats to the United States, whether it is the rise of new economic powers or the unsettling use of the tools of global communications by Al Qaeda and other terrorist groups. Yet even as globalization changes in character, almost every element of it – whether it is the remarkable increase in flow of digitalized information via the Internet, the diversification of transnational civil society, or the heightened movement of service industries across borders – implies some sort of rule-of-law development as either a facilitator or a counterweight.

In this context of ever-increasing interest and often enthusiasm for rule-of-law development among Western policymakers and aid practitioners, a tendency exists toward uncritical and sometimes wishful thinking about the subject. Some of these lines of thought represent what can be described as temptations, temptations to believe certain things about the rule-of-law and its place on the international stage that are misleading and sometimes unhelpful. At least four such temptations – concerning consensus, reductionism, sequencing, and ease – are identifiable and deserve attention.

Consensus

The degree of apparent international consensus on the value and importance of the rule-of-law is striking. Almost all other parts of the Western donor consensus on what is good for other countries are hotly debated. For example, the desirability of "the Washington consensus" as an economic prescription for developing countries is argued about constantly in both developed and developing countries. What is informally termed "a consensus" is in fact a constant source of controversy. On the political front, although liberal democracy appeared for a time to be gaining near-universal normative acceptance, it is questioned these days, whether by practitioners of "authoritarian capitalism," Bolivarian democracy, Islamic revolutionary democracy, or other alternative political systems. In contrast, almost no leader anywhere is openly against the rule-of-law or will publicly mount an argument that the rule-of-law is a bad idea for their society. And ordinary citizens almost everywhere will respond very positively to commitments by politicians to strengthen the rule-of-law.

This wide consensus of the rule-of-law is impressive. Yet one must be careful about attributing too much significance to it. In the first place, affirmations by powerholders of commitment to advancing the rule-of-law often do not translate into real action. Many leaders in developing or post-communist countries are elected these days on the basis of promises to reduce corruption, restore law and order, and implement other elements of a rule-of-law agenda. In fact, anticorruption has become one of the key issues in electoral campaigns in many countries, developed or developing. Yet these stern promises tend to melt in the heat encountered when new leaders confront the entrenched, countervailing interests that undergird the existing patterns of corruption. And dispiritingly often, the new leaders end up reproducing the old forms of corruption, or inventing their own. Hugo Chávez came to power decrying Venezuela's endemic corruption, yet his rule has come to be marked by equally or even greater corruption. Relatively few citizens of countries in the former Soviet Union, South America, sub-Saharan Africa, South Asia, and elsewhere would say that the apparent global consensus on the importance of the rule-of-law has translated into actual marked improvement of the state of law in their societies.

Second, even to the extent that all the many stated commitments by politicians, donor representatives, and others to the rule-of-law are real, the concept is so capacious that it is open to significantly different interpretations and operational emphases. Sometimes the differences are rooted in ideology. Conservatives often embrace the rule-of-law as a desirable developmental objective because they find in it things they especially value, such as property rights, fair treatment of foreign investors, strong police, and a general emphasis on law and order. Persons on the left read the concept differently. They see in it a focus on rights and on fair and equal treatment for all, a focus that will help boost disadvantaged people and empower citizens generally. Centrists are drawn to the rule-of-law as a technocratic ideal, one that encompasses key elements contributing to good governance, such as governmental accountability, transparency, and anticorruption.

These ideological differences exist both among donor actors supporting rule-of-law development and among persons within the society in question. In Colombia, for example, rule-of-law reform has been intensely politicized for many years. This is true among the various US actors engaged in the subject, which range from the US Department of Justice and the US Agency for International Development to various US human rights groups. It is similarly true within Colombian society itself, where the contending political forces have often disagreed about the best approach to rule-of-law reform.

Differences over the meaning of rule-of-law development are not necessarily always ideologically based. Sometimes they simply reflect varied professional perspectives. When asked to contribute to rule-of-law reform, for example, judges will tend to emphasize the importance of judicial reform. Police will argue for the need to supplement resources for law enforcement. Lawyers will highlight the potentially valuable role of bar associations. Mediation specialists will note the value of increased emphasis on arbitration and mediation. And so forth. Furthermore, different aid organizations that support rule-of-law development also have their own specialties and preferences within the diverse corpus of rule-of-law development activities. Within one country context, different organizations will tend to push for their own varied areas of specialization.[1]

As a result, when diverse national and international actors gather and agree that they are all committed to helping build the rule-of-law in a particular country or context, they usually agree on much less than it initially appears. They may all proceed with a putatively common rule-of-law agenda but in practice pursue quite different preoccupations, either in relative isolation from each other or sometimes at cross purposes.

Reductionism

As international attention to rule-of-law development increased across the 1980s and 1990s, the definition of rule-of-law became more inclusive. Early on, some rule-of-law aid actors, particularly those who came to their work primarily out of a concern for economic development, inclined toward a relatively formalist or proceduralist conception of the rule of law. Such a conception stresses procedural fairness and institutional inefficiency. It leans in the direction of rule *by* law as much as rule *of* law. Over these two decades, however, supporters of a broader conception of the rule-of-law gained ground in international development circles. This broader conception holds that the rule-of-law is about substantive outcomes, not just procedural norms. It views basic political and civil rights as essential to ensuring justice and an integral part of the rule of law[2].

The growing inclusiveness helped tie the rule-of-law agenda together with the democratization agenda. Promoting rule-of-law development entailed supporting the institutionalization of core democratic rights. And supporting democracy helps bolster basic elements of rule-of-law development. Some organizations engaged in rule-of-law support, such as the World Bank, maintained an official neutrality regarding political development. In practice, however, the broadening of their work on the rule-of-law made it increasingly compatible with and sometimes similar to rule-of-law work carried out by organizations that expressly incorporated a pro-democracy rationale.

In this decade that process of inclusion has met a countertrend. As more authoritarian and semi-authoritarian governments publicly embrace a rule-of-law agenda, they tend to prefer the more reductive, proceduralist conception. They promise citizens fairness and efficiency but steer clear of the rights element of the rule-of-law. Thus they seek to break the tie between advancing the rule-of-law and building democracy. This is evident with the two largest challengers of the Western democratic line, the current governments of Russia and China. Vladimir Putin came to office in Russia promising a rule-of-law presidency and he held to that line (at least rhetorically) even as he moved the country away from its earlier democratic experiment. Russia's new president, Dmitry Medvedev, has struck a similar note, emphasizing his commitment to rule-of-law reform, even as he continues the pattern of limited political openness. China's rulers have been responding to rising citizen anger and unrest over corruption and poor local governance by carrying out some rule-of-law reforms, yet they continue to restrict political contestation and political freedom. In all these countries, strong-hand rulers have found that the rule-of-law works well as an alternative objective to democratization, not one that complements it but rather one that will help preserve authoritarian or semi-authoritarian rule. Thus in this decade, the continued growth of international attention to the rule-of-law in some countries involves greater reductionism rather than inclusion. The growing attention is thus as much about the fraying of an international consensus on political values as it is about a growing political convergence. Western policy actors, often eager to find signs of positive change or at least positive intent from those governments, salute their rule-of-law promises, overlooking the damage that the reductionism may cause to the health of the broader rule-of-law agenda.

Sequencing

Another unhelpful temptation concerning the rule-of-law that has gained ground in international policy circles in this decade is that of sequencing – the idea that transitional countries should not pursue rule-of-law development and democratization together but rather in sequence, first building the rule-of-law and only after that turning to democratization. The thinking is that until a country enjoys a reasonable level of economic development, the rule-of-law, and a well-functioning state, it is not ready for democracy. The growing reach of this idea connects to the tendency toward reductionist thinking about the rule-of-law – seeing rule-of-law development and democratization as distinct processes rests on a narrow, proceduralist conception of the rule-of-law.

The new enthusiasm for sequencing on the part of some influential Western scholars and policy experts reflects their concerns over what they see as the high risks involved when countries with weak states and weak rule-of-law, and little experience with political pluralism, attempt rapid processes of democratization (see, e.g., Mansfield and Snyder 2005 and Zakaria 2003). Such risks include the emergence of illiberal democracies and the outbreak of civil or interstate conflict. The cases of genocide in Rwanda and Burundi in the early 1990s are cited as examples. So too are the cases of conflict among the former Yugoslav republics in the 1990s. Sequentialists believe that by first developing the rule-of-law, traditionally authoritarian societies will create the necessary mechanisms and habits of control and restraint to ensure that potentially chaotic or unpredictable processes of mass political participation do not get out of hand. They buttress their arguments in favor of sequentialism for transitional countries with the argument that this was the pattern followed in the eighteenth and nineteenth centuries by what are now the well-established democracies of Europe and North America.

Sequentialism is indeed appealing not only to scholars and policy experts concerned about economic and political transitions going awry. Authoritarian and semi-authoritarian powerholders also readily embrace the idea. Chinese officials are fond of stressing the need for China to modernize its state and achieve progress in the rule-of-law before democratizing. Arab autocrats like Egyptian president Hosni Mubarak make the same argument. It gives these leaders a principled justification for blocking or avoiding democratization. In the sequentialist paradigm, putting off democratization, which usually means imposing and maintaining repressive political control, becomes not an authoritarian maneuver but actually the correct path toward eventual democratization.

Sequentialism is indeed an appealing idea. It promises to bring order and rationality to what might otherwise be uncertain, dangerous processes of sociopolitical change. Unfortunately, however, it is a flawed idea.[3] Certainly societies need a certain basic level of order and the presence of basic institutions of a state before they should attempt the establishment of political pluralism and active political contestation. Yet the idea that societies should live with authoritarianism until they develop full-fledged rule-of-law and a well-functioning state is mistaken.

The core flaw in this idea is the notion that authoritarian leaders will in fact take their societies along the road to the rule-of-law. The image of the austere, wise autocrat who slowly but systematically builds the rule-of-law may be attractive, but it is much more the exception than the rule. The developing world is crowded with countries that have suffered punishing abuses and developmental failures under authoritarian leaders who promised to advance the law and build the state as a foundation for eventual democratization. The chronic weakness of the state and of the rule-of-law in almost all of Latin America, for example, is the consequence of generations of authoritarian rule there, rule which often claimed to be seeking the strengthening of the state and of law. The same is true in sub-Saharan Africa. Only a few autocratic leaders of developing countries have in fact delivered on such pledges, primarily in a small set of Asian countries that are exceptional in various ways. In general, presenting continued authoritarianism as a cure for what is in fact a characteristic weakness of authoritarian rule – haphazard state building and low respect for the rule-of-law – is a curious idea.

Although autocrats' strong emphasis on order and control may seem a natural lead-in to rule-of-law development, in fact authoritarian leaders have strong structural reasons to abridge and avoid true rule-of-law development. They may like to use law as an instrument of state control. But cardinal features of the rule-of-law – establishing a truly independent judiciary, subordinating government officials to the law, treating all citizens in accordance with basic principles of legal fairness, and respecting political and civil rights – threaten the power and hold of authoritarians. As a result, they usually resist and undermine reforms that would take their country closer to such practices, no matter how lofty their promises of commitment to the rule-of-law. The arc from gilded promise to open failure on rule-of-law development is all too familiar in the developing world.

The rule-of-law is by no means easy or automatic for democracies. Fledgling democratic governments certainly struggle with rule-of-law development. New political elites getting into power for the first time often fall into corruption. Democratic governments may focus only on short-term survival rather than longer-term institutional reform. Popular pressures on such governments for anticrime measures may lead more to abridgments of rights rather than to genuine rule-of-law reforms. Even well-established democracies fall short on the rule-of-law. Italy has been a democracy for generations yet suffers from some chronic deficiencies in this regard. The United States in recent years has been the subject of withering criticism from other countries for its abuses of the rule-of-law at counterterrorism detention facilities in different parts of the world.

Nevertheless, unlike autocratic governments, democratic governments do not face any intrinsic or structural clash between the rule-of-law and their hold on power. Creating alternative centers of power, treating citizens evenhandedly, and respecting rights are all integral not just to building the rule-of-law but also to deepening democracy. Moreover, certain elements of democracy actively help foster the rule-of-law. Alternation of power, for example, helps break up established concentrations of influence and control within state institutions, reducing corruption and increasing accountability. Freedom of the press, which rarely exists under authoritarianism but often under democracy, is a powerful mechanism for bringing attention to legal abuses by powerholders and helping build the rule-of-law.

A related flaw in the sequentialist outlook is the notion that democratization can simply be put off for some extended time while the rule-of-law is achieved. This idea ignores the fact that over the last two decades the norm of democratic participation has spread widely in the world. When authoritarian governments lose their grip and collapse, such as Indonesia in the late 1990s, citizens usually push for elections, no matter how ill-prepared the country may be for democracy according to classic "preconditions analysis." Some authoritarian governments are able to put off citizen pressures for greater participation through successful economic performance. In most cases, these are oil-rich states benefiting from revenue bonanzas, although China and Vietnam have managed to do so through impressive economic growth generated through manufacturing export-driven growth.

Finally, the idea that sequentialism is the formula that produced successful, stable democracies in the West is at best an oversimplification and in fact largely myth. Take the United States as one example. The young United States did not first achieve a well-functioning rule-of-law and then gradually add democratization bit by bit on top of that foundation. The rule-of-law and democracy developed in a complex interactive process in which both moved ahead by fits and starts. During the nineteenth century, the United States fell short in significant ways in both the rule-of-law (frontier justice in the American West hardly represented a well-functioning rule-of-law) and in democratization (slavery being the most egregious but hardly the only violation of democratic principles). It was only in the twentieth century that both a relatively well-functioning rule-of-law as well as a relatively well-functioning democracy came to define the American national experience. Sheri Berman (2007a) argues that the same pattern of complex interweaving of rule-of-law development and democratization also characterized Europe's path in the modern era.

Ease

As attention to the promotion of the rule of law as a growing element of international assistance has continued expanding in this decade, it has moved well beyond the circle of development and democracy specialists into the broader foreign policy community. Diplomats, military officials, law enforcement agents, policy pundits, politicians, and others now regularly join the international conversation about rule-of-law development, offering advice and opinions. As the conversation widens, one hears more references that imply that the task of rule-of-law building is relatively straightforward and even quick, at least compared to democracy-building. Thus, for example, the laments in Western policy circles that a better outcome in Russia would have occurred if Western governments had focused more on rule-of-law development immediately after 1991 imply that the rule-of-law could have come about more easily and expeditiously than democracy.

The notion that helping another country foster the rule of law is a relatively feasible task is a familiar idea, one that existed within the aid community in the 1960s, at the start of the first wave of rule-of-law aid programs, the Law and Development Movement, and in the 1980s in the early years of the current generation of rule-of-law programs. It was rooted in the tendency common among US rule-of-law enthusiasts to see rule-of-law development as either a naturalistic process that will unfold expeditiously once the correct ideas are injected into the target country or a technocratic process that can proceed almost by logic alone. In both cases, however, the difficult experience of trying to convert noble donor ambitions into successful accomplishments chastened practitioners. They learned that rule-of-law assistance is, like almost all forms of external aid, at best a modest helping hand and that processes of rule-of-law development almost always encounter formidable obstacles. Although practitioners have not given up in the face of the chastening that they have experienced, they have largely recalibrated their expectations about what can be accomplished and in what time frame, ratcheting them downward to more realistic levels.

In contrast, the wider circle of people coming into the arena of rule-of-law development in the past ten years lack this experience and often appear determined to repeat the same cycle of overly optimistic starting assumptions and eventual chastening experience. It is enough to read the accounts, for example, of the simplistic sorts of rule-of-law building programs that the US military put in place in Iraq after the ouster of Saddam Hussein – sending over groups of US judicial experts with no experience in the Arab world and no grounding in Iraqi legal culture to advise on a rapid rebuilding of the Iraqi judicial system – to see this pattern at its worst.

What Western policymakers, diplomats, military officials, political observers, and others are overlooking in their enthusiasm for the rule-of-law as a response to troubled transitions is that achieving the rule-of-law involves far more than getting judges trained, putting modern police equipment in place, and reprinting and distributing legal texts. It is a transformative process that changes how power is both exercised and distributed in a society and thus a process inherently threatening to existing powerholders. It also involves basic changes in how citizens relate to state authority and also to each other.

Arguably, achieving the rule-of-law is a more complex and deep-reaching challenge than democratization. In its bare-bones forms, democratization is primarily a process of organized political contestation which can leave many other societal structures relatively intact. In contrast, law cuts through almost every part of the political, economic, and social domains. Elites in many societies have demonstrated the ability to accommodate to democratization without either losing their privileged place in society or changing their ways very much. Yet they have often resisted or evaded key rule-of-law reforms, like subordinating power to law, as being too threatening.

Conclusions

The rule-of-law agenda has tremendous potential value and importance on many fronts. It is an area that was relatively neglected for many years in the existing development paradigms, both those focused on economic development and those on political development. It can serve as a vital connective tissue linking many elements of concern in societies emerging from authoritarian rule in today's globalizing world. It has a usefully non-ideological appeal in an international climate of heightened sensitivity about ideological imposition. It is precisely because of these qualities, however, that it is easily the object of the various temptations described herein. These include overestimation of the level of consensus about what rule-of-law building means in practice, a tendency toward reductionistic views that narrow the rule-of-law to rule by law, the false promise of sequentialism, and underestimation of the difficulty of the task. These temptations do not represent potentially fatal threats to the agenda or grave dangers to the countries involved. They do, however, risk sending rule-of-law promoters down wrong paths that can result in wasted efforts and bad policy decisions. These temptations are a result of a complicated and sometimes clashing mix of factors. To some extent they are the product of enthusiasm – the enthusiasm of many rule-of-law assistance providers who believe fervently in the centrality and naturalness of the rule-of-law agenda. Yet they are also in part a result of cynicism, the cynicism of powerholders in unfree or partly free societies who use the rule-of-law banner to legitimate their own anti-democratic actions. They are also almost inevitable products of an international context in which a driving overall force – globalization – both points countries all over toward a common set of rule-of-law concerns yet also entails fissiparous tendencies of division and fragmentation in many specific domains, such as identity and ideology.

Moving ahead, it is essential to keep a sober eye on the uses and abuses of the rule-of-law theme, to ward off unrealistic expectations, simplistic formulas, and other similar traps. As with other parts of the world of international policy and assistance that seek to do good on many fronts at once, a healthy dose of analytic as well as practical restraint is likely to increase the longevity of key themes and priorities relating to the rule of law in the years ahead.

Notes

1 On the diversity of agendas in rule-of-law reform and assistance, see Carothers 2001: 4–16.
2 For an overview of the debate on the competing definitions of the rule of law see Carothers (2006).
3 For a broader critique of sequencing, see Carothers 2007a. For replies to this critique, see Mansfield and Snyder 2007; Fukuyama 2007; Berman 2007b; and Carothers 2007b.

Chapter 2

Why developing countries prove so resistant to the rule of law

Barry R. Weingast[1]

Introduction

Why do developing countries prove so resistant to the rule-of-law and, more generally, good governance? The problem is all the more paradoxical because the institutional technologies for providing the rule-of-law – systems of property rights, civil rights, and personal liberties, general incorporation laws, corporate governance structures, contract law, and judicial systems – are relatively well known. To address these questions, I draw on the new approach developed by North, Wallis, and Weingast (2009) – NWW – to suggest how the rule-of-law emerged in the West and why the rule-of-law cannot readily be transplanted into developing countries.

The traditional approach to development in economics, political science, and law sees developing societies as incomplete versions of developed ones; that is, as lacking essential ingredients of mature developed societies. Economists, democrats, and legal scholars all recommend that new institutions and policies be transplanted from developed societies into developing ones – typically capital, technology and competitive markets; parties and elections; and rights, constitutions, and judicial institutions. And yet these reforms rarely succeed in producing long-term economic growth, stable democracy that polices public officials, and rule-of-law institutions with efficient justice.

The NWW approach provides a new explanation for why it is so difficult to transplant these institutions from developed societies into developing ones. This framework divides today's societies into two different types of social orders, arguing that developing countries differ dramatically in their organization from those of developed ones. Missing from traditional approaches is how societies reduce or control the problem of violence. The most common social order throughout history, the limited access order or natural state, solves the problem of violence through rent-creation, granting powerful individuals and groups valuable rights and privileges so that they have incentives to cooperate rather than fight. The resulting rents, limits on competition, and limited access to organizations hinder long-term economic development of these societies. In contrast, open access orders use competition, open access to organizations, and institutions to control violence and are characterized by rent-erosion and long-term economic growth.

I focus on two aspects of the rule-of-law in this chapter: first, the ideas of certainty, equality before the law, and the absence of arbitrary abuse by authority; and second, a dynamic component missing from most treatments that emphasizes that the rule-of-law must hold not only today, but also tomorrow. The dynamic issue raises the problem of turnover in the ruler or dominant coalition of a state: what binds new political officials to honor existing rules and institutions? This issue is especially problematic in authoritarian regimes but is relevant in all natural states, including nominally democratic ones: the inability to bind successor regimes to today's rules and institutions is a fundamental barrier to establishing the rule-of-law. No matter how attractive are today's institutions or rights, they are no good in the long term if tomorrow's regime can alter them at will. This issue is intimately tied to the issue of creating a perpetually lived state, a state whose characteristics and institutions do not depend on the identity of leaders or dominant coalition.

Too often, students of the rule-of-law focus on the form of rights – for example, the nature and specification of the law – or the form of institutions that should implement and oversee those rights – for example, the nature and specification of judicial institutions. They fail to study how to sustain these institutions and protect them from abuse by political officials. Leaders in natural states typically have the power to undo these institutions when they prove inconvenient, as witnessed by Nazi Germany's Adolf Hitler, Russia's Vladimir Putin, Venezuela's Hugo Chávez, or Zimbabwe's Robert Mugabe. Similarly, many natural states' leaders grabbed power by force, and these leaders often directly compromise existing institutions; examples include Chile's Augustin Pinochet and Spain's Francisco Franco. Finally, many natural states fall into civil war, which also ends continuity of institutions, as illustrated by the former Yugoslavia in the early 1990s, Rwanda in 1994, and Somalia since the early 1990s. All three forms of instability hinder the natural state's ability to create the rule-of-law. These examples show that maintaining the first part of the rule-of-law – equality and the absence of arbitrary abuse – critically depends on the creation of a perpetual state in which the rules and institutions of government do not depend on the identity of political officials.

The chapter's main lesson is that natural states cannot create the rule-of-law by adopting the institutions and governance structures possessed by open access orders. To gain the rule-of-law, natural states must begin to transition to open access orders. Rule of law emerges as part of this transition when the society transforms from one based on personal relations and personal exchange to one based on impersonal relations and impersonal exchange. Part of the transition is institutional. Indeed, creating the rule-of-law requires two separate institutional changes: institutions to provide for the law; and a set of credible commitments that protect those institutions and ensure that they survive.

This chapter proceeds as follows. Section 2 sketches the North, Wallis, and Weingast framework. Section 3 defines the aspects of the rule-of-law used in this study. Section 4 applies this framework to the emergence of rule-of-law in a historical perspective, showing its intimate connection to the transition and how the societies of the West grappled with these issues as they made the transition from natural states to open access orders. Section 5 explains why the procedures, rights, and institutions of the rule-of-law cannot be transplanted into developing countries. My conclusions follow.

The conceptual framework for interpreting recorded human history

To understand how societies are organized and function, I rely on the conceptual framework developed by North, Wallis, and Weingast (2009) – NWW.[2] The NWW framework distinguishes among *social orders*, distinct patterns of organizing society. Each social order represents a particular pattern of human relationships structured in a way to constrain violence. The method by which a society constrains violence affects the entire society. The concept of a social order provides a framework within which we can understand how the political, economic, and other systems relate to one another. The framework integrates fundamental concepts: violence, institutions, organizations, and beliefs. Central to the framework are the questions of how and whether violence is controlled or contained; how societies are organized and what institutions support them; in particular, how they support organizations and who gets to form organizations; and finally, whether interactions are based on personal or impersonal relationships.

Human history has witnessed three social orders. In the *foraging order*, which reaches back long before recorded human history, people existed in small bands, typically of 25 to 100. The *limited access order*, also called the natural state, emerged with recorded human history about 10,000 years ago and is associated with the first social revolution creating the first civilizations. In this social order, the political system manipulates the economic system to create rents so as to control violence and sustain order. By allocating the rents to those with violence potential, these societies significantly reduce the problem of violence. Finally, the *open access order* relies on competition in the political and economic systems to sustain order. This social order first emerged during the second social revolution, also called the knowledge or industrial revolution.

Persons and personhood

Relationships in natural states are personal relations; specifically, relationships among members of the dominant coalition are personal: they depend on the identities of the individuals. How the natural state treats an individual – his or her rights, privileges, rents, and duties – depend on that individual's identity, so these rights, privileges, rents, and duties typically differ across individuals. These states build on repeat-play interaction among individuals to help build personal knowledge and trust and to enforce exchange. Because everyone and every relationship is different, repeated interaction is necessary to enforce exchange. Cooperation and exchange break down when these relationships are infrequent.

A person has two parts. First, every human possesses a unique corporeal body, including size, appearance, and intelligence. Second, every person has a set of socially ascribed characteristics based on their position, power, privileges, rights, and duties.[3]

A society is dominated by personal relationships when each individual's social persona is unique. In contrast, a society is dominated by impersonal relationships when the social persona of large classes of individuals is the same.

The natural state

All states must control the fundamental problem of violence. In natural states, a dominant coalition of the powerful emerges to solve this problem.[4] The coalition grants members privileges, creates rents through limited access to valuable resources and organizations, and then uses the rents to sustain order. Because fighting reduces their rents, coalition members have incentives not to fight so as to maintain their rents. Natural states necessarily limit access to organizations and restrict competition in all systems. Failing to do so dissipates rents and therefore reduces the incentives not to fight.

We call this order the *natural state* because for nearly all of the last 10,000 years of human history – indeed, until just the last two centuries – the natural state was the only solution to the problem of violence that produced a hierarchical society with significant wealth.[5] In comparison with the previous foraging order, natural states produced impressive economic growth, and even today we can see evidence of wealth amassed by many of the early civilizations. In contrast to open access orders, however, natural states have significant, negative consequences for economic growth.

Personal relationships characterize both politics and economics in natural states. Within the dominant coalition, all relationships are personal. More powerful members, for example, gain more valuable privileges. Natural states that fail to distribute benefits in this way risk violence. When the power relationships are out of balance with the distribution of benefits, those with more power than benefits are likely to demand a larger share; and, if it is not forthcoming, they are then tempted to fight for it. Patronage networks typically connect those with less power to those with the most power: anyone without power must be connected to an organization with power in the event that violence breaks out. Personal relationships also characterize most economic relationships. The principal mode of enforcing economic exchange is repeat play. Rule of law institutions, such as courts, only begin to emerge in mature natural states, and these are largely for organizations rather than individuals.

Natural states are stable, but not static. They regularly adjust as circumstances change. Various shocks – dramatic weather events, changes in demographics, changes in relative prices, technological change, or military events – all have implications for the fortunes of coalition members. As some members become more powerful and others weaker, the coalition must adjust the distribution of benefits and rents. Failing to do so risks violence as those members whose rents, privileges, and rights do not match their power threaten violence to gain what they believe is their fair share. Because the world is changing, natural states therefore regularly have dramatic adjustments in rights, privileges, and ruling coalitions, often associated with the expropriation of assets and privileges of some elites which are then granted to others.

A typology of natural states

The NWW framework distinguishes among three types of natural states, depending on how they treat organizations and, in parallel, their institutional sophistication. In *fragile natural states*, the only organization supported by the state is the state itself, the dominant coalition. These states have little differentiation and hence little economic specialization and exchange. Fragile natural states are poor and prone to violence, and they have a limited range of institutions and credible commitments. Examples include Chad, Iraq, Mozambique, Somalia, and the Sudan.

Basic natural states support a set of organizations, all of which are closely associated with the state. These organizations create considerable specialization, such as tax collection, religious activity, and specialized economic functions, including mineral extraction or long-distance trade. Basic natural states have a wider range of institutions to support state organizations, and they are more resilient to shocks than fragile natural states. These states may also have a range of public institutions, such as succession rules for new leaders, or rules that regularize taxation rates, or the division of spoils from conquest. To the extent that these states have enterprises, they are state-run enterprises. All of these issues hold the potential for violent disputes, and rules that institutionalize decisions about them reduce the chances of violence. Examples of basic natural states include the Aztec empire, the Medieval Carolingian empire, Iraq under Saddam Hussein, the former Soviet Union, and Egypt.

Finally, *mature natural states* develop sophisticated private organizations that exist apart from the state. Merchant organizations and other private firms may exist independently of the state rather than being state-run enterprises. In parallel with private organizations is a system of private law and contract enforcement that supports these organizations. Nonetheless, mature natural states limit access to private firms as part of the rent-creation process. Only members of the dominant coalition have access to private organizations, and this access remains a valuable privilege. Mature natural states are more resilient to changing circumstances than are basic natural states; as with all natural states, however, they too have crises and periodic coalition adjustments of rights and privileges. Examples include seventeenth-century England and modern-day Argentina, Brazil, Mexico, and India.

Moving across the progression of natural states, from fragile to basic to mature, states become wealthier. This greater wealth occurs for several reasons. First, the range of organizations and the degree of specialization and exchange is richer across this progression. Second, the degree of violence diminishes across the progression. Lower levels of violence have a direct effect and an indirect effect on wealth. Directly, lower levels of violence destroy less wealth. Indirectly, lower levels of violence mean that greater numbers of potentially profitable exchanges take place because parties that would lose if violence broke out become willing to make the exchange when the risk of violence diminishes.

Nonetheless, the need of all natural states to use limited access to control violence necessarily limits access to rights and to organizations; these limits, in turn, restrict competition in the economy. These states also limit competition in the polity, in turn reducing the production of new ideas and means of solving various political and other dilemmas that all societies inevitably face.

Open access orders

Open access orders sustain open entry to political and economic organizations. As a result, they exhibit political and economic competition, and this competition is central to political order and the prevention of violence. In contrast to the natural state, all citizens in open access orders have the ability to form contractual organizations and to use the state's courts to enforce the organization's contracts. Open access therefore creates and sustains a rich civil society. Competition and open access in the economic system reinforces competition and open access in the political system, and vice versa.

Standard views in both economics and political science fail to understand the open access order because they typically focus on one system alone. Economists attempt to understand economic stability by focusing on the equilibrium properties of markets without reference to the political system, ignoring the problem that property rights, the legal system and contract enforcement, and macroeconomic stability are all products of political and democratic choices. Political scientists study the properties of democratic systems in open access orders taking them as given, failing to explain both how democracy sustains competitive markets and how democracy is sustained when it fails in most countries.[6]

Open access orders are sustained in part by a belief system that emphasizes equality and incorporation. In the nineteenth century, these beliefs were embodied by incorporating citizens within the law, markets, and democracy where elites had previously excluded them. In the twentieth century, these beliefs include impersonal equality before the law so that the rule-of-law is enforced impartially for citizens. Further, these beliefs have actualizations in a wide range of policies and public goods that create explicit sharing: public goods (such as education), social insurance (such as health, unemployment, old age, and workers' accident insurance), and the provision of infrastructure (such as access to a wide range of local public goods). Although not all people living within the society's borders need be citizens for open access to be sustained, a large portion must be. Nonetheless, to be an open access order, all citizens must be equal; that is, the state must treat them impersonally.

Equality, incorporation of citizens, and policies for sharing all lower the demand for crippling redistribution that might destroy an open access order. The means by which open access orders share – public goods, social insurance, and infrastructure – all complement competitive markets and have significantly lower costs than pure redistribution (Lindert 2005). This observation parallels the argument that all successful constitutions limit the stakes of power (Weingast 2006). Because powerful groups are less likely to be threatened by incumbent regimes, constitutions that limit the stakes are subject to fewer coups as these groups support coups to protect themselves.

Open access orders sustain political competition in the form of a competitive party system. The success of this competition depends on open access not only to parties but to organizations. Open access to organizations fosters the civil society, allowing citizens to mobilize and defend their interests when threatened. Organizations of all types – benevolence societies, churches, soccer leagues, firms – are potential political tools for mobilizing interests in the face of political threats. Political parties not only organize the electorate, they police one another. The political opposition is central to a successful democracy. Not only does the opposition formulate alternative plans, but the credible threat from the opposition forces incumbents to adapt their own policies in the face of new circumstances. This competition of ideas and policies affords open access orders a degree of adaptive efficiency (North 2005; NWW: ch. 4) not possessed by natural states.

Open access orders also sustain competitive markets. These societies therefore produce long-term economic growth. Competitive markets have strong feedback mechanisms that limit the ability of political systems in open access orders to create too many rents. Market competition erodes many rents. Fiscal interests produce incentives in open access states for governments to limit their rent-creation. Massive programs to create rents that impose significant harm on the economy have immediate feedback: a shrinking economy lowers tax revenues to support redistribution and public goods; and a shrinking economy directly harms voters. Both of these effects have historically turned voters against incumbents in stable democracies. Mobile resources and international competition reinforce these effects.

Finally, consider the relationship between open access orders and the growth of government. Following beliefs in equality and inclusion, policies for social insurance have meant substantial increases in government spending to finance these programs. Underlying these programs is the ability of open access orders to provide benefits to impersonal categories of citizens. Because natural states lack the ability to treat citizens impersonally, they face great difficulties in providing public goods. Similarly, inclusion in open access orders leads to the provision of infrastructure in the form of wide-ranging local public goods and services (roads, electricity, telephones, water, sewage, garbage), and public education, all of which require significant expenditures. Open access orders have bigger governments than do natural states, in large part because they provide more public goods and services to their citizens (Lindert 2005). More generally, open access orders have larger governments because of trust and reliance – citizens believe the government will provide public goods rather than dissipate expenditures on patronage, so they have a greater willingness-to-pay for government services than do people in natural states.

Natural states versus open access orders

Natural states have many of the same institutions as open access orders, such as parties, elections, markets, and judiciaries. Why do they work differently in open access orders? The answer is that natural states have limited access to organizations, lack competition, and lack a perpetual state.

Limited access to organizations and the creation of privilege hinders markets. While natural states may have some markets, these markets are typically hindered by cumbersome restrictions, far more so than in open access orders. Legal systems in these states typically fail to enforce contracts or mediate disputes among individuals and organizations based on rule-of-law principles. Indeed, most natural state judiciaries are just another corrupt rent-generating organization. Finally, the absence of a perpetual state means that the state itself hinders markets with arbitrary action. As Haber *et al.* (2008) illustrates for Mexico, the government regularly grants extensive privileges and monopoly privileges in banking, only to expropriate the banks during times of crises and then repeat the cycle anew. The inability of the state to honor a stable system of property rights greatly compromises markets in natural states.

Similarly, many mature natural states hold elections, some for decades (as in Mexico since 1930 or Chile prior to 1973). But here too, elections differ systematically from those in open access orders. As mentioned, the incumbent regime may compromise the opposition's ability to compete in various ways. Limited access to organizations hinders the civil society, compromising the ability of citizens to express their views. The absence of a judicial system that operates under rule-of-law fundamentally transforms the legislature in these countries. This absence makes it difficult for the legislature to pass laws controlling the bureaucracy, for there is no way to enforce such laws. This allows executive dominance of the government, greatly diminishing the effectiveness of the separation of powers and the ability of the legislative branch to act as a check on executive power.

Another problem with natural states is the inability to provide benefits on an impersonal basis. This hinders their ability to provide public goods, making it much more difficult to provide the most common policies of open access orders that complement markets: the public goods of social insurance, education, and infrastructure noted above.

Finally consider what Hayek (1960) and North (2005) call "adaptive efficiency," the ability of states to respond to various shocks. All states face problems and crises. How do they respond? First, because open access orders have better means of controlling violence, violence is far less likely to break out when a crisis occurs. Citizens are therefore much less likely to respond by protecting themselves. In contrast, where violence is likely or a possibility, citizens or groups in natural states may well respond quickly to the prospect of violence by protecting themselves so as not to be vulnerable if another group initiates violence. This feedback means the potential for violence makes these societies volatile.

Second, open access orders exhibit competition for ideas. Parties compete for solutions to crises, and the open access to organizations within the civil society means that individuals, groups, and organizations independently produce many new ideas which can be debated throughout the society. Opposition parties and interest groups in particular have strong incentives to monitor, criticize, and provide alternatives to the solutions proposed by incumbents. Open access orders therefore make it far easier than natural states to discard bad or failed ideas.

Third, by virtue of being able to make credible commitments more readily, open access orders are more likely to create new pacts in the face of crises. Indeed, the history of all open access orders is replete with pacts that solve crises; to name a few: the creation of the French Fifth Republic in 1959, the Compromises of 1820, 1833, 1850, and 1877 in the nineteenth-century United States, and the various nineteenth-century Reform Acts in Great Britain.

The force of this subsection is twofold. First, natural states possess many of the same institutions as open access orders, such as markets, elections, and judiciaries. But these institutions work very differently in natural states because they limit access, lack a perpetual state, and cannot deliver benefits to citizens on an impersonal basis. Second, open access systems are not perfect, and in practice all open access states produce significant rents. But – in comparison to natural states – the open access order's competitive mechanisms work relatively well and provide a far better means for long-term economic growth and resiliency to various problems and crises faced by the society.

The transition from limited to open access

The NWW perspective redefines the process of economic and political development as the transition from a limited access order to an open access order.

The transition is a difficult process, and only two or two-and-a-half dozen states have successfully completed it. As I use this material only sparingly, I only briefly describe the transition (see NWW: chs 5 and 6 for further details).

Because the transition begins with the natural state, the early part of the transition must be consistent with the logic of the natural state. Some natural states move into positions in which a series of changes toward open access can be sustained. Within a natural state, conditions may arise that enable impersonal relationships to develop among elites. When this occurs, elites may find it in their interests to institutionalize these relationships.

NWW divides the transition process into two parts, the doorstep conditions and the transition proper. There are three doorstep conditions:

DC 1: Rule of law for elites

Some mature natural states institutionalize relations among elites so that privileges are regularized in a way that they transform into elite rights; put another way, privileges move from being personal and idiosyncratic to being impersonally applied equally to all elites. As discussed below in greater detail, English medieval land law provides an illustration. In the eleventh century, rights to land reverted back to the king on the death of the lord. For a negotiated payment – depending on both the value of the land and the expected relative power of the heir – the heir could purchase the rights to the land. Over time, this process became standardized and impersonalized in fees. Similarly, competition among different court systems in England for revenues led courts to innovate, leading to rules that better served elite interests. Importantly, legal rules emerged granting landowners the right to control how land passed among various heirs when they died, including the ability to grant rights to land on conditions (whereby if the conditions failed, the land reverted to another heir).[7]

DC 2: The perpetual state

Almost all natural states are mortal in the sense that, as the dominant coalition and rulers change, so too do fundamental aspects of the state, such as the rules governing political choice. These states have limited ability to make credible commitments to honor various rights and rules that bind successor coalitions and leaders, so that new leaders often make dramatic revisions in the nature of institutions, rights, and policies. The idea of perpetuity is to create aspects of the state that live beyond the lives of the current officeholders so that the institutions do not depend upon the identity of the officials that hold them.

An especially important aspect of perpetuity is the creation of perpetually lived organizations, organizations whose existence extends beyond the lives of the individuals that create them. Partnerships, the dominant form of business organization throughout history until the mid-nineteenth century, require that the organization be dissolved or reorganized on the death or voluntary exit of one of the partners. Creating corporations with tradable shares and allowing the shareholders to pass their shares to heirs upon their deaths solves this problem, creating perpetually lived organizations. Corporations therefore allow substantial risk-pooling and have much longer time horizons than partnerships.

DC 3: Consolidated control over violence and the military

The third doorstep condition is at once the most difficult to understand and to achieve. Without consolidated, political control over the varied sources of violence, including the military, neither of the other doorstep conditions can hold. Neither the rule-of-law nor credible commitments can exist as long as one faction can use force to bend others to their will. Few discussions of the rule-of-law mention this problem. And yet, as critical as this condition is, we know too little about how this consolidation takes place (NWW: ch. 5).

The transition

The transition proper occurs when sufficient numbers of people become citizens in the sense that the state treats a large category of people impersonally and identically. At the same time, processes must begin that afford citizens access to organizations in both politics and economics, granting them the ability to compete as they wish in either system. In the United States, this process occurred over several generations, spanning the colonial era through the Constitution and well into the nineteenth century. Indeed, the idea of party competition with a legitimate opposition party in politics did not emerge until the middle of the nineteenth century, around the 1840s (Hofstadter 1969; NWW: ch. 6). Similarly, general incorporation laws, allowing anyone to form a corporation, also arose first in the 1840s (NWW: ch. 6). Events in Great Britain were not far behind the United States; and in France, they occurred by the 1880s.

Vexing problems in creating the rule-of-law

Scholars use the term "rule-of-law" to mean different things in different contexts, and this label is sometimes used to encompass all good things, including good governance, democracy, and human rights. For the purposes of this chapter, I emphasize two core aspects of the rule-of-law: first, the impersonal aspects of law: the certainty or predictability of the law, including the absence of arbitrary actions by the state against individuals; transparency; and the requirement that the state treat individuals as citizens with equality before the law. Second, a dynamic aspect of the rule-of-law which requires that the state be able to honor these aspects of the rule-of-law tomorrow even if it experiences turnover in officials.

By this definition, natural states have substantial difficulties creating the rule-of-law. First, this definition contrasts with the typical natural state dominated by personal relationships. In natural states, people's identity determines how they are treated; in particular, the state treats more powerful individuals and groups differently than weaker ones. For example, the privileges of Duke A differ from those of Dukes B and C – as a matter of de jure or de facto – and all dukes are treated differently from knights, let alone from all peasants.

Second, natural states have difficulty creating the predictability necessary for the rule-of-law. Because these states are built around a dominant coalition, as the needs and power relations of the coalition change, so too do rules, policies, rights, and privileges. Similarly, the absence of perpetuity makes it very difficult for natural states to commit to long-term rules, institutions and policies.

Third, natural states often seem to act arbitrarily. This behavior typically reflects the logic of the dominant coalition of the natural state. For example, as the fortunes of the various coalition members rise and fall, the ruler adjusts their rights, privileges, and rents, often redistributing them from some members to others. From the open access perspective, these choices seem arbitrary; policies and rights appear to be too closely associated with choices by the ruler bound not by rules but seemingly by whim. The identity and power characteristics of the individuals and groups are central to this natural state behavior. Reflecting the dynamics of the natural state coalition logic, this behavior is the opposite of the rule-of-law.

Finally and perhaps most importantly, the rule-of-law involves the dynamic component, for the issue of the certainty of the law concerns not only what the law is today, but what it will be tomorrow. We take this feature of the rule-of-law for granted in open access orders, but those living in natural states cannot.[8] The dynamic issue raises several concerns. First, from an economic and political standpoint, consider expropriation. Investors of all kinds care not just what the rules are today – property rights and tax rates, for example – but what they will be tomorrow. Investments profitable under today's rules may not be under tomorrow's, particularly if the government acts opportunistically by using these policies to expropriate the value of the investment. Farmers in Ghana, for example, fear that their long-term investment in coffee trees profitable under today's tax rates will be expropriated if the government raises the tax rate as the trees mature and start bearing fruit.

Second, a political complication concerns the problem of changes in the dominant coalition and ruler: natural states have too few institutions that bind new coalitions and their leaders to today's rules. This is especially problematic in authoritarian regimes. As discussed in the next section, this problem is intimately tied to the issue of creating a perpetually lived state.

The concept of credible commitment provides the answer to both of these problems. States cannot simply announce impersonal rules and rights, for their rulers – or those rulers' successors – may alter them tomorrow. Creating a state that honors rules today and tomorrow requires institutions with two characteristics. First, these institutions must commit the state – political officials, judges, bureaucrats – to honor these rules and rights. Second, they must commit all major players in society to respect the constitutional rules. In particular, anyone with access to violence and the ability to overturn the regime must have incentives to refrain from doing so. Similarly, those in power must have incentives to respect the rules, including the rights of the opposition, and, if a democratic society, to give up power if they lose elections. These incentives are intimately connected with creating the credible commitments necessary for a perpetual state and the dynamic aspects of the rule-of-law. Unfortunately, this type of credible commitment eludes most natural states and typically occurs only for those that begin the transition.

Historic emergence of the rule-of-law in the West

The emergence of the rule-of-law coincides with the transition from the natural state to the open access order. Natural states have only a limited ability to provide the rule-of-law; they cannot make either extensive credible commitments to institutions and rules that provide for certainty expectations or impersonal rules that treat a wide class of citizens equally. Whereas the rule-of-law requires that the state treat citizens impersonally, natural states treat people personally and hence differentially. Natural states also emphasize power; and as power shifts, not only does the membership in the dominant coalition adjust, so too do privileges, rents, institutions, and policies. These adjustments can be seen in the coalition changes in seventeenth-century England, as the Stuart kings redistributed power and rents from one faction to another, but also in modern natural states, such as Russia under President Putin and Venezuela under Hugo Chávez.

A natural state cannot sustain impersonal rights of a large group of citizens who are equal under the law. Nor can today's natural state bind a successor regime. Rights and reforms in a natural state fail when the ruler needs to adjust the coalition in response to changing circumstances. Thus, even if today's regime in a natural state institutes the appropriate reform, it cannot commit itself or its successors to maintain these reforms.

Natural states entering the transition, however, change as they begin to assume the doorstep conditions. All three of the doorstep conditions are central to the emergence of the rule-of-law. The first doorstep condition is rule-of-law for elites, in which various forms of elite privileges are transformed into elite rights. Consider early English medieval history.[9] Immediately following William the Conqueror's invasion in 1066, the king dispersed rights to land to his followers from Normandy. These holdings did not displace existing landlords, but instead forced existing landlords to pay tribute to and share rents with the newcomers. At the death of these men, the rights to the land reverted to the king, who might return land rights to the original holder's heir, typically for a payment. But the king might instead redistribute rights to the land. If, for example, the fortunes of the original holder had fallen (say the heir was seen as a weak leader) while those of another had risen (say he had done favors for the king and deserved a reward), the king might grant the land to the other instead of the heir. In this way, the logic of maintaining the dominant coalition in the natural state dictated the allocation of rights to land, which worked as a system of privilege to the powerful rather than as a set of rights. England at the time was a fragile natural state; it had few organizations outside of the state.

Over time, as relationships stabilized, new institutions and organizations associated with the state grew. Although the king sought to retain his flexibility with respect to rights to use the land, the great lords had a collective interest in stabilizing the rules. Moreover, wealth would rise if rights could be made more secure; everyone, the king included, could be made better off, if rights were made more secure. And so, over a considerable period of time, rights to inherit the land became more secure.

This same scenario played out with respect to a wide variety of aspects of rights associated with land. As another example, consider the ability to devise property by will. Although heirs could inherit land in medieval England, the law did not allow the owner flexibility in terms of dividing land among many heirs or granting land under particular conditions such that, if unmet, the land reverts to another heir. Here too the evolution of secure, flexible elite rights to devise property by will took several centuries. In the end, rights to land became secure slowly over many centuries, and were considerably secure as England became a mature natural state in the seventeenth century and then began the doorstep conditions.

As a final example, consider the emergence of rights to sell and trade corporation shares. Originally, corporate shares emerged as a privilege associated with a unique corporation created to capture rents associated with a particular opportunity, such as the East India Company or the Bank of England. But once a corporation was created, holders of its shares had an incentive to foster the right to trade these shares and to extend the right to own them to a substantially larger group of people: doing so would enhance the value of their shares. In other words, although these corporations began as personal, natural state creations, they provided incentives to create impersonal securities markets to enhance the value of the firms and to increase the liquidity of the owners' capital.

Each of these cases illustrates the transformation of elite privileges into elite rights. Each also involves the transformation of the state so that it creates a system that enforces these rights and hence attains an aspect of rule-of-law for elites.

The second doorstep condition, perpetually lived states and organizations, is also central to the rule-of-law. Unfortunately, this critical aspect of the rule-of-law is largely neglected in literature, in part because the literature fails to study the problem of maintaining the rule-of-law over time.

Put simply, *the absence of a perpetual state allows future natural state officials to dishonor the rules, laws, and institutions devised by today's state.* As natural states adjust to changing circumstances, they violate the basic features of the rule-of-law. Perpetuity is therefore an obvious condition necessary for states to maintain the rule-of-law. Indeed, many of the classic figures in the rule-of-law have articulated sentiments that fit with this logic. When Aristotle (1988: 90–1) condemns rule by people rather than rule by law in *Politics* he seems to be referring to the absence of perpetuity. Similarly, Locke (1980 [1690]: 17), in his *Second Treatise*, says,

> Freedom of men under government is, to have a standing rule to live by, common to every one of that society, and made by the legislative power erected in it ... and not to be subject to the inconstant, uncertain, arbitrary will of another man.

All of these ideas depend on the certainty of law, itself dependent on the perpetuity of the state.

Because natural state rulers, representing the dominant coalition, face relatively fewer credible commitments than rulers in open access orders, they can remove or undo laws and institutions that they find inconvenient. Former president Vladimir Putin systematically did this in Russia, transforming a mature natural state with many organizations independent of the state back toward a basic one where survival requires that organizations have close ties to the state. A wide range of once independent private organizations have lost their independence. Similarly, a range of political institutions that once stood as moderate checks and balances on former Russian president Boris Yeltsin either no longer exist or are much weaker, including the Russian Duma, the governors, the press, and the civil society. The absence of these checks has allowed Putin to remove his political opponents and take undisputed control over Russia, even as he has nominally stepped down from the presidency and allowed a successor, Dmitry Medvedev, to be elected to the presidency. Because these institutions lacked perpetuity, they could be dismantled. President Hugo Chávez of Venezuela has overseen a similar if less thorough transformation in Venezuela, as has President Robert Mugabe of Zimbabwe. In the 1930s, Adolf Hitler engineered a similar if far more sinister transformation of the Weimar regime, a mature natural state, into Nazi Germany, a basic natural state. These leaders accomplish their goals in response to changing circumstances, such as a depression or a significant increase in state revenue,[10] that allow them to consolidate their position by eliminating privileges of other coalition members whose support is no longer needed to survive.

Creating perpetuity requires establishing various credible commitments by which the ruler and dominant coalition have incentives to honor the institutions and rights. The incentives created by the credible commitments imply that the institutions and rights do not depend on the identity of political officials or members of the dominant coalition. As the rulers, political officials, or coalitions change, state institutions and citizen rights nonetheless survive and elements of the rule-of-law can be sustained.

As perpetuity is the most novel aspect of the rule-of-law, I give several illustrations of this concept. First, consider the creation of the second doorstep condition, a perpetual state, among one of the first movers, England, in the Glorious Revolution of 1688–9. This revolution was not only a coup removing one king and inviting in another, but also a constitutional revision by which the erstwhile divided English elite settled many of their differences over which they had fought for much of this century (including a bitter civil war in the 1640s, the beheading of the king in 1649, the formation of a parliamentary republic that failed, followed by the restoration of the monarchy in 1660). The divided elite settled many of their differences in a way that placed bounds on the powers that the king, as head of the dominant coalition, could exercise. In particular, the status of laws of Parliament and Parliament's control over taxation – both contested issues during the previous century – became sacrosanct. The portion of the Glorious Revolution known as the Revenue Settlement announced that any king who ignored a law of Parliament risked being replaced (Jones 1972: 318; North and Weingast 1989). The new consensus created the credible commitment binding the king to the new rules.

Backed by a threat of an elite united against the crown, the Revolution Settlement created a central aspect of a perpetual state. Laws of Parliament now bound the current king as head of the natural state coalition. Importantly, the settlement also bound all future kings (Weingast 1997).

The parliamentarians negotiating the Revolution Settlement were backward-looking, attempting to solve the problems of the previous century. But by endowing the state with perpetuity, the institutional changes had immense forward-looking effects.

The effects of perpetuity are readily seen in three important illustrations. First consider the issue of sovereign debt. Prior to the Glorious Revolution, sovereign debt represented a natural state personal exchange between the king and the lenders. Being the sovereign and above the law, the king chose whether to pay back creditors. If he wanted to lower the interest rate, delay payment, or default on the loan altogether, it was at his personal discretion. As a consequence, the king was credit-rationed; creditors would lend only limited funds. After the Glorious Revolution, new debt issues became laws of Parliament. Legally, this meant that altering the terms of debt required a new law of Parliament. If the king unilaterally sought to alter the debt terms, such as default on an interest payment, he would violate a law of Parliament. The new arrangements greatly raised the cost to the king of altering the debt terms: disregarding a law of Parliament threatened a coup. The new arrangements therefore provided the king with strong incentives to honor them; loan repayment was therefore more credible. As a consequence of the increased credibility to repay, the credit available to the government went up enormously. Debt rose by nearly an order of magnitude in a few short years (1689–97), from roughly 5 percent of estimated GNP to roughly 40 percent (North and Weingast 1989). This debt allowed England to hold off France in the war that began with the Glorious Revolution, preventing (among other things) France from restoring the deposed king.

Second and perhaps most central for the rule-of-law, consider the independent judiciary. This independence is one of the most difficult institutions for today's natural states to accomplish. Although many developing countries announce independent judiciaries in their constitutions, few can sustain them, and most developing countries compromise their independence when it proves inconvenient.[11] Indeed, the seventeenth-century Stuart kings had long openly fired judges for ruling against them – famously, Chief Justices Coke (1616–17) and Crew (1627) (see Hirst 1986). The crown was personally responsible for the day-to-day operation of the government, so it paid the judges. As they served at the crown's pleasure, the Stuart kings used their power to influence the judges' decisions. In the end, this threat of being fired produced compliant judges. Following the Glorious Revolution, judges became more independent of the crown. In 1701, Parliament passed the Act of Settlement, granting judges official independence of the crown. Here too perpetuity protected judicial independence. Parliament, as representatives of the dominant coalition, sought to protect judges by passing a law officially recognizing the independence of judges from the crown. Royal manipulation of judges now risked violating a law of Parliament and hence the threat of a coup, making judges far more independent. Using event-study methods, Klermen and Mahoney (2005) provide statistical evidence demonstrating the importance of this Act.

Third, an important implication of a perpetual state is that it can create perpetually lived organizations. These organizations greatly increase the amount of wealth that the society can generate. For example, perpetuity allows insurance companies to pool vast quantities of risk and thus substantially reduce risk to individuals and firms. It allows corporations to pool capital and create organizations that make long-term investments that live beyond the lives of the existing partners. Because partnerships must be renegotiated on the death of any partner, they become very cumbersome as they begin to pool large amounts of capital from a large number of investors.

More generally, perpetuity is central to the process of creating a long-term time horizon for a society. As is well-known, short time horizons lead to decisions by state leaders with bad economic consequences (North 1981: ch. 3; Bates 1983; Olson 1993). The absence of long-term horizons greatly hinders the ability to make long-term investments, which are critical to long-term economic development. Put simply, investors cannot have long time horizons and make long-term investments if the state is not perpetual and has a short time horizon. The absence of a perpetually lived state therefore implies the absence of perpetually lived organizations.

Creating perpetuity is therefore a central feature of the rule-of-law. It is a necessary component of creating a state that moves beyond the personal rule of individuals, where the institutions and policies of the natural states depend upon the identity of the dominant coalition and who runs the state. Creating perpetuity requires credible commitments that institutionalize political and social mechanisms that create incentives for both political officials and citizens to honor the rules so that not only do today's officials honor the rules but so too will tomorrow's. This is clearly part of the essence of satisfying the two conditions of the definition of the rule-of-law articulated earlier.

The third doorstep condition, consolidated control over the military, is another obvious precondition for the rule-of-law. Indeed, as NWW (North *et al.* 2009: ch. 5) argue, the other two doorstep conditions cannot be sustained if this condition is not firmly in place. The absence of consolidated control over the military allows those with access to military resources to grab what they like, if not always when they like, at least when circumstances are propitious. As long as this type of military intervention remains possible, the rule-of-law cannot hold. Strongmen with access to violence have the ability to evade the law, so the rule-of-law necessarily remains incomplete. Although perhaps the most important of the three conditions, we know least about this doorstep condition.

Implications

The emergence of the rule-of-law is intimately connected with the transition from natural state to open access order. Each of the three doorstep conditions, which represent the beginning of the transition, is necessary to achieve the rule-of-law. Natural states have great difficulties establishing and maintaining institutions capable of sustaining the rule-of-law. They cannot deliver benefits on an impersonal basis. The absence of perpetuity means that they cannot commit to long-term policies, so that these states witness great transformations in institutions and policies, whether following dramatic coups, such as Chile (1973), the severe financial crises of Argentina (2001) and Thailand (1997), or the more subtle and prolonged transformations of present-day Russia, Zimbabwe, Venezuela, Kenya, and South Africa. Each of these natural state transformations reflects the absence of perpetuity, allowing leaders to adjust institutions, policies, rents, and privileges as the needs of the dominant coalition change in order to maintain political stability (or, sometimes, a mere modicum of political stability in the face of threats of more severe disorder). Frequently accompanied by dramatic policy reversals, these shifts wreak havoc with investment and the economy; they may also end freedoms overnight, such as democracy. All too frequently, the institutions designed to promote the rule-of-law are a casualty.

Why the rules, rights, and institutions supporting the rule-of-law in the developed (open access) world cannot be transplanted into the developing (natural state) world

Natural state systems of privilege and rent-creation do not arise simply because people are greedy, malevolent, or corrupt. Instead, privilege and rent-creation arise because they are the solution to the problem of violence. Rents grant powerful individuals and groups with access to violence incentives to cooperate with other members of the dominant coalition. In comparison with disorder, all members of the society benefit from the peace that follows.

Into this world come reformers with the best of intentions – economists promoting economic reform, democrats promoting elections and democracy, and lawyers promoting legal reform and the specification of citizen rights. These reformers argue that their proposed reforms will make citizens better off. But they are wrong. The reason is that their reforms are institutions and policies from the world of open access orders. In pursuing their programs, reformers seek to transplant a subset of open access institutions into natural states without understanding why natural states systematically differ from open access orders and in particular, why natural states fail to be open access orders.

These reforms virtually always fail for two reasons: violence and the absence of perpetuity. I consider these problems in turn.

Reform efforts typically fail to understand the role of violence in structuring the natural state

Reform efforts almost always ignore the problem of violence that the natural state political and economic systems solve. The systems of privileges, rents, and limited access are not arbitrary; they serve a valuable and necessary – if costly – purpose; they are the means of controlling the problem of violence. Transplanting open access order institutions – such as markets, elections, and legal systems – cannot create an open access order. This type of reform has been tried hundreds of times, and it typically does not succeed. The problem is that these reforms seek to dismantle the natural state systems of privilege and limited access; they therefore threaten violence and disorder. Rather than making everyone better off, as the reformers intend, these reforms threaten to make everyone worse off.

Consider the problem of market reform. Existing market privileges are part of the larger system of privileges and limited access granting elites incentives to refrain from violence. Market reform that removes these restrictions eliminates these rents; reforms that promote open entry into markets erode these rents. Both types of market reform remove the incentives that sustain elite cooperation. The likelihood of violence rises, particularly in times of crisis. Similar effects arise from electoral reform that increases political competition and legal reform, again threatening to undo many of the privileges that hold the society together.

Because these reforms threaten a society with violence, people in these societies resist them. The paradox is that not only will those who benefit directly from the rents fight reform, so too will those who are exploited by the natural state privileges. The reason is that being exploited in a peaceful society is typically better than living under disorder. For this reason, none of the major open access institutions – markets, democracy, or legal systems – can be transplanted directly into developing countries qua natural states. This is also why, despite hundreds of billions of dollars, the best intentions, and the best development advice, the World Bank, the IMF, and USAID have relatively few success stories.[12]

Democracy and elections serve as a major check on government in open access orders. Although many mature natural states sustain elections for significant periods – including Argentina, Brazil, Chile, India, Russia, and Venezuela – elections in these states do not seem to curb corruption, serve as a check on government abuse, protect citizen rights, or more generally foster the rule-of-law. Indeed, these states frequently constrain the opposition's ability to compete, such as limits on freedom of the press, limit on open access to organizations so that groups cannot organize in support of opposition parties or candidates they favor, or directly hinder candidates from competing (sometimes they are jailed).

Students of democracy are only beginning to learn what makes democracy work in open access orders. Most new democracies fail, and we have only a few clues about what makes some democracies succeed while most do not. One condition, however, is that all successful democracies seem to reduce the stakes of political conflict. The reason can be seen in Chile in 1973, Spain in 1936, or Kenya in 2007–8. When the stakes are too high, powerful groups whose interests are threatened by legitimately elected governments provide support for coups or violent movements that destroy democracy. Democratic constitutions that limit the stakes therefore make democracy more likely to survive because they make coups and violence less likely (Weingast 2006).

This same principle applies in another way, sometimes called "tragic brilliance" (Diaz-Cayeros *et al.* 2008), in which natural states engineer the delivery of highly valued local public goods, such as water, so that they depend on whether citizens in a locality support the government. Failing to support the government leads it to cut off these citizens' water. In this case, citizens nominally possess the freedom to participate in elections, but they cannot exercise full freedom of choice because of the government's credible threat to punish them if they support the opposition. In a study of Mexican municipalities in the mid-1990s, which received on average 80 percent of their budgets from higher governments, the localities that failed to vote for the incumbent Institutional Revolutionary Party, known by its Spanish acronym the PRI, received one-quarter less funds (Diaz-Cayeros *et al.* 2008). The PRI used this technique to manipulate voters to support it during its long-term dominance of Mexican politics (1930–2000). Similarly, Rodriguez (1995) and Ward (1995) showed that when the first two Mexican municipalities elected opposition mayors in 1983, they experienced a budget drop in the order of 50 percent. This system is at once tragic and brilliant because it forces citizens who prefer the opposition to support a corrupt, incumbent regime.

In contrast, open access orders provide local public goods impersonally on the basis of citizenship, not on the basis of political support. The impersonal delivery of services at once lowers the stakes of power and prevents the incumbent regime from manipulating citizens by threatening to cut off valuable public goods and services. Elections in natural states therefore do not work in the same way as those in open access orders, and they often fall far short of the democratic ideal.

The absence of perpetuity

Central to creating the rule-of-law is creating a perpetual state whose institutions, rules, and policies do not depend on the identity of current officials or dominant coalition. The problem with natural states in the developing world is that almost none have perpetual states. Consider the most institutionalized and sophisticated natural state, ones that in the NWW framework are mature natural states. A great many mature natural states have constitutions that specify separation of power systems with elections, legislatures, presidents, and independent judiciaries. The problem is that these institutions fail to work as specified in the constitution or as they do in open access orders. Nearly all of the mature natural states – for example, Argentina, Brazil, Chile, India, Mexico, Russia, and Venezuela – have experienced constitutional breakdowns or subversion of constitutional institutions in the last three decades. The absence of open access to organizations means an absence of a civil society to help police political officials. Legislatures cannot effectively police the executive without a working judiciary – no institution exists to enforce legislative restrictions on the executive – so the corrupt judiciaries of natural states hinder the separation of powers system.

The absence of perpetuity reflects the absence of credible commitments that bind political officials to honor political institutions and the rights they protect. When these institutions or rights become inconvenient, political officials ignore, abuse, or rescind these rights. I have already mentioned Russia under Putin. In recent years, a host of Latin American countries – including Chávez in Venezuela and President Carlos Menem in Argentina – have defied their supreme courts, either by directly ignoring rulings; or, in parallel with the Stuart kings, firing judges who fail to give favorable rulings; or by simply packing the supreme court with compliant judges so as to obtain desired rulings. India's President Indira Gandhi did so in the 1970s. So too have many African leaders.

Along with the absence of the other doorstep conditions, the absence of perpetuity in most natural states helps explain why most attempts over the past four decades to transplant markets, elections, and judicial institutions into a great many natural states have failed to produce thriving markets, vibrant democracies, and independent judiciaries throughout the developing world. These reforms may last for a few years, but they cannot be sustained. When the natural state reaches a crisis, they typically go by the wayside.

Let me illustrate this point with the failure of democracy; when, for example, incumbents refuse to abide by election results (or commit fraud to remain in office) or opponents take power by force. In each of these instances, the rule-of-law fails as fundamental rules of the society are set aside. Examples abound: the fall of the Second Spanish Republic in 1936 into Civil War, the dramatic Chilean coup of 1973, and the PRI's electoral fraud in the 1988 election.

The recent events in Kenya illustrate this point. Many observers had thought Kenya had turned a corner, moving from the brutal dictatorship of Daniel arap Moi to democracy in a series of steps from the early 1990s through the early 2000s. New organizations and a civil society flourished. A range of economic reforms and economic growth followed so that by 2007 Kenya seemed a symbol of hope for sub-Saharan Africa. And yet much of this progress fell apart following the elections at the end of 2007. In part because the stakes were too high, the incumbent party resorted to electoral fraud, refusing to cede power. The result was widespread violence.

Kenya's progress followed by relapse illustrates the dynamic problem of the rule-of-law emphasized in this chapter. Natural states may exhibit periods of reform, democracy, and economic growth; but the absence of perpetuity means that, when the situation becomes difficult, incumbents or outsiders with access to violence break the rules as a means of furthering their own interests in the face of large threats. Maintaining the rule-of-law is not simply about what the rules are today, but whether perpetuity and credible commitments exist so that these rules can be sustained in the future.

How natural states today differ from the historic transitions

The existence of open access orders in today's world transforms the problem of development and creation of the rule-of-law. Most obviously, the existence and wealth of open access orders provides an understanding of what can be achieved in ways that were missing during the historic transitions of the first movers. More subtly – and paradoxically – the existence of open access orders combines with globalization to *reduce* the demand in many of today's natural states for rule-of-law. The reason is that elites and middle class can outsource the credible commitments to open access orders by holding assets in open access order banks rather than those at home and by partnering with multinational companies that, as an enticement to invest domestically, are given special privileges that protect their investments (North *et al.* 2007).

Conclusions

The central feature of the rule-of-law – creating certainty and equality of the law with an absence of arbitrary abuse – requires not only the supremacy of the law as traditional arguments emphasize but a dynamic component by which the law holds not only today but also in the future. Sustaining the rule-of-law therefore involves creating perpetuity. To sustain the rule-of-law over time, the state must become perpetually lived; that is, state institutions must survive beyond those who create them so that the identities of political officials do not matter. To have this ability requires the appropriate form of credible commitments that provide political officials with the incentives to honor these institutions and the rights they protect so that turnover in officials does not result in major alterations of institutions and rights.

This perspective shows why it is so difficult to transplant the rule-of-law into developing countries; and, further, why developing countries often actively resist attempts to secure the rule-of-law. Natural states solve the problem of violence by granting powerful members privileges and rents. These states adjust to changing circumstances by adjusting the distribution of privileges. Big changes in circumstances, for example, following crises, often require big adjustments in privileges, institutions, and policies. These adjustments are often accompanied by violence or threats of violence. Governments fall, coups occur, rights are altered, assets expropriated, constitutions are arbitrarily changed or ignored, and policies altered. Natural states also lack a perpetual state. The absence of perpetuity means that these states do not have the necessary credible commitments that provide political actors with incentives to honor the constitutional rules, making it difficult for these states to sustain many rights and institutions.

Even when natural states adopt all the right constitutional provisions of democracy, separation of powers, and the specification of individual rights, they cannot create a perpetual state so they cannot sustain these provisions over the long term. The problem with most reforms is that they attempt to transplant the rules, rights, and institutions from open access orders directly into natural states. These attempts nearly always fail because they cannot alter the basic structure and incentives of the natural state. When natural states face crises, they inevitably go through dramatic transformations that revise institutions, rules, and policies, making it difficult to sustain the rule-of-law.

To gain the rule-of-law, natural states must enter the transition from limited access order to an open access order.[13] This means the fragile natural states must first become basic ones; basic natural states become mature ones; and mature natural states begin the transition with the doorstep conditions. Only at this stage of development are states capable of beginning to create the institutional and organizational basis for the rule-of-law.

The tenor of this chapter is thus a pessimistic one. It suggests that creating the rule-of-law involves the transition from limited to open access order which has proven quite difficult. Natural states have dominated history and represent the vast majority of states in existence today. Although natural states have existed for 10,000 years, only a little over two dozen states have succeeded in this transformation, with most clustered in Europe.

Notes

1 The author gratefully acknowledges helpful comments and conversations with Lee Cabatingan, Margaret Levi, Robert Nelson, Douglass North, Jed Stiglitz, John Wallis, and Steven Webb.
2 North *et al.* (2007) elaborate some of the implications of the framework for the problems of economic development.
3 Moreover, the law may endow non-corporeal persons, such as organizations, with personhood so that they have legal standing under the law. A legal person is an entity capable of bearing rights and duties. Western law since the Romans has recognized legal persons as combinations of both sets of attributes.
4 In this chapter, I use the term "power" to refer to those who control organizations capable of exercising coercion and violence.
5 Some earlier states, such as Ancient Athens and the Roman Republic, had begun the transition, but none completed the transition to an open access order.
6 Most new democracies fail. To the extent that open access orders can sustain stable democracy, something must be different about them. Yet the literature fails to provide a compelling case for what and why. See Weingast (2006) for details.
7 These issues are quite complicated, both in terms of the various forms of rights (breaking property into different groups; placing different conditions on different pieces of property), different forms of legal rules, and so on. See NWW (NWW: ch. 3).
8 This dynamic component is not always assured in open access orders. The Bush Administration's handling of suspected terrorists demonstrates that, at the margin, these rules can be compromised when open access orders face difficult circumstances.
9 This discussion of English medieval land rights draws on NWW (NWW: ch. 3).
10 The set of such circumstances is large – what North (1981: ch. 1) refers to as changes in relative prices: demographic shifts, natural disasters, the outbreak of war, and the invention of new technologies.
11 Manipulating the judiciary is common in the natural states of today's developing world, including Chávez in Venezuela, former president Carlos Menem of Argentina, former president Pervez Musharraf of Pakistan, former president Indira Gandhi of India, and Putin in Russia.
12 Easterly (2001) provides a sobering assessment of aid programs and their systematic lack of success.
13 These ideas about the transition are further developed in North *et al.* (2007).

Part II

Global justice and the world community

Chapter 3

Global justice[1]

Amartya Sen[2]

"Injustice anywhere is a threat to justice everywhere," wrote Dr Martin Luther King, Jr, 45 years ago in April 1963, in a letter from Birmingham Jail. It would be hard to find a more urgent intellectual agenda today than the demands of world justice. But world justice is not an easy subject. Nor is the notion of "the rule-of-law" which motivates this research initiative. I think I should begin with a few remarks on the idea of justice in general and that of world justice in particular, as well as on the idea of the rule-of-law.

It is, I would argue, useful to distinguish between (1) an *organization-focused* understanding of justice, and (2) the basic idea of *realized justice*. Sometimes justice is conceptualized in terms of certain organizational requirements – some institutions, some regulations, some rules (for example, free speech, or free trade, or progressive taxation, depending on a particular understanding of the structural demands of justice). This can be fine enough as far as it goes, but going beyond institutions and structures, we also have to examine what actually does emerge, influenced by institutions and organizations, but also by other features of the society (such as behavior modes, social norms and practices, and so on).

In classical Sanskrit, two distinct words – *niti* and *nyaya* – help to differentiate two separate concentrations. Words such as *niti* and *nyaya* have been used in many different senses by different legal theorists in ancient India, but one of the main uses of the term *niti* is organizational propriety. In contrast, the term *nyaya* stands for a more comprehensive concept of realized justice. In this line of vision, the role of institutions, important as it is, takes a subsidiary and partial role. For example, the ancient Indian legal theorists talked disparagingly of what they called *matsyanaya*: "justice in the world of fish" – a society of fish where a big fish can freely devour a small fish. This is outlined as what is to be avoided, and it is seen as imperative that the "justice of fish" cannot invade the world of human beings. So *nyaya* is the subject matter of the kind of society that the social institutions and practical rules should be aimed at, working with other influences. The realization of justice in the sense of *nyaya* is not just a matter of judging institutions and rules, but of judging the societies themselves. Whatever the propriety of established organizations, if a big fish remains free to devour a small fish, then this is a violation of human justice, no matter to what the causation of that transgression is traced.

In the inclusive perspective of *nyaya*, there is little room for judgments like Ferdinand I's famous sixteenth-century maxim: "Fiat justitia et pereat mundus" (let justice be done, though the world perish). If the world does perish, there would not be much to admire in this development in the perspective of *nyaya*, even though the austere *niti* leading to this result could be defended with very sophisticated arguments of different kinds. The distinction is important, even when *niti* and *nyaya* complement each other. For example, setting up many more schools for children in educationally deprived countries would be an important *niti*, but what would be celebrated in the perspective of *nyaya* is the achievement that boys and girls are actually educated and have the freedom that comes from that accomplishment. Similarly, reforming the counterproductive patent laws for medicine to make urgently needed drugs against preventable diseases affordable by the poor of the world would be an excellent departure in *niti*, but it is the actual overcoming of those diseases (through the combination of cheaper drugs, more targeted research, better delivery and use, and so on) that would demand inclusion in the vision of *nyaya*.

It is easy to see that the pursuit of world justice would need a great many institutional developments and organizational changes around the globe, but underlying our interest in institutional analysis must be some idea of the overall demands of global justice itself. The distinction between *nyaya* and *niti* is, thus, important for the subject of world justice.

Something similar can, in fact, be said of our understanding of the "rule-of-law," the basic idea behind our research initiative. The challenge is not confined only to making sure that the laws, as they exist, apply to all and are followed by all, though these demands too can be very important (as Frederick Marryat put it famously in 1830 in *The King's Own*, "there cannot be one law for the rich and another for the poor"). But going beyond that, we must also take on board the need to scrutinize the kind of comprehensive justice (in the sense of *nyaya*) that emerges from practices of the rule-of-law. As James Heckman, Robert Nelson, and William Neukom point out, it is necessary to examine "fundamental normative questions as what defines a good life and what the ultimate ends of a rule-of-law system might be" (2007). The subject matter of this volume is, thus, both complex and momentous.

Contemporary political philosophy

We are not, of course, working in an intellectual vacuum, for these subjects have engaged attention over a very long period of time. There are also well-developed bodies of literature on the theory of justice in political philosophy, in jurisprudence and legal philosophy, and in welfare economics. That large literature has much relevance to the challenge that this project is attempting to address.

Even though the inspiration for contemporary works on justice goes back to classic contributions of the stalwarts of the European Enlightenment, for example the contributions of Jean Jacques Rousseau, Immanuel Kant, Jeremy Bentham, and Thomas Jefferson, the modern discipline of the theory of justice has been most strongly influenced by the writings of John Rawls, whose path-breaking book, *A Theory of Justice*, published in 1971, has set the stage for much of the present-day animation in the theory of justice. Even those of our leading contemporary political philosophers, such as Ronald Dworkin, Thomas Nagel, Robert Nozick, and Thomas Scanlon (to name a few), who have proposed rather different ways of dealing with the issues identified by Rawls in his famous contribution, have tended to a great extent to see the requirements of a theory of justice in basically Rawlsian co-ordinates. John Rawls is clearly the dominant influence in the contemporary philosophy of justice.

I must admit that I too have, until fairly recently, tended to agree on the centrality of the Rawlsian perspective on justice, seeking departures mainly in the form of different answers to essentially Rawlsian inquiries. I now believe that this is a serious mistake, despite the profundity of Rawls's ideas and the debt that we owe to him.[3] It is, I believe, quite useful to examine why the skepticism of the Rawlsian basic framework may be justified, and why there is an urgent need for foundational departures from the prevailing theories of justice in contemporary political philosophy. These departures are necessary for the theory of justice in general, but they are particularly important for addressing the challenges of world justice.

Rawlsian theory of justice as fairness

The starting point of Rawls's formulation of the theory of justice is his insistence that the idea of justice – and the institutions needed for it – should be based on the demands of a more foundational concept than justice, namely fairness. It is on the foundations of fairness (as characterized by Rawls) that the Rawlsian principles of justice are developed. Fairness involves a demand to avoid bias in our assessments, and in particular the need to escape being influenced by our respective vested interests or personal advantages. It is, in this sense, a demand for impartiality. Rawls's explication of the demands of impartiality makes use of an imaginary device, which he calls the "original position." The original position is a postulated situation of primordial equality, when the parties involved have no knowledge of their respective personal identities *within* the group as a whole. They have to choose, under this devised "veil of ignorance," what exact rules should govern the society they are, as it were, "establishing." The influence of individual vested interest or personal gain is "kept out" through the insistence that the deliberations on the choice of rules occur under ignorance of each person of his or her own personal interests and particular desires. This is how Rawls gets to his principles of justice.

Rawls's principles of justice, thus chosen, are aimed at the selection of the basic institutional structure of the society. He characterizes in the following way the exact principles that he expects would emerge in the "original position," with a priority for the first principle over the second, in the case of any conflict.

> (1) Each person has an equal right to a fully adequate scheme of equal basic liberties which is compatible with a similar scheme of liberties for all. (2) Social and economic inequalities must satisfy two conditions. First, they must be attached to offices and positions open to all under conditions of fair equality of opportunity; and second, they must be to the greatest benefit of the least advantaged members of society.
>
> (Rawls 1993: 291)

It will be readily seen that the principles of justice, which are aimed at setting up "just institutions," take the form of specifying organizational requirements mainly in the sense of *niti*, rather than judging the societies as a whole, in the sense of *nyaya*. That, as will emerge, is indeed a problem, but I must also emphasize that despite this rather limited focus, Rawls does also provide plentiful discussion of the kind of just society we might hope to see as emerging from these appropriate institutional choices.

More substantively, it can be seen that the principles of justice identified by Rawls include the priority of liberty (the "first principle") giving precedence to maximal liberty for each person subject to similar liberty for all. Other issues of institutional choice are taken up through a compound set of requirements that are combined in the "second principle," but the "priority of liberty" comes first.

Among the important features of this set of principles for just institutions is the special role that Rawls gives to the claims of personal liberty. This is given priority over the demands of the second principle related to the equality of certain general opportunities and to the need for equity in the distribution of other general-purpose resources.

The first part of the second principle is concerned with the institutional requirement of making sure that public opportunities are open to all, without anyone being excluded or handicapped on grounds of, say, race or ethnicity or caste or religion. The second part of the second principle (called the "Difference Principle") is concerned with distributive equity as well as overall efficiency, and it takes the form of making the worst off members of the society as well-off as possible.

Rawls's analysis of equity in the distribution of resources is done through an index of what Rawls calls "primary goods," which are *general-purpose means* to achieve a variety of ends (whatever resources would be generally helpful in getting what people would want, varied as they might be). Rawls sees primary goods as including such things as "rights, liberties and opportunities, income and wealth, and the social bases of self-respect" (1971: 60–5).

Some questions

Rawlsian theory of justice has been a major constructive force in political philosophy, welfare economics, and legal theory. Even though I must argue for the need for several radical departures from the Rawlsian understanding of the theory of justice, I must also emphasize how much our thinking on justice has benefited from Rawls's constructive work – both affirmatively and dialectically. Also, there are elements of Rawls's theory that, I would argue, cannot but be central to any plausible theory of justice. For example, I would strongly support Rawls's chosen starting point, to wit, the need to consider the demands of fairness as a prelude to the scrutiny of justice. Even though I shall presently suggest that the particular way Rawls proceeds to characterize fairness has several difficulties, I concur with his general belief that some exacting demands of impartiality must be incorporated in the foundations of justice.

I The discipline of comparison

I proceed now to a number of critical issues that are problematic in the Rawlsian framework. The first question is extremely simple but, I would argue, rather far-reaching: *what do we want from a theory of justice*? In his analysis of justice, Rawls takes the principal task of a theory of justice to be aimed at identifying the "just society." This leads to what can be called a "transcendental" approach to justice that focuses on identifying perfectly just societal arrangements, rather than offering a way of comparing not entirely just societies against each other (the kind of societies we might actually encounter in the world – to decide on what we should actually do. The transcendental approach goes back at least to the writings of Thomas Hobbes, and to his insistence that we cannot talk about justice without invoking a sovereign state, since we cannot fulfill the exacting requirements of a perfectly just society without the help of unimpeded sovereignty. So this is in line with a transcendental approach (focusing on the unsurpassably just), but there were, in fact, many other approaches in political philosophy that emerged during the Enlightenment which did not take the transcendental route (for example, those proposed by Adam Smith, or Condorcet, or Mary Wollstonecraft, or William Godwin, or Jeremy Bentham, or James Mill).[4]

However, in Rawls's work, and in the theories that have followed his identification of the requirements of a theory of justice, the attention of modern political philosophy has tended to be relentlessly focused on addressing the transcendental question (and quite often *only* that question). In contrast, what can be called a "comparative" approach would have concentrated instead on ranking alternative societal arrangements (whether some arrangement is "less just" or "more just" than another, so that we get guidance on what to do), rather than focusing exclusively – or at all – on the identification of a fully just society. Modern social choice theory takes a robustly comparative approach.[5] I shall call this "the comparison question."

2 Room for disagreement

The second question concerns the type of agreement that can be reasonably expected to emerge from public reasoning under conditions of fairness (in Rawls's case through his device of the "original position"). Can we really expect that everyone in the original position would proceed to accept some one specific set of rules – principles of justice – as the only way to go? Is it sensible to assume that all our disagreements really arise from our respective vested interests (so that once they are taken out of action, we would all come to exactly the same conclusion)? Could it be that some of our differences are linked with basically different conceptions of justice, focusing on different grounds of justice? I shall call this the "room for disagreement question."

3 Individual interest, social parochialism, and open impartiality

The third issue concerns Rawls's way of characterizing the demands of fairness. How do we specify these demands so that the evaluation of justice and the choice of principles of justice, under those conditions, guarantees the necessary impartiality? The issue of impartiality relates both to eliminating the influence of vested interest across the board, and also to eradicating the impact of local parochialism – an issue of some importance not only for global justice, but also for local or national justice in a global world. Rawls keeps his exercise of fairness confined to the limits of each polity on its own, that is, roughly speaking, separately for each nation state. While fairness in the treatment of all the persons in a nation (or "a people," as Rawls calls that collectivity) is pursued by Rawls through vigorous elimination of individual vested interests, others who do not belong to this nation or people do not come into consideration in the same way at all.

That is problem enough, but there is in addition a second problem as well. The exclusive focus on eliminating the influence of individual vested interest, as opposed to that of community-based parochialism, makes the pursuit of impartiality and fairness in the Rawlsian framework that much more limited. I shall call this "the impartiality question."

4 Freedoms and capabilities

Fourth, since Rawls concentrates on a person's holding of "primary goods" (like income, wealth, etc.) to judge the overall advantage that he or she enjoys compared with others, there is some serious overlooking of the fact that different persons, for reasons of personal characteristics or environmental influence, can have widely varying "conversion" opportunities of external objects (like income and wealth) to their respective capabilities – what they can or cannot actually do. A person with a proneness to illness, or living in an epidemiologically challenged environment, may get far less out of a given amount of income than another who is not similarly afflicted.

Rawls does talk about the eventual emergence of special provisions for "special needs" (for example, for the blind or for those who are otherwise clearly disabled), at a later phase – the "legislative phase" – of his multi-stage story of Rawlsian justice. This is good rectification as far as it goes, but (1) these corrections occur (if they do) only after the basic institutional structure has been set up through the Rawlsian "principles of justice" (which are not influenced by such "special needs"), and (2) even at a later stage, when special note is taken of "special needs," there is no attempt to come to terms with the *pervasive* variations in conversion opportunities between any two different persons.

Transcendental versus the comparative

The transcendental and comparative approaches are quite distinct, and neither approach, in general, subsumes the other.[6] This is unfortunate for the transcendental approach, since no matter what other characteristics a theory of justice might sensibly have, it must also, for use in practical reasoning, help us to address comparative assessments of justice, such as: how can we make a country, or the world, less unjust? The pursuit of justice in the world can never take the form of jumping in one go to some perfectly just society. Despite that, the Rawlsian framework, and nearly all the theories of justice in contemporary political philosophy, are exclusively devoted to identifying "the perfectly just," rather than being concerned in any direct way with comparative assessments.

The intellectual interest in, and practical relevance of, comparative questions about justice are hard to deny. Investigation of different ways of advancing justice in a society (or in the world), or of reducing the manifest injustices that may exist, demands comparative judgments about justice, for which the identification of fully just social arrangements is neither necessary nor sufficient. To illustrate the contrast involved, it may well turn out that in a comparative perspective, the introduction of social policies that eliminate widespread hunger (or remove rampant illiteracy) is widely seen as a manifest advancement of justice. But the implementation of such policies would still leave the societies involved far away from the transcendental – or unsurpassable – requirements of a fully just society (since transcendence would have many other demands regarding equal liberties, distributional equity, and so on).

To take another example, instituting a system of health insurance in the United States that does not leave tens of millions of Americans without any guarantee of medical attention at all may be judged to be an advancement of justice, but such an institutional change would not turn the United States into a "just society," since there would remain a thousand other transgressions to remedy. Some non-transcendental articulation is clearly needed.

But, it can be asked, do we not need a transcendental pure theory to have an intellectually adequate theory of comparative assessment of justice? There seems to be fairly widespread belief among many of the practitioners of Rawlsian and other transcendental theories of justice that comparative questions can be answered only with the help of a transcendental identification of a perfectly just society. It is, however, not at all easy to see why this should be the case. Indeed, the two exercises are quite distinct and neither need throw much light on the other. You cannot get anything like the richness of a comparative approach from identifying a transcendental possibility. For example, you may firmly conclude that Leonardo da Vinci is the best painter ever in the world (including Picasso, Braques, and so on), but it won't tell you how to rank Picasso against Braque. Conversely, you could not necessarily get the unsurpassable (or the transcendental) alternative from the totality of our comparative judgments. We may be able to make a great many pairwise comparisons, but not quite all. We may be able to rank, say, Picasso against Braque, or Dali, and make many other such judgments, and yet we may fail to identify the "very best," or the "absolutely right" choice, because of an inability to rank some pairs of alternatives, say Picasso against Van Gogh (if the two are competing for the top position).

This is not to reduce in any way the importance of the inspiration that Rawls's transcendental theory has provided in drawing general attention to many issues of practical importance, such as the critical role of social institutions, the special status of personal liberty, or the centrality of poverty removal as a social concern. And yet if we want to use that theory not just for inspiration, but for guidance in making judgments about the enhancement of justice through institutional reform or behavioral transformation, we would not, alas, get any specific comparative implications from the identification of a transcendental alternative.[7]

Disengagement from world justice in transcendental theories

It is not hard to see that world justice demands many reforms and many new institutions and practices. But the mere identification of the "perfectly just society" would not tell us much about what to do to pursue the advance of justice in the world in which we live. Indeed, the concentration on the transcendental approach has had, I would argue, a seriously negative effect on practical discussion of justice in general and global justice in particular. We can think of many changes that would manifestly advance world justice as we see it, without getting us to "the perfectly just world." However, that kind of discussion would appear to be just "loose talk" to those who are persuaded by the Hobbesian–Rawlsian claim that justice is about the perfectly just society, and that we need a fully sovereign state to apply the principles of justice with its extensive institutional requirements, which is a consequence of taking questions of justice to be exclusively issues of transcendental justice.

Consider the strongly argued dismissal of the relevance of "the idea of global justice" by one of the leading contemporary philosophers, Thomas Nagel (from whose work I have learned so many things). His argument draws on his understanding that there are extensive institutional demands to think cogently about justice which cannot be met at the global level at this time. As Nagel puts it, "It seems to me very difficult to resist Hobbes's claim about the relation between justice and sovereignty," and "if Hobbes is right, the idea of global justice without a world government is a chimera" (Nagel 2005: 115). In the global context, Nagel concentrates, therefore, on clarifying other demands, distinguishable from the demands of justice, such as "minimal humanitarian morality" (ibid.: 130–3, 146–7).

In the Rawlsian approach too, the application of a theory of justice requires an extensive cluster of institutions that determines the basic structure of a fully just society. Not surprisingly, Rawls actually abandons his own principles of justice when it comes to the assessment of how to go about thinking about global justice. In a later contribution, *The Law of Peoples*, Rawls invokes a "second original position," with a fair negotiation involving representatives of different polities – or different "peoples" as Rawls calls them – who serve as parties under this second veil of ignorance (1999). However, Rawls does not try to derive principles of justice that might emanate from this second original position, and concentrates instead on certain general principles of humanitarian behavior.

Thus, the theory of justice, as formulated in this transcendental approach, reduces many of the most relevant questions of justice in the world as being simply inadmissible when they would seem to be most strongly needed. This is a pity: when people across the world agitate to get more global justice, they are not clamoring for some kind of "minimal humanitarianism."

Incomplete orderings and the use of comparative judgments

Am I overstretching the dichotomy between the transcendental and the comparative? The former may be neither necessary nor sufficient for the other, but should not a sequence of pairwise comparisons invariably lead us to the very best? That presumption has some appeal, since the superlative might indeed appear to be the natural end point of a robust comparative. But this is, in fact, a non sequitur. It is only with a "well-ordered" ranking (for example, a complete and transitive ordering over a finite set) that we can be sure that pairwise comparisons must ultimately identify a "best" alternative.

We must, therefore, ask: how complete should the assessment be, for it to be a systematic discipline of evaluation? In what can be called a "totalist" approach that characterizes the standard theories of justice (including Rawls's), incompleteness tends to appear as a failure, or at least as a sign of the unfinished nature of the exercise. Indeed, the survival of incompleteness is sometimes seen as a defect of a theory of justice, which calls into question the positive assertions that such a theory makes. In fact, however, a theory of justice that makes systematic room for incompleteness allows one to arrive at possibly quite strong judgments (for example, about the injustice of continuing famines in a world of prosperity, or of persistently grotesque subjugation of women), without having to find highly differentiated assessment of every political and social arrangement in comparison with every other arrangement (e.g. addressing such questions as: is a top income tax rate of 39 percent more just or less just than a top rate of 38 percent?)

I have discussed elsewhere why a systematic and disciplined theory of normative evaluation, including assessment of social justice, need not take a "totalist" form (Sen 2000; see also Sen 1970; 1997; 1999b; and 2004b). Incompleteness may be of the lasting kind for several different reasons, including unbridgeable gaps in information and judgmental unresolvability involving disparate considerations that cannot be entirely eliminated, even with full information. For example, it may be hard to resolve the overall balance of the comparative claims of equity considerations, when different considerations conflict in subtle ways. And yet, despite such durable ambiguity, we may still be able to agree readily that there is a clear social injustice involved in the persistence of endemic hunger or exclusion from medical access, which calls for remedying for the *advancement* of justice (or reduction of injustice), even after taking note of the costs involved. Similarly, we may acknowledge the possibility that liberties of different persons may, to some extent, conflict with each other (so that any fine-tuning of the demands of equal liberty may be hard to work out), and yet strongly agree that torturing people in custody would be an unjust violation of liberty, and such policies demand immediate rectification.

There is a further consideration that may work powerfully in the direction of making political room for incompleteness of judgments about social justice, even if it were the case that every person had a complete ordering over the possible social arrangements. Since a theory of justice invokes agreement between different parties (for example, in the "original position" in the Rawlsian framework), incompleteness can also arise from the possibility that different persons may continue to have some differences, even after agreeing on a lot of the comparative judgments. Even after vested interests and personal gains have been somehow "taken out" of consideration through such devices as the "veil of ignorance," there may remain possibly conflicting views on social priorities, for example in weighing the claims of need over entitlement to the fruits of one's labor.

Room for disagreement: an illustration

Conflicts of distributive principles that are hard to eradicate can be illustrated with an example. The illustration is concerned with the problem of deciding which of three children should get a flute about which they are quarrelling – you have to adjudicate between these different claims. Child A claims it on the ground that she is the only one of the three who knows how to play the flute (the others don't deny this). If that was all you knew, the case for giving it to the first child would be strong.

However, child B expresses his claim to the flute on the ground that he is the only one among the three who is so poor that he has no toy of his own, and that the flute will give him something to play with (the other two concede that they are much richer and well-supplied with engaging amenities). If you had only heard child B and none of the others, the case for giving it to child B would be strong.

Child C, on the other hand, argues that she has been working for many months to make the flute with her own labor (the others confirm this), and just when she had finished her work, she complains, "these Johnnies came along trying to snatch the flute away from me." You might have given it to child C if her statement was all you had heard.

However, having heard all three you do have a problem. Theorists of different persuasions – *utilitarian* or *egalitarian* or *libertarian* – may believe that a just resolution can be readily spotted here, though, alas, they would respectively see totally different resolutions as being "obviously right."

The main point to note in the present context is that the different resolutions all have serious arguments in support of them, and we may not be able to identify, without some arbitrariness, one of the alternative arguments as being the only one that must invariably prevail. Different impartial judges may take different views in this decisional problem (unrelated to their respective vested interest or hope of personal gain). And the problem of choice in this case is ultimately one of priorities in the principles of justice, so that the decisional dilemma reflects a deeper problem of conflict of unrejectable principles that would need to be accommodated.

And yet in many particular cases, there will be no decisional dilemma to resolve, even when none of the underlying reasons is summarily rejected. It may turn out that the child who has made the flute is also the poorest, or the only one who knows how to play the flute. Or it might be the case that child B's deprivation is so extreme, and his dependence on something to play with so important for a plausible life, that the poverty-based argument might come to dominate the judgment of justice. There could be what can be called "circumscribed congruence" despite the varying weights that different impartial judges apply to the conflicting considerations.

Rawls has shown, rather convincingly in my view, why liberty has a special place that cannot be ignored when comparing the claims of liberty against other considerations, including the avoidance of inequality and poverty. Rawls went on to argue for giving total priority to liberty in *all* cases. It is much easier to be persuaded that such a priority would be quite right when the violations of personal liberty happen to be extremely serious, whereas issues of economic inequality are not at all matters of life and death. And yet when the transgressions against liberty are rather marginal, and the inequalities involved can cause extremely tragic deprivations, then, as Herbert Hart, the Oxford legal philosopher, argued in a famous critique of Rawls, the case for giving invariable priority to liberty would be hard to defend (Hart 1973). In his later writings, Rawls was willing to make some concessions to Hart's argument (Rawls 1993: Lecture VIII), and yet his theory makes that very hard to do.

Open impartiality and global public discussion

I turn now to the third issue, the impartiality question. The role of impartiality in the evaluation of social judgments and societal arrangements is well recognized in moral and political philosophy. There is, however, a basic distinction between two quite different ways of invoking impartiality. With what I would call "closed impartiality," the procedure of making impartial judgments invokes only the members of a given society or nation or what Rawls calls a "people." The Rawlsian method of "justice as fairness" uses the device of an "original contract" between the citizens of a given polity. No outsider is involved in such a contractarian procedure, or is a party to the original contract (either directly, or through representatives). For the members of the focal group, the "veil of ignorance" requires them to be ignorant of their respective identity *within* the focal group, and this can be an effective procedure for overcoming *individual partialities* within the focal group.

However, even under the veil of ignorance a person does know that he or she belongs to the focal group, and is not someone outside it – indeed he or she could be anyone in that particular group – and there is no insistence at all that perspectives from outside the focal group be invoked. As a device of structured political analysis, the procedure is not geared to addressing the need to overcome group prejudices or parochialism.

In contrast, in the case of "open impartiality," the procedure of making impartial judgments can (and in some cases, must) invoke judgments *inter alia* from outside the focal group. For example, in Adam Smith's use of the device of "the impartial spectator," the requirement of impartiality requires the invoking of disinterested judgments of "any fair and impartial spectator," not necessarily (indeed, sometimes ideally not) belonging to the focal group (Smith 1976).

Adam Smith was particularly concerned about avoiding the grip of parochialism in jurisprudence and moral and political reasoning. In a chapter entitled "Of the Influence of Custom and Fashion upon the Sentiments of Moral Approbation and Disapprobation," Smith gives various examples of how discussions confined within a given society can be incarcerated within a seriously narrow understanding:

> the murder of new-born infants was a practice allowed of in almost all the states of Greece, even among the polite and civilized Athenians; and

> whenever the circumstances of the parent rendered it inconvenient to bring up the child, to abandon it to hunger, or to wild beasts, was regarded without blame or censure ... Uninterrupted custom had by this time so thoroughly authorized the practice, that not only the loose maxims of the world tolerated this barbarous prerogative, but even the doctrine of philosophers, which ought to have been more just and accurate, was led away by the established custom, and upon this, as upon many other occasions, instead of censuring, supported the horrible abuse, by far-fetched considerations of public utility. Aristotle talks of it as of what the magistrate ought upon many occasions to encourage. The humane Plato is of the same opinion, and, with all that love of mankind which seems to animate all his writings, nowhere marks this practice with disapprobation.
>
> (ibid.: V.2.15, 210)

Adam Smith's insistence that we must *inter alia* view our sentiments from "a certain distance from us" is, thus, motivated by the object of scrutinizing not only the influence of vested interest, but also the impact of entrenched tradition and custom. While Smith's example of infanticide remains sadly relevant in some societies even today, many of his other examples have relevance to other contemporary societies. This applies, for example, to Smith's insistence that "the eyes of the rest of mankind" must be invoked to understand whether "a punishment appears equitable" (Smith 1978: 104). Scrutiny from a "distance" may be useful for practices as different as the stoning of adulterous women in Taliban's Afghanistan, selective abortion of female fetuses in China, Korea, and parts of South Asia (see, e.g., Sen 2001), and plentiful use of capital punishment in China, Singapore, or for that matter in parts of the United States (with or without the opportunity for celebratory public jubilation).

While we are not likely to have a global state or a global democracy any time soon, Smith's emphasis on the use of the impartial spectator has immediate implications for the role of global public discussion in the contemporary world, to arrive at some important comparative judgments. Global dialogue, which I believe is central for world justice, comes today not only through institutions like the United Nations or the WTO, but much more broadly through the media, through political agitations, through the committed work of citizens' organizations and many NGOs, and through social work that draws not only on national identities but also on other commonalities, like trade union movements, cooperative operations, or feminist activities.

Primary goods versus capabilities

I turn, finally, to the capability question. In comparing the relative advantage of two persons in applying the Difference Principle of Rawls, we are directed by Rawls to proceed on the basis of the holdings of primary goods the two persons respectively have. But he focuses on command over general-purpose resources, rather than the actual ability of the person to do this or be that. In a series of contributions the Rawlsian approach of focusing on primary goods has been fairly extensively challenged in recent years by the alternative perspective of what is called the "capability approach" (see, e.g., Sen 1985 and Nussbaum and Sen 1993).[8] In that line of vision a central role is given to the person's actual ability to do the different things he or she has reason to value. These attainments in human living (like being well nourished, avoiding premature mortality, taking part in the life of the community, and so on) are called human functionings. We have to concentrate on those functionings which we value and have reason to value, and the focus is specifically on a person's capability to achieve particular combinations of valued functionings. All the achievable combinations of functionings are called a person's capability set, and it is on this that the capability approach concentrates.

Through this elementary procedure, the capability approach focuses on human life, and not just on some detached objects of convenience, such as incomes or commodities that a person may possess, which are often assumed to be the main criteria of human success. Since the income-oriented approach is quite standard in economics in particular, the capability approach proposes a change – a serious departure – away from concentrating on the *means* of living, to the *actual opportunities* of living.

It is not hard to see the reasoning underlying the understanding that the departure in favor of capability can make a significant – and constructive – difference. For example, if a person has a high income but is also very prone to persistent illness (for inherited, acquired or environmental reasons), then the person need not necessarily be seen as being very well off on the mere grounds that her income is high. She certainly has more of one of the means of living well (that is, a lot of income), but she has difficulty in translating that into good living (that is, living in a way that she has reason to value) because of the adversities of illness and physical handicap. We have to look instead at the extent to which she can actually achieve, if she so chooses, to be healthy and well, and to do various things she would value doing.

To understand that the *means* of satisfactory human living are not themselves the *ends* of good living, helps to bring about a momentous extension of the reach of the evaluative exercise, especially for world justice. And the use of the capability perspective helps to pursue these extensions.

It is important to emphasize that the focus of the capability approach is not just on what a person actually ends up doing, but also on what she is in fact capable of doing, whether or not she chooses to make use of that opportunity. For example, in terms of being undernourished, a famine-stricken victim may be just as deprived of food and nourishment as a person who voluntarily fasts, for political or religious reasons (despite having the ability to buy and eat plenty of food). Their manifest undernutrition may be much the same, but the capability of the well-off person who chooses to fast to be actually well-nourished (if she were to choose to go that way, instead) is much larger than that of the person who starves involuntarily because of poverty and destitution. The idea of capability is, thus, oriented towards freedoms and opportunities (to wit, the capability to live the kinds of lives that people have reason to value), rather than being concerned only with the one particular life that the person chooses to live.

World justice and the rule-of-law

The focus of this chapter has been on linking the understanding of justice to the nature of the society and the kind of opportunities and freedoms that people actually have, not just to institutions and practices (that too, but not just that). In this sense my concentration has been on *nyaya*, rather than only on *niti*. Terrible things happen in the world in which we live – from illiteracy and starvation to torture and violence. They arise from a variety of causes, which demand investigation, but the ultimate test of success is not whether the rules or institutions we can dream up are plausible, but what opportunities, what real capabilities people actually have in the world in which they live, based on all the influences that work on society.

To conclude, I have argued against giving the theory of justice a transcendental form – concerned only with characterizing "the just society." We have reason to try to address as many questions of comparative assessment as we can. Agreement on many major issues of world justice can emerge even when there are other matters in which we continue to differ and disagree. When Adam Smith and Condorcet argued for the abolition of slavery, or for free public education for all, including for women, they were not claiming that these changes would make the world perfectly "just" – but only *more just*, in an identifiable way, than the world they saw around them. A comparative perspective that makes use of incomplete rankings (with the discipline of using partial orders that modern social choice theory has extensively explored) has much more to offer to the understanding of the demands of world justice (strictly, removal of world injustice) than the transcendental approach of Hobbes and Rawls, which is forced to abstain from judgments of world justice to concentrate on the fluffy characteristics of "minimal humanitarianism."

I have also argued against considering the question of impartiality in the fragmented terms that apply only within nation states – never stepping beyond the borders. This is important not only for being as inclusive in our thinking about justice in the world as possible, but also to avoid the dangers of local parochialism against which Adam Smith warned nearly two and a half centuries ago. Indeed, the contemporary world offers a much greater opportunity to learn from each other, and it seems a pity to try to confine the theorization of justice to the artificially imposed limits of nation states. This is not only because (as I earlier quoted Martin Luther King as saying) "injustice anywhere is a threat to justice everywhere" (though that is hugely important as well).

But in addition we have to be aware of how our interest in others across the world has been growing, along with our growing contacts and increasing communication.

Already in the 1770s, David Hume noted the importance of increased intercourse in expanding the reach of our sense of justice. He had put the issue thus (in his chapter "Of Justice," in *An Enquiry Concerning the Principles of Morals*):

> again suppose that several distinct societies maintain a kind of intercourse for mutual convenience and advantage, the boundaries of justice still grow larger, in proportion to the largeness of men's views, and the force of their mutual connexions. History, experience, reason sufficiently instruct us in this natural progress of human sentiments, and in the gradual enlargement of our regards to justice, in proportion as we become acquainted with the extensive utility of that virtue.
>
> (Hume 1966: 25)

The search for world justice is a central challenge in the world today not merely because our lives are interconnected, but also because the very presence of our interconnections makes us inescapably interested in and involved with each other. The "natural progress of human sentiments" and "the gradual enlargement of our regards to justice," which David Hume saw in the 1770s, did not come to an end in the eighteenth century.

Notes

1 This article was produced for the American Bar Association as part of the ABA's World Justice Project, funded by generous grants from the Bill & Melinda Gates Foundation and the William and Flora Hewlett Foundation.
2 For helpful suggestions, I am grateful to Dr Pedro Ramos Pinto and to Kirsty Walker.
3 The outline of a very different approach to the theory of justice is the subject matter of my forthcoming book, *The Idea of Justice* (2009).
4 The emergence of alternative approaches is discussed in my forthcoming book, *The Idea of Justice* (2009).
5 Social choice theory, in its modern form, has been pioneered by Kenneth Arrow (1951) (see also Sen 1970). The analytical priority of the comparative can also be seen in the early formulations of social choice theory in the eighteenth century, particularly by Marquis de Condorcet (see de Condorcet 1785).
6 For a demonstration that identifying a perfectly just society is *neither necessary nor sufficient* for answering comparative questions in justice, see Sen 2006b.
7 The mathematical "disconnect" here is discussed more fully in Sen 2006b.
8 There is a huge literature and extensive active research engagement on this and related subjects in many different countries in the world, with regular meetings organized by the Human Development and Capability Association (HDCA).

Chapter 4

The rule of law in Islamic thought and practice

A historical perspective

Timur Kuran[1]

The rise of movements to restore Islamic law and broaden its reach constitutes one of the most significant events of our time. These movements have spawned vast literatures, energized political movements that have shaken the global international order, and provided rationales for religious militancy. The architects of these campaigns, known as Islamists, view the holy law of Islam, the sharia, as the answer to assorted social, moral, political, and economic problems.[2]

Without necessarily endorsing Islamist goals or values, diverse other groups have supported, or at least tolerated, Islamist campaigns for reasons of their own. Many multiculturalists are sympathetic to reinstituting Islamic law on the ground that diversity is inherently good and cultures cannot be ranked. Assorted democrats support peaceful Islamist parties that prove their popularity through elections. Western military strategists abet selected Islamists as counterweights to secular opponents deemed particularly dangerous; the American support of the Taliban against the Soviet army offers a case in point. Certain constitutional scholars view Islamic law as a vehicle for instituting political checks and balances capable of turning autocracies into stable democracies.

For all this support, Islamic law is very poorly understood. Few people know much about its content or about the means by which it is supposed to achieve results. Surprisingly little comparative research focuses on the identification of its advantages and disadvantages in relation to alternative legal systems or evolving conditions. The goal of this chapter is to advance the comparative agenda by evaluating Islamic law in one particular context, its compatibility with the rule-of-law. To what extent, and in what ways, does Islamic law satisfy the principles of the rule-of-law?

The task requires specifying what these principles entail. As I understand the term, it encompasses government accountability, equal access to justice and the political process, efficient judicial and political systems, clear laws, generally stable laws, and the protection of fundamental human rights.[3] To what extent does Islamic law, in theory and in practice, conform to these principles?

Like the rule-of-law, Islamic law has meant different things to different people. Its applications, too, have varied enormously. The law enforced by the Islamic courts of sixteenth-century Istanbul differed in content and complexity from that enforced in the first Islamic state of seventh-century Arabia. Whereas the Taliban see Islamic law first and foremost as a vehicle for preserving a puritanical lifestyle, constitutional scholars consider its chief virtue to lie in its political functions. Every group gives priority to particular aspects of the Islamic heritage, downplaying, ignoring, or simply overlooking much else. Nevertheless, the various conceptions of Islamic law share certain characteristics that allow useful generalizations. Besides, it is instructive to consider how Islamic law has fared according to certain criteria that are widely considered desirable.

Government accountability

The sharia subjects all human beings – male and female, rich and poor, educated and illiterate – to the same rules. It makes no exceptions, not even for rulers. If people of means are to pay an annual tithe, so must they. If it is wrong to discriminate among Muslims on the basis of tribal affiliation, rulers, too, must pursue tribe-blind policies. If employers must pay their workers a fair wage, rulers are to obey the same standards of fairness vis-à-vis government employees (Rahman 1979: ch. 4; Vikør 2005: chs 1, 10; Lewis 1988: chs 2, 3; Weiss 1998: ch. 2).

A central concept in Islamic political thought is that an Islamic ruler must not only enforce Islamic law but obey it strictly himself. The legitimacy of his rule depends critically on his adherence to the sharia. If he fails to uphold Islamic law through either his policies or his personal life, he must be deposed. Centuries before the issuing of the English Charter of Liberties (Magna Carta) in 1215, in Islamic thought the law was considered a force above government and independent of the whims of individual rulers. In principle, Muslim rulers were accountable for their actions.

To lay down a principle is not the same thing as putting it into practice. The most basic obstacle to implementing the sharia lies in its content. Consisting of a mix of very general and highly specific rules, it covers less than most people realize, and many of the rules are subject to interpretation. Most modern promoters of the sharia consider interest un-Islamic. They thus infer that the officials of an Islamic state should work to eradicate interest-based transactions. But what credit instruments qualify as interest-free? No consensus has emerged, making it impossible to judge conclusively whether any particular government is respecting the presumed interest ban (Kuran 2004; Imber 1997: 145–6).

In the course of Islamic history the promoters and enforcers of Islamic law have understood that its provisions are seldom self-explanatory. Accordingly, they have developed various methods for resolving ambiguities. During Muhammad's lifetime, interpretations were facilitated through new verses of the Koran, Muhammad's own pronouncements, and examples set by his actions. With his death in 632 CE these means ceased to be available with respect to new controversies. For a while people who knew him, or his acquaintances, or acquaintances of his acquaintances, could come forward with recollections of his words or deeds. Whatever the veracity of these recollections, they served to dampen ambiguities and resolve impasses. With every passing generation, of course, new recollections lost credibility. It also became increasingly unlikely that the situations demanding resolution had parallels in Muhammad's time and milieu. Hence, for all practical purposes, the sharia progressively lost its usefulness as a source of guidance in everyday life (Zubaida 2003: ch. 1; Rahman 1979: chs 4, 5). Today, fourteen centuries after the birth of Islam, both rulers and the ruled routinely encounter issues unresolvable by consulting the Koran or remembrances of the Prophet's life. A vast array of issues demand fresh thinking.

Very early in Islamic history, just a few generations after Muhammad, a solution presented itself. An expanding group of religious scholars, known as ulama (in Arabic, '*ulamā*', plural of '*ālim*') asserted the right to settle controversies over the law. Over the course of a couple of centuries, they succeeded in getting caliphs and the wider Muslim community to recognize them as the guardians, transmitters, and interpreters of Islamic law. In the process, they effectively gained control over the evolution of legal doctrine, making their collective judgments serve roles once fulfilled by the Koran and Muhammad's wisdom. From then on, it was they who determined how the law applied to novel situations.

In acquiring the right to settle legal controversies, Noah Feldman (2008) notes, the religious scholars also placed limits on the executive dominance of caliphs. Although caliphs, and later sultans, who ruled over Muslim communities retained extensive administrative authority, they came to share power with ulama. Rulers became accountable to religious scholars, who could now undermine their legitimacy merely by pronouncing state policies un-Islamic or their implementers impious.

Precisely because Muslim rulers were accountable under Islamic law, Feldman considers Islam's traditional form of government to have provided, for a while, a version of the rule-of-law. He also imagines that in principle a modern Islamic state could institute the rule-of-law by returning to the community of religious scholars the authority that they lost as a result of secularization and political centralization. Restoring to religious scholars their traditional rights could make Muslim governments less arbitrary and less despotic.

This optimism rests on the assumption that other constituencies would passively accept the shift of political power back to ulama. Historically, they never did. Rulers tried, often successfully, to gain control over scholarly interpretations. Diverse other groups, including soldiers, landowners, merchants, and craftsmen, took positions that influenced scholarly discourses. As in every known society, past and present, controversial issues thus got decided through give-and-take among multiple constituencies. Sometimes the ulama managed collectively to constrain policy decisions, control public opinion, and shape political fortunes by granting religious legitimacy to certain individuals and denying it to others. At other times they fell under the control of successive rulers who bought them off through perks or weakened them by exploiting their differences.

The Ottoman Empire provides abundant examples of the latter pattern. In certain periods the ulama managed to act as a pressure group that constrained Ottoman sultans (Zilfi 1988: chs 3, 4). At times they went so far as to depose those who harmed their interests or failed to satisfy their sensibilities. However, far more often, and increasingly over time, they served them as loyal civil servants. Ebu's-Su'ud, for three decades in the mid-sixteenth century the chief judicial officer (*şeyhülislam*) of the Ottoman Empire, gave sultans vast discretion by dutifully issuing a supportive religious opinion (*fetva*) whenever secular considerations made it expedient to change course (Imber 1997; Coşgel *et al.* 2009). One factor that facilitated the subordination of religious scholars is that as individuals they owed their positions to the sultan's patronage. Another is that the enforcement of property rights was in the hands of secular authorities. Still another is that in executing laws the sultan could abide by scholarly interpretations selectively, in self-serving ways. Each of these factors gave sultans leverage over the ulama, undermining their ability to constrain government.

In recent decades Al-Azhar, Egypt's leading Muslim institution of jurisprudence and higher learning, has helped to legitimize government policies through supportive statements laced with religious motifs (Barraclough 1998). In Saudi Arabia, too, the ulama have participated in the legitimation of policies motivated by secular considerations (Al-Rasheed 2002: chs 3–5; Steinberg 2005; Vogel 2000). True, they have resisted certain technological changes, and grumbled about Saudi military alliances with non-Muslims. But these are exceptions that prove the point. They have accepted every major technological advance that initially they opposed, including television and the telephone; and the Saudi government secured their approval even of placing non-Muslim soldiers on Saudi soil. Like Ottoman history, the modern records of Egypt and Saudi Arabia thus show that granting the community of religious scholars the right to veto government policies does not make rulers accountable for their actions in practice.

None of these cases implies that the ulama have lost social relevance. In serving the state they legitimize not only state policies but also the principle of anchoring social institutions in Islam. As such, they make it harder for the government to pursue policies that the public considers un-Islamic. For example, they make it effectively impossible for their governments to defend the expressive freedoms of people deemed, in the public imagination, to have violated a religious taboo. They thus distort government policies in domains removed from those in which they are asked to lend support.

Precisely for that reason, there exist constituencies who can be expected to resist the empowerment of Muslim religious scholars. The secularists of Turkey stand out as the most obvious example of a constituency opposed to reinstituting Islamic law in any form and loath to give religious functionaries control over their lives. Similar constituencies exist in other countries, though they are generally less vocal in their opposition to Islamic rule. In Iran, where religious scholars have enjoyed veto power over executive decisions since the Islamic revolution of 1978–9, political pressures have muted public expressions of anti-Islamic sentiment.[4]

In sum, both the historical record and contemporary patterns suggest that the balance of power implied by the concept of rule-of-law cannot be achieved simply by declaring government accountable to the ulama. Major constituencies will try to frustrate any attempt to increase the powers of religious functionaries. Soothing their fears would require institutional innovations that are not part of the Islamic heritage. It would also require reinterpretations of Islam itself. Modern Islamic thought has not yet generated the essential innovations, notwithstanding the ongoing transformations in religious traditions all across the Islamic world (Zaman 2002).

Equal access to justice and the political process

Our second rule-of-law principle is that the process through which laws are enacted, administered, and enforced must be both accessible and fair. As with government accountability, this principle is satisfied in the abstract. Under Islamic law all segments of society, regardless of gender, wealth or status, are entitled to sue in an Islamic court, to defend themselves if sued, and to be treated fairly. Moreover, everyone is entitled to participation in the political process. In theory, therefore, the enactment, administration, and enforcement of laws obey rules of impartiality (Khadduri 1984).

Yet barriers exist to the implementation of Islam's impartiality objectives. In a state committed to Islamic law, under its most common interpretations, two groups are bound to suffer legal and political discrimination: women and non-Muslims.

Islam emerged in a society in which women enjoyed fewer political rights than men. In seventh-century Arabia, women who participated in the marketplace and the political process generally did so under the protection of male relatives. Although the Koran contains provisions that improved the social status of women and gave them new economic rights in the Arabian milieu, it stops short of calling for economic gender equality. Its inheritance rules assign to a female inheritor a share equal to half that of a male in the same category; for instance, a daughter gets half as much as a son (Coulson 1971; Fyzee 1964).

Invoking the Koran, along with Islamic history, most contemporary promoters of Islamic law seek to maintain forms of gender inequality that are withering away in economically developed parts of the world, even elsewhere.

No major Islamist party favors the liberalization of female attire, or removing restrictions on women's mobility and social interactions. On the contrary, constraining women's freedoms stands out as one of the defining characteristics of modern Islamism. More to the point, no Islamist group considers the inheritance shares recorded in the Koran to be nonbinding, or subject to revision. For all practical purposes, then, restoring the sharia is a recipe for instituting gender inequality in political and economic life. It is bound to place women at a disadvantage with respect to controlling assets and, hence, in politics and the courts.

The claim that non-Muslims are bound to face discrimination in a state governed under Islamic law may appear overdrawn, because for most of Islamic history Muslim-governed states treated religious minorities quite well by the prevailing global standards. In Spain under the Moors and in Ottoman Turkey, lawsuits that pitted a Muslim against a Christian or Jew frequently ended in favor of the latter; for certain periods the Islamic court registers show no evidence of systematic discrimination in adjudication on the basis of religion.[5] Nevertheless, Islamic states did not meet modern standards of impartiality. Non-Muslims were generally excluded from high reaches of the administration and military command, unless they accepted conversion. Even in the most tolerant Islamic regimes, including those just mentioned, Islamic courts drew their staffs from Muslims, generating inevitable biases on matters involving intercommunal conflict. There is no guarantee, then, that in a modern state governed under Islamic law non-Muslims would have equal access to justice, or that they could participate in the political process on an equal footing with Muslims.

The root problem is that Islam recognizes no basis for nationhood except religion. Having declared tribalism illicit from the start, it has been committed to building and strengthening ties of religious brotherhood. This alone has made religious equality inconceivable in administration, the military command, and the judiciary (Zaman 2002: 4–50). Although non-Muslims may be granted protection of life and property, and allowed to participate in exchanges as equals, they cannot be given the means to subjugate Muslims, or allowed to make policies or engage in legal interpretations of consequence to Muslims.[6]

Efficiency of the legal and political systems

To turn now to matters of efficiency, historically a distinct characteristic of the Islamic court system was its ability to settle disputes quickly. The litigation procedures of an Islamic court are simple by modern standards and highly transparent. There is no jury. A single judge, trained to handle both civil and criminal disputes, listens to the litigants and their witnesses, reviews any documents presented, and pronounces a verdict, possibly after conducting investigations or having experts do so on his behalf. He does not have to deliberate with other judges, or justify his decision. He may even avoid pronouncing one side right, and seek instead to have the litigants reach a compromise. Litigants are not constrained in regard to the presentation of evidence. The absence of a jury contributes to the simplicity of the proceedings (Rosen 1989: chs 3, 4; Tyan 1960: chs 1–7).

Modern life is replete with interpersonal disputes that could be settled efficiently through the simple procedures of a traditional Islamic court. However, in a wide range of contexts the complexity of the disagreements would overwhelm the capacities of an unspecialized judge trained in classical Islamic law. Cases involving environmental damage, corporate responsibility, high technology, and international business often turn on concepts, or involve actors, absent from classical Islamic jurisprudence. On such cases, the disadvantages of incompetent litigation could easily overwhelm the advantages of speedy resolution. That is why, beginning in the nineteenth century, specialized courts have emerged all across the Islamic world. These courts have effectively secularized wide areas of the law, narrowing the jurisdiction of Islamic courts to a subset of the domains present at the rise of Islam, such as marriage.

A political system in which the government is accountable to the ulama could work smoothly, especially insofar as the latter were organized hierarchically. Hierarchical organization would give them the capacity to judge government decisions systematically and communicate evaluations without delay. Whether the screening improves the quality of government – as measured, for example, by the delivery of public goods – would depend on the capabilities of individual scholars doing the screening. For the same reason that religious scholars lack the training to adjudicate complex disputes, they are unequipped to evaluate government policies involving complex tradeoffs.

The substance of Islamic training has varied across time and space. Though fixed in principle, in practice it has adapted to changing needs and circumstances. Yet nowhere have reforms been extensive enough to qualify the graduates of religious schools for monitoring government policies. To gain relevance to policy matters, Muhammad Qasim Zaman (2002: ch. 3) has observed, the religious content of Islamic legal training would have to make way for the natural and social sciences; in other words, the training would have to incorporate knowledge developed outside of distinctly Islamic realms, becoming less Islamic.[7] Yet many modern reforms have gone in the opposite direction by distinguishing between religious studies and secular knowledge, and making a point of excluding the latter from the curriculum. Moreover, some reforms have led to a redoubled emphasis on Islam's original sources, with the effect of increasing the detachment of students from policy controversies of the present. A modern training in Islamic law does not provide the skills to evaluate policies involving the money supply, the global trading system, food safety, or building codes, to name just a few of the issues that governments address.

In sum, instituting Islamic law need not improve the efficiency of the processes whereby a society governs itself and settles its disputes. Although it might do so in contexts similar to those present in the medieval social systems that produced Islamic law, in a wide range of contexts characteristic of modernity the costs could easily outweigh the benefits.

Many of the functions that religious scholars performed in the Middle Ages, and would be re-assuming under some current proposals, are now the province of specialized agencies: central banks, currency boards, global trade organizations, zoning boards, and myriads of other agencies with specialized staffs. The skills in question are not obtainable by studying Islam or, for that matter, Christianity or any other religion. This does not mean that religion has lost its usefulness as a political tool and instrument of social advancement. Islam still serves as a source of morality, a rhetorical tool kit, and an organizational medium. In parts of the Arab world, societies to help battered women raise money in mosques by invoking verses of the Koran and Muhammad's calls for charity toward the downtrodden. Their officials find that people are more responsive to religious appeals than to ones framed in secular terms. Charitable organizations seeking to finance scholarship programs and health services find, likewise, that religion motivates people to become more philanthropic.

So the issue is not whether Islam, or religion in general, remains socially useful. It is whether Islamic law, as commonly understood and practiced, can be the basic ingredient of a social system that satisfies the rule-of-law principles identified at the outset. Having addressed three of these principles, I now turn to the remainder.

Clear laws

Considered divine law, Islamic law is supposed to offer a universally comprehensible blueprint for human behavior. Over the ages its promoters have intimated that this condition is generally satisfied. There is a single law, they have suggested, which can be discovered and understood through study; and although interpreting the law may challenge the average person, especially in novel situations, the ulama are available to resolve ambiguities and fill in perceived gaps. Trained to reason by analogy and seek consensus among themselves, the ulama have been viewed as qualified to overcome confusion, whenever it arose. In assisting with interpretation, they are expected to extend the clarity of the law to an ever widening set of areas (Vikør 2005: chs 4, 5).

In various contexts, the system has worked as envisaged. In the Middle Ages it was common for Muslims to consult a mufti on matters pertaining, say, to divorce. This remains the case today, all across the Islamic world. Yet, the legal clarity ideal has never been satisfied generally, in every domain. In certain domains the Islamic legal tradition has been considered irrelevant to resolving controversies. In other domains the problem has been that Islam's fundamental sources, or interpretations of their content, point in multiple directions, making it difficult to obtain authoritative advice.

To start with the first category of problems, in domains far removed from the content of traditional Islamic jurisprudence, religious scholars cannot credibly identify what Islamic law requires, because they have little to draw on, beyond abstract principles and remotely pertinent historical cases. In modern times such domains have included, among many others, mass production, industrial regulation, environmental preservation, medicine, and energy policy. Thus, most practicing Muslims look primarily to secular authorities for guidance regarding policy choices in these domains. Rarely do they approach muftis, teachers, judges, or other Islamic functionaries. It is common knowledge that these functionaries lack the training to offer meaningful advice, are unaccustomed to handling queries, and have produced few relevant writings.

In modern countries with functioning sharia courts, the perception that Islamic law is irrelevant to a broad array of distinctly modern issues gets reflected in government constraints imposed on their jurisdiction. Consider Pakistan, whose successive constitutions have required laws to be compatible with Islam. Pakistan's Sharia Court may rule on the Islamic legitimacy of policies, but only on issues that the High Court, which has been dominated by Western-trained modernist judges, considers it competent (Zaman 2002: 88–93). As a matter of practice, the Sharia Court has jurisdiction only in domains considered integral to religious life, narrowly defined. It is kept out of domains that classical Islamic jurisprudence did not address directly.

To turn now to the traditional domains of Islamic jurisprudence, they present the problem of indeterminacy. People seeking clarity from religious scholars may well encounter mutually inconsistent rulings and opinions. The root of this problem is that in certain contexts Islam's fundamental sources are too thin to guarantee a unique interpretation. After all, the Koran offers mostly moral guidelines. It provides few explicit instructions pertinent to the types of decisions people face on a daily basis in the marketplace, at work, in the political arena, and in social interactions. Moreover, recollections of Muhammad's words and deeds cannot possibly fill in every perceived gap. First of all, they pertain to a pre-industrial society with relatively simple political and economic institutions. Second, ulama of the past have offered myriads of inconsistent opinions concerning issues already present in the Prophet's lifetime. Finally, modern life has compounded the possibilities of discord. It differs so radically from life in seventh-century Arabia that leading modern scholars routinely disagree on the practical implications of Islamic traditions to such issues as market freedoms, income distribution, and the state's economic role (Vikør 2005: ch. 16; Haneef 1995; Behdad 1994).

Historically, when scholars faced with the silences and ambiguities of Islam's traditional sources reached a consensus, they often did so by granting Islamic legitimacy to an existing local tradition (*'urf*). Commercial regulation offers cases in point. The Koran and Muhammad's life both contain certain specifics on pricing, bargaining, and contracting. These specifics relate to bilateral exchanges involving commodities of commercial significance in seventh-century Arabia, such as dates, camels, and gold. During Islam's long expansion, Muslim scholars had to address matters involving commodities without significance in seventh-century Arabia. They also faced controversies concerning practices, institutions, and conditions unknown in the early years of Islam. They had to rule, for instance, on disputes involving the just price of fur, the rights of craft guilds, and property claims after major urban fires. Generally they resolved the conflicts by granting Islamic legitimacy to what happened to be customary and appeared widely acceptable, rather than by appealing dogmatically to some variant of Islamic doctrine (Udovitch 1985).

The opinions and commentaries that legitimized customs were aimed at solving problems of daily life rather than at upholding a fixed interpretation of the law. This practical orientation is evident in the nature of the differences among interpretations. They have differed precisely because needs and conditions varied across space and time.

The very success of past efforts to achieve legal clarity in particular locations and periods has had a downside from the standpoint of subsequent needs. Insofar as they produced variations in interpretation, they made it harder to reach a consensus later, in new circumstances. On any given issue, modern Muslims trying to make sense of the Islamic legal tradition encounter a panoply of possibly pertinent interpretations in historical records. The richness of those records raises the probability of disagreements.

To summarize, Islamic law does not necessarily satisfy the clarity principle in practice. In relation to modern life, it is not comprehensive. Besides, although Islamic jurisprudence is equipped with mechanisms for resolving legal ambiguities and responding to new situations, issues addressed in the past voluminous precedents can complicate legal interpretation today.

Stable laws

The legal stability principle of the rule of law is easily misunderstood. Although the terminology connotes fixity, what it requires is only that laws be resistant to modification. Laws must be difficult though not impossible to change. Implicit in the principle is a tradeoff between the predictability and adaptability of laws. They must be sufficiently stable to facilitate planning for the future, but also flexible enough to permit timely adaptation to changing conditions.

On the surface, Islamic law satisfies the stability requirement, as just identified. Under Islamic tradition, Muhammad was the last of a long line of prophets, and the Koran, the unalterable word of God, constitutes the final divine revelation to humanity. By implication, Islamic law is eternally fixed. Yet the law can be reinterpreted from time to time, as new situations and challenges present themselves.

As already noted, over time new institutions and practices were incorporated into the Islamic legal system. For example, a century or so after the rise of

Islam a distinct form of trust, the waqf, gained Islamic legitimacy; under successive regimes, and in various places, new taxes were absorbed into the system under one guise or another; and more than a half millennium after Muhammad craft guilds began to gain recognition as legitimate associations.

So Islamic law supports what one may call "adaptive legal stability" – legal fixity in general along with some capacity to change with the times. Whether it achieves an optimal balance between the conflicting needs for stability and change is a different matter. There are innumerable ways to reach a balance. The founding fathers of the United States sought the right balance through high hurdles for amending the Constitution: the approval of both houses of Congress by two-thirds votes along with that of three-fourths of the states within seven years. Since 1791 more than 10,000 proposed amendments to the US Constitution have failed as a result of these hurdles, but 17 have been approved. It is easy to identify advantages of the resulting legal stability as well as inefficiencies caused by the stringent requirements for making amendments.[8]

In Islamic legal history, too, it is easy to identify both efficiency-enhancing adaptations over time and adaptational failures that have been harmful with regard to economic development, social peace, or democratization. The development of the waqf as an Islamic institution promoted economic growth by making it easier for wealth holders to shield property from state predation. By the same token, some of the waqf's key characteristics – lack of legal personhood, inability to restructure itself or modify its objectives without court approval – turned into economic handicaps as the modern global economy took shape (Kuran 2001). More generally, Islamic law equipped Muslim-governed societies with institutions that enabled them to function remarkably well within the global economy of the Middle Ages. However, as the global economy evolved it did not undergo the adaptations necessary for Muslim communities to remain economically competitive. For most of the second millennium, a time when western Europe was developing modern financial and commercial institutions, Islamic contract law remained essentially stagnant. Hence, by the nineteenth century the most dynamic Muslim merchants and investors considered it archaic. Most of them approved of the legal reforms that effectively moved commerce and finance beyond the jurisdiction of Islamic courts.

If excessive stability has been harmful in certain contexts, inadequate stability has been a major problem in others. Taxation offers a case in point. During the expansion of Islam, rulers sometimes found it convenient to retain the existing tax practices of conquered territories. At the same time, they retained the flexibility to alter tax rates and forms in response to changes in taxable capacity. The lack of constraints on taxation would have lowered incentives to invest and accumulate.

The taxes imposed arbitrarily in the early Islamic centuries include ones without Islamic precedent. The ulama accepted most of them without serious objection (Ashtor 1976). Continuing this pattern of permissiveness, the ulama of the Ottoman Empire formalized the state's authority to alter tax rates by recognizing a parallel legal system meant to exist side by side with the sharia: state law (*kanun*). Matters essential to the health and survival of the state would fall within the jurisdiction of state law. Although the ulama retained the right to veto state policies and regulations in conflict with the sharia, this right did not always carry practical significance. When governments had a vital interest in changing legal practices, they usually prevailed (İnalcık 1970).

Earlier we saw that in many contexts Islamic law has lacked clarity, that gaps and silences have required reinterpretations, and that these led to a diversification of legal understandings and practices. The myriads of reinterpretations have also bred legal instability. As the challenges facing Muslim communities changed over time through such factors as urbanization, commercial expansion, conquests, and technological change, rulers were able to alter, essentially as they saw fit, laws critical to state power, size of government, and their own survival. Ordinarily they did so with the consent of religious scholars.

Many luminaries have shown that efficiency in governance requires constraints on the state's powers (Hayek 1973–9; North and Weingast 1989). "Leviathan" has to be chained in the interest of preserving individual incentives to produce. The task of chaining Leviathan has entered modern discourses on Islamic law mostly in relation to subordinating rulers of the distant past to Islamic law. The finer challenges of binding modern states of the Islamic world, most of which are authoritarian, has received much less attention. The proposed concrete measures are mostly dated. This is particularly remarkable in view of a phenomenon noted by Seyyed Vali Reza Nasr (2001): the use of Islamic symbolism to suppress dissent and expand state powers.

Protection of fundamental rights

The protection of fundamental human rights is a basic element of almost every version of the rule-of-law. Islamic law guarantees both personal security and private property rights. Only people who stray from the path of righteousness can be fined, imprisoned, or killed, it holds; and private property cannot be restricted arbitrarily (Khadduri 1984: chs 2, 6). Our focus here will be on the implied economic rights. The Koran provides a sound basis for protecting private property. In addition, it explicitly tolerates various types of material inequality: between men and women, masters and slaves, and merchants of different ability.

In turning to how basic rights have been interpreted within Islamic discourses, we begin to encounter elements at odds with common modern understandings. Slavery, a legitimate institution under classical Islamic law, is incompatible with the almost universally accepted modern principle that individual freedom should be denied only for a proven crime. However, slavery is now illegal throughout the Islamic world, and modern Islamists do not want to restore its legitimacy. Islamic law has been reinterpreted in this regard by turning a blind eye to Koranic verses and historical precedents that accommodate slavery (Lewis 1990).

A more significant difficulty stems from Islamic principles in conflict with basic individual rights enshrined in classical Islamic law. In recognizing private property rights, the Koran also treats God as the owner of the universe. The principle of divine ownership can be invoked to restrict privileges that are central to modern notions of private property. For much of Islamic history, in fact, it served to deny peasants the right to sell land or pass it on to their heirs. In the early Arab empires, as in the Ottoman Empire that followed, a small farmer held land as a temporary trust, provided he kept it in production. If he ceased cultivation, his plot reverted to the state for reassignment. At his death, likewise, the state reclaimed his farm. Although officials usually let his heirs take it over, the state retained the right to take the farm away from his family (İnalcık 1994: 103–78).

Lack of private ownership in small plots did not mean that peasants always worried about expropriation. Ordinarily the state lacked a reason to drive away productive and tax-paying farmers. Following a conquest, the new ruler would leave peasants alone, so long as their taxes started accruing to him. The groups threatened most seriously with expropriation were large landowners and successful merchants. For these wealthy groups, the danger of confiscation varied across periods and regions, and also according to political circumstances. It tended to rise in times of financial crisis or military threat. Expropriations of substantial estates were especially common.[9]

Until modern times, taxation was also relatively arbitrary. New taxes could be imposed, or rates changed for specific groups, under the rubric of state law, to transfer rents from producers, or assets from the wealthy, to the state. Maqrizi, an Egyptian historian of the fifteenth century, considered expropriation commonplace in his surroundings. Ibn Khaldun thought the same about Tunisia and Egypt in the fourteenth century (Ibn Khaldun 1379/1958; Allouche 1994). In the seventeenth century the greatest source of government revenue in the Ottoman Empire became the avarız – a generic name for an extraordinary tax imposed by imperial edict, without a religious basis, but with the endorsement of ulama (Darling 1996).

States resorted to arbitrary taxation and expropriations partly because they could not borrow easily. In turn, that difficulty reflected the ineffectiveness of the political checks and balances that the ulama were supposed to provide. As Douglass North and Barry Weingast (1989) have shown, states subject to appropriate constraints tend to repay their loans, developing a reputation as credit-worthy; consequently, they can borrow at low cost and have few incentives to expropriate. Whatever the governance benefits that the ulama supplied historically, clearly their oversight failed to protect property rights adequately by modern standards. This does not imply that rulers had incentives to grab any and all resources in their reach. Political considerations made them limit certain levies. Thus, Ottoman sultans generally capped the tax burden on the peasantry, in order to trim the resources available to potential political rivals, namely provincial officials who exercised tax collection rights in return for military and other services (Karaman 2009).

In brief, although classical Islamic law allowed private property rights, these conflicted with a principle that facilitated state predation: God's ownership of everything. When the state took measures to advance material security, as when it imposed and enforced tax ceilings, it did so for self-serving reasons, not merely to abide by Islamic law.

An early Islamic institution to strengthen property rights

The Ottoman sultans who imposed tax ceilings in the countryside did so by invoking their own prerogatives under state law. However, they also appealed opportunistically to the Islamic legal heritage. During Muhammad's lifetime, Islam had established an institution to cap taxation and make it predictable. Known as zakat and still counted among Islam's five fundamental requirements, this institution provided a religious basis for limiting state predation. Why did zakat prove ineffective? Exploring the mechanisms at play will identify the shortcomings of Islamic law as an enforcer of property rights.

Zakat consists of regulations designed to systematize transfer payments. Requiring certain groups to pay taxes, it entitles a few constituencies to subsidies. As implemented by Muhammad and his first few successors, zakat taxed major sources of income and forms of wealth at fixed rates, with exemptions for the poor and reductions for high-cost producers. Because zakat revenue was meant to finance all expenditures of the Islamic state, except those met through booty, the fixity of the rates capped individual tax obligations. This fixity also limited the state's economic reach (Kuran 2003).

It mattered that taxes collected under the rubric of zakat entailed not a general levy on income and wealth but, rather, a levy on their forms known in seventh-century Islam to the peoples of western Arabia. Because the underlying principles of equity were not made explicit, it is the specific rates and forms of taxation that entered Islamic teachings, not the principles of mild progressivity and predictability. Specifics came to be treated as sacred, rather than the underlying goals. That choice quickly lessened zakat's relevance to economies with characteristics significantly different from those of seventh-century Arabia. Thus, as the early Arab conquests brought the cities of Syria and Iraq into the Islamic fold, their governors discovered that taxing the incomes of artisans required going outside the zakat system. Having breached the evolving Islamic fiscal regime in that context, they then found it easy to adjust agricultural taxes as well (Løkkegaard 1950). To do so, they did not have to challenge zakat rates. They could do so through new taxes, such as labor dues. Before long, Muslim rulers were adjusting taxes more or less at will.

At the inception of the zakat system, taxation was mildly progressive. Small farmers and herders were exempt, and farmers who needed to maintain water canals paid less than those who relied only on rainfall. The subsequent arbitrariness of rates made the tax systems of Islamic states decidedly regressive. Within a century after the rise of Islam, the wealthiest officials were exempt from taxation, town-dwellers were being treated leniently to reduce the likelihood of revolt, and peasants were paying relatively high taxes. These transformations occurred at a time when increasing numbers of high officials were Persian. They amounted to a grafting of the ancient Persian system of taxation onto the original Islamic system. What historians of Seljuk Turkey, the Ottoman Empire, and Safavid Iran identify as variants of the Islamic system of taxation are actually forms of a pre-Islamic system. Unlike the zakat system, the core element of taxation in the Prophet's lifetime, what came to be known as "Islamic taxation" gives the ruler considerable discretion in setting tax rates and forms.

The upshot is that zakat did not become a permanently effective weapon against government predation. Formulated in relation to conditions of seventh-century Arabia, rather than as a general transfer system, it served merely as a temporary barrier to arbitrary taxation. This failure to impose general limits on taxation also affected the evolution of legal discourse. In allowing states to exercise discretion in setting taxes in new territories and economic sectors, it also kept Islamic legal discourse from focusing on the development of checks and balances. Today, fourteen centuries after the advent of Islam, texts on zakat written by expositors of "Islamic economics" spell out the early rates without identifying general principles that those specifics were meant to serve. Moreover, they refrain from addressing the challenge of protecting individual property rights in general (Kuran 2004: 19–28).

The trust as a substitute for property rights

The inadequacies of zakat as a barrier to state predation were bound to stimulate searches for alternative institutions to protect private wealth. Indeed, by the eighth century prosperous Muslims were looking for alternative institutions to secure private property. The most important innovation had drawbacks of its own. It had unintended consequences that undermined the rule of law in ways still visible, more than a millennium later.

About a century after the rise of Islam, a form of trust known as waqf emerged as an antidote to weak private property rights. The owner of an income-producing property founded a waqf by endowing it in perpetuity to finance a designated social service. Regardless of the nature of the service, income-yielding assets endowed as waqf were considered sacred. Nevertheless, the founder was allowed to appropriate some of the income. In combination, these two provisions made the waqf a wealth shelter. On the one hand, they gave the assets considerable immunity against taxation and confiscation. On the other, they allowed the founder to maintain personal control over some of the assets. The waqf thus represented an ingenious implicit contract between the state and its wealthy subjects. The rich received the material security they craved, in return for providing social services. For its part, the state freed itself of the need to supply public goods, in return for accepting constraints on predation (Kuran 2001).

Over a millennium, this wealth-sheltering function resulted in the conversion of private property into waqf property on a massive scale. Waqfs were established to finance a vast range of social institutions – mosques, schools, fountains, soup kitchens, hospitals, and much more. Depending on the region, up to half of all real estate ended up in waqfs. This transformation strengthened property rights insofar as it limited the productive assets available for predation.

Against this benefit, there were also rising costs, as measured by effects on the rule of law. The waqf's manager–trustee enjoyed little discretion over the deployment of assets, presumably to prevent misuse. Consequently, organizations established as waqfs could not renew themselves easily as conditions changed, as they could if they were corporations. Over time they tended to become dysfunctional. Also, whenever adaptations did occur, they involved acts that skirted the law. These illegal acts contributed to a culture of corruption, which raised the cost of enforcing laws. Even today, certain laws enforced at low cost elsewhere – for example, rules against littering – are poorly enforced in the Islamic world. Also, corruption remains very common by global standards.[10]

The deeds of waqfs kept them from participating in political causes. That limited their contributions to political movements that might have strengthened the rule-of-law. Nor was this the sole long-term effect. Given the enormous economic weight of the waqf, its failure to become self-governing left the Islamic world without the intermediate social structures that form what we now call "civil society." Civil society is essential to the establishment and preservation of democratic rights. Early in Islamic history, in the eighth century, the waqf system had put in place a key ingredient of a strong civil society: the freedom to found nongovernmental organizations of one's choice. But it inhibited another condition: organizational autonomy. Meanwhile, the waqf limited pressures for stronger property rights also directly, by providing wealth shelters. Access to wealth shelters lowers incentives to seek stronger private property rights.

Conclusions

At the end of this excursus on whether Islamic law satisfies the core principles of the rule of law, three broad themes stand out. First, the early development of Islamic law involved a panoply of institutions that served these principles. For each principle we can identify one or more early Islamic institutions that were meant, at some level, to promote it. Second, the institutions in question were not flawless as measured by long run success in sustaining the rule-of-law. Over time they lost effectiveness. Finally, the relevant Islamic institutions now tend to be out of date. Hence, Islamic law, as it is now understood, does not offer an efficient variant of the rule-of-law.

In reaching these conclusions, the argument has appealed to evidence from various periods and places. The purpose has been to underscore a point to which contemporary Islamic discourses pay inadequate attention, if at all: the performance of a society's institutional complex depends critically on the available technologies, the external environment, and the knowledge that governs individual choices. This point, which will not surprise social scientists, implies that Islamic law could satisfy any given rule-of-law principle in the early Islamic milieu without meeting its requirements in the present. The imposition of Islamic law on a society in any one of its pre-modern formulations would result in massive failures, at least as measured by the extent to which the rule-of-law principles are satisfied.

To this day, much of Islamic thought, which consists of discourses grounded self-consciously in Islamic sources and traditions, has been wedded to the notion of a fixed Islamic law, based on a divine text. However, the practice of Islamic law has never ceased to evolve. The promoters and practitioners of Islamic law, past and present, have enriched, modified, and updated it in various ways. Quite obviously reformers have been motivated by a desire to overcome emerging deficiencies. Yet the reinterpretations have not been extensive or imaginative enough to make Islamic law compatible with the rule-of-law principles.

To start with government accountability, in the centuries immediately following the rise of Islam, the community of Muslim religious scholars managed to check certain abuses of government power. However, neither rulers nor other constituencies passively accepted the instituted limitations on their prerogatives. Muslim rulers managed to establish, and then maintain, substantial control over the ulama in their realms. The records of modern regimes that formally give ulama veto power – Saudi Arabia offers an example – prove that the political processes responsible for limiting government accountability in early Islam remain operative today. Moreover, the promoters of Islamic law have developed no strategy for instituting the checks and balances that Muslim-dominated modern regimes generally lack.

All variants of Islamic law formally promote equal access to justice and the political process. However, the concept of equality is restricted by modern standards. Muslim men have greater political rights than women, who are subject to special social controls, and non-Muslims, who are considered unfit to govern or deliver justice. Although historically the inevitable biases did not handicap either group in every context, the inequities were certainly not harmless, and they would not lack significance in a modern regime.

Evaluated from the standpoint of efficiency, Islamic law presents further shortcomings. For more than a millennium the Islamic courts rendered justice quickly and cheaply. But the complexity of most modern disputes far surpasses what judges trained in Islamic law are equipped to handle. The same logic, applied to the political balancing role of the ulama, suggests that whatever their contributions to political efficiency in the Middle Ages, they lack the expertise necessary to judge government actions involving distinctly modern technological and institutional complexities. It is possible, of course, to redesign the curriculum through which religious scholars are trained. However, the requisite curricular reforms have not taken place. In any case, there is reason to question the desirability of training religious scholars to exercise what have become distinctly secular functions everywhere, including the Islamic world. If nothing else, there would be a duplication of social functions. A more efficient alternative would be to accept restrictions on the jurisdiction of Islamic law and leave political balancing to secular actors.

The legal clarity requirement of the rule-of-law is never fully satisfied, and early Islamic history offers no exception. Yet early Islam did develop procedures for resolving ambiguities. A common method for promoting legal clarity was to treat customary practices as consistent with Islamic law. This method would be much less reliable in modern settings, because the issues that require resolution are far more removed from those to which the fundamental sources of Islam speak. True, Islamic law has been broadened to subsume new institutions, such as banks and stock markets. However, nowhere has the broadening gone far enough for the purpose of guiding a person who wants to live by Islamic law. In none of its forms does Islamic law provide a comprehensive guide to daily life, and the boundaries of its authority remain undrawn.

Under the conditions of early Islam, even those of later centuries, the reliance on Islamic law stabilized its applications to daily life in a wide range of contexts. But the exceptions have carried great significance. One involves taxation. Because Islam's rules of taxation were developed in relation to a particular milieu, they quickly lost their relevance to government; this allowed states great discretion in taxation – precisely the opposite of the apparent original intention. Islamic thought has yet to come to terms with such unintended consequences of classical Islamic institutions. Nor has it considered the proper scope of legal flexibility, with attention to particularities.

Islamic law recognizes private property, one of the fundamental rights enshrined in the rule-of-law. At the same time, it is committed formally to the principle that the universe belongs to God alone. In some contexts, the latter principle has served to weaken the former. On the ground that the ruler is the best judge of God's will, major Muslim empires denied peasants the right to transfer land at will. In other contexts, private property rights have effectively trumped divine ownership. Limits on wealth and income taxation, where enforced, kept most assets under individual control. But the significance of these limits eroded over time because they were specific to particular types of wealth and income.

There have been other Islamic institutions devised to provide material security to wealth holders. By far the most important has been the waqf, which imposed barriers against state predation. However, in substituting for property rights, the waqf undermined the rule-of-law in other ways. Its restrictions on resource reallocation stimulated corruption, which weakened the judicial system's perceived commitment to equal treatment. Meanwhile, in providing a wealth-sheltering function, it dampened incentives to strengthen property rights directly.

Notes

1 A draft of this chapter was presented at the World Justice Forum in Vienna, 2–5 July 2008.
2 In practical usage, the sharia encompasses all legal pronouncements of trained Muslim jurists. This is the sense in which the term is being used here. Historically the term represented more than a system of law. It was also a discursive tradition (Messick 1993).
3 Each of these appears within the rule-of-law definition of the World Justice Forum. See Dam (2006) for accounts of what the principles entail.
4 Although political repression makes it difficult to measure the extent of hidden opposition, the Iranian regime appears vulnerable to an explosion of the type that has toppled other modern regimes, including the Iranian monarchy and the communist regimes of Eastern Europe (Kuran 1995: chs 15–16, 19). On the political functions of the Iranian clergy after the Islamic Revolution, see Rahnema and Nomani (1990: chs 6, 7) and Zubaida (2003: ch. 6).
5 In the court records of seventeenth-century Istanbul, one finds a huge number of lawsuits that pitted one or more Muslims against one or more Christians. The plaintiff won 59 percent of the cases in which the suing party was Muslim, but 68 percent of those where the suing party was Christian. This evidence is based on a data set developed by the author. It involves more than 10,000 observations.
6 Religious discrimination remains common all over the world, even in countries where the law explicitly bans it. As a case in point, in the modern United States a professed Muslim stands no chance of getting elected to high office. Witness the lengths to which Barack Obama traveled to assure voters that he is a practicing Christian, and not a Muslim.
7 For similar points, see Rahman 1982: chs 2–3.
8 Constitutional stability lowers the risk of investing in the United States. An unimplemented efficiency-enhancing change is the presidential authority to veto line items in Congress-approved budgets.
9 This practice could be considered a violation of the Islamic law of inheritance, so usually it was justified on the ground that the deceased was not the rightful owner of his estate. The deceased could not defend himself, and his descendants were not necessarily privy to pertinent facts. This is what made states resort to it so frequently.
10 In the 2006 World Corruption Index of Transparency International, the three largest countries of the western Islamic World – Iran, Egypt, and Turkey – all rank as more corrupt than each of the five most populous countries of the European Union.

Part III

Rule of law and economic development

Chapter 5

The viability of the welfare state[1]

James J. Heckman

Introduction

The welfare state is a late nineteenth-century invention. Its provisions for economic security are now accepted as rights in many countries. Franklin Delano Roosevelt proclaimed Freedom from Want as one of his Four Freedoms. The Universal Declaration of Human Rights adopted by the United Nations goes further in guaranteeing the right to work, the right to a standard of living with adequate health and well-being, including food and medical care in the event of an emergency. Many perceive such social rights as an integral aspect of a well-functioning state, and covered under the rule-of-law.

The case for the welfare state that motivates these proclamations is that it protects its citizens against the consequences of risks beyond their control (Agell 1999). The case against the welfare state is that it blunts incentives and reduces productivity. Supporting this point of view is that the economic performance of many welfare states has been poor. There has been a rapid runup in unemployment in most Western European welfare states in the past 20 years. When properly measured, many Western European welfare states have much higher rates of unemployment than are reported in the official statistics. Incentives to withdraw from work, to go underground, to evade taxes, to retire early, and not to produce, are high.

Immigration levels are also high in many European countries. There are serious problems with immigrant assimilation created in part by welfare-state policies. There is slow growth in human capital – a vital ingredient for a modern economy. In addition, there are low rates of business formation, weak incentives for entrepreneurship, and low levels of research and development. There are high taxes on labor and, in many countries, on capital. Poverty traps are often created that discourage work.

The forces creating the pressure on the welfare state are globalization and an inability to tax internationally mobile factors of production. The increase in the unpredictability in trade and technology, the increasing openness of economies, and the secular bias against unskilled labor in trade and technology are also the forces that create the demand for the welfare state as an insurer against risk, and as a protector against the reduced wages that the unskilled experience when the demand for their skills is reduced. As economies become more open, it is much more difficult to shelter workers and firms from the rigors of the market. And in fact, less-sheltered economies like the US and UK have shown substantial increases in wage inequality and social inequality due, in part, to these trends.

In the current environment, a premium has emerged for flexibility and responsiveness of economies. High levels of workforce skill and a regulatory environment that supports change allow economies to benefit from new opportunities. An economic order that was well adapted to the more stable and predictable environment of the 1950s and 1960s and that had a large role for unskilled labor to play has become dysfunctional in the early twenty-first century. The opportunity cost of security and preservation of the status quo – whether it is the status quo technology, the status quo trading partner or the status quo job – has risen greatly in recent times. While reforms have been made in Europe, they have mostly been small-scale in nature. Europe has to run and not walk to keep up with the pace of global change, and it is barely even walking, although by European standards, it is rapidly reforming.

Not all welfare states have lagged, or at least they have not all lagged in the same way. It is fruitful to examine differences in economic performance among different welfare states. This is the topic of the chapters. The key to a successful welfare state lies in devising proper incentives to encourage actors at all levels of the economic system to respond to the new opportunities. In principle, a welfare state can provide the proper incentives for productivity and at the same time afford a measure of security and dignity for its citizens. But it has to respect incentives.

Themes of this chapter

This chapter develops five broad themes. First and foremost, people respond to incentives, and responses are often very strong. It is very dangerous, when designing laws and regulations, to underestimate the ingenuity of economic agents in pursuing their self-interest, the responsiveness of the economic system, and the broader consequences of regulation on all members of society. Many advocates of the rule of law promote principles like universal economic security, the right to organize trade unions, or the right to a minimum standard of living without accounting for the economic costs of such provisions. The rights granted to some, if they are enforced, often reduce the welfare of others. For example, trade unions often raise benefits to members at the cost of higher prices for consumers, lower profits for shareholders, and lower wages for nonunion workers. The welfare state often benefits insiders at the expense of outsiders (Lindbeck and Snower 1989).

Second, the debate about the welfare state often poses a false dichotomy. It compares the US (or the Anglo-Saxon bloc of countries) to Europe. It frames the debate as a choice among systems in place. The US, Canada, the UK,

Australia, and New Zealand are, of course, welfare states. They have made their share of mistakes in devising incentives and protecting their workers. The relevant issue is *not* whether Europe should adopt the Anglo-Saxon model, or whether the Anglo-Saxons should adopt the European model. Rather, it is which features of the welfare state reduce inequality and provide insurance against uncertainty in an efficient way.

Third, the term "welfare state" is far too broad. At least four models are often mentioned (see Sapir 2006) and these categories are surely too crude.

(1) The Nordic/corporatist model (Scandinavia, Finland, Netherlands), which provides a high level of security for workers, heavy reliance on active labor market policies, low inequality, high levels of taxation of labor income, relatively low levels of taxation of capital income, very high levels of education and high levels of government activity, generous grants that are not means tested, high levels of wage compression, centralized unions, and high levels of concentrated unions and wage setting.
(2) The Continental model (Austria, Belgium, France, Germany, and Luxembourg). Its features are heavy reliance on insurance-based nonemployment benefits and old-age pensions, strong unions that are not all centralized, lots of regulation, inflexibility in labor markets, and compressed wage distributions. It shows a marked inability to adjust to change.
(3) The Mediterranean model (Italy, Spain, Portugal, Greece). It is characterized by reliance on employment protection (lifetime jobs), with union-covered sectors with compressed wages, concentrated spending on old-age pensions, and high segmentation of entitlements and status.
(4) The Anglo-Saxon model (United States, Canada, United Kingdom, New Zealand and Australia). It is characterized by social assistance only in the last resort, low levels of job protection and minimum wages, high levels of cross-section wage inequality, considerable social spending on old-age pensions, and high levels of segmentation of entitlements and status.

For close observers of the welfare state, these four categories are far too broad in many respects. For example, Ireland is a corporatist state often lumped into the Anglo-Saxon camp.[2] It has implemented strong incentives, especially for capital. It also has a lot of wage coordination. The four categories of welfare state are thus, at best, a rough cut.

Fourth, comparing alternative economic systems is a dangerous practice. Different baseline and terminal periods can produce very different ratings of the performance of any economy. Yesterday's success is often today's failure. Recall the love affair with the Dutch Polder model ten years ago that still lingers on in some quarters. There was an even earlier fascination with Japan and, earlier yet, a fascination with the USSR.

Many European think tanks and the Organisation for the Economic Cooperation and Development (OECD) have embraced the "Nordic model" or the closely related "corporatist model." For example, the recent 2006 OECD Jobs Report, which updated the influential 1994 OECD Jobs Report, trumpets the "corporatist model" as being coequal in efficiency with the Anglo-Saxon model. An influential paper by Andre Sapir (2006) of the Bruegel Group made the same endorsement, and has had a big effect on the European discussion. This praise is echoed by Jeff Sachs (2006) in a recent column in *Scientific American*:

> Half a century ago, the free-market economist Friedrich von Hayek argued that a large public sector would threaten democracy itself, putting European countries on a "road to serfdom." Yet the Nordic states have thrived, not suffered, from a large social welfare state, with much less public-sector corruption and far higher levels of voter participation than in the US. Von Hayek was wrong. In strong and vibrant democracies, a generous social-welfare state is not a road to serfdom but rather to fairness, economic equality and international competitiveness.

Sweden's economic performance in the past decade has been impressive. So has that of Finland. Denmark's "flexicurity" system promotes job mobility. It gives generous unemployment benefits and, at the same time, provides sanctions to promote rapid return to work among the unemployed. It has attracted a lot of attention among the policy pundits. The recent fascination with Scandinavia is typical of a mentality of many policy analysts who look to a working model as a system for adoption, rather than looking at basic principles that transcend any economy to explain the successes and failures of a particular model. This chapter looks at those basic principles to draw general lessons from many models rather than to extol the virtues of one system currently in place in comparison with any other system.

Fifth, I make a basic methodological point that affects the way analysts should use and interpret the available evidence. A large literature on the European welfare state relies on arbitrarily constructed indices to examine incentive effects of different policies. Many of these studies claim to prove that the incentives ("institutions") that basic economic theory suggest should matter, do not in fact matter. These conclusions are a statistical mirage. They are consequences of using bad data. When incentives are properly measured, they matter, and they matter a lot.

Students of Latin American labor markets have measured the costs of regulation more carefully than students of the European welfare state. Latin America has experienced more dramatic regime changes and policy shifts than any that have occurred in Europe. The Latin American data clearly show strong adverse effects of perverse incentives.

The plan of the rest of the chapter

The rest of the chapter proceeds in the following way. Given the current romance with Nordic and corporatist models, I look at their performance and the performance of welfare states more generally. It is useful to examine long-run trends to supplement the short-run time series that attract so much attention in policy discussions. Nordic performance is *not* impressive, especially if one looks at long-run trends. Policies in place often *conceal* rather than solve problems and create problems for the future. Problems of flawed measurement create serious problems in making meaningful comparisons across alternative systems. Long-run trends in skill accumulation, in attitudes toward work, in research and development, in adoption of new technology, benefit dependency, and dependence on government employment are not encouraging and portend serious problems in the future for many quarters of Europe, even for Scandinavian Europe.

The performance of the European welfare state in the past 20 years

First consider the labor market. A new OECD Jobs Report, released in 2006, shows that some of the reforms suggested in the 1994 Jobs Report (OECD 1994) have been implemented. It claims that those reforms partially account for the improved state of European labor markets. European unemployment rates post-1994 are lower but they are still very high. See Figure 5.1, which plots the "open" (official) unemployment rates over time. Starting in the early 1980s, the overall Western European OECD unemployment rate rose. It has not fallen to its previous level. However, unemployment appears to be much

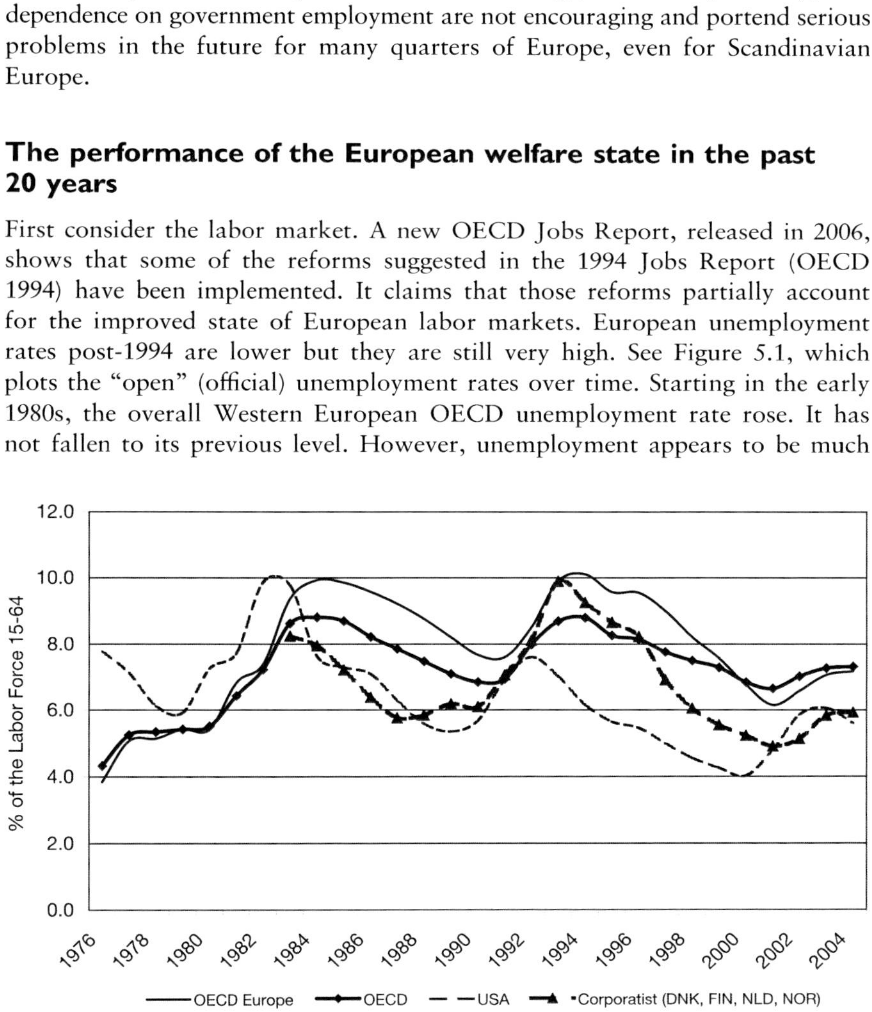

Figure 5.1 Open unemployment rates in the OECD.
Source: Author's calculations from Organisation for Economic Co-operation and Development (2006a)

lower in corporatist Europe. This has led to calls by some to adopt the corporatist model as a way to conduct economic policy.

Average productivity growth is lower in the EU than in the US. However, it is high in the "flex market" Nordic countries (see Figure 5.2).

However, GDP growth is lower in the past five years in the EU than in the US. This is true even for corporatist Europe (see Figure 5.3).

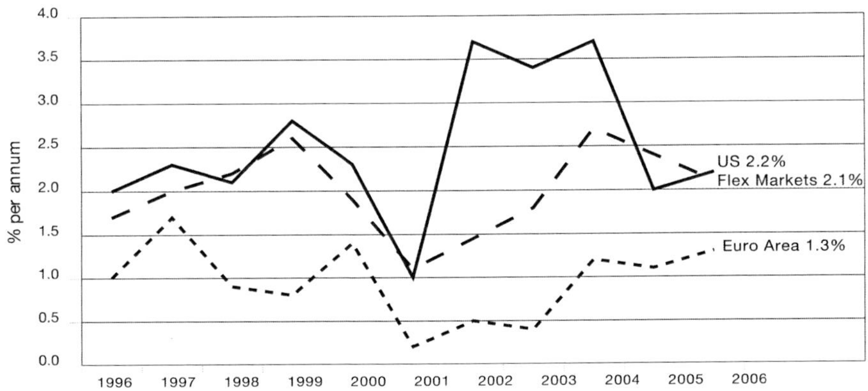

Figure 5.2 Labor productivity growth in the business sector.
Source: Author's calculations from Organisation for Economic Co-operation and Development (2006a)

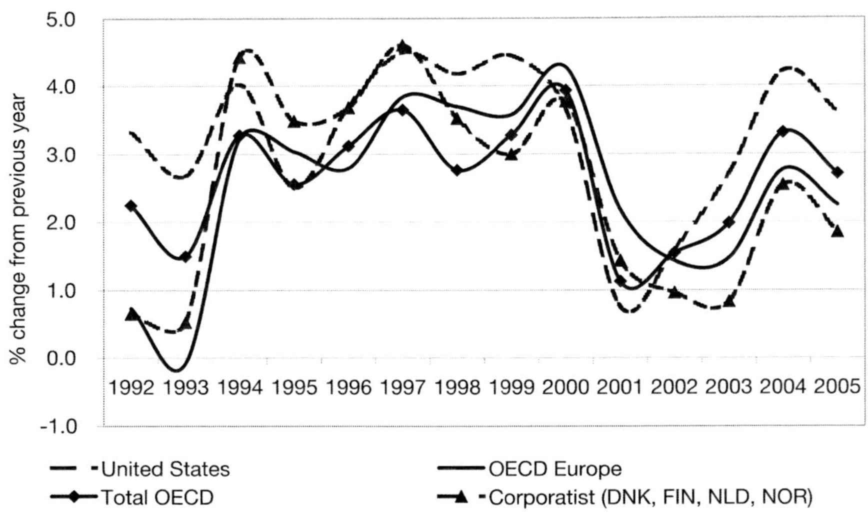

Figure 5.3 Real GDP growth.
Source: Author's calculations from Organisation for Economic Co-operation and Development (2006a)

Consider, in particular, the performance of one of the "Nordic miracle" countries – Sweden, the Nordic country most often studied. It has recently seen improvement in its economic performance after the deep recession of the early 1990s. However, its recovery is not strong. Placed in historical perspective, the story of Sweden is one of relative decline and a mild recent recovery. Figure 5.4 shows the decline in PPP – adjusted GDP per capita in Sweden as a percentage of the OECD average since the Second World War. Sweden has shown secular decline, which has only recently been arrested, and its recent boom is modest in historical perspective. Figure 5.5 reveals that, until recently,

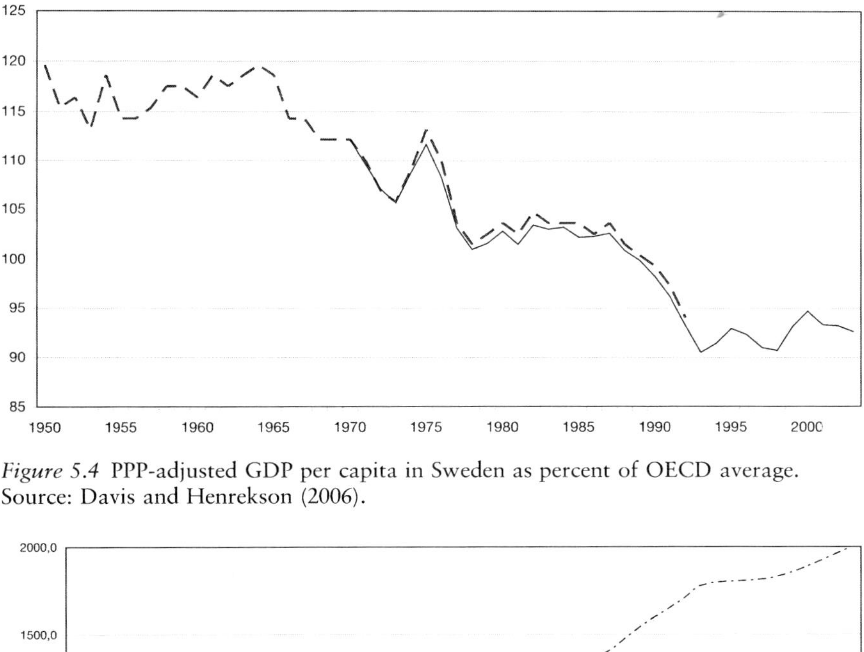

Figure 5.4 PPP-adjusted GDP per capita in Sweden as percent of OECD average. Source: Davis and Henrekson (2006).

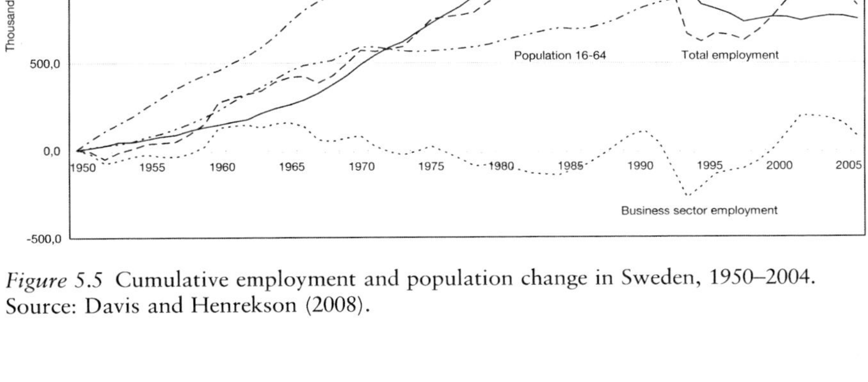

Figure 5.5 Cumulative employment and population change in Sweden, 1950–2004. Source: Davis and Henrekson (2008).

it was growth in government employment that fueled Swedish employment growth. Figure 5.6 shows that growth in employment, adjusting for population, lags the US and the OECD excluding the US.

Sweden is far from being a basket case. Capital taxation there is relatively low and was cut substantially in the reform of the early 1990s. Levels of education are high. The international trade sector is competing effectively in world trade, especially in the Information and Computer Technology (ICT) sector, though it is dominated by a few big successful companies. Sweden's world leadership in information technology comes largely from the success of a few established firms.

The partial reforms instituted in the Swedish economy in the past decade were effective. A lot of Swedish (and Finnish) growth is recovery growth – a rebound from a depression as deep as anything in the 1920s and 1930s. However, since the crisis of the early 1990s, Sweden has moved toward increasing incentives. This has helped to fuel growth.

Sweden has moved towards a more incentivized state. The introduction of incentives is an important ingredient of recent Swedish performance. However, a recent study concludes that there is still a lot of scope for reform and improvement in Sweden (Freeman *et al.* 2006).

Focusing on Sweden or the Nordic countries neglects the most vibrant European economy – Ireland. Compared to Ireland, a country not often mentioned as a model for Europe by policy pundits but much admired by many smaller Eastern European countries, the growth in employment in Sweden has been very limited. See Figure 5.7, which contrasts the GDP per capita growth of Ireland with that of the Nordics, Figure 5.8, which contrasts Irish and Nordic civil employment growth, and Figure 5.9, which compares Irish and Nordic productivity growth rates.

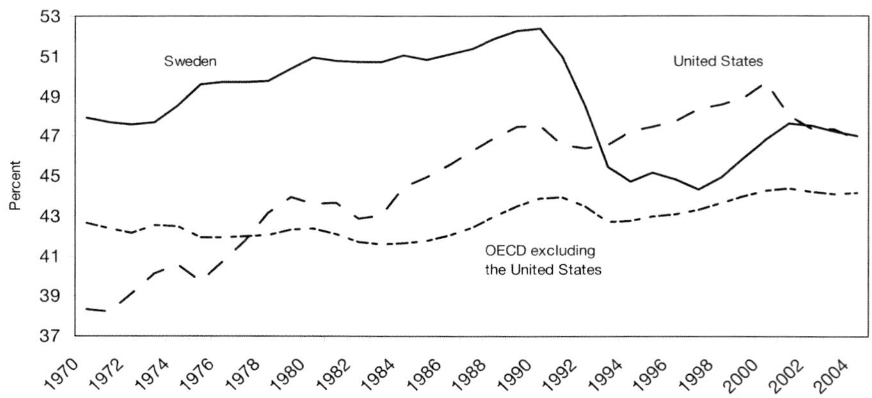

Figure 5.6 Employment as a share of total population in Sweden, the United States, and the OECD, 1970–2004 (%).
Source: Davis and Henrekson (2006).

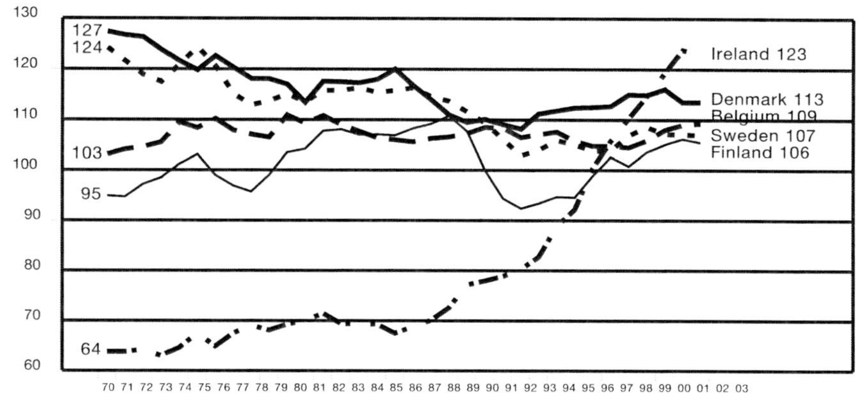

Figure 5.7 Prosperity levels 1970–2003 (OECD = 100) – GDP per capita using current prices and current Purchase Price Parities.
Source: Author's calculations from Organisation for Economic Co-operation and Development (2006a)

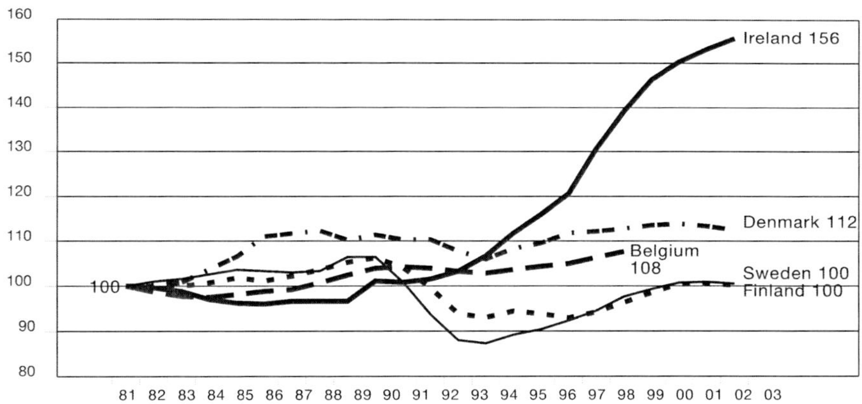

Figure 5.8 Job creation – total civil employment (1981 = 100).
Source: Author's calculations from Organisation for Economic Co-operation and Development (2006a)

Put in context, the Swedish miracle is not so miraculous. Ireland substantially reduced taxes on capital, raised its educational stock, and opened itself up to world trade. It is heavily unionized and follows a corporatist model. It was proper attention to incentives that produced the Irish miracle. Unlike the recent economic recoveries of Finland and Sweden, the Irish experience cannot be interpreted as a rebound from a deep depression in the 1980s. The Irish economy was stagnant for decades before the 1980s. As occurred in the reforms in Sweden, the UK, New Zealand, Australia, Chile,

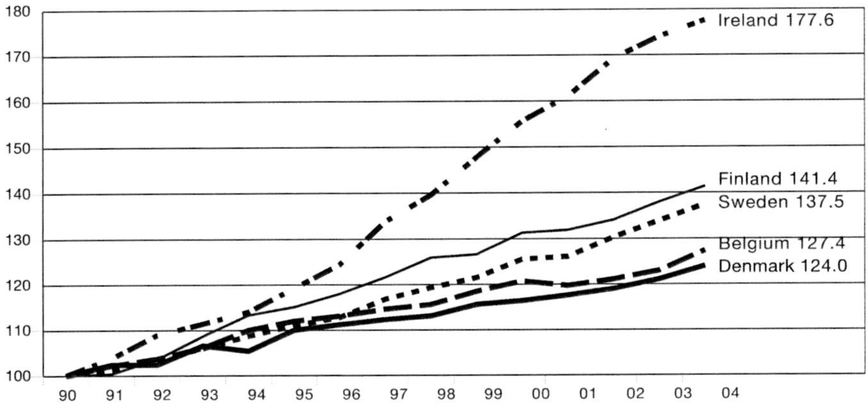

Figure 5.9 Productivity per working hour (1990 = 100).
Source: Author's calculations from Organisation for Economic Co-operation and Development (2006a)

and Ireland, social partners cooperated in a time of crisis. It is important not to underrate the value of crises in producing reforms. The question is, can one avoid crises and still make meaningful reforms? I return to this question, but I first examine the official statistics that are the basis for the recent praise of the Nordic model more closely.

Understanding what the statistics reveal and conceal

The official statistics on Nordic welfare states are highly distorted. The lower levels of unemployment found there are misleading and conceal deep problems in those societies. Consider active labor-market programs which are widely regarded in policy circles as a source of success of Nordic (and other) economies. There has been a substantial commitment to expenditure on active labor-market programs (ALMP) in many European countries and especially in corporatist Europe. Figure 5.10 shows that ALMP programs account for more than 4 percent of GDP in some corporatist economies. The OECD (2006b) and many commentators have endorsed these programs in their official publications. They attribute lower unemployment in the Nordic areas in part to ALMP.

A large array of studies surveyed in Heckman *et al.* (1999) and Martin and Grubb (2001), as well as more recent studies, show that ALMP programs at current levels of funding have at best minor long-term effects on wages and employment. Most do not survive a cost–benefit test. Few programs lift most participants out of poverty. A recent paper by Forslund and Krueger (2008) shows that *none* of the recent recovery of the Swedish economy can be attributed to ALMP programs.

ALMP accounting boosts reported Swedish GDP in a spurious way. Persons in training programs are counted as government employees and their wages are

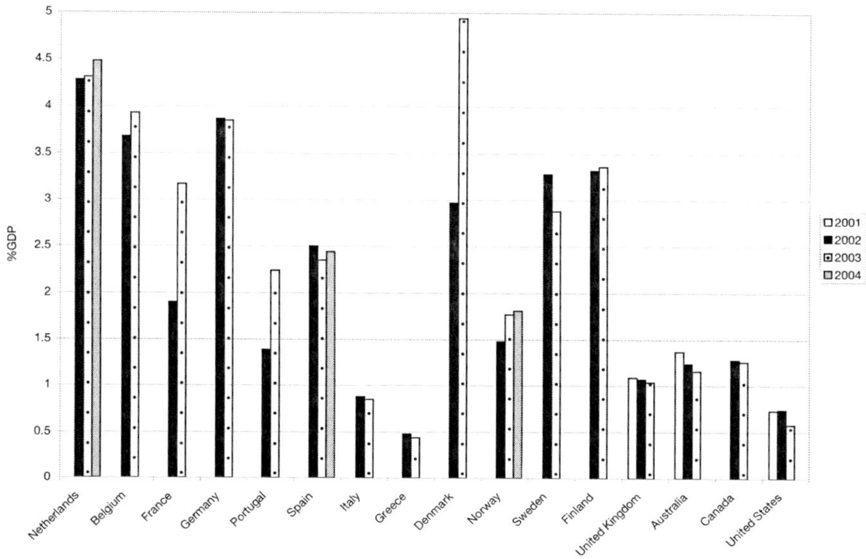

Figure 5.10 Total expenditure on training and passive/active labor market programs (% GDP).

Source: Author's calculations from Organisation for Economic Co-operation and Development (2005a, 2005b, 2006a, 2007a, and 2007b)

counted in Swedish GDP. This artificially inflates employment figures. Adjusting "open" unemployment by disguised unemployment produces a very different image of the performance of corporatist Europe compared to the performance of the US than is given in the official account of the success of the Nordic model. Figure 5.11 shows that adjusting the padded statistics boosts corporatist unemployment rates by a full four percentage points. Adjusting European unemployment rates for ALMP substantially increases true European unemployment rates (Figure 5.12).

ALMP programs that conceal unemployment are only part of the reason for lower "open" Nordic unemployment rates. Europe, and Nordic Europe in particular, has many more persons dependent on government programs than the US. Consider just one program. Expenditure on disability is much higher in the EU than in the US. In Holland, at its peak, some 14 percent of all potential workers were collecting disability insurance. On top of the high expenditure on ALMP, expenditure on disability commands a substantial chunk of OECD expenditure (see Figure 5.13). The data for 2004 show that disability take-up rates among potential able-bodied workers reach levels as high as 10 percent in many countries (see Figure 5.14).

More generally, dependency rates for social programs are much higher in the EU, and the structure of dependency is different. Participation in welfare and

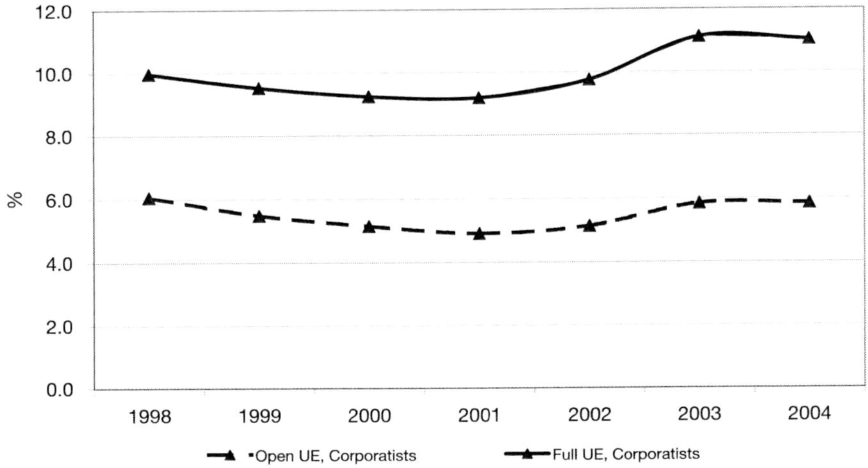

Figure 5.11 Open and full employment.
Source: Heckman, Ljunge, and Ragan (2006)

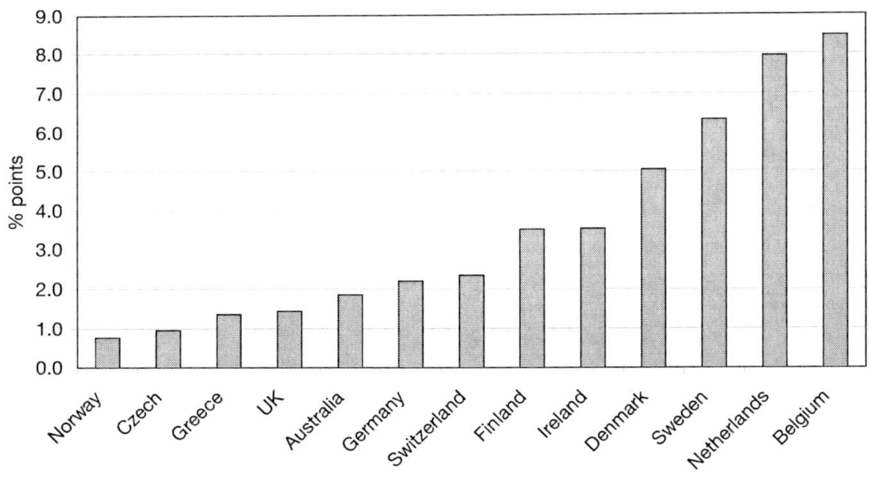

Figure 5.12 Differences between open and full unemployment, 1998–2004 averages.
Source: Heckman, Ljunge, and Ragan (2006)

transfer programs in the EU tends to be much more long-term than in other welfare states. In many EU states, the rate of dependency on transfers is high, and has increased. Participation in a variety of welfare-state programs has produced lower rates of employment in many OECD countries. They reduce unemployment by buying people out of the workforce. When the data are adjusted for employment subsidies, the true employment rate of the corporatist states

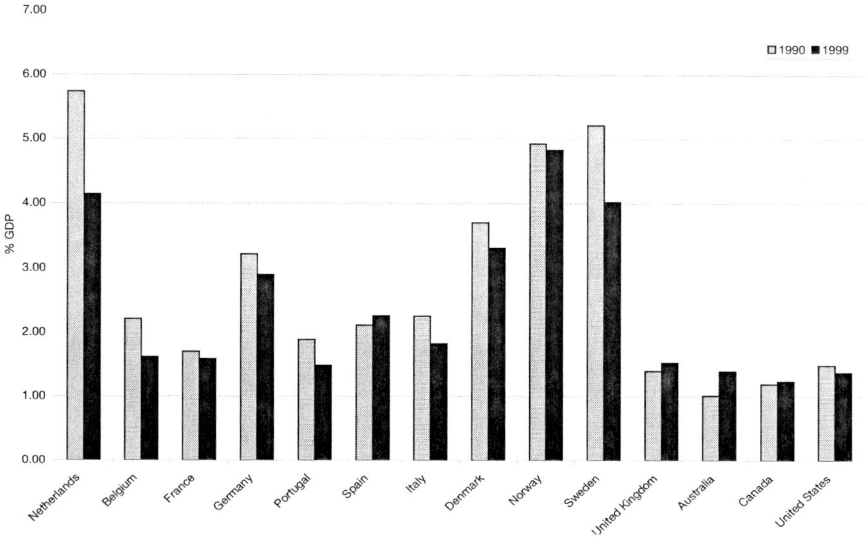

Figure 5.13 Disability-related expenditures (% GDP) in 1990, 1999.
Source: Author's calculations from Organisation for Economic Co-operation and Development (2005a, 2005b, 2006a, 2007a, and 2007b)

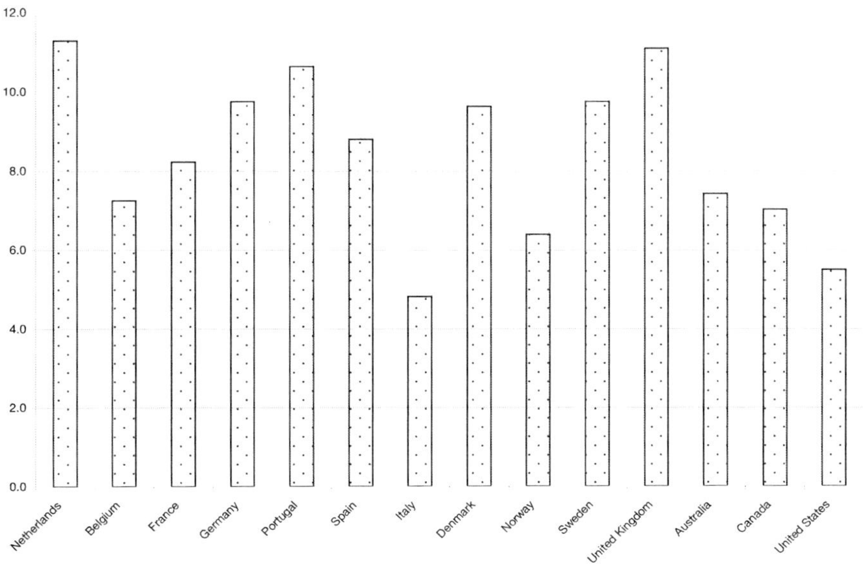

Figure 5.14 Nonemployed disabled workers (% of labor force).
Source: Author's calculations from Organisation for Economic Co-operation and Development (2005a, 2005b, 2006a, 2007a, and 2007b)

substantially declines (see Figure 5.15). The effects on Western welfare-state employment rates are substantial (see Figure 5.16).

A larger fraction of employment the EU — especially corporatist EU — is in the government sector (see Figure 5.17). Government employment is an index of regulatory activity, and in most sectors, government employment is not productive, although measurement of productivity in governments' activity is a tricky issue.

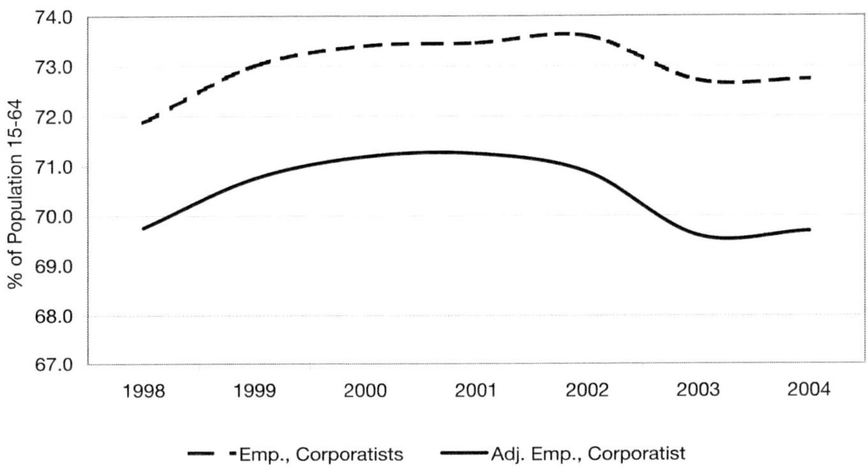

Figure 5.15 Open and adjusted employment rates in a subset of European countries. Source: Heckman, Ljunge, and Ragan (2006)

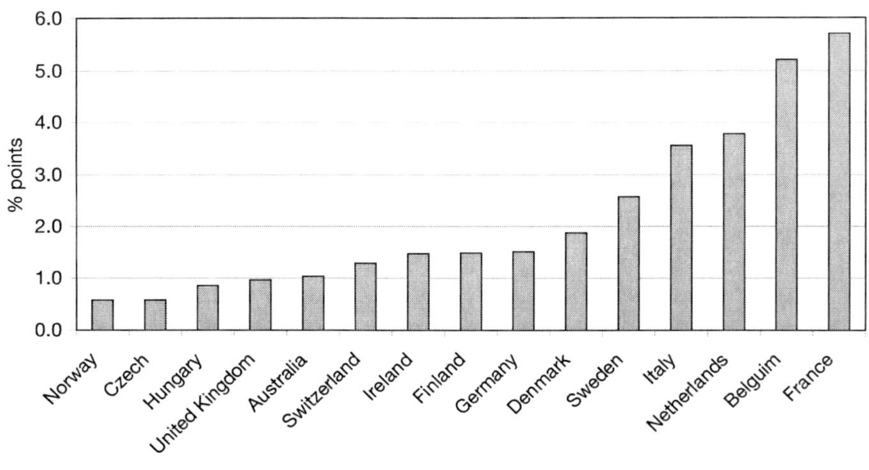

Figure 5.16 Differences between open and full employment rates, 1998–2004 averages. Source: Heckman, Ljunge, and Ragan (2006)

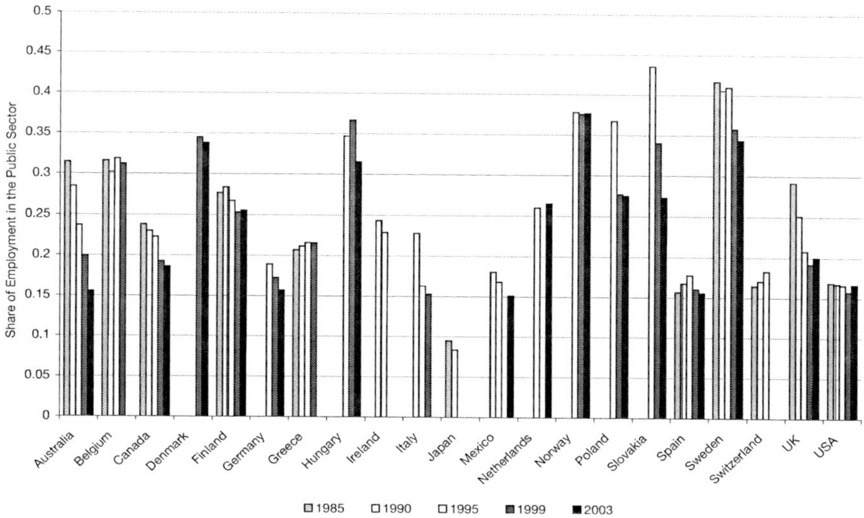

Figure 5.17 Public sector employment share.
Source: Heckman, Ljunge, and Ragan (2006)

The growth in dependency on government creates a serious problem of political economy in democratic welfare states. If one adds current dependents to government workers, one sees that there is considerable inertia to protect the status quo. Moreover, to finance the high level of benefits and the ALMP programs, tax rates are high (see Figure 5.18). The total share of spending on government is substantial, although it has begun to decline (see Figure 5.19). The disincentives for work and the timing of work over the life cycle and investment in human capital are substantial. Retirement benefits are perverse at a time when the population is ageing. It has been estimated that, in Denmark, for the median person, 75 percent of the taxes are repaid in benefits but both taxes and benefits distort margins throughout the life cycle at many margins (see Bovenberg *et al.* 2008). Incentive schedules often create poverty traps.

There is an inverse relationship between the size of the government sector and the growth of GDP (see Figure 5.20). It turns out on closer analysis that transfers are the culprit, and not government expenditure per se. Recognition of the often harmful role of a large government sector has led to trends in the OECD against public spending as is evident in Figure 5.19.

Education is a major determinant of long-run employment and unemployment. More educated workers are more adaptable, innovative, and easily employed. Educational expenditure per student in tertiary education (college) is much lower in the EU than in the US. The relatively low rate of educational attainment in the OECD countries is due to high progressive taxation of income with reduced incentives to acquire skills. In addition, there is exclusive

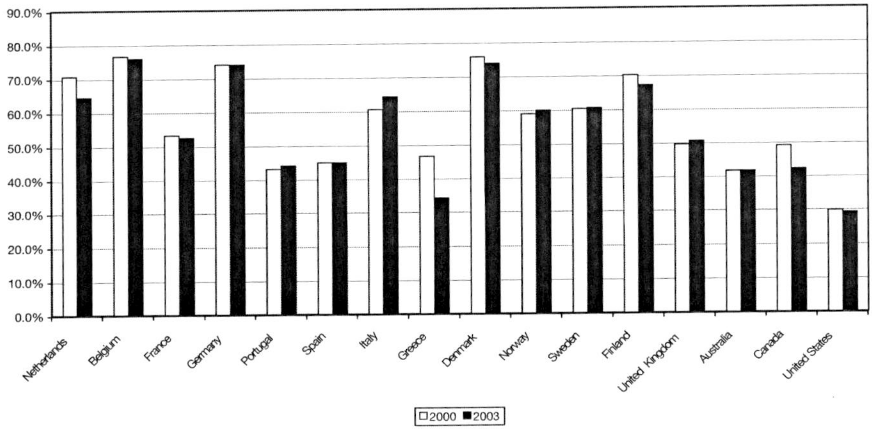

Figure 5.18 Total marginal tax wedge on personal income, including consumption taxes (% of income) for a single worker earning the average production wage without children (US: no cons. taxes available).
Source: Author's calculations from Organisation for Economic Co-operation and Development (2005a, 2005b, 2006a, 2007a, and 2007b)

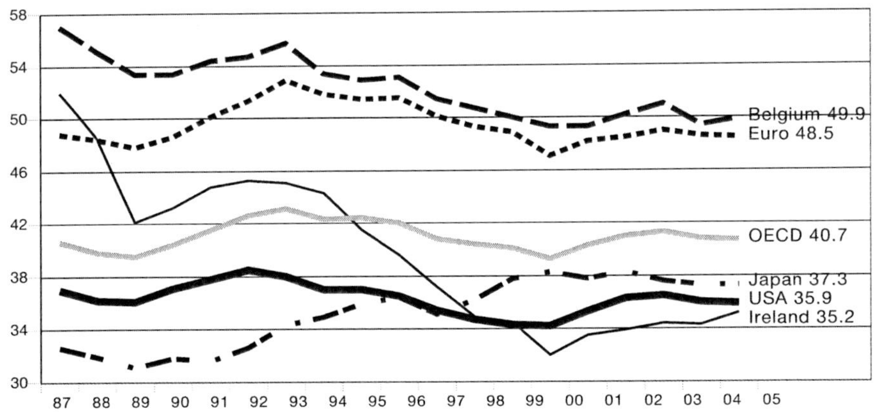

Figure 5.19 Public spending as a percentage of GDP.
Source: Author's calculations from Organisation for Economic Co-operation and Development (2006a)

dependence on public-sector resources to support education in a period when government resources are limited. Fees are not charged, and there is little reliance on the private sector as an engine of revenue, unlike the case in the US. Student fees are a source of revenue and screen into schooling students with high demand for it. Joint ventures with business are limited. Sweden partially offsets this disincentive by generous subsidies to education. However,

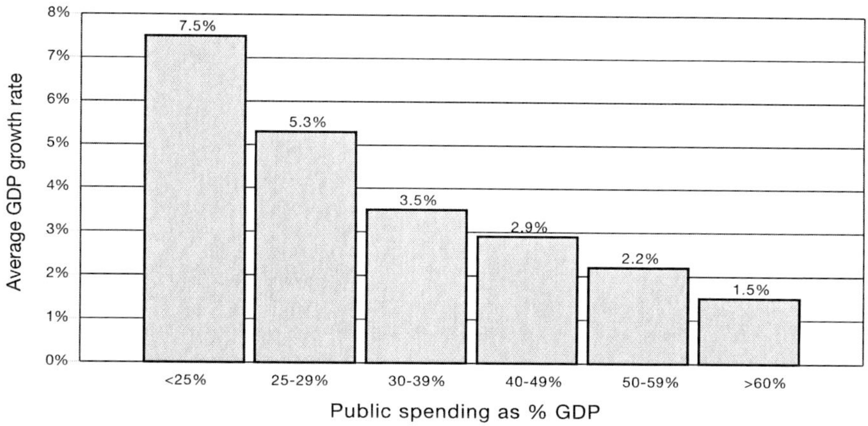

Figure 5.20 Correlation of growth and public spending – 30 OECD countries, 1960–2005. Source: Author's calculations from Organisation for Economic Co-operation and Development (2006a)

this policy runs the risk of training people for British, US, and Canadian jobs. (See Figure 5.21, Figure 5.22.)

Participation in generous welfare states leads to erosion of the work ethic and withdrawal from participation in the social contract. There is evidence of cohort drift in welfare participation. Those cohorts who have lived a greater fraction of their lives under the generosity of the welfare state come to accept its benefits and game the system at higher rates. Martin Ljunge (2006) studied

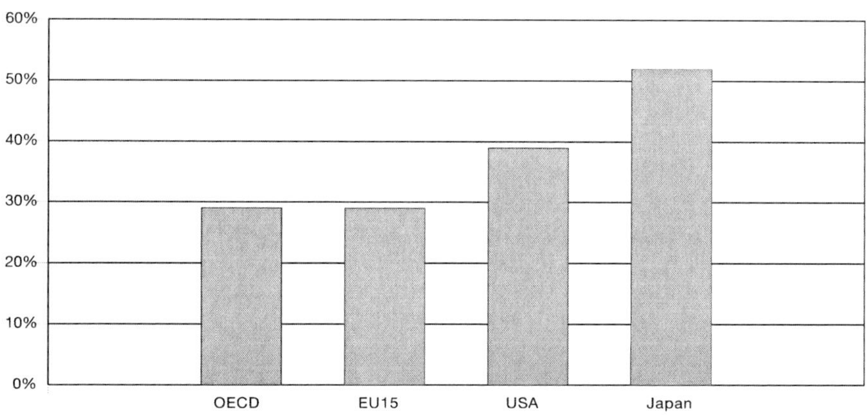

Figure 5.21 Proportion of 25–34 age group with university education.
Source: Author's calculations from Organisation for Economic Co-operation and Development (2005a, 2005b, 2006a, 2007a, and 2007b)

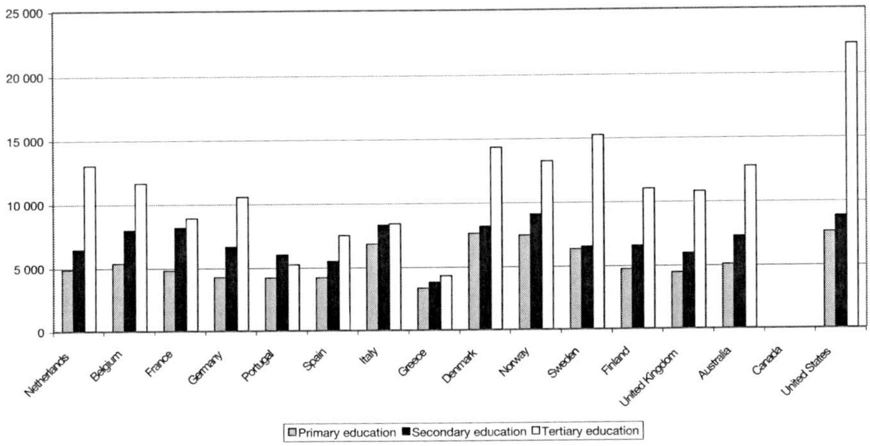

Figure 5.22 Real expenditure per student in US$.
Source: Author's calculations from Organisation for Economic Co-operation and Development (2006a)

the use of sick leave for three cohorts of Swedish workers. The incentives to use the system have been the same for 40 years. Yet, as Figure 5.23 reveals, the take-up rate at the same age has increased for recent cohorts. This is a serious long-term problem for the European welfare state. Problems of an eroding work ethic are compounded by the lack of assimilation of many immigrant populations. In truth, the welfare state creates inequality, and has self-perpetuating features.

Bad measures lead to weak conclusions; good measures lead to strong conclusions

The OECD and many students of European economic performance analyze the effectiveness of alternative economic systems by relating performance to various *ad hoc* measures of the incentives created by institutions. There is a large literature on cross-country panels that uses these measures to explain variation in European unemployment and other issues (see, e.g., Blanchard and Wolfers 2000; Layard *et al.* 1991). The countries studied are very heterogenous and the time series analyzed are typically very short. Many measurements of institutions are indices formed for entire countries. These studies do not analyze incentive effects on firms and workers at the levels at which the incentives operate. The analyses are conducted at aggregate levels using a "representative agent" framework that ignores basic heterogeneity in society. Such evidence is fragile and unreliable.

It would be fruitful for students of OECD labor markets to follow the lead of students of the Latin American labor market and quantify the costs and incentives of institutions governing labor markets.[3] Such studies would reveal the

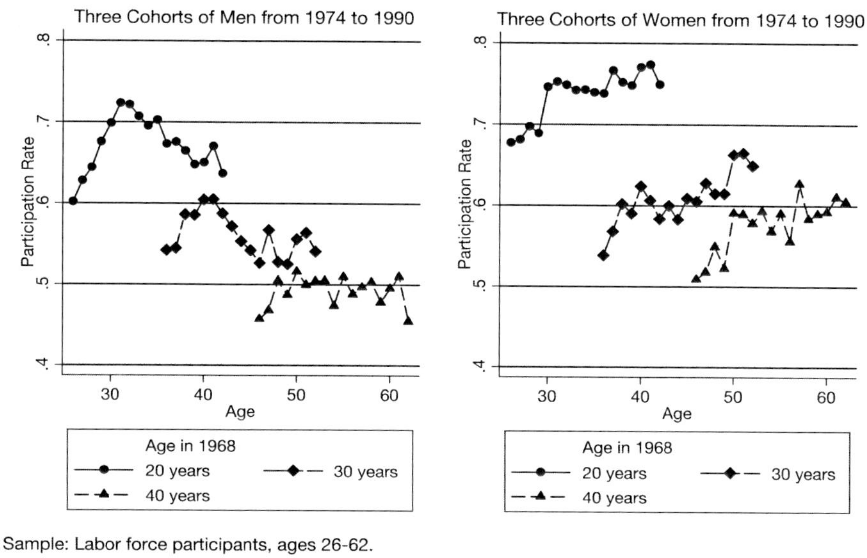

Figure 5.23 Sick leave participation for men and women.
Source: Ljunge (2006).

quantitative insignificance of the reforms made in Europe in the past decade. Scholars of Latin America have collected micro data on costs, employment, wages, and turnover in their countries. Policy instability in the region produces some radical economic experiments with much greater variability than any natural experiments or policy experiments that have been observed in Europe. Many of these natural experiments are plausibly exogenous. From these experiments we can learn about the basic economics of incentives that applies universally even if the details of the policy environment vary from episode to episode.

Consider the substantial variation in labor costs in Peru in the last decade associated with various Fujimori governments. Figure 5.24 shows the range of variation in non-wage costs due to policy shifts in Peru from the first quarter of 1987 to the first quarter of 1997.

Using these and other data, the costs of institutions (unions, labor market regulations, severance payment schemes, minimum wages) can be quantified and estimated on microeconomic models of firms. Translating regulations into costs allows analysts to summarize a variety of features of labor market institutions using an interpretable cost schedule. The cost data can be used to estimate the impact of regulation on the labor market. In the best studies, the analysis is highly disaggregated and applied to the firm or industry level.

Studies that measure labor cost precisely establish that labor demand curves are downward sloping, i.e. higher labor costs mean fewer workers demanded.

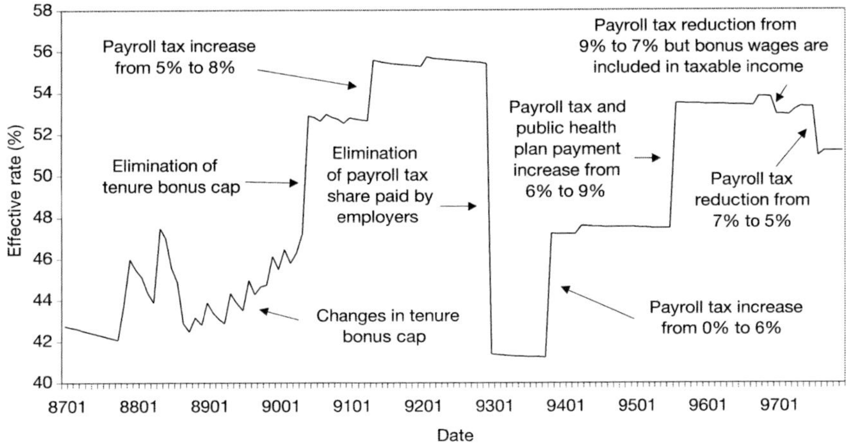

Figure 5.24 Evolution of nonwage costs paid by employers – Peru.
Note: Non-wage costs paid by the employer include payroll tax, tenure bonus, public retirement plan payments, and public health plan payments. Vacations and holiday bonuses are included in the effective rate, although they were not modified during the period and stand for 25 percent of non-wage costs paid by the employer (two bonus wages and one month of paid vacation per year).
Source: Saavedra and Torero (2004).

This relationship has been found for economies around the world. The elasticity of demand for labor with respect to wage is 0.7 (Hamermesh 2004). Regulations and unions raise labor costs and reduce employment. A 10 percent increase in labor costs leads to a 7 percent reduction in employment. Contrary to a folklore that many embrace because it is politically convenient to do so, binding minimum wages reduce employment as do payroll taxes that are imposed in countries without wage flexibility. The current practice of using *ad hoc* measures of the costs of institutions on highly aggregated statistics from very heterogenous countries is guaranteed to produce the finding that "institutions don't matter" when in truth they do.

Payroll taxes

Payroll taxes are a substantial fraction of total labor cost in most modern welfare states. The disemployment effects of payroll taxes depend on what economists call "pass-through." The proportion of the cost of the payroll tax that is borne by firms and, therefore, the extent of disemployment, depends on how flexible wages are, and on how wisely funds are spent (do workers value the benefits?). One cost of corruption and bad governance is that firms bear a greater share of their payroll tax. This reduces employment.

Studies of union reforms corroborate the value of disaggregated studies

Consider the benefits of redefining the role of unions. Reforms of this sort have been put in place and analyzed using data at the individual plant level (see Pencavel 2004; Nickell *et al.* 1992). Studies show the value of exploiting local knowledge and incentives. The more decentralized the locus of collective bargaining, the more economically productive is the worker–firm relationship and the less rent-seeking behavior there is by unions. Public policy toward unions should be even-handed and not favor one party over another. Governments should allow parties to set the rules and not impose uniform rules on all bargaining pairs.

One important exception to this rule is that, in times of crisis, it is possible – as in wartime – for centralized unions to act in the public interest and hold down wage demands. This observation motivates in part the claim of a "U" shape in optimal union density, i.e. that the best social arrangements are 0 percent union or 100 percent. Studies of unions find little evidence that monopoly unions operate in an enlightened fashion in the long run (see Pencavel 1999). They can operate constructively in the short run in times of crisis but maintaining the cooperation in a period of sustained success has proved to be difficult.

Pencavel (1999) documents the effect of union reforms in the UK that moved bargaining to the local level. They raised productivity of firms, both union and nonunion. The moral of Pencavel's study is not to eliminate unions, but to change the union–firm relationship to focus on creating *incentives* to enhance productivity locally. Reforms in the union sector were complementary with product market reforms (see Pencavel 1999). Uniform wage setting in Italy (south and north), East Germany, and Northern Sweden that is not sensitive to local demands leads to high rates of unemployment in lower productivity regions.

The burden of regulation

Many economies around the world operate under a heavy burden of regulation. These regulations raise adjustment costs of labor and promote inflexibility. Regulation leads to sluggish employment responses. Employment protection laws that are popular in LDCs and in the Mediterranean welfare states reduce labor mobility. Deregulation raises mobility and flexibility. Regulation reduces employment overall, but raises employment for protected workers. It produces a protected enclave of insiders (see Lindbeck and Snower 1989).

Moreover, as noted by Nicoletti and Scarpetta (2003), product-market and labor-market regulation are highly correlated (see Figure 5.25). This array of regulations reduces innovation and impairs adoption of technology (see Figure 5.26). Regulation reduces entry of firms (see Djankov *et al.* 2002; Freeman 2002) (see Figure 5.27). These barriers have substantial long-run, perverse effects on growth in productivity.

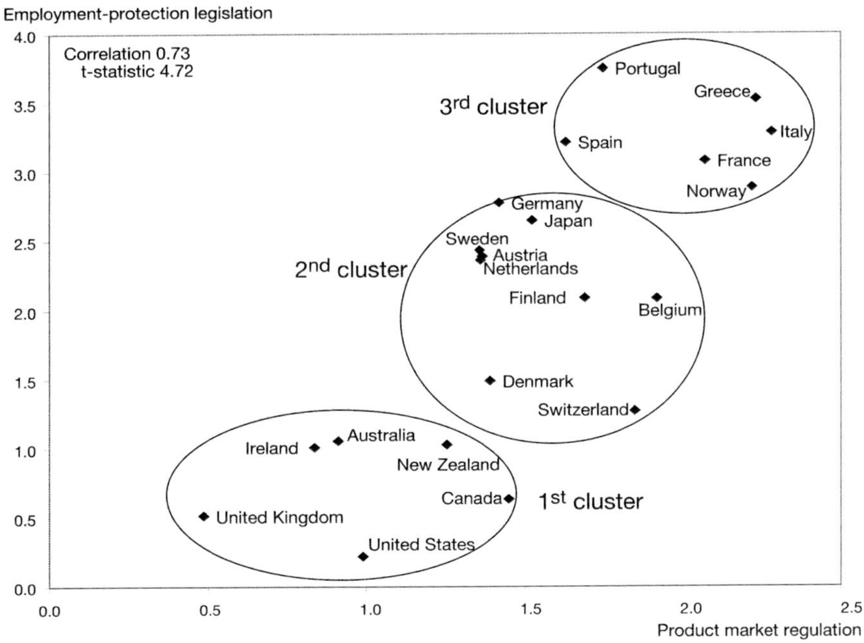

Figure 5.25 Product-market regulation and employment-protection legislation.
Source: Nicoletti and Scarpetta (2001).

The inequality argument for the welfare state re-examined

A principle argument in support of welfare states is that they reduce inequality and promote social inclusion. In practice, the welfare state often excludes people, creates inequality, and reduces competitiveness (see Heckman and Pagés 2004). Incentives in place often retard immigrant assimilation and reduce inclusion.

Incentives that protect the status quo reduce mobility over the life cycle.The rigidities of the welfare state raise lifetime inequality. Cross-sectional inequality (over people at a point in time) is much larger in the US than it is in Italy. However, in Italy, jobs are protected for life. Mobility out of a bad starting job is much lower than in the more flexible US labor market. The gap in lifetime inequality between the US and Italy is much less than the cross-section gap (see Flinn 2002).

Crisis is the mother of all welfare-state reforms

The political economy of the welfare state is rigged against reform because so many persons are its beneficiaries. Reforms that have occurred in most welfare

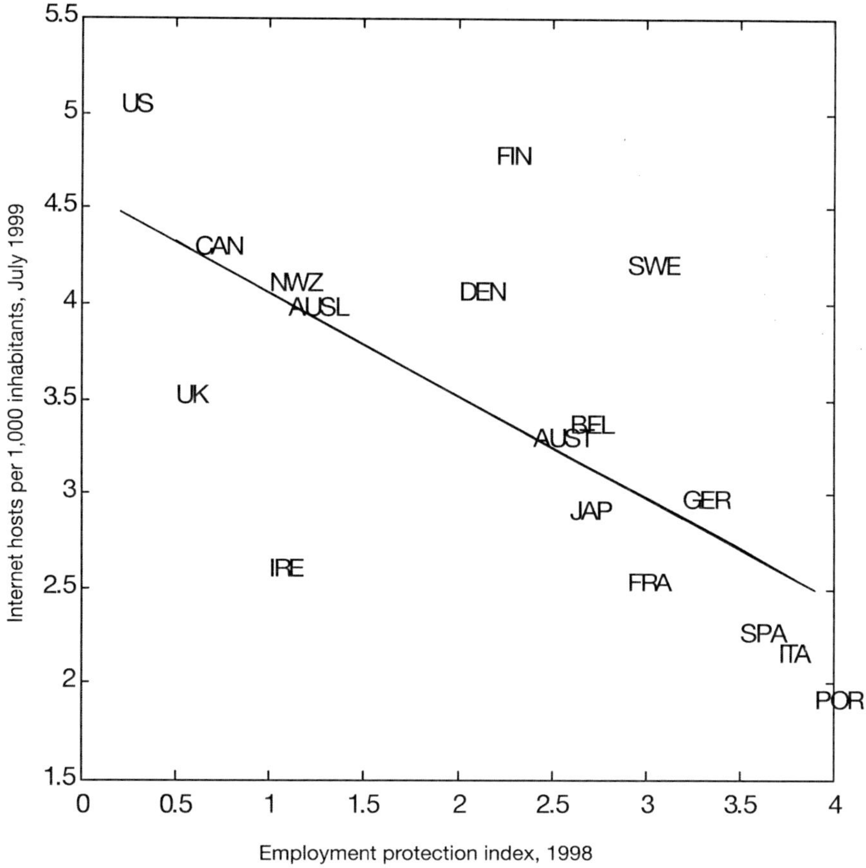

Figure 5.26 Internet usage and employment protection.
Source: Samaniego (2006).

states have been quite modest. Most reforms have come in the wake of an economic crisis. There is little internal capacity for democratic societies to reform themselves without a crisis.

Summary

Provisions of the welfare state, such as the right to economic security, are often interpreted as basic human rights that implement the rule-of-law. Rights that improve the lot of all or most in society should be distinguished from rights that benefit some at the expense of many. Many provisions of modern welfare states favor some while harming others. Programs that pay workers to

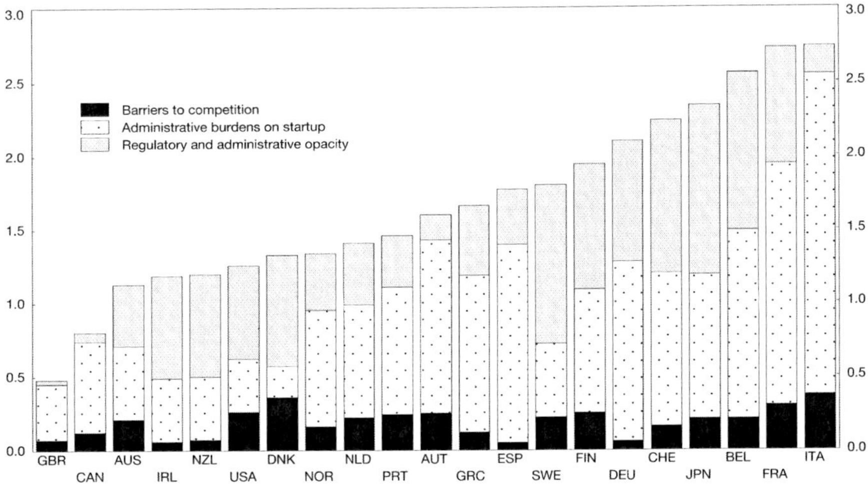

Figure 5.27 Barriers to entrepreneurship: cross-country comparison based on 1998 data. Source: Nicoletti and Scarpetta (2001).

withdraw from economic activity while others work to support them are examples of such provisions.

This chapter elevates the discussion of the welfare state beyond the level of endorsing one system over another. I have presented the essential features that underlie the success of aspects of many different systems. Systems that respect the basic incentives of economic life are the most successful. These incentives provide restraints on the freedoms possible under a welfare state.

Incentives include rewards for production of output, for creation of new ideas and institutions; for work rather than politicking; incentives to seek jobs when economic conditions favor reallocations (e.g. sanctions in the Netherlands and Denmark); incentives to invest as opportunities arise, to venture, to build for the future; and incentives to move when economic conditions call for it (as in the flexicurity system).

Long-run trends in Western welfare states are not favorable even in the Nordic countries. This is especially clear once the distorted nature of the published statistics is exposed. High levels of taxation, protection, and generosity of benefits erode the dynamism of any society. They build a culture of dependency that erodes innovation. They create a level of complacency that erodes the work ethic and mutes incentives to invest in skills and in the larger society. They create a system that protects the status quo and is very difficult to change except when a crisis emerges. Most reforms of welfare states (e.g. Ireland, Finland, Holland, and Sweden) came in moments of crisis.

There is much room for creative policy innovation. One can create incentives for mobility, but at the same time give workers some security as in the

Danish "flexicurity" system. One can create incentives to work (WTC, UK; EITC, US) and not participate in welfare. Such incentives boost productivity and raise levels of well-being and social integration. One can use social insurance accounts that insure, but at the same time introduce flexibility into the system.

The welfare state is a relatively new creation. It is not surprising that early versions of it sometimes created perverse incentives. Such perverse incentives are not intrinsic to it. Innovation, reform, and experimentation will improve it. Attempts at reform and regulation should respect the power of incentives and promote efficient social insurance.

Notes

1 This research was supported by a grant to the World Justice Project from the William and Flora Hewlett Foundation, Grant #2008–2244. This chapter draws in part from a paper presented at the OECD Conference in Toronto on the 2006 Jobs Report (Heckman *et al*. 2006).

2 Ireland has centralized bargaining in trade unions.

3 See the papers in Heckman and Pagés 2004.

Chapter 6

Comparing legal and alternative institutions in finance and commerce[1]

Franklin Allen and Jun "QJ" Qian[2]

Introduction

Transiting from a central-planning to a market-based economy, China's economic achievements in the past three decades have been remarkable. Its economic growth, lifting hundreds of millions of people out of poverty in the process, represents one of the greatest economic transformations in history. India is also successful in terms of economic growth during the past two decades. At the end of 2007, China and India together accounted for 40 percent of the world population and about 20 percent of the world GDP in Purchasing Power Parity terms. With growth rates among the highest of all countries, these two countries will play an increasingly important role in the world economy for years to come.

The conventional wisdom is that to be successful in terms of long-run economic growth a country needs good institutions. In particular, it needs a good legal system that enforces contracts and resolves disputes and a good financial system including financial markets and a banking sector to fund firm growth. In earlier work (Allen, Qian, and Qian (AQQ) 2005, 2008; Allen, Chakrabarti, De, Qian, and Qian (ACDQQ) 2008), we have documented that China and India do not have these. In fact, the governments of these countries are notoriously corrupt, the legal systems are ineffective, and the financial markets and banks are small relative to their economies and inefficient.

Most observers would characterize the economic performance in China as "successful *despite* the lack of Western-style institutions." By contrast, we argue in this chapter that China has done well *because of* this lack of Western-style institutions – in that conducting business outside the legal system in fast-growing economies, such as China and India, can actually be superior to using the law as the basis for business transactions. We develop our main theses by comparing and contrasting two different sets of systems, with the focus on dispute-resolution and contract-enforcement mechanisms. In one system, observed in developed and democratic countries such as the US, there is a commitment to use the law as the basis for finance and commerce, with legal institutions serving as the ultimate source for resolving disputes and enforcing contracts. Moreover, any fundamental changes to the law must be approved by the legislature and electorate. In the other system, with China providing the primary example, there is no clear definition of private property rights at the highest level and, in place of the law, nonlegal mechanisms based on reputation, relationships, and trust rather are the norm for conducting business.[3]

We first present a number of examples on how alternative mechanisms work. The practice of corporate sectors in China and India shows alternative mechanisms can substitute for legal mechanisms. Based on earlier work, we show that despite the differences in their history of developing laws and formal institutions, the legal environment for business is characterized by an underdeveloped legal system (China) or a sophisticated legal system on paper but of limited use in practice (India). Within the corporate sectors of these countries, state-owned enterprises and publicly listed firms have much easier access to legal institutions, banks and financial markets than nonstate, nonlisted firms. To a large extent these nonstate, nonlisted firms, most of which are small and medium firms, conduct business outside the legal system and do not rely on financial markets or banks for most of their financing needs. Instead, they use nonlegal methods based on reputation, relationships, and trust to settle disputes and enforce contracts and rely on alternative financing channels such as trade credits and funds from family and friends to finance their growth. Yet in both countries, and especially in China, it is the nonstate, nonlisted firms that provide most of the economic growth and employ most of the labor forces. The insignificant role of the law and legal system during periods of rapid economic development has also been documented in other East Asian economies such as Japan and Taiwan.

In another set of examples we show that alternative mechanisms can handle disputes that arise from complicated transactions. The diamond industry has historically operated outside the legal system of any one country and flourished worldwide despite the lack of transparency of most of its dispute resolutions. Another industry that has relied on out-of-court mediations and arbitrations to settle disputes is reinsurance. In recent years it appears that selecting objective arbitrators has become a lengthy process that significantly delays the arbitration process, particularly in large-scale transactions, and the industry has been revising the traditional procedure in order to expedite the process without losing sight of fairness.

Next, we focus on examples in developed countries, such as the US, to highlight the problems of using the law and legal system as the basis for finance and commerce. The reason for this choice is obvious. If there are significant deficiencies in using the legal system in countries with the most developed institutions, these deficiencies are likely to be magnified in developing countries with poor institutions.

A central concept in the legal paradigm and institutions is (private) property rights. One of the intensely debated topics on property rights is intellectual property rights including patents and copyrights. The practice of enforcing intellectual property rights by courts is much more vigilant and prevalent in developed countries than in developing countries. There is a widespread belief in developed countries that such protection is essential for promoting innovations, but this belief is not shared in the developing world. What is the empirical evidence? An extensive literature in industrial organization in economics has found mixed results on the relationship between patent/copyright protection and the pace of innovations. On the one hand, exclusive property rights provide strong incentives for innovations and do lead to more innovations in some industries such as chemicals and pharmaceuticals. On the other hand, such a positive relationship between protection and pace of innovations is not observed in many other industries; instead, excessive protection deters competition, which is another important factor in spurring innovations. One of the problems with the patent/copyright and litigation systems is that they induce rent-seeking behaviors by vested interest groups and individuals. With abundant resources they can undertake various measures and use the legal system to block competition and innovations from other individuals or smaller companies, and this type of behavior reduces social welfare.

Another potential problem of using the law lies in the legal-system capacity and fixed costs associated with revising the law as may be required by changes in the economic environment. In democracies, the legislature must approve any revisions in the law before corporations and investors can freely implement new techniques in their activities and transactions in practice. However, in any given period politicians have limited time and effort to devote to one area of the law, implying a fixed cost in revising the law. A good example illustrating such limited capacity and fixed costs is the US payments system. At the beginning of the twenty-first century the US had a nineteenth-century payments system, relying mostly on paper checks and the mail, and significantly lagging behind other developed nations. Checks had to be physically transported from where they were deposited to a central operations center, then to the clearer and then back to the banks they were drawn on. This process significantly delayed business transactions as compared to electronic methods.

Despite repeated calls for changes from the banks and businesses, it appeared that the US Congress was not interested in solving this seemingly simple yet costly problem, until 11 September 2001. After the terrorist attack all commercial flights in the US were grounded for several days, completely halting the check clearing process. The Check Clearing for the 21st Century Act was signed in October 2003, allowing electronic images to be a substitute for the original checks, thereby offering the clearing process a means to circumvent the mail and transportation system.

These examples motivate our analysis on the advantages and disadvantages of a system based on rule-of-law and legal institutions versus a system relying on alternative, nonlegal institutions. Using the law and the legal system as the basis of finance and commerce has many well-known advantages. The legal system of a democracy ideally allows equal and full access by all and fairness in trials and settlements. With powerful enforcement mechanisms including civil and criminal penalties, disputing individuals, firms, and organizations have strong incentives to follow the resolutions backed by courts and the government. This in turn provides long-term stability on how things should be done in practice. By using the entire legal operator and system, the marginal enforcement costs for an additional case can be low, and this improves overall efficiency.

However, there are also disadvantages in using the law and legal institutions. First, recent research on political economy factors – in particular, work by Rajan and Zingales (2003a, 2003b) – argues that rent-seeking behaviors by vested-interest groups can turn legal institutions into barriers to changes. We expect these problems to be much more severe in developing countries, where the costs of building good institutions can be enormous. We argue that one way to solve this problem is not to use the law as the basis for finance and commerce but instead to use alternative mechanisms. Second, as shown by the example of US payment system reform, the capacity of the legal system and legislature can impose significant fixed costs in revising the law and thus delaying the pace of innovations. These fixed costs can further increase if the people in charge of revising the law (e.g. politicians and judges) lack expertise in business transactions. In addition, interest groups with more resources may receive more protection than individuals, and this asymmetric protection system induces more rent-seeking behaviors and further deters innovations.

In the context of a fast-growing economy, such as that of China or India, characterized by frequent, fundamental changes in the economic environment, the disadvantages of using the legal system can overshadow its advantages, and it may be better to conduct business without using the law and legal system. In addition to minimizing the political economy costs associated with legal institutions, using alternative mechanisms is advantageous in that such mechanisms can adapt and change much more quickly than the law. In particular, competition among different networks and institutions can ensure the most efficient prevails, and it is not necessary to persuade the legislature and the electorate that the law needs to be revised when circumstances change.

There are also limitations to alternative mechanisms. By design these mechanisms often exist within a network (or networks) of firms and investors and may be inaccessible to outsiders. The limited access can come with the price of biases favoring insiders. With frequent changes and limited enforcement (since penalties cannot be imposed with authority), these systems generate instability and hence weak long-term incentives. While in a fast-growing economy profit-sharing in the long run and reputation-based mechanisms can ensure "good" (cooperative) behavior, these mechanisms may be insufficient to induce such behavior in environments with limited long-term profits. On the other hand, in such static environments with infrequent changes to the fundamentals (e.g. a developed economy with low growth rates), the fixed costs of using the legal system are relatively small (especially in large transactions); hence the law and legal system become superior to the alternative mechanisms.

Overall, we conclude that while legal mechanisms are an important part of developed economies' institutions, alternative mechanisms play a much more prominent role in emerging economies and can be superior to legal mechanisms in supporting business transactions in certain industries or entire economies. Therefore, our main policy implication is that in emerging economies, alternative dispute-resolution and contract-enforcement mechanisms should be encouraged and developed alongside the development of legal and other formal institutions. The coexistence of alternative and legal mechanisms can also foster competition among (legal and nonlegal) institutions, which in our view is essential for creating an environment conducive for innovations. Competition from alternative institutions can also exert positive impact on the development of legal institutions, so that they are less likely to be captured by interest groups and become more efficient in adapting to changes.

Examples of alternative mechanisms and problems with the legal system

In this section we first provide a set of examples on how alternative mechanisms work and substitute for legal mechanisms in different industries and countries. We then present examples that illustrate potential problems with using the law and legal system as the basis for finance and commerce. As indicated earlier, we focus on examples in developed countries such as the US in order to emphasize the nature of the inefficiencies of legal institutions.

Alternative mechanisms in China and India

In the first set of examples we describe how alternative mechanisms substitute for legal mechanisms in China and India. Using information from the IMF, Table 6.1 presents GDPs based on simple exchange rates and purchasing power parity (PPP) and the growth rates in GDPs and per capita GDP (both in constant prices) during 1990–2007 for the top 20 countries in *each* category. China is leading the world in terms of growth rates of both GDP and per capita GDP over this period. At the end of 2007, China's PPP-adjusted GDP is the second largest in the world. If current growth rates persist, China's economy (PPP-adjusted) will overtake the US to become the largest economy in the world in 2010 and will double the size of the US economy by 2020. While economic growth has widened the income and wealth gap in China as compared to the pre-reform period, it has elevated hundreds of millions of people from absolute poverty.[4] India's records in economic growth are not as impressive as those of China, but its growth rates in GDP and per capita GDP are the third and fifth highest in the world, respectively, during 1990–2007. At the end of 2007, India's PPP-adjusted GDP is the third largest in the world.[5]

Table 6.1 The largest 20 economies in the world: GDP and growth

	GDP in 2007 (simple Exchange rates)		*GDP in 2007 (PPP)*		*GDP growth: 1990–2007 (constant prices)*		*Per capita GDP growth: 1990–2007* (constant prices)*	
Rank	*Country /Region*	*US$ Billion*	*Country /Region*	*Int'l $ billion*	*Country /Region*	*Annual growth*	*Country /Region*	*Annual growth*
1	U.S.	13,794	U.S.	13,543	**China**	**10.3%**	**China**	**9.3%**
2	Japan	4,346	**China**	**11,606**	Vietnam	7.6%	Vietnam	6.0%
3	Germany	3,259	**India**	**4,727**	**India**	**6.3%**	Korea	4.7%
4	**China**	**3,249**	Japan	4,346	Malaysia	6.2%	Taiwan	4.5%
5	U. K.	2,756	Germany	2,714	Chile	5.6%	**India**	**4.4%**
6	France	2,515	U. K.	2,271	Korea	5.5%	Chile	4.2%
7	Italy	2,068	France	2,040	Taiwan	5.3%	Poland	3.9%
8	Spain	1,415	Brazil	2,014	Bangladesh	5.2%	Sri Lanka	3.8%
9	Canada	1,406	Russia	1,909	Sri Lanka	5.0%	Malaysia	3.7%
10	Brazil	1,295	Italy	1,888	Yemen, R.	5.0%	Thailand	3.6%
11	Russia	1,224	Spain	1,310	Thailand	4.6%	Bangladesh	3.1%
12	**India**	**1,090**	Korea	1,250	Pakistan	4.6%	Indonesia	3.0%
13	Korea	950	Mexico	1,250	Egypt	4.5%	Peru	2.9%
14	Australia	890	Canada	1,217	Iran	4.5%	Iran	2.9%
15	Mexico	886	Indonesia	1,054	Peru	4.4%	Argentina	2.8%
16	Netherlands	755	Taiwan	750	Indonesia	4.4%	Egypt	2.3%
17	Turkey	482	Australia	731	Turkey	4.0%	Turkey	2.3%
18	Belgium	443	Turkey	723	Argentina	4.0%	Pakistan	2.3%
19	Sweden	432	Argentina	691	Poland	3.9%	Spain	2.2%
20	Switzerland	414	S. Africa	664	Philippines	3.8%	Australia	2.2%

Source: IMF World Economic Outlook Database 2008.
* = Countries with population less than 20 million or GDP less than US$ 20 billion are excluded from this ranking.

With 40 percent of the world's population and the two largest emerging markets in the world, China and India are expected to play an increasingly important role in the global economy for years to come.

The remarkable economic performances of China and India also present significant counterexamples to existing literature on law, institutions, finance, and growth. The conventional wisdom is that a necessary condition for long-run economic growth is good (Western-style) institutions, including laws that protect small investors, a legal system that enforces contracts and resolves disputes, a financial system with efficient financial markets and a banking sector, and a democratic and benign government. However, AQQ (2005) and ACDQQ (2008) document that both China and India have ineffective legal systems, banks, and markets that are small relative to the economies and have played a limited role in allocating resources to most efficient uses, and governments that are among the most corrupt in the world.

While there are many factors that have contributed to the economic growth in these two countries, we want to emphasize the role of financial systems in funding the growth of different corporate sectors.[6] In our earlier work (AQQ 2005; 2008 on China; ACDQQ 2008 on India), we document that state-owned enterprises and publicly listed firms in these countries have much easier access to the legal system, banks, and financial markets than nonstate, nonlisted firms. Most of the nonstate, nonlisted firms are small and medium firms, and to a large extent conduct business outside the legal system and rely on nonlegal methods based on reputation, relationships and trust to settle disputes and enforce contracts; most of these firms' financing comes from alternative channels such as trade credits and funds from family and friends. Interestingly, nonstate, nonlisted firms account for most of the economic growth and employ most of the labor forces in both countries. The dominance of this sector over state and listed sectors is particularly pronounced in China. These findings suggest that for nonstate, nonlisted firms alternative financing channels and nonlegal mechanisms might be superior to the bank and market finance and formal legal institutions utilized by the larger state-owned, publicly listed firms. We formalize and discuss this argument below.

China and India present distinctly different cases in their histories of developing Western-style legal and other formal institutions. Transiting from a socialist system to a market-based system, China had no formal commercial legal system and associated institutions in place when its economy began to take off in the 1980s. However, historically China had highly commercialized societies without the development of Western institutions. India, on the other hand, has a long history of Western legal institutions and financial systems due to its colonial ties to the UK. Based on the British judicial system, India's formal legal system dates back more than two centuries. The State Bank of India, the largest commercial bank in the country in terms of deposits as well as assets, is over 200 years old and thriving. The Bombay Stock Exchange (BSE), at 130 years, is the oldest in Asia. Yet, Indian firms, like Chinese firms, generally conduct business with little reliance on the legal system.

What economic lessons can be learned from the remarkable performance of China and India? Are they simply applying the conventional wisdom, or are they doing something fundamentally different that (Western) economists have yet to fully understand? In this regard, China presents the extreme example. In the West, we take it for granted that finance and commerce should be undertaken using the law as the basis for contracts. Many would agree that the same should be applied for China: "The modern corporation based on a Western model would be the essential vehicle for private economic development" (China 1904).

Interestingly, this statement was not written today but was the view of China's first Company Law in 1904 (*Gongsilü*), drafted by the then newly created Ministry of Commerce (*Shangbu*) of the waning Qing government and aimed at promoting China's industrial development. Several subsequent versions of the Company Law (1904–46) tried to promote the development of shareholding corporations with limited liabilities, but despite these attempts the model of Western-style corporations was never taken up in China. An important factor is that the philosophy of having a disperse ownership that included outsiders ran directly against the traditional Chinese model of keeping business within the family. Indeed, most firms' fear of incorporation stemmed from their distrust of government and unwillingness to let strangers gain partial control of the firm.[7]

Despite the lack of rule-of-law in finance and commerce and their separation from the legal system, China had a highly commercialized society. The earliest form of capitalism can be traced back to the late Ming Dynasty (seventeenth century), with commerce initiated in the Zhejiang–Jiangsu area and further developed during the Qing Dynasty (seventeenth to early twentieth century). The Opium War (1840s) between China and Great Britain destroyed China's sovereignty, but it brought Western-style legal and capital systems into China's coastal areas (until 1949). During this period, foreign systems and the Chinese system coexisted and commerce boomed. Yet, despite the entrance and development of numerous Western-style courts in Shanghai and other major coastal cities, most business-related disputes were resolved outside courts. Since the Qing Dynasty, dispute resolution by guilds (merchant coalitions), families, and local notables based on explicit and implicit regulations of guilds, family traditions, and social norms was commonplace. Chinese firms on the mainland (pre-1949) and later in Taiwan (after 1949) did not use the provisions of the law but again conducted commerce outside the formal legal system. Modern equivalents of these dispute- and contract-enforcing mechanisms are arguably behind the success of Chinese firms since 1979.

The development of China's financial system from the late-nineteenth century to the early-twentieth century was highlighted by the emergence of Shanghai as the financial center of China and Asia. With thriving entrepreneurial and trading activities, financial institutions proliferated and financial innovations surged. Merchants used up to 11 currencies in their transactions, some of which were printed by local banks. The exchange rates of local currency saw wide fluctuations; many unregistered local banks (*diaotang*) engaged in high-leverage credit transactions with little capital reserves and defaulted frequently. At the same time, merchants' fear of risk spawned an active insurance industry, which was first introduced by the British. Insurance on real estate, ships, and goods became routine, with collateral and personal guarantors accompanying large transactions to reduce the risk of nonpayments. To alleviate the problems of asymmetric information, foreign merchants hired Chinese middlemen (and guarantors) to select Chinese merchants. Chinese and foreign merchants also devised the "commission indent system," an early form of trade credit allowing firms and institutions to operate with minimum financial resources. The stock exchange in Shanghai was the largest in Asia for most of the 1920s and 1930s.

To summarize, relying on alternative mechanisms, China has a long history of developing finance and commerce outside the legal system. In fact, most of the development of the sophisticated financial system prior to 1949 coincided with one of the most volatile periods in Chinese history characterized by political turmoil and (civil and foreign) wars. In recent years, there has been a concerted effort by the government to improve China's legal system, including passing new laws in finance and commerce similar to those in Western countries. In our view, however, these laws have very limited impact in practice other than "window dressing" for Western investors who do not understand China.

A good example illustrating the ongoing legal reform is the bankruptcy law. A trial version was first passed in 1986, applying to state-owned enterprises (SOEs) only. There were very few bankruptcy cases, in part due to possible adverse effects on workers. The current version of the Enterprise Bankruptcy Law was passed in 2006 and became effective in June 2007. A much more comprehensive version than the trial version, it applies to all enterprises except partnerships and sole proprietorships. In many aspects it resembles bankruptcy codes in Western developed countries. For example, secured creditors are paid ahead of employee claims and allowed to vote in the reorganization plan. However, more than 2,000 financially distressed SOEs won a stay of execution by being excluded from the new law until the end of 2008, since workers' wages and benefits would still take precedence over creditors' claims. Moreover, in most of the bankruptcy cases, creditors have little influence on the process and are treated inconsistently; deviations from the stated priority rules are commonplace, and final decisions are left to local judges, who often handle the cases not following the bankruptcy law, but rather other regulations from the State Council (see, e.g., Li (2001) for more details).

A review and comparison of India's corporate sectors also provide an example of the effectiveness of alternative mechanisms and problems with legal institutions. The Indian economy is unbalanced relative to other large economies, in that 52 percent of output is from services, 26 percent is from manufacturing, and 22 percent is from agriculture (67 percent of workforce). Manufacturing industries have not done well, and a widely accepted reason is that they are constrained by unions and traditional political economy factors, including corruption and bureaucracy in the government and legal system.[8] New industries like software have done much better because they are not constrained by political economy factors as much and rely more on alternative mechanisms.

ACDQQ (2008) have conducted detailed surveys of more than 200 firms from the small and medium enterprises (SMEs) sector in India, and the results clearly favor the use of alternative mechanisms over the law and legal system. For example, when asked about their preferred actions following defaults, breaches of contract, and disputes initiated by their business partners, over 80 percent of surveyed firms say they do not use the legal system at all. Out-of-courts channels of dispute resolution play a far more important role for these firms. About 50 percent of the firms surveyed do *not* have a regular legal adviser. When pressed for a reason, 63 percent of respondents who did not have legal advisers claimed they did not need lawyers as they knew all their business partners and could deal with them fairly. Clearly, the formal legal system takes a back seat while reputation, trust, and informal personal relationships are the driving factors in screening potential business opportunities.[9]

The survey responses further indicate that not only is the law a disfavored means to resolve a breach that has already occurred or a dispute that has already arisen, but it also plays a weak role in dissuading future breaches and disputes. To this end, the survey findings indicate that legal sanctions are far less important than the demands and responsibilities of the networks within which they exist and function. For instance, in the case of default, late payment, and a breach of contract, the primary concern is loss of future business opportunities or reputation; the fear of legal consequences (adverse court sentence or jail term) is the *least* important concern, below even threat to personal safety.

Overall, the picture that emerges of the SME sector in India clearly indicates that the sector has little confidence in the legal system. It relies little on the courts in settling disputes and enforcing contracts and is minimally concerned about legal consequences of infractions. Nonlegal sanctions, on the other hand, are far more effective. This is also the finding of the Chinese corporate sectors today.

The limited role played by the law and legal system in the economic growth of China and India has been found in other prominent East Asian economies. Upham (2002) shows that Japan had developed economic and political systems operating outside the formal legal system before World War II. After WWII, despite the influence of the US, Japan's formal legal system actually shrank during the high economic growth period, and alternative mechanisms, similar to those in China and India, were the main force in finance and commerce. In addition, some researchers argue that during early stages of development, it was informal relationships of trust, rather than law as commonly believed, that promoted the development of the financial systems in Western European countries.[10]

Alternative mechanisms can work in complicated transactions

One may wonder if the limited role of the legal system documented above is limited to simple financial and business transactions and a few developing countries. We next provide two examples to demonstrate that nonlegal mechanisms can deal with complicated, international transactions. First, the global diamond industry has historically operated outside the legal systems and systematically ignored state-created laws (e.g. Bernstein 1992). This is in part due to the fact that legal contracts cannot be enforced since the value of each transaction (a particular diamond) is highly idiosyncratic and most diamond traders do not have access to capital markets, and hence calculated damages based on "what if" contingencies are not applicable. Moreover, it generally takes too long for courts to issue their decisions. In its place, the sophisticated diamond traders (belonging to trading clubs or bourses) who dominate the global industry have developed an elaborate, internal set of rules, complete with distinctive institutions and sanctions, to handle disputes. The arbitration process within the DDC (diamond dealers' club) based on the rules is usually straightforward and quick, with rulings often involving parties simply splitting the differences in estimated damages. Typically, the private arbitration system keeps all judgments secret as long as payments are promptly paid. Given the long-term relationship of members and their interest in preserving their reputations, these simple rules work much better in the long run (even though they may not be fair in individual cases) and save costs. In recent years, the World Association of Diamond Bourses (WADB) has successfully shifted from the traditional relationship-based DDCs to a worldwide information technology-based regime (a database containing reports of arbitrations from 20-plus member countries, many of which are in Asia). Only rarely do a state's laws enter the discussions about the reform.[11]

Another industry that has relied on out-of-court mediations and arbitrations to settle disputes is reinsurance. Reinsurance is the practice where an original insurer, for a definite premium, contracts with another insurer or insurers to carry a part or the whole of a risk assumed by the original insurer. While the earliest reinsurance contract can be traced to fourteenth-century Italy (e.g. Kopf 1929), the first use of an arbitration clause in an insurance contract was, by most accounts, the one in the Insurance Company of North America in 1793 (e.g. Winn and Davis 2004). The original arbitration system requires each party to appoint their own arbitrator and typically requires the two party-appointed arbitrators to appoint a third arbitrator referred to as an "umpire." In practice, however, it is the parties and their outside counsel who play a large role in the selection of the umpire. This often results in disagreements, especially in large transactions, which delay the appointment and hence the arbitration process as a whole.

In recent years the industry has been revising the traditional procedure in order to expedite the process while still preserving its fairness. Industry experts have turned to other industries where arbitration has been used most successfully, such as securities arbitration wherein the New York Stock Exchange and the National Association of Securities Dealers disseminate and continually refine and improve a set of rules (e.g. Kondo 2007). The Dispute Resolution Protocol, developed by the Conflict Prevention and Resolution International Industry for the reinsurance business, reflects these new ideas and changes. It is non-legally binding for members. Based on best practices from the field, the Protocol, among other things, simplifies and standardizes the process of selecting neutral arbitrators and has been endorsed by leading companies such as Lloyd's. This example demonstrates the importance of adapting to changes quickly as a main condition for the long-term viability of a dispute-resolution mechanism.

Intellectual property rights and innovations

As discussed earlier, one of the cornerstones of Western law and institutions is property rights. A "hot-button" issue in property rights is the protection of intellectual property rights and their role in economic growth, which is also at the center of our comparisons between the two different systems of finance and commerce. Because of space limitations we cannot review all the evidence on intellectual property rights (see, e.g., the OECD, Directorate for Financial and Enterprise Affairs of the Competition Committee (2005) report and the Bessen and Meurer (2008) book for excellent reviews). We focus on two aspects of intellectual property rights. First, whether the protection of exclusive rights (through patents, copyrights, trade secrets, trademarks, etc.) has a positive impact on the pace of innovations, and second, the problems of using the law and legal institutions as the basis for disputes related to intellectual property rights.

In almost all the countries with laws on intellectual property rights, the scope of patentable subject matter has traditionally *not* included fundamental scientific discoveries. A frequently mentioned rationale for this omission is that, given the far-reaching impact in many fields of these discoveries, it would be impossible to outline the boundaries of the patent protection. In fact, whether the boundary of a patent can be precisely defined is an important determinant of effective enforcement of the patent law (e.g. Bessen and Meurer 2008). Once the patent is approved and issued, the primary forum for resolving disputes is the (federal) courts, which have exclusive jurisdiction over disputes involving the infringement of patents and appeals of court decisions.

There is an extensive literature in industrial organization in economics examining the relationship between the protection of intellectual property rights and the pace of innovations during the past three decades, and the research yields mixed findings. In the chemicals and pharmaceuticals industries, stronger and more effective protection has been found to lead to more research and development spending and innovations in developed countries. This positive relation is attributed to the fact that most patents are valuable with clearly defined boundaries. This, in turn, helps keep litigation costs (of alleged infringers) low. However, it is unclear whether the most important inventions and discoveries in the chemicals and pharmaceuticals industries were made under the protection of property rights. Table 6.2 presents the development of some of the most important (and profitable) medical breakthroughs during the past 150 years. It is interesting to see that the majority (especially before 1950) of the discoveries was made by university researchers (not affiliated with corporations), and the initial invention was *not* protected by any patents. In some of the cases the patent holder is not the original inventor or discoverer.

As an example, the process of discovering and producing penicillin is illuminating. While it is widely believed to have been discovered by Alexander Fleming (as shown in Table 6.2) in 1928, several others had discovered its

Table 6.2 Major Medical inventions and history of patients

Name	*Purpose of Use*	*Inventor*	*Invention Time*	*Have a patent?*	*Patent Holder*	*And When?*
Ophthalmoscope	Instrument used to examine the eye	Charles Babbage	1847			
		reinvented: Hermann von Helmholtz	1851			
		refined: William Allyn & F. Welch	1915	US Patent: 4065208	Welch Allyn	1915
Hypodermic needle	A hollow needle used with a syringe to inject substances into the body	Charles Pravaz & Alexander Wood	1853			
		Disposable syringes: Arthur E. Smith	1949–1950	8 US Patents	Arthur E. Smith	1949-1950
		Disposable syringes: Phil Brooks	9-Apr-74	US Patent	Phil Brooks	9-Apr-74
		Hypodermic needle: K. Simm & D. Emis	31-Aug-04	US Patent	K Simm & D Emis	31-Aug-04
Carbolic acid (phenol)	sterilize surgical instrument to clean wounds	Joseph Lister		US Patent: 1950359		
Rabies vaccination	To prevent rabies (viral neuroinvasive disease)	Louis Pasteur	Jul 6, 1885	No		
Contact Lens	A corrective, cosmetic or therapeutic lens	Descriptions of lenses: Leonardo da Vinci	1508			
		Corneal contact lens: Rene Descartes	1632			

(continued on next page)

Table 6.2 (continued)

Name	*Purpose of Use*	*Inventor*	*Invention Time*	*Have a patent?*	*Patent Holder*	*And When?*
		Water-filled glass tube with lens: T. Young	1801			
		Invented and made: Adolf Eugen Fick	1887			
		Grinding to fit eye's surface: John Herschel	1827			
		US made plastic lens: W. Feinbloom	1936			
		Plastic lens: Kevin Tuohy	1948			
		Soft and gas-permeable lens	1970s			
X-ray	Used for diagnostic radiography	Wilhelm Conrad Rontgen	Nov 8, 1895			
Electrocardiogram	Graphic produced by an electrocardiograph of the electrical activity of the heart	String galvanometer: Willem Einthoven	1901	US Patent: 4457309	Elemeskog; Alf U.	Feb. 1982
Sphygmomano-meter	A device used to measure blood pressure	R. H. Miller	1948	US Patent: 2560237	R. H. Miller	10-Jul-51
		Pocket sphygmomanometer: Man S. Oh	2002	US Patent: 6752764	Pocket: Man S. Oh	22-Jun-04
Penicillin	Treatment of bacterial infections	Sir Alexander Fleming	28-Sep-28	US Patent	Andrew J. Moyer	25-May-48

(continued on next page)

Table 6.2 (continued)

Name	*Purpose of Use*	*Inventor*	*Invention Time*	*Have a patent?*	*Patent Holder*	*And When?*
Artificial pacemaker	An electrical device to regulate heart beating	Earl Bakken & C. Walton Lillehei	1957	US Patent: 4009721	Alcidi; Mario	23-Apr-76
Heart Transplant	Procedure for patients with heart failure or severe coronary artery disease	Christiaan Barnard	Dec, 1967	No		
MRI & fMRI	Imaging technique primarily used in Radiology	Paul Lauterbur & Peter Mansfield	1970	US Patent	R. Damadian	1974
CAT scan	Medical imaging using tomography	Godfrey Newbold Hounsfield Allan Mcleod Cormack	1967–1972	US Patent: 3922552	Robert S. Ledley	25-Nov-75
Ultrasound scan	An ultrasound-based diagnostic imaging	Lan Donald	1953–1958	US Patent: 5860925	D. Liu; (conversion)	27-Jun-97
Artificial Heart	Prosthetic device implanted to replace heart	Robert Jarvik	1970's–1980's	US Patent: 3097366	Paul Winchell	16-Jul-63

bacteriostatic effects as early as 1875. The real challenge of the new "wonder drug" was how to produce it in large quantities. This probem was magnified at the outset of WWII, during which penicillin significantly decreased the number of deaths and amputations caused by infected wounds among Allied forces. Because of the large demand and costs of mass production, the price soared and a large amount was reserved for military use. A team of British and American scientists finally made a breakthrough in the early 1940s allowing rapid production of the drug. Penicillin production was quickly scaled up and made available in quantities necessary to treat Allied soldiers wounded on D-Day. As production rose, the price dropped from being nearly priceless in 1940, to US$ 20.00 per dose in July 1943, to US$ 0.55 per dose by 1946. Andrew Moyer, a member of the research team, was granted a patent in the US for a method of mass production of penicillin in May of 1948, after the commercial value of the drug had plummeted. Other researchers and producers of penicillin had applied for patents in other European countries but the applications were turned down, as it was deemed unethical to provide exclusive rights for an invention that can save lives. In fact, the attitude of governments and societies toward using patents and copyrights became increasingly pro-rights holders only after World War II.[12]

Outside the chemical and pharmaceutical industries, prior economic research finds that in many developed countries, there is no positive relation between the protection of intellectual property rights and the pace of innovations. Instead, excessive protection deters competition, which is another important factor in spurring innovations, and small inventors do not benefit from the laws on intellectual property as much as large corporations. In addition, based on changes in patent laws and enforcement regulations, Lerner (2002, 2005), among others, finds only weak or no evidence that *strengthening* patent rights and the enforcement of patent laws spurs the pace of innovations across developed countries.

Research in developing countries also generally fails to establish a positive relationship between the protection of intellectual property rights and the pace of innovations. This is due to weak enforcement of such rights and the lack of other relevant institutions.[13] China is often singled out as notoriously bad in protecting intellectual property rights, as copying and imitation via reverse engineering is a prevalent strategy across industries. Legal actions by foreign firms have been nearly useless in preventing these activities.[14] As argued above, despite concerted efforts by the government to pass new laws and strengthen existing ones, including those on intellectual property rights, in part as a response to mounting international pressure, it is doubtful that these efforts will have any system-wide impact. First, there is no systematic statement of the law of property or clear definitions of private property rights. Second, law enforcement is likely to be ineffective because of the intrinsic conflict of interest between fair play in practicing law and the monopoly power of the single ruling party, especially in cases in which government officials or their affiliates are involved (e.g. Clarke *et al.* 2008). Notably, though, while the protection of intellectual rights in China has been poor, the pace of innovations has been furious because of the pressure of competition.

One of the main problems of the patent system based on the law is that it motivates rent-seeking behaviors by interest groups. An example to illustrate such behavior is that companies, especially large corporations with abundant resources, come up with numerous *nonessential* inventions to pad the one significant (patented) invention or establish a new standard in production (e.g. Dewatripont and Legros 2007). The creation of such a standard can impact the use of many different technologies – in the case of mobile technology, for instance, a production standard on a new handset requires the use of more than a thousand technologies protected by patents. By jamming the patent system with extra patents or standards, the patent holders can essentially block or delay innovations by competitors. This is what has led to the FRAND concept – "fair, reasonable and non-discriminatory royalties."

Another form of rent-seeking behavior is that patent holders, especially those with more resources, seek the best possible legal venue to maximize the likelihood of winning a lawsuit against patent or copyright infringements. This type of behavior runs against the principle that the legal system within a democracy should be based on fair procedures and should allow equal access to all. The rise of Marshall, a small town in eastern Texas, as the center of patent-related litigation is an interesting case study (e.g. Creswell 2006). According to LegalMetric (2008), a legal data and analysis company, the Federal Eastern District of Texas (which also includes the rural towns of Tyler and Texarkana), now handles the largest amount of patent litigation cases in the country – up to one third of all new cases and an even higher fraction of all cases involving a US firm suing foreign firms or individuals, surpassing courts in Chicago, Manhattan, and Los Angeles, historically home to the largest number of new patent cases.

Many attribute this phenomenon to T. John Ward, the federal judge in Marshall. Since he joined the Eastern District of Texas, the district has seen a tenfold increase in patent cases since 1999 (14 cases in 1999 and 234 in 2006). Judge Ward has been described as pushing cases through quickly, and his court has been described as a "rocket docket" for its speed – each side in a case might receive between 9 and 15 hours for evidence, compared to other courts in which it may take a month or more to do the same. While there is disagreement as to whether the jurors from the district are "patent friendly," most observers believe that plaintiffs, especially US firms suing foreign firms and individuals over patent infringements, have a significant advantage because they hire lawyers or legal consultants who are familiar with Judge Ward's style and know the jurors and benefit from that information. Overall, plaintiffs (patent holders) have won much more frequently (and have done so in a short period of time, no less) in the district than anywhere else in the country.

In our final set of examples illustrating problems of intellectual property rights, we examine recent innovations in communications and knowledge industries based on Internet revolutions. Some of these inventions are free of charge and are not protected by patents or copyrights, while others do charge and are protected. As discussed above, when it is difficult to determine whether an invention has broached the boundary of a patent, as is often the case for Internet-related innovations, enforcement efforts become ineffective and may cause rent-seeking behaviors to escalate.

On the knowledge front, SSRN (Social Science Research Network) and JSTOR are great academic inventions that bring new working papers and published articles, in electronic format, to individual researchers worldwide essentially free of charge (based on institutional subscriptions). For the general public, Wikipedia, a multilingual, web-based platform with free content, is quickly becoming the most useful encyclopedia. Written collaboratively by volunteers from around the world, the Wikipedia articles provide links to guide users to related pages with additional information and offer a useful point to begin research on almost any subject (including some of the topics discussed in this chapter). Since its creation in 2001, it has grown rapidly into one of the largest reference websites, attracting over 600 million visitors annually by 2008.

While the growth of Wikipedia has met with little resistance from the traditional media companies, it is a totally different situation with Google's equally ambitious "Print and Library Project." Under the "fair use doctrine" of the US Copyright Law, Google's ambitious plan has two components: Google Publisher Program, in which a publisher holding copyrights to a book can authorize Google to scan the entire book into Google's search database; and Google Library Project, where some of the largest libraries (Harvard, Oxford and Stanford Universities, University of Michigan, and the New York Public Library) allow Google to scan materials. According to Google, for books/print materials in the public domain (not subject to copyright) from the libraries, Google will display the full text of the book with the search result; for those that are still covered by copyrights, readers can only see a few sentences of the text around the search item; copyright holders can also exclude selected books from Google Print. Ever since the initial idea of the Project floated around, it was met with disdain from publishing companies. The Association of American Publishers, including well-known companies such as Penguin, McGraw-Hill, Pearson Education, Simon & Schuster, and John Wiley & Sons, and the Authors Guild, the nation's largest organization of book authors, filed suits against Google in the second half of 2005. The legal action came after months of talks failed to hammer out an agreement and has held up the implementation of the Project indefinitely. Even if Google wins in the US it may be sued again in other countries (e.g. in EU countries) with different and perhaps even more stringent copyright laws.

Another example is the Linux operating system, started in 1991 by Linus Torvalds. A Unix-like computer-operating system, Linux is one of the most prominent examples of free software and open source development. Typically all underlying source codes can be freely modified, used, and redistributed. Historically, Linux has mainly been used as a server-operating system and has risen to prominence in that area. How does Linux stack against the Windows system, the most prominent operating system released under a proprietary software license by Microsoft? Not surprisingly, Windows dominates the desktop and personal computer markets with about 90 percent of market share, as compared to 1 percent market share by Linux. In the servers market, Windows had a share of 36 percent (fourth quarter of 2007) while Linux had a share of 12.7 percent. As of November 2007, Linux powered 85 percent of the world's most powerful supercomputers; in February 2008, Linux powered five of the ten most reliable Internet hosting companies. Proponents of free software argue that the key strength of Linux is that it respects what they consider to be the users' essential freedom – to run, study, change, and to redistribute copies with or without changes free of charge.[15]

Our final example regards music (and movie) downloads, both legal and illegal, and the status of the music (movie/entertainment) and recording industries. Downloading music first became popular with the file-sharing technologies such as peer-to-peer networks, with individuals possibly knowingly or unknowingly violating copyright laws by not obtaining permission or payments. The Recording Industry Association of America (RIAA) claims that this practice is damaging the industry, and a series of lawsuits led to many of these networks being shut down – with perhaps the best-known example being Napster. Going after companies such as Napster is one thing; going after millions of people downloading and sharing music on a daily basis is another. However, RIAA and the recording companies are certainly trying, and have taken their crusade against pirating to a new level recently. In its federal case against Jeffrey Howell, who kept a collection of about 2,000 music recordings on his personal computer, the industry maintains that it is *illegal* for someone who has *legally* purchased a CD to transfer that music into his own computer (Fisher 2007).[16] Many observers of the industry believe that RIAA's campaign against its own customers is a classic example of an old media company clinging to a business model whose time is past.

We end this subsection with a comment on the effectiveness of using lawsuits to protect patents and copyrights. As in the case of music downloads, the efforts by vested-interest groups seem to be largely ineffective when the public is engaged in the illegal act at low costs, but these efforts become more effective when a single company is leading the implementation of new technologies (e.g. Google's Print Project). The contrast in these cases, however, suggests that using the law as the basis for the protection of intellectual property rights can induce rent-seeking behavior by the interest groups that will have the most to lose given the new technologies, and their efforts can become significant barriers to changes and innovations.

Limited capacity of the legislature

Another potential problem of using the legal system in a democracy is that when there are fundamental changes in an economy so that the law and/or regulation must be revised, the legislature must approve any revisions before corporations and investors can freely implement new techniques in their transactions and interactions (without worrying about breaking the law). However, politicians have limited time and effort that can be devoted to any given area of the law, and hence there is a legislature capacity and a fixed cost in revising the law. The following example illustrates that such limited capacity and fixed costs can singlehandedly slow down the pace of financial and business transactions in practice.

Figure 6.1 compares payments systems in major developed economies. At the start of the twenty-first century the US had a nineteenth-century payments system, relying mostly on checks and the mail, and significantly lagging behind other developed nations. While countries like Germany, the Netherlands, Sweden and Switzerland had almost completely abandoned checks (and rely instead on electronic payments systems), about half of all the payments in the US were still in the form of paper checks. Under the old Uniform Commercial Code, the only legally acceptable proof of payment was cancelled checks, or checks processed by both the deposited and paying financial institutions. Hence, checks had to be physically transported from where they were deposited to a central operations center, then to the clearer and then back to the banks they were drawn on. This check-and-clearing process significantly delayed business transactions as compared to electronic methods.

How costly was this backward payment system? Using information from Humphrey *et al.* (1996) and Bolt *et al.* (2008), we can conduct a back-of-the-envelope calculation. From cross-country comparisons and analysis, these researchers suggest that there are savings of about 1–2 percent of GDP when a

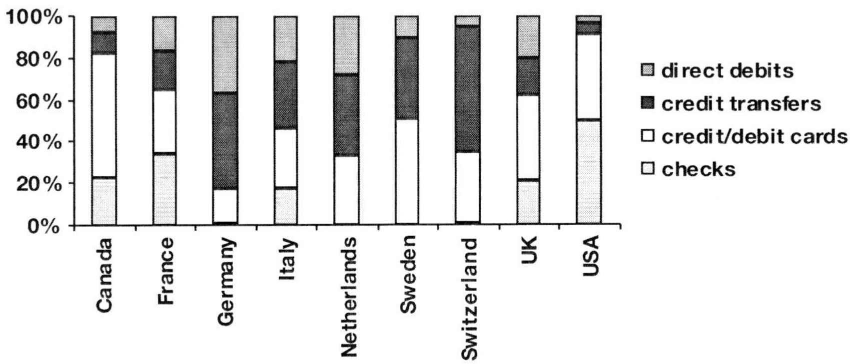

Figure 6.1 Comparing payments systems in developed countries in 2006.
Source: Bank for International Settlements 2008.

country moves away from paper checks (e.g. the US) and towards electronic-based methods. From Table 6.1, the US 2007 GDP was $13,543 billion, which indicates the magnitude of savings from reforming the payment system to be $135 billion to $270 billion per year. With a 5 percent discount rate (roughly the risk-free rate in the US), the discounted present value of this savings (assuming a ten-year growing annuity of 2 percent per year to control for inflation) is between $1.1 trillion to $2.2 trillion; in other words, the magnitude of the savings is comparable or higher than the total cost of the most recent Iraqi war.

Despite years of calls for changes from the banks and businesses, the US Congress appeared not in a hurry to solve this seemingly simple yet costly problem. Without the approval of the legislature, banks cannot expedite the payment process because of the fear of lawsuits. Then, the tragic events of 11 September 2001 occurred and served as a catalyst for change. After the terrorist attack all commercial flights in the US were grounded for several days, completely halting the check clearing process. After the flights resumed, the call for change in the payments system finally resonated with Congress. The Check Clearing for the 21st Century Act ("Check 21 Act") was signed in October 2003 and became effective one year later. The Check 21 Act allows electronic images of both sides of paper checks to be a "legally equivalent" substitute for the original checks, and these "substitute checks" can be exchanged among financial institutions including banks, clearing houses, and the Federal Reserve Bank (see, e.g., Board of Governors of the Federal Reserve System (2008) for more details). Therefore, the clearing process is no longer dependent on the mail and transportation system.

To summarize, in this section we presented examples to highlight two potential problems of relying on the law as the basis for finance and commerce: rent-seeking behaviors by vested-interest groups and limited capacity of the legislature in approving changes to the law. We also argue that these problems are likely to be worsened in developing countries until they can develop sound legal and other related institutions. We also present examples to illustrate that alternative systems can work well outside the legal system in both developing and developed countries.

Legal institutions versus alternative mechanisms: comparisons and policy implications

The above examples motivate our comparisons of two different sets of systems. The first system, employed by developed and democratic countries such as the US, commits to use the law as the basis for finance and commerce and legal institutions as the ultimate source for resolving disputes and enforcing contracts; further, changes to the law must be approved by the legislature and electorate. In the second system, symbolized by countries such as China, there is no systematic definition of private property rights or property law, and, in practice, nonlegal mechanisms are the norm for conducting business; the process of change in finance and commerce is often bottom-up rather than top-down. We make these classifications to better differentiate these two systems and facilitate the comparisons, but they may not be mutually exclusive when we look at a particular country. In fact, as the literature on legal pluralism (see, e.g., Merry (1988) for a review) shows, in many countries these two systems can coexist but do not necessarily work to improve each other.

In what follows we compare the advantages and disadvantages of conducting finance and commerce in these two systems. We then discuss conditions under which one of the two systems is superior. Finally, we provide discussions on policy implications based on our analysis.

Comparing legal and alternative mechanisms

There are well-known advantages of using the law and legal system as the basis for finance and commerce. The legal system of a democratic society allows equal and full access by all and promises fairness in trials and settlements. Backed by the government and legislature, the legal system also has the ultimate authority in its decisions on any and all disputes. The legal system is endowed with powerful enforcement mechanisms, including criminal penalties, such as imprisonment, as well as civil laws and financial penalties to affect people's behaviors. These enforcement mechanisms and penalties provide strong incentives for individuals and organizations to follow the resolutions endorsed by the legal system, which in turn provides long-term stability in the economy. The legal process, including resolution and enforcement, can be anonymous (e.g. details of a settlement of a dispute may not be disclosed) or transparent (the entire procedure of a high-profile trial may be covered by media). By using the entire legal system, the marginal costs for resolving an additional dispute and enforcing an additional contract can be reduced, and this improves overall efficiency.

However, there are also disadvantages in using the law and legal institutions. First, recent research on political economy factors suggests that rent-seeking behaviors by vested-interest groups can turn legal institutions into barriers to changes. For example, Rajan and Zingales (2003a, 2003b) suggest that development of a formal financial system may trigger political economy costs, causing a disconnection between the level of financial market activity and economic development. Similarly, Acemoglu and Johnson (2005) find that while "contracting institutions," or laws protecting contracts between individual parties, do not affect long-term growth, "property rights institutions," or laws and regulations restraining powerful elites and the government, do affect economic growth. We expect these problems to be much more severe in developing countries, where the costs of building good institutions can be enormous. We argue that one way to solve this problem is not to use the law as the basis for finance and commerce but instead to use alternative mechanisms, as the experience in China and India documented earlier.

Second, in democracies there can be a lengthy political process before significant changes can be approved (by the majority of the electorate or legislature), and the people in charge of approving or disapproving changes (e.g. politicians and judges) may lack expertise in the business transactions under scrutiny and have limited capacity (time and effort) to study the proposed changes. The process of passing the Check 21 Act epitomizes this capacity issue. In addition, as demonstrated in examples in the previous section, interest groups with more resources may receive more protection than individuals and organizations with fewer resources. This asymmetry in protection induces more rent-seeking behaviors and further deters innovations.

Unlike the legislature, which has monopoly power and authority in revising the law, one of the main advantages for alternative mechanisms, along with the bottom-up process for changes, is that such mechanisms are more likely to foster competition among different mediation/resolution agencies/organizations. Competition can ensure that the most efficient mechanism prevails – for example, only experts are involved in the rule-changing process. Competition can also limit rent-seeking behaviors by one or more groups. Clearly, alternative mechanisms as described can be much faster in adopting new rules to deal with changes in finance commerce since these changes do not require the permission from the legislature or electorate.

One of the main disadvantages of the alternative mechanisms is the lack of enforcement power and authority. Without the backing of the government and judicial system, alternative mechanisms can only rely on reputation along with economic and financial incentives (e.g. avoiding future losses due to sanctions by other members of the network or coalition) and mutual monitoring to enforce contractual agreements. These methods may be insufficient to ensure good behavior if future losses are not substantial relative to the gains that can be made today, or if these losses can be recuperated by entering other lines of business or networks. Another negative for alternative mechanisms is that by design they exist among a network and thus may be inaccessible to outsiders; partial access by outsiders may come with the price of biased outcomes in dispute resolution favoring insiders. In addition, frequent changes adopted by a network (or networks) create instability in the entire economy and hence weak long-term incentives.[17]

These advantages and disadvantages lead to the tradeoffs of the two systems in different economic environments. In *static* environments with infrequent and predictable changes (i.e. mature and slow-growing economies and industries), the advantages of the legal mechanisms dominate the disadvantages. First, the strong incentives provided by the enforcement mechanisms of the legal system imply that efficient systems can be designed that do not rely solely on positive monetary incentives. Second, the fixed costs of using the legal system when changes occur can be negated by the infrequent revisions of the law and by a few large-scale transactions; the legislature and the judicial system can appoint experts to be involved with the process of changing the law and grant them the authority in decision-making. The combination of effective enforcement and infrequent changes also implies that there is stability in the system, which in turn creates strong long-term incentives for economic agents to play by the (universal) rule.

In *dynamic* environments with frequent and unforeseen shocks (i.e. new industries and/or emerging, fast-growing economies such as China and India), however, the disadvantages of legal mechanisms are magnified and can outweigh their advantages. The lengthy approval process by the legislature and electorate of any change to the law, along with the limited capacity and possible lack of expertise by the judges and politicians, means that the legal system is slow in reacting to changes. Moreover, a legal system captured by interest groups can in fact oppose changes, and with its monopoly power it can become a barrier to competition and innovations. On the other hand, alternative mechanisms can adapt to changes much more quickly, since competition ensures that the most efficient mechanism will be implemented quickly, and this process does not require the approval of the legislature. Weak enforcement power and long-term incentives of the alternative mechanisms can be significantly strengthened by effective reputation mechanisms as long as there are long-term profits to be made and shared by participating individuals and organizations.

The interaction between legal and alternative mechanisms is another reason why alternative mechanisms can promote economic growth and improve social welfare. Since most of the laws are adopted from best practices, having a viable system of alternatives can thus improve the efficiency of legal institutions, especially in dynamic environments. Competition among formal and alternative mechanisms can also ensure that the best mechanism will be eventually adopted in the entire economy, and this is especially important in environments where special-interest groups can easily capture the legal system. A fair and functional legal system can also improve the effectiveness of alternative mechanisms by adopting the best rules and enforcing the changes in the entire economy and by instilling stability amid frequent changes.

Policy implications

It is not our intention to downplay the importance of the role of the law and legal system in finance and commerce. Our ultimate goal is to help design the optimal combination of legal and alternative institutions that best suit a country's needs. To this end we have compared the advantages and disadvantages of two systems operating based on the law and legal institutions versus alternative mechanisms. We conclude that legal mechanisms are an important part of developed economies' institutions, providing stability and strong long-term incentives. This conclusion is based on the premise that there are infrequent shocks to the economy that cause fundamental changes in ways that business is conducted and that the legal system allows full access by all and promises fair resolution of disputes, and enforces the rules uniformly.

However, the assumptions making legal institutions the optimal system in developed countries are unlikely to hold in many emerging economies. A fast-growing economy, such as that of China and India, is often characterized by frequent shocks to the fundamentals of the economy, which make repeated changes to the practice of finance and commerce a requirement, not a choice. Given that it typically takes years to build a well-functioning legal system and other formal institutions, the fixed costs of using the legal system can be quite high in a dynamic economy, even if the system provides fairness and expertise when dealing with changes in the law.

A much more severe problem with the legal system, perhaps, is the political economy factor. It would be much easier for interest groups to capture the legal system and government in a country with underdeveloped institutions than in a country with developed institutions. As a result, an economy relying on law and legal institutions as the sole basis for commerce may find that such reliance is, in fact, a barrier to change and innovation.

Therefore, we argue that alternative mechanisms play a much more prominent role in emerging economies and can actually be superior to legal mechanisms in supporting business transactions in certain industries or entire economies. Our main policy implication is that in emerging economies, alternative dispute-resolution and contract-enforcement mechanisms should be encouraged and developed alongside the development of legal and other formal institutions. In particular, measures that help foster competition and reduce entry barriers are welfare enhancing. The coexistence of and competition between alternative and legal mechanisms can also exert positive impact on the development of legal institutions, so that they are less likely to be captured by interest groups and become more efficient in adapting to changes.[18] Whether and how a transition from a system dominated by alternative mechanisms to one using the law and legal institutions as the focal point depends on the country's economic history and growth potential, as well as the workings of many other social and cultural factors that help build the social norms in the society and business communities.

Concluding remarks

In our view China and India's economic success contains important lessons. While the use of the law and legal institutions in the finance and commerce industries has become a widely accepted idea, it is based on the history of institutional development in the West. We have argued that it can be optimal in static environments with infrequent changes. In dynamic environments such as China and India, however, it may be better to use other mechanisms that do not rely on the law, as these alternative mechanisms can reduce the inefficiencies associated with political economy factors. Designing economic institutions, therefore, that do not rely on the legal system and, thus, minimize political economy problems is one of the keys to fast economic growth.

Notes

1 We appreciate detailed comments from Katharina Pistor that significantly improved the chapter. We also received useful comments from Colleen Baker, Lee Cabatingan, Jim Heckman, Mudit Kapoor, Curtis Milhaupt, Bob Nelson, and participants at the NYU–Penn Conference on Law and Finance, Summer Research Conference at the Indian School of Business and World Justice Project scholars' meeting in Vienna. Research assistance by Sailu Li and Chenying Zhang, as well as financial support from the American Bar Association, Boston College, and the Wharton Financial Institutions Center are gratefully acknowledged. We are responsible for all remaining errors.

2 Corresponding author: Finance Department, Carroll School of Management, Boston College, Chestnut Hill, MA 02467. Phone: 617-552-3145; fax: 617-552-0431; e-mail: qianju@bc.edu

3 These classifications are made to facilitate the comparisons between legal and alternative mechanisms, and not meant to be mutually exclusive when studying a given country. Indeed, in many countries, a combination of the two systems could be working in practice.

4 For example, using different metrics Ravallion and Chen (2004) report steep declines in the proportion of rural Chinese living in absolute poverty over the period 1980–2001.

5 The World Bank adjusted downward its PPP-based estimates of GDP for large emerging countries such as China and India in 2008; a third source, the CIA, produces PPP-figures that are in between those from the IMF and the World Bank. See Heston (2008) for a review and comparison of different PPP-based GDP figures and methodologies.

6 For an excellent review of China's economic growth during the past thirty years, see the book, *China's Great Economic Transformation*, edited by Brandt and Rawski (2008).

7 For more descriptions of China's current financial system see AQQ (2005b, 2008). For more anecdotal evidence on the development of China's financial system in the period discussed, see, for example, Kirby (1995) and Lee (1993).

8 For example, an estimated 25 million cases are pending before the courts in India, and it will take more than 300 years to clear the backlog (Bearak 2000).

9 However, the courts, while not the most popular method of dispute resolution, appear to have some utility as a negotiating tool. When asked what a firm does to ensure payment or repayment (more than one response allowed), about 59 percent replied that they would go to court while leaving negotiation possibilities open.

10 Greif (1989, 1993) documents the important role of reputation, trust, and implicit contractual relations in the growth of Mediterranean traders' organizations in the eleventh century. Mayer (2008) offers a review of how similar mechanisms were behind the development of financial markets in the UK and the banking sector in Germany in the early-twentieth century.

11 There is the argument that the bypassing of the national legal systems by the diamond industry has led to lack of accountability and transparency in diamond producing countries, especially concerning miners in Africa (see, e.g., the Smillie *et al.* (2000) report on Sierra Leone). However, the expansion of WADB has actually restricted the monopoly power of the DeBeers Cartel, the largest supplier of diamond worldwide, which has its own dealers (Bernstein 1992).

12 Thomas Jefferson, a prolific inventor and founding father of the US Constitution, was known for his suspicion of granting monopoly power to inventors ("no patent for ideas"). During his term as the Examiner of American Patents, he insisted on thorough examination of the originality and novelty of an invention applied for patents. During the second half of the nineteenth century, an abolitionist movement,

which promoted free trade and viewed patents as anti-competition analogous to tariffs on imports, halted the adoption of patent laws in European countries. In particular, the Netherlands repealed its patent legislation in 1869 and did not reinstate the patent system until 1912 (e.g. Khan 2005).

13 See, for example, Djankov and Murrell (2002) for a review on the obstacles in the development of commercial laws and legal system in the economies of transition in Eastern Europe and Vietnam.

14 For example, the Chinese car Chery QQ appeared six months before the Chevy Spark, which it was a copy of, and the Shuanghuan Automobile's CEO model is remarkably similar to a BMW X5. For more details and other Chinese "knock-offs" of Japanese, European, and American cars, see Kimes (2008).

15 Nobody registered the name Linux until August 1995, when William Della Croce Jr applied for a trademark and demanded royalties from Linux distributors. Mr Torvalds and other affected organizations sued him and the case was settled in 1997. Mr Torvalds has stated that he trademarked the name to prevent others from using it, but was bound in 2005 by the US trademark law to take active measures to enforce the trademark. As a result, the Linux Mark Institute, holder of the name, had to request a fee be paid for the use of the name and a number of companies have complied.

16 Interestingly, researchers (e.g. Oberholzer-Gee and Strumpf 2007) have found that Internet music piracy not only does not hurt legal CD sales, it may even boost sales for some types of music.

17 See Dixit (2004) for an excellent review of the advantages and disadvantages of the alternative mechanisms.

18 Qian and Weingast (1997) argue that government decentralization since 1979 has helped foster competition among local officials and preserve market incentives in China. Allen and Qian (2008) argue that competition among officials from different regions curtails the negative impact of corruption on economic growth in China.

Chapter 7

Law, finance, and the first corporations

Ron Harris[1]

The English East India Company (EIC) and the Dutch East India Company (VOC) were incorporated by state charters two years apart, in 1600 and 1602 respectively. They were involved in similar business activities, oceanic trade in high value goods between Europe and Asia, via the Cape Route. They were both organized as joint stock corporations, with huge capital and hundreds of shareholders. In fact they were by an order of magnitude the largest business corporations of their era. The formation of the companies was situated in a crucial junction in the history of business organizations and stock markets. Yet, while the formation of the VOC led to the appearance of a secondary market in shares in the Dutch Republic, in England a share market emerged only a century after the organization of the EIC.

The present chapter focuses on a main organizational challenge faced by the two companies, the facilitation of long-term impersonal cooperation between active entrepreneurs and passive investors. It will study the manners by which legal and political environmental factors were translated into the detailed financial and governance structure of each of the two companies. It will explain the distinct English and Dutch paths to the creation of share markets through these environmental and organizational differences.

My approach and case study will be encountered with three influential, theoretically oriented approaches to the relationship between law and institutions and the development of the stock market. The approaches are those of Schleifer and his collaborators (hereafter LLSV) that emphasize the effect of legal origins on investor protection, of North and Weingast that view the ability of the state to convey credible commitments as a key to the development of stock markets, and of Rajan and Zingales that focus on market infrastructure and on the power of social and interest groups. The purpose of this encounter is twofold; first, to enrich our understanding of the reasons for the historical divergence between the two countries; and second, to analyze these leading theories in light of the empirical findings of our pivotal case study.

The chapter will first communicate with the three above mentioned approaches in order to extract from them direct arguments and implicit predictions with respect to the historical case that I am studying. It will next survey the development of government-bond markets in the Netherlands and England. It will then analyze the raising of capital by the EIC and VOC in the primary market, after that explain the emergence of a secondary market in company shares in the Dutch Republic and the absence of such a market in England for another century, and finally conclude from the history, theory and policy viewpoints.

Theories of law, finance and economic development

Economic theory long assumed that stock market development allowed the transfer of capital from investors to entrepreneurs and contributed to economic growth. In the last two decades, empirical studies have provided clear support not only for the claim that stock market development and economic growth are correlated, but also for the direction of the causality, from stock market to growth. More recently, a rapidly growing body of literature has established the claim that stock market development results from a supporting legal and institutional framework.[2] The historical argument is that by designing the appropriate investor protection law, enforcement system, and stock market institutions, developed economies achieved fast and sustainable growth in the last two or three centuries. Today it is recommended, on theoretical, empirical, and historical grounds, that lesser developed countries (LDCs) do the same, in order to achieve growth in the future.

The definition and protection of property rights by law is essential for investment and for economic development. Individuals are willing to invest more labor and capital in their property when they are assured that the increase in value and in revenues will be captured by them and not by the state or by third parties. Protection of property rights is also good for investment in the stock market. However, investors in the stock market have more particular concerns. The specific concerns of investors in government bonds are different from the concerns of investors in shares of business corporations.[3] The main concern for investors in government-bonds is that the state will suspend payment or even write off the debt. In other words, the risk is that the state will expropriate bondholders' intangible property rights in the bonds. A greater obstacle to the development of a government-bond market is that states, as absolute and unconstrained sovereigns, cannot credibly commit not to expropriate.[4]

In investment in company shares, a misalignment of interests between insiders and outsiders creates significant agency problems. The main concern for these investors is that insiders will shirk and steal, leaving outsider equity holders with less than their share in the profits or even with a loss of the investment.[5] Personal relationships between investors and insiders provide social and other nonlegal mechanisms to moderate the problem; however, when the relationship between the insiders and the outsiders is impersonal, the problem is more acute. The law can reduce these concerns. Significant asymmetry in information between insiders and outsiders augments the agency problem. Outsiders need a law that will provide them not only with protective contractual rights but also with an institutional structure that enables them to get verifiable information that they are being defrauded.

The LLSV brand within the law and finance literature (La Porta *et al.* 1997, 1998) finds that legal origins matter. Equity capitalization, disperse or concentrated share ownership structure, and economic growth are predicted by the legal origins of the current legal system of a state. To put it differently, the family of legal systems to which a legal system belongs determines its capital markets volume and economic performance. Systems whose modern law is based on French law, through migration of people, colonial imposition, or voluntary transplantation, fare worst. Systems whose legal origin is German have better economic performance. Anglo-American systems lead to the best performance.

What can explain this? Here, LLSV offer two versions. The first version points to differences in the role of the government in the legal system. The more dominant the state, the less supportive of financial development is the legal system. Where the state was stronger, say France under its absolute monarchs, as manifested in a dependent judiciary, inquisitorial trial procedure, or disrespect for private property, the legal system ended up being less investor friendly. Where the judiciary was independent, the trial procedure adversarial and private property rights respected, as in early modern Britain, the system ended up being more protective and supportive of investors.

The second LLSV version points to the mechanisms of change that characterizes each type of legal system (Schleifer and Glaeser 2002). The case law-based common-law system responds faster to changes in economic needs than statute or code-based civil-law systems. This version has much in common with the thesis initially articulated by Posner, according to which the mechanisms of common-law litigation lead to the inherent drive to efficiency of common-law rules.

Both versions suggest not only that law matters but also that history matters. What determines present performance are the past features of the legal system. The relevant questions here are: was the state strong in the past? Was the judiciary independent in the past? Was the mechanism of change in the past based on court decisions? The crucial period in the past is the twelfth through thirteenth centuries, when common law diverged from continental law and, within a short formative stage, acquired the characteristics that distinguish it from continental law until today. What matters is the legal origin.[6]

North and Weingast, coming from a New Institutional Economics perspective, identify solving the problem of credible commitment by the state as a key to explaining economic development (North and Weingast 1989; North 1990). The British solved this problem around the time of the Glorious Revolution of 1688. The solution marked the emergence of an expanding stock market and the beginning of a century and a half of continuous and unprecedented economic growth. Countries such as France, which were unsuccessful in solving the problem, muddled.

A strong and unconstrained state cannot credibly commit not to expropriate its creditors. The British solved the problem partly by re-designing their constitution so as to limit the power of the state. They weakened their Crown by shifting powers to Parliament through the Bill of Rights, and establishing a constitutional monarchy. But their constitution was not paramount or entrenched, and the empowered Parliament could still expropriate by way of legislation. The British needed additional shackles. These were created by forming institutions that would counterbalance Parliament, notably the Bank of England. The Bank administered the national debt of Britain, ensuring that bondholders will be repaid through tax revenues and be protected from expropriation. Interest groups of politically powerful investors that organized around the Bank and other financial institutions clustered around Parliament and the Crown to prevent them from defaulting and expropriating. Three layers, constitutional, institutional, and interest groups, constrained the state and made its commitments credible.

Rajan and Zingales claim that governments don't always want to develop mechanisms for conveying credible commitments (2003b). The knowledge of how to design mechanisms that would prevent governments from withdrawing their commitments was available in the Dutch Republic in the late-sixteenth century and in Britain in the late-seventeenth century. It could have been transferred to other places. The fact that the mechanism did not spread throughout Europe indicates that there was opposition to its adoption. Interest and class groups did not want to encounter a strong state. For credible commitment to be adopted, the aristocracy had to be weakened, the gentry had to emerge, and Parliament had to become a more powerful coordinating body. While for North and Weingast, the state is an agent of change, for Rajan and Zingales it is only an arena, which different social groups try to control. While for North and Weingast learning how to design institutions is central, for Rajan and Zingales overcoming opposition to change is central. Law matters for finance, but it serves as a tool whose use is determined politically. It is not an exogenously and historically provided system as it is for LLSV. Rajan and Zingales go beyond the constraining of expropriation, which is a precondition. For financial markets to expand, they need infrastructure. This infrastructure includes transactional standards, information disclosure, legal constructs (such as collaterals and bankruptcy law), and contract enforcement. The infrastructure is a public good. Thus, it can best be provided by the state. Note that this infrastructure can serve the secondary market in government bonds and the secondary market in corporate shares. I shall return to this point below.

When do stock markets emerge and where? The three theories do not all aim to predict timing. But I will try to identify their implications, even if implicit, regarding timing. For LLSV, the stock market was likely to emerge earlier in England. The twelfth-century divergence of the common law, and the development of the basic characteristics of the common law during the formative period that ended with the death of Edward I in 1307, created the preconditions. How long it should have taken for the maturation of conditions and the development of the necessary legal protection for investors is not altogether clear. But one would imagine that it should not have taken too long. For North and Weingast, the precondition is the creation of credible-commitment devices. These are associated with the rise of Parliament, with the seventeenth-century upheavals and with the Glorious Revolution. For Rajan and Zingales, the key period is the reign of the Tudors in the sixteenth century, when Henry VII, Henry VIII, and Elizabeth I weakened the aristocracy and opened the way to the rise of the gentry and eventually to pro-market, pro-financial market merchants and investors. In their view, opposition to the stock market was sufficiently weakened by the turn of the seventeenth century. But they assert that for a stock market to develop, elimination of opposition or even protection of investors is not enough. Market infrastructure has to be supplied as a public good by the state. They claim that the infrastructure was not in place before the late-seventeenth century.

What about the Dutch Republic? It receives less attention from all three. For LLSV, the Dutch are of inferior continental legal origin. For North and Weingast, the Dutch did not go through a Glorious Revolution and did not solve the credible-commitment problem. For Rajan and Zingales, what is most crucial is not what is peculiarly English – the common law or the English constitution. If the Dutch had been able to weaken the aristocracy and put a market infrastructure in place, they could have been the first to develop a stock market.

Which market was likely to appear first, the share market or the government-bond market? Here the prediction of the three theories is not clear because each of them has a different emphasis. LLSV focus on the share market. North and Weingast focus on the bond market. Rajan and Zingales do not always distinguish between the two.

The demand for a stock market may arise separately for government finance and for corporate finance. The government needs to borrow in the market when government expenses increase. In the pre-modern setting, the main cause for this is wars. Longer, more frequent or more costly wars create new demands. Wars were funded by collecting military services from feudal lords, by turning the feudal duties to financial, by taxation, or by sale of lands, offices, monopolies, and the like. The feudal services and dues could fluctuate with wars. Other sources of income were more constant. Loans could smooth out the fluctuations, provide the needed resources rapidly in wartime, and be paid gradually out of the stream of constant revenues in the peace time that followed. Loans could be obtained on a personal basis from those well connected with the state, could be arranged through intermediaries such as corporations (guilds, cities, etc.) or banks, or through the market. We shall see that the demand for market-based government loans was created in the Dutch

Republic in the last quarter of the sixteenth century. In England, it was created in the last decade of the seventeenth century. We will consider the possibility that in England, demand was created in earlier periods as well, but was not supplied.

Demand for a market in corporate shares emerges when the cost of doing business increases; for example, when economies of scale provide more advantages or when entry barriers become higher or when risks are greater. This demand can be met internally. It can be met externally on a personal basis. It can be met by intermediaries. But when these are unavailable, the market could be used for raising impersonal external finance. We shall see that both in the Dutch Republic and in England, impersonal external finance was sought with the beginning of the oceanic trade with Asia in the closing years of the sixteenth century.

The focus of this chapter is on the founding of the EIC (1600) and the VOC (1602), and the relationship between their organization and the formation of stock markets in England and the Dutch Republic. The two companies were larger by an order of magnitude, in terms of capital and number of shareholders, than any earlier merchant company in existence in England and the Dutch Republic. They were the largest business corporations in Europe for the next two centuries and served as the basis for the formation of the British and Dutch Empires.[7] As widely held public corporations, their development could be linked to the development of a primary and a secondary market in shares. But here they diverge. The VOC relied on a preexisting market in government bonds, and its formation marked the origin of the Dutch share market. The EIC did not rely on a preexisting bond market and did not contribute to the formation of a share market in England.

The EIC and the VOC are usually viewed in the literature as similar joint-stock companies – the forerunners of the modern public corporation. They are contrasted in the literature with the older forms of organizing Eurasian trade, the Silk Road caravans, the medieval merchant ship partnerships of the Asians, and the state-owned enterprises of the Iberians. A main purpose of this chapter is to identify and analyze the major institutional differences between the companies. I will explain these differences by dissimilarities in the political, legal, and stock market environments in which the two companies were formed.

The present chapter will also connect the growing literature on the role of law, the government and institutions in the development of stock markets with the crucial historical juncture in which these first large corporations were formed in the two soon-to-be-leading economies in Europe. The purpose of this connection is to gain insight from the literature and to challenge it through this pivotal historical case study. The challenge is not posed here by systematic, large-scale econometric empirical testing. Such tests have been performed elsewhere by others.[8] It is hoped that the historical study can enrich the theory and contribute to the contemporary policy discussion.

The Dutch and the English government-bond markets

Dutch bond market

The Dutch revolt against the Habsburg Empire that began in 1568 placed new demands on public finance. The tax burden had to be increased, and wartime gaps in tax collection had to be filled by borrowing. As the federal government did not have the administrative apparatus or the political power to collect taxes, the seven provincial states that comprised the United Provinces had to carry the burden. They negotiated a formula to split this burden among them through a quota system. Each of the provinces, in turn, allocated part of the burden to the city magistrates and tax farmers within its territory (de Vries and van der Woude 1997: 91–129).

Wartime gaps in tax collections had to be filled by borrowing. The mechanism used in taxation – of shifting the burden down from the federal to provincial governments – was used for borrowing as well. By 1574, the public debt of Holland, by far the largest (and best-documented) province, stood at 1.4 million guilders. In 1600, it reached nearly 5 million guilders (Tracy 1985; 't Hart 1993). The debt kept rising throughout the seventeenth century (see Figure 7.1). Much of the borrowing was from lenders with close ties to the

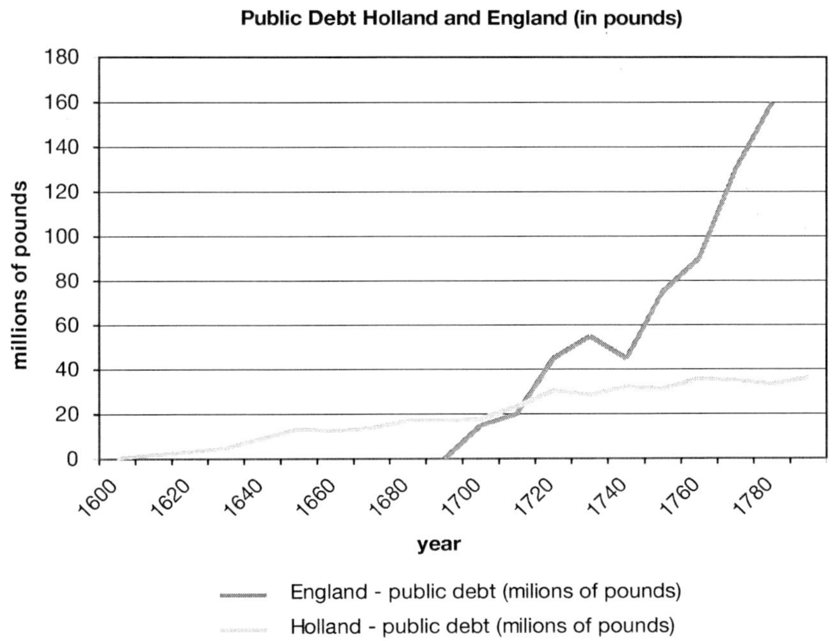

Figure 7.1 Timing of creation of public debt in Holland and England.
Source: De Vries and van der Woude (1997); Brewer (1990).

state. Some of it was forced upon involuntary lenders. The province facilitated the creation of a secondary market in its bonds in order to allow liquidity to its coerced creditors. It followed in this a practice that was developed in previous centuries in Italian city-states such as Venice, Florence, and Genoa. As we shall see, a similar order of things and similar motivation allowed the formation of a market in shares in the Dutch Republic. The secondary market in bonds would make use of the well-developed commodities marketplace with its regularly published (since 1583) price list and other information-flow and transaction-cost reducing institutions. By the end of the sixteenth century, Amsterdam, the dominant city in Holland and in the federation as a whole, was an active marketplace for commodities, freight, insurance, foreign currencies, and government bonds (Braudel 1982: 100–6; Kohn 1999). Shortly after the formation of the VOC, its shares were also traded there. The Amsterdam Beurs building was built in 1611, shortly after the establishment of the Bank of Amsterdam (Wisselbank) in 1609. The Tulip Mania of 1636–7 manifested the sophistication and centrality of the Amsterdam markets (de Vries and van der Woude 1997: 147–58; Garber 2000: 15–83).[9]

The fundamental change in taxation and borrowing that took place in the Dutch Republic in the late-sixteenth and early-seventeenth centuries is often referred to by historians as the financial revolution. It is viewed as a key to the economic growth and political power of the Dutch Republic in its seventeenth-century Golden Age. There are a number of disagreements with respect to the exact nature of this revolution.[10] These may have led North and Weingast not to interpret it as solving the basic problem of conveying credible commitment. But there is agreement with respect to the fact that this revolution predated the English financial revolution by almost a century. It is agreed that the creation of public debt was a precondition for the creation of a market for trading in public-debt instruments. It is agreed that a significant public debt was created in the Dutch Republic long before it was created in England. Tracy (1985), 't Hart (1993), and others date the formation of a market for government bonds in the Dutch Republic a few decades before the formation of the VOC. This enabled the market for VOC corporate shares, when it emerged, to free ride on institutions that were already in place. Even Fritschy's revisionist account of the Dutch financial revolution, that delays its timing and downplays its extent, concludes that public finance played a role in the development of Dutch financial markets. She notes that, "Holland's 'post-revolt' public credit and the Amsterdam stock market were apparently born around 1600 as Siamese twins!" (Fritschy 2003: 80).

English bond market

How and why did English sovereigns manage their public finance until then without Dutch-type borrowing and a Dutch-type bond and share markets? It is now common wisdom that England's commercial credit market, intended for small-scale, short-term overseas transactions and based on bills of exchange, followed advances on the Continent. This was not the case with public finance. The massive sale of church lands during the Reformation enabled Henry VIII and Elizabeth I, during whose reign the EIC was formed, to be less heavily dependent on borrowing than were later English monarchs or the Dutch. In hard times, such as wars, when they needed liquidity, they resorted to foreign lenders. Henry and Elizabeth raised all of their loans in the period 1544–74 in Antwerp, the leading financial center of the time. Between 1574 and 1588, Elizabeth was able to avoid borrowing altogether. When war resumed against the Spanish Armada in 1588, she had to return to limited domestic borrowing. This borrowing did not rely on a functioning stock market. Elizabeth used archaic, cumbersome, and unpopular methods to coerce loans from wealthy individuals and from the Corporation of London. Of the £461,000 she borrowed after 1588, all but £85,000 was raised at zero interest and only £10,000 at market terms (Outhwaite 1966, 1971). The early Stuarts gradually increased their loans but maintained the same practice of raising money from corporate bodies such as the City of London, and by receiving advances from tax farmers (Ashton 1960: 79–131; Braddick 1996). Thus, at the time of the formation of the EIC and in its years of infancy, the financial needs of the state were met without the existence of a government stock market. State loans were based on personal connections, on ad hoc intermediaries, on coercion, and on short-term borrowing. A domestic secondary market, which is essential for the creation of public debt that is based on long-term, irredeemable, and voluntary bonds because it allows liquidity, did not exist.

As conflicts between the Crown and Parliament intensified with the progression of the Stuart reign, and as the stock of land for sale decreased, so did the creditworthiness of the state. The use of voluntary loans declined. Strict parliamentary control over taxation after the 1660 Restoration forced Charles II to seek new lenders (Wheeler 1996). After the Glorious Revolution of 1688, public finance entered a new phase. Expenses rose because of prolonged wars with France, and tax incomes, with the excise leading the way, increased, but an unprecedented degree of borrowing was nevertheless needed to bridge the deficit gap.

A variety of institutional novelties coupled with the changing tax system to bring this about. These included the subjection of the Crown to parliamentary supervision through the Bill of Rights; the linking of loans to specific taxes that were supposed to provide the assured stream of income out of which interest would be paid – the so-called funded debt; the incorporation of the Bank of England as a pivot that connected private lenders with the Exchequer, and the evolvement of interest groups that used their political power to prevent expropriation of lenders. These political–constitutional–institutional changes were inspired by the Dutch model, which was well known to the newly arrived King William of Orange. An effective market for government bonds developed within a few years that introduced brokers, a marketplace, price reports, transaction techniques, and a volume of trade to allow liquidity. All these changes and others amount to what is known as the Financial Revolution (Mathias and O'Brien 1976; Dickson 1967; Brewer 1990; North and Weingast 1989; Harris 2004; O'Brien 1988). The national debt mounted from around £1 million in 1688 to £15m a decade later, to £78m in 1750, and to £244m in 1790 (see Figure 7.1).

The timing of the Financial Revolution in England has been thoroughly researched by leading economic and political historians. Unless one is to challenge this timing, one has to acknowledge that throughout most of the seventeenth century, the Dutch had an effective stock market while the English did not. This timing fits North and Weingast's credible-commitment theory well. But the timing generates two puzzles. Did the Dutch solve the credible-commitment problem a century before the English, and if so, how? How could widely held English corporations function throughout the seventeenth century, before the development of a government-bond market and apparently also a share market? Rajan and Zingales do not have a problem with the Dutch being able to develop a bond market before the English and as early as the sixteenth century. LLSV do not have a clear prediction as to timing, but the order of emergence of bond markets, in which the Dutch appeared before the English, does not fit their theory. I will deal below with the puzzles generated by North and Weingast's theory.

From its inception, the VOC functioned in an environment that included a bond market that could be utilized for its shares, and the EIC functioned in an environment that did not have such a market. The VOC was formed after the appearance of a bond market and simultaneously with the market in shares; the EIC predated a bond market and a share market by close to a century. As I will show below, the absence of an effective share market in England did not altogether prevent the transfer of shares in the profits of the EIC.

Financing the formation of the companies – the primary share market

The Dutch and the English were attracted to the lucrative Asian–European trade that promised considerable profits due to the vast arbitrage gaps in high value luxury goods between the two markets. Merchants of both nations were dismayed at being excluded by the Portuguese and Spaniards, who had dominated the oceanic trade since its establishment at the beginning of the sixteenth century. The direct Iberian trade with Asia, which amounted to buying Asian goods at source, put English and Dutch traders who bought spices at the western terminals of the Silk Road and other old caravan routes and from Spaniards and Portuguese in Europe, at a considerable disadvantage. The Iberian dominance also extended to controlling the network that distributed Asian goods, particularly spices, in Europe. In the closing decades of the sixteenth century, there were signs of a weakening of the Iberian holding of the sea routes to Asia. These were manifested in the defeat of the Spanish Armada at the hands of the English, the advance of the Dutch Revolt, and the crisis of the Portuguese State-owned Asiatic trade enterprise – the *Estado da India.*

Based on the historical context and theoretical considerations, I will now try to characterize the financial needs of the companies and the modes by which they could be supplied. In order to enter the oceanic Cape Route trade with Asia, the Dutch and the English had to overcome not only navigational and military obstacles but also financial and organizational ones. This trade required a leap in capital investment compared with shorter-distance trade. The merchants had to finance larger ships, a larger quantity of export goods (mainly silver), and, particularly, they had to be able to provide this finance for a longer period of time – typically two to four years per round-trip voyage that included several Asian stops. The Eurasian trade also involved greater uncertainties and higher risks than short-distance trade. These were incurred by oceanic currents and monsoons, by pirates, by inhospitable Asian rulers, and by unknown market conditions.

Direct state ownership based on the Iberian model was not an option. It seems that the English state was not even willing to provide significant trade infrastructure and protection. The Dutch were willing to provide some indirect support. While the Iberians funded their Asian trade primarily by plundering their American colonies and sending the silver from there to Asia, the Dutch and English states had to raise money by way of unpopular taxes or loans. They preferred that this will be done by private or semi-private trade entities and not directly by the state.

The promoters of both companies needed external finance because of the high-entry barrier into this long-distance trade, because of wealth and particularly liquid-wealth constraints (much of their wealth was held in land), and because they wanted to limit their risk and spread some of the risks to others. Thus, both Dutch and English merchant-entrepreneurs aimed at raising capital from a wider circle of passive investors. It is impossible to fully reconstruct the social networks of family, kin, neighbors, and business partners of the insiders. But it is quite safe to assume that capital of such magnitude could not be raised only based on personal relationships. The task, then, was to raise long-term external and impersonal investment. It also seems likely that this had to be mainly equity and not debt investment. While credit could be built into some of the supply and service transactions, the main funding for ships and goods had to come from the new companies themselves. They did not have the option to borrow from just a few individuals or from a large intermediary bank.[11] Debt finance had to come mainly from the offering of bonds to the public. This would involve market access problems similar to those of raising share capital from the public. Investors in bonds would not share in full the upside payoffs that would attract equity investors for such risky enterprises. The uncertainty involved in Asian voyages would make it hard to price ex-ante the risk premium and fix the interest. Usury laws would cap the maximum interest possibly below the level that risk would justify. Lenders would on the other hand assume much of the downside risk together with the equity investors.[12] The promoters searched for market and institutional mechanisms that would bring hundreds of investors into their conceived enterprises: the VOC and the EIC. But while the Dutch entrepreneurs could benefit in some way from the existence of a market in government bonds, the English could not.

Dutch East India Company

The VOC was formed on top of earlier business entities. The Dutch used various kinds of partnerships in their short-distance maritime trade (Riemersma 1950, 1952). At first, the Dutch Asian trade was organized into partnerships that were, in retrospect, called *voorcompagnieën* or pre-companies. These were based on two classes of partners, active *bewindhebbers* and passive *participanten*. The passive partners were not members of the undertaking and did not participate in decision-making. They invested through active partners who, supposedly, represented them. These pre-companies were a variation on the *commenda* or limited partnership form.[13] The intense competition between these pre-companies raised prices in Asian markets and lowered the prices of Asian goods in Dutch and other European markets and was wasteful in terms of infrastructure. The desire to form a cartel, to save in costs, and to coordinate the struggle against the Portuguese and the English, led to the integration of six city-based pre-companies into the United East India Company (the VOC) in 1602 (Steensgaard 1977; Prakash 1985; de Vries and van der Woude 1997).

The VOC was chartered on 20 March 1602 by the States-General, the federal assembly of the Dutch Republic. It was established for 21 years. The first account was set to take place after ten years. Investors were allowed to withdraw their capital from the company at that stage but not before. At that stage their exit was dependent on raising capital from the new investors in the second joint stock. The investors of the first joint stock were not allowed to just strip and divide the VOC assets in 1612. The VOC was granted by the state a trade monopoly for the entire area between the Cape of Good Hope and the Straits of Magellan. The VOC structure reflected the fact that it was a merger of six pre-companies. It had six city-based chambers that were in charge of raising capital and fitting ships. Each chamber had two classes of shareholders *bewindhebbers* and *participanten*. The former had the status of governors and took an active role in management of the chamber;[14] the latter had no voting rights and did not take part in decision-making (hereafter referred to as active shareholders and passive shareholders respectively). The united company had a central management, the Heren XVII (17 Directors), that was in charge of general policy (Gaastra 2008). Only chamber governors, that is active shareholders, were eligible to serve as VOC Directors (Figure 7.2 sketches the VOC governance structure). Passive shareholders were not entitled

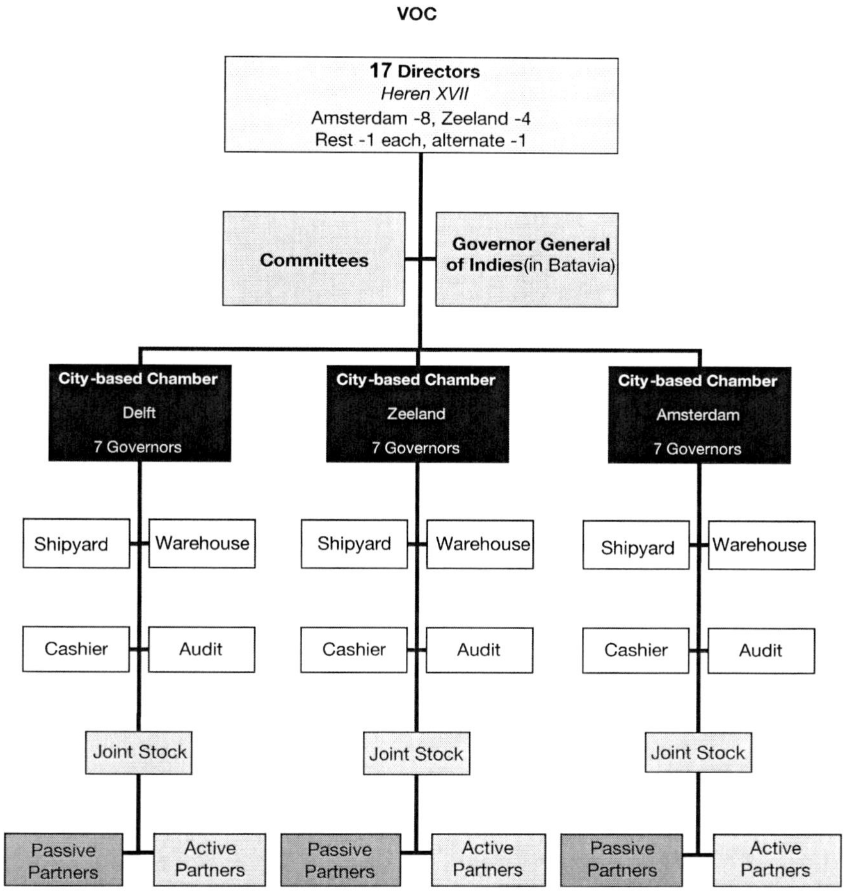

Figure 7.2 Governance structure of VOC.
Note: The Rotterdam, Hoorn and Enkhuizen Chambers, which were identical to Delft's, are not shown in the Figure.
Source: VOC Charter 1602.

to accounts at the end of each voyage, which meant that they were not entitled to information or dividend. Dividend was at the discretion of the active shareholders. In fact, dividends were distributed only once in the first ten years, in 1610, and then they were in kind, pepper, and not in cash.

Each city-based chamber opened its own register. The active members of the VOC, those who were active partners in the pre-companies, led the marketing of shares and opened subscription offices. The news about the new company, the lucrative Asian trade, and government support were circulated in various ways. By the last week of August, a mania erupted. Altogether, 6,424,588 guilder were raised in all six chambers. The number of subscribers in

Amsterdam was 1,143 and in Zeeland 264.[15] The capital and the number of investors were far higher than in any previous enterprise.

What can explain this accomplishment? A fundamental puzzle that this chapter addresses is: why were the outside investors willing to buy an inferior type of shares in the VOC? Why did they invest without receiving in return voting rights, information, or at least a better defined right for dividend? The VOC possibly relied on three methods for raising initial capital: social networks, prior business reputation, and government inducement and support. I am unable to assess what is the role played by each. Initial capital for the VOC was raised in August of 1602.

The Dutch Republic already had, as discussed above, a bond market in 1602 that VOC promoters could make use of. But at the primary share market initial offering stage, the bond market infrastructure did not have a lot to offer. The bond market could not offer a legal framework for the formation of the VOC or for the designation of property rights in its shares. The bond market did not offer a protective regulatory system to passive investors in the VOC. Its professional brokers, meeting places, trading practices, and information dissemination methods would be relevant, as I will show below, only to the formation of a secondary market in company shares. But the preexistence of a bond market may have widened the pool of individuals that were willing to consider investing in intangible assets such as bonds and shares.

The two-stage process, beginning with pre-companies, made the raising of equity capital more gradual. The investors in the pre-companies were natural candidates for investment in the VOC. The reputation acquired by the active partners could be used to convince the passive partners to reinvest. The prospects for high profits based on past success could also attract new investors who by now knew more about the risks and expected payoffs. Asymmetry in information between insiders and outsiders could be reduced due to the first stage. The formation of the VOC was gradual in another sense as well. Payment for the shares was made in four installments over the years 1603–7 (den Heijer 2005; VOC Charter (1602: 60–1). The installments were paid according to the need to send annual voyages to Asia. This structure may have made investors sense that the VOC was not dramatically different in its financial structure from the pre-companies.

The organization of the pre-companies and the two types of investors of the VOC may suggest that the raising of capital was based on hierarchical social networks. It can be suggested that each active member raised capital from his kin and associates through reputation mechanisms (coupled with social sanctions) that were not based on the trading entities. Each passive shareholder invested equity capital with an active shareholder whom he knew and trusted. It is very likely that some of the money came through social networks. But the number of investors, the fact that many of them came from professions that were not connected to trade, and the wide geographical area from which investors came, suggest that they were quite heterogeneous (van Dillen 1958: 42–59; den Heijer

2005: 70–80). It seems that many investors decided to deposit money with an anonymous company – with business plans – and not with familiar faces. This was a shift from personal to impersonal cooperation.

The success of the VOC was important to the government. The VOC promoted the policy aims of the Dutch Republic by expanding Dutch influence into the Indian Ocean and by diminishing the political and naval power of Iberian and English competitors (Israel 1989). It did so not at the expense of the government. On the contrary, if profitable, it could generate additional revenues for the Republic. The federal government assisted by coordinating among the city-based pre-companies and by granting them a monopoly (Mansvelt 1922: 54). The grant of the monopoly was a signal for government commitment to the enterprise. It also indicated potential monopoly rents. The monopoly had an additional effect as a device for attracting investors. The federal government collided with the promoters to ignite interest in the company and optimism about its prospects. But the government played, according to my interpretation, another, unnoticed, role. After luring investors to invest in the company, it locked them in. The VOC Charter issued by the federal government locked in the invested equity capital for ten years (VOC Charter 1602). As it turned out, during these years, the passive investors did not receive financial accounts, and even at the end of the first joint stock, accounts were partial and unaudited (den Heijer 2005: 66–68). They took no part in corporate management. They were paid dividends for the first time only in 1610 and then, in spices.

Based on the current literature, it is impossible to determine which of the factors discussed above were more important in facilitating the raising of initial capital. It is likely that a combination of factors – the pre existing bond market, government support, social networks, and the gradual transformation from pre-companies, all contributed to the successful raising of capital.

English East India Company

The EIC could not rely on a pre existing bond market, on significant state support, or on a gradual transformation from earlier business entities, as could the Dutch. As we saw, the government-bond market developed in England only around the Glorious Revolution of 1688.

As a result of the expanding Portuguese oceanic trade between Asia and Europe, the overland caravan routes of Central Asia and the Middle East, notably the Silk Road, and the Red Sea route that supplied the English Levant and Russia companies with Asian goods became outmoded. The success of the Dutch pre-companies served as a final warning to English merchants with established interests in Asian goods (Chaudhury and Morineau 1999; Chaudhuri 1965; Scott 1912; Furber 1976). In September 1599, a group of London merchants, dominated by members of the Levant Company who felt it was crucial for them to enter the oceanic trade with Asia, held a number of meetings that in retrospect turned out to be the founding meetings of the EIC. The promoters negotiated with the Privy Council for a Charter of Incorporation, customs privileges, license to export specie, monopoly, and possible political and military support. The Crown was not highly supportive. In 1599, Elizabeth refused the promoters' request because she thought that the presence of English merchants in the Indian Ocean could damage improving relations with Spain. The following year, because relations with Spain worsened, she changed her mind, and on 31 December 1600, the EIC was formally chartered (Harris 2005a: 224–34). But Elizabeth promised no investment or naval support. The company was on its own.

The first recorded meeting of the EIC promoters was devoted primarily to raising capital. Potential external investors were invited and asked to invest in joint stock of the company in return for a proportional share of the profits. By the time the Charter was granted, there were 219 Charter members, presumably all subscribers. By the time of the departure of the first voyage, total invested capital had reached £68,937 (Harris 2005b; Scott 1912).

The Charter of Incorporation defined the basic governance structure of the EIC. This included a governor, a deputy governor, a committee of 24 – also called the "Court of Committees" (and after 1709, the "Court of Directors") – and a General Court (for the governance structure of EIC, see Figure 7.3). The

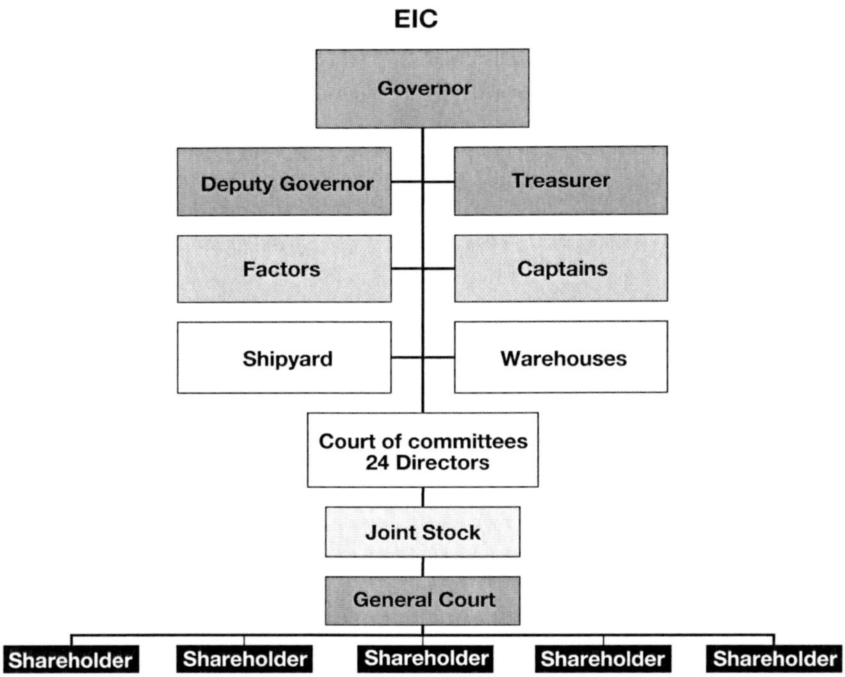

Figure 7.3 Governance structure of EIC.
Source: EIC Charter 1600.

General Court was composed of all members of the company. Every member, of whatever status and however large a share in joint stock, had one vote in the General Court. The Court was to convene at least once a year, in the first week of July, and elect the governor, the deputy, and the committees. The General Court was empowered by the Charter to remove from office the governor or any of the members of the committees on the grounds of "not demanding themselves well in their said office" (EIC Charter 1600). Committees (Directors) of the EIC, unlike those of the VOC, could come from among all shareholders, were nominated for only one year, and could be removed from office. There was only one class of shares. Voting in the General Court, for committees and on other issues, was based on one vote per member. Only gradually, beyond our period, was the strict equality of the EIC voting system altered.

The Charter, together with the bylaws, created a participatory framework for managing the EIC (Harris 2005b). Membership in the EIC afforded both voting rights and information. Members received information on EIC affairs in Asia and in London on a regular basis. The records of the early days of the company are packed with examples of how information that reached the executives was in fact shared with the committees and members according to the prescription of the Charter and the bylaws (Harris 2005a). Members could elect directors and officers and be elected as such, and elections were conducted annually. The EIC was a democratic and egalitarian company compared with the oligarchic, two-shareholder classes, governance structure of the VOC. Subscription to the joint stock of a specific voyage entitled the subscriber to receive a proportional share in the company's profits. Principal and profits were shared at the end of each voyage, unless it was decided explicitly, on a case-by-case basis, by the General Court to carry capital from one voyage to the next. In this respect as well, the EIC was substantially different from the VOC that locked-in capital for ten years.

The VOC and the EIC faced different challenges when raising their initial capital. The VOC benefited from the preexistence of a bond market, from government support and assistance in locking-in investors, and from the gradual development from pre-companies to a united company. The EIC had to raise external finance without these benefits. It had to develop institutional means for fostering impersonal cooperation. The better starting point of the VOC was not foreseen by LLSV, who expected the common-law origin to provide England with a better investor protection law. Rajan and Zingales emphasize the capture of the state by classes and interest groups. For them, the fact that in England the aristocracy was dominant while in the Dutch Republic the merchants were dominant is conclusive for predicting that the Dutch would develop business corporations and share markets earlier. For North and Weingast, the fact that the Dutch Republic gave rise to a major corporation and to a primary market would be a surprise as the English were the first to solve the credible-commitment problem. For them, there are three ways around this. First, they would say that they have predictions primarily regarding bond markets. Second, they might say that they were willing to reconsider their tentative conclusion that the Dutch did not solve the credible-commitment problem earlier than the English. Third, they would say that even though the Dutch were able to develop as large a corporation as the VOC and a secondary market, these were in fact traditional coercive institutions while the EIC was a modern institution based on voluntary and informed cooperation. With these insights from the literature, I shall turn to a discussion of the rise of the secondary market.

Secondary share market

The VOC and the rise of the share market

In the Netherlands, despite the preexistence of a stock market, the VOC did not simply raise equity capital on a purely voluntary basis in that market. Its promoters relied on the networks and reputation that served the pre-companies and on the support of the state. More than this, they wanted to raise long-term capital without deterring outside investors. They did not reveal this intention in full, and they changed the rules retroactively. The state was willing to issue a charter that did not disclose in full the disempowerment of the passive investors, the state assisted the insiders to lure the passive investors, and eventually the state was willing to legitimize the change in the rules of the game and the lock-in of the passive investors. Why did the insiders lock in, with the support of the state, the external investors of the VOC? Because the mechanism that had performed quite well in the earlier period – that of per-voyage partnerships and pre-companies – could not survive the transition to a long-lasting enterprise. The VOC was not formed for a single voyage. On the contrary, it was formed as a perpetual enterprise. The intention was to send annual voyages to Asia and to maintain permanent agencies and warehouses – fortified, if needed – in India and Indonesia. For this reason, its Charter incorporated a new and separate legal entity that would exist for at least 21 years. Further, the Charter created joint stock that would exist for ten years and would not easily dissolve even at that stage. The VOC was formed in order to assure continuity, from voyage to voyage, in the flow of commodities between Asia and Europe; to coordinate among competing Dutch city-based companies; and to overcome Portuguese and English competition.

This shift from a single voyage to a long-term enterprise was motivated by factors that did not correspond well with voluntary cooperation with outside investors. The institutional reorganization had a negative effect on the ability to raise capital. The insiders and the state tried to blur this effect. As we saw, passive investors were asked to put in their money in annual installments over a four-year period. These installments may have conveyed to the passive investors that it was business as usual despite the formation of the VOC, and that they were still investing per voyage. But, in fact, they were not. They were locked in. They could not withdraw their money at the end of every year or every voyage. Further, once they had subscribed, they were legally obliged to pay all four installments in full, irrespective of the performance of the VOC. As described above, even when the VOC was doing well and making profits, its dividend policy was very restrictive. The active shareholders retained control of the joint-stock capital of the VOC through the City Chambers and the Heren XVII for no less than ten years. They offered passive investors no voting rights, no information on trade, no account of profits, and thus no share in control. The active shareholders used their positions as both merchants and city magistrates to exercise political influence on provincial and federal governments and to unilaterally lock in the external investors by way of the Charter. They could, and in fact did, lock in the passive investors again at the end of the ten-year period by using their political clout to amend the terms of the original Charter and extend the duration of the joint stock.

Once locked in, the passive investors became dissatisfied and agitated. They were dissatisfied with their legal status. But many of them were also dissatisfied because they realized that the VOC did not aim only at maximizing profits and returns. The VOC was also used by the financial-political elite to promote the military, religious, and political aims of the Republic and the leading provinces (Adams 2005: 52–61). The VOC financed armed ships to attack the Spanish–Portuguese fleet in the Indian Ocean and capture territorial strongholds. The passive investors sensed that profits were compromised at the expense of political aims. Investment in territorial strongholds and in war could be interpreted as one that intended to promote longer-term profits and not necessarily as non-business investment. But for the passive investors it was another indication that they were not going to see money anytime soon and that they were locked in and powerless.

It was not easy for them to organize. But in time, they protested the fact that they lacked voice and information and were not paid dividends. Following protests by Isaac Le Maire and a short selling of shares that led to price downfall, the company distributed the first dividend (van Dillen 1935). This was a dividend in kind, not in cash. The 1610 dividend was in mace, the 1612 dividend was in pepper and nutmeg, and only 7.5 percent was in cash. The dividend in spices advantaged the active investors, who, as merchants, could accumulate stock and had better access to the market. The demand of the passive investors to participate in management was avoided throughout the first joint stock, and, even in 1612, the state assisted the active shareholders to delay and eventually refuse the demand (den Heijer 2005; Gepken-Jager 2005). On these two fronts, the passive investors did not achieve much; however, they were more successful with the exit option.

We don't know of significant trading in shares of pre-companies, probably for two main reasons: the pre-companies were limited in time to one venture, and the number of members of each was small and they were personally connected and unwilling to include outsiders. The VOC was a much larger and more impersonal enterprise. Its shares were not bearers' and no certificate was issued to holders (van Dillen 1958: 32–4). Thus, no physical asset was conveyed by private contract. However, its Charter included a clause that allowed transfer by registering the transfer in the VOC books in the presence of two directors and paying a small fee. Thus, in contrast to the EIC, while passive shareholders had no voice in VOC affairs and their initial investment was locked in for ten years, they were able to exit the company by selling their shares. Because a clause in a Charter cannot in itself assure liquidity, the emergence of a market for government debt instruments before 1600 was crucial in facilitating this option.

A recent study (Gelderblom and Jonker 2004) convincingly documented the volume of Amsterdam Chamber VOC shares that were traded in the years 1603–12 (see Figure 7.4). Roughly 0.5 percent to 1.5 percent of the shares of the company were traded every month. Nearly 33 percent of the shares changed hands in the first decade. The Amsterdam market was sophisticated, with full-time brokers, a meeting place, and several non-spot transactional designs (Gelderblom and Jonker 2004, 2005). One may argue that the availability of a government-bond market led to the introduction of the exit option for VOC passive investors, that the trade in VOC shares was a natural advance over the

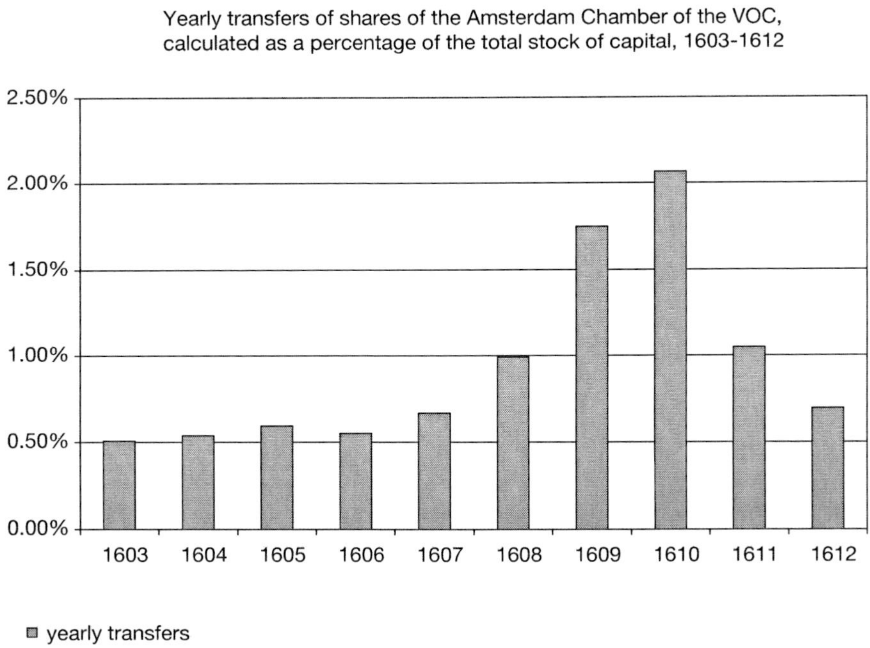

Figure 7.4 Transfer of shares in VOC.
Source: Gelderblom and Jonker (2004); (2005).

nontraded shares in the pre-companies, and that a share market naturally follows a bond market. My reading is that this explanation is not sufficient. The exit option and the transfer of shares were introduced because the previous cooperation system, based on reputation, recurring transactions, and social networks, had collapsed. They were used with growing frequency because of the dissatisfaction of passive investors with the lock-in of their money and because they were nevertheless deprived of share in control. The exit partly offset the oligarchic and cooperation-damaging effects of the other institutional features of the VOC.

The EIC as a preshare market corporation

In order to attract external investors, the EIC offered them voice and information on a level far higher than in the VOC, in an attempt to offset the lack of liquidity in the absence of an effective market for shares in 1600s England. Further, the EIC was designed in a manner that would allow its members an exit option despite the lack of a preexisting stock market. This option had to be formulated in an unusual way, unfamiliar to modern scholars who view exit through the market as the standard form of exit (Harris 2005b). Members of the EIC were given the option to invest, or not to invest, in any voyage beyond the first. Some invested; others did not. Often, when not enough capital was raised from existing EIC members, resort was made to outsiders who were invited to invest in the stock and join the corporation. In this sense, the corporation was a club of potential, though not necessarily actual, investors. All potential investors (members) had a voice in the decision to undertake a new voyage and to raise more money. They then received an option to join by investing in the voyage.[16] Those who decided not to subscribe for a specific voyage could not get a share of its profits. Different groups of individuals, all supposedly members of the corporation, contributed to each of the first twelve voyages (1600–12). There was significant overlap between the groups of investors, but they were not identical in composition. Membership allowed potential investors to receive first-hand information about the outcome of past voyages, the status of ongoing voyages, and the prospects and business plans with respect to future ones. Their primary exit opportunity did not involve selling their shares in a non-existing market, but rather lay in receiving their original investment and profits at the end of a successful voyage and deciding whether to join additional unfolding business opportunities.

To exit their initial investment while a voyage was still out in Asia, an exit of a secondary importance, members had to match up with buyers – without benefit of a functioning market or of pre-structured low-cost transactions. Networks based on kin and family connections always assisted in this. The transfer of interest was subject to approval by the EIC, approval that in the first few years was not always granted without delay. This was not an adequate solution for the widely held corporation that the EIC turned out to be. This secondary option for exit was somewhat facilitated by the institutional structure of the EIC that served as a participatory meeting place for potential sellers and buyers. In a way, the regular meetings of its courts were a good marketplace for company shares. There, potential buyers could locate a seller, obtain information on the quality of the goods (shares) offered by learning about the state of affairs in Asia, and get some sense of the market price of the goods. These meetings functioned more like annual fairs than like modern capital markets. It is important to remember that the sale of shares was subject to approval by the corporation and to registration in its books. The primary mode of exit, at the end of a voyage, was not.

I have constructed a database, the first of its kind, of transactions in EIC shares based on reports in the EIC minutes on transactions that were presented for approval in the EIC Court. In 1607, the number of such transactions was 47. For the period until the introduction of the new EIC Charter in 1609, I identified 100 transactions altogether, not including the allocation of shares in profits to employees (see Figure 7.5). Taking into account that the EIC minutes for the period 1604–6 were lost and that 1600 and 1609 were not full years, the annual average can be extrapolated to be around 40 transactions. This number is high for an environment that was devoid of a stock market. Still, liquidity

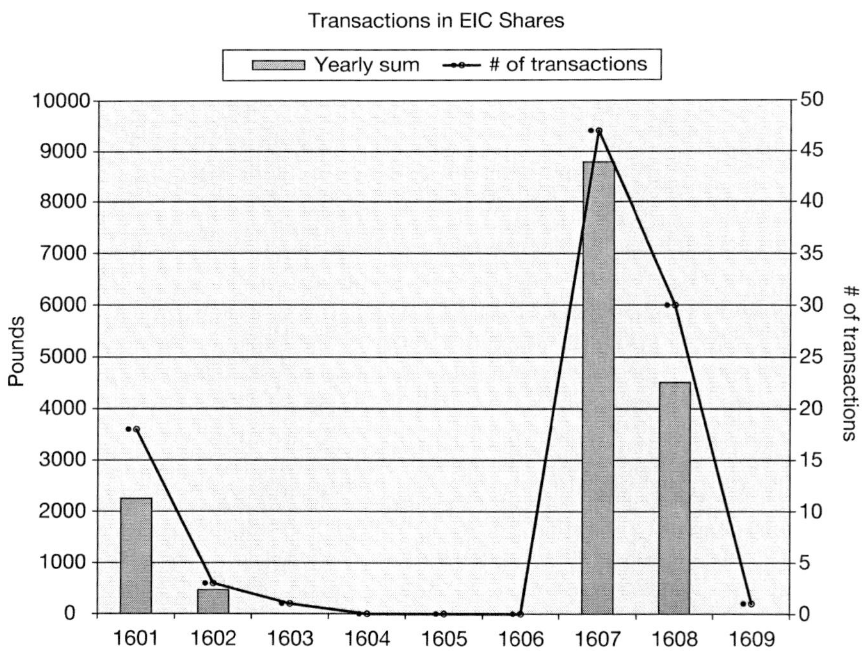

Figure 7.5 Transfer of shares in EIC.
Source: Harris (2005) database, based on Calendar of State Papers.

was limited. If a transaction could not materialize, either for lack of approval or for failure to match a buyer, the investor had to hold his share until the end of the voyage, hoping that it would be successful and that there would be a final settlement of accounts for the voyage. Thus, the more viable exit option at this stage in the history of the EIC still involved opting out of a specific voyage rather than exiting the corporation altogether. The real challenge for the promoters of the EIC, because of the exit option at the end of each voyage, was not to convince investors to subscribe £68,373 for the initial voyage, substantial as that sum was by contemporary standards, but rather to maintain the relationship so that investors would be forthcoming in future voyages. Almost £400,000 was raised in the years 1603–12 for voyages 2–12, about six times the initial investment. With free access to an effective market, the liquidity of VOC shares was higher than that of EIC shares. But the liquidity of EIC shares was higher than any historians, economists, or legal scholars have hitherto attributed to pre-1688 England.

Throughout much of the seventeenth century, the shares of the EIC were traded in company meetings, on a personal basis, or by ad hoc matching. There is no evidence of the creation of an infrastructure for a secondary share market in EIC shares or in the shares of any other corporation before 1688. After the Glorious Revolution, things changed. A market in government debt emerged, as described above. Thereafter, a handful of corporate shares, the EIC, Bank of England, Royal African Company, and Hudson's Bay Company, free rode the government-bond boom and were traded in this market place in the 1690s. Only with the South Sea boom of 1720 did a larger number of companies, mostly short-lived bubbles, make use of the English stock market (Neal 1990; Chancellor 1999; Harris 2000; Michie 1999; Morgan and Thomas 1969).

Conclusion

The analysis of the formation of the EIC and VOC and of the development of the stock markets in England and the Dutch Republic confirm the general thesis that law and the state matter. The Dutch government bond market developed more than a century earlier than the English because of a variety of demand- and supply-side factors, including wars, the federal structure of the Republic, the balance of powers between classes, and the creation of facilitative institutions by the state. We observed a close link between the legal and political environment and the development and design of the two corporations. The VOC, supported by the state, could lock in investors and legitimize a hierarchical and oligarchic governance structure. The English company, lacking strong state support, could not lock in investors, had to provide an exit option at the end of every voyage, had to base itself on fully voluntary cooperation, and to offer outside investors a more democratic and participatory governance structure. The VOC had to provide the locked-in passive and voiceless investors with an exit option by developing a liquid secondary share market. The VOC offered liquidity that did not amount to withdrawing the initial investment (and in fact even the accumulated profits) while the EIC offered a full withdrawal option. The EIC did not give rise to a secondary share market in England. But it gave rise to a path in which a widely held corporation existed for nearly a century in a pre-share-market setting.

This analysis challenges the existing literature on law and finance in several respects. First of all, it does not conform to LLSV's conclusion that the common law as judge-made law better supports the development of a stock market. Both the bond market and the stock market developed earlier in the Dutch Republic, a country that applies continental law, than in the birthplace of the common law – England. In addition, the markets developed in both countries on the margins of the legal system. They did not develop within core province of judge-made law in England or of civil code-based law on the Continent. They did not benefit from the allegedly superior mechanisms of change of the common law. They developed out of charters – constitutional and administrative tools. They developed in interaction with merchant law and maritime law, which were not very different on both sides of the Channel.

Second, LLSV predict that an active and dominant state, such as the typical continental state, would discourage the development of a share market. We have seen that the Dutch state was much more involved in trade and in the economy than the English state. Was this detrimental, as LLSV predicted? This chapter suggests a mixed bag. On one hand, Dutch state involvement assisted in raising huge sums by contemporary standards. It convinced investors that VOC prospects were good, and it locked in unwary investors.[17] State support allowed the VOC to maintain annual voyages to Asia and to fund military operations. The VOC could send more ships than the EIC, to capture larger markets, grow faster, and be more profitable (and destructive). But the state support inhibited the development of a more innovative and cooperative institution. In the long run, the inactivity of the English state forced entrepreneurs and investors in England to design an institution that would better protect external investors and would serve as the basis for the modern public corporation. In the present case, LLSV predicted the long run but not the short to medium term.

Third, North and Weingast are correct in identifying the resolution of the credible-commitment problem as a precondition for the rise of a government-bond market. They focused on the Glorious Revolution in England, but nothing in their theoretical analysis rejects the possibility that the Dutch Republic could solve the problem a century earlier even if not through a grand constitutional revolution. They are also correct in predicting a synergy between the development of the bond market and the development of the share market. But the relationship between the two can be refined. The ability of the sovereign to make a credible commitment was only partially relevant for the development of a share market. The creation of stock market infrastructure, to which Rajan and Zingales referred, was at least as important. The Dutch secondary share market was able to free ride the bond-market infrastructure. The formation of joint-stock companies with numerous shareholders was a precondition. The search for liquidity in the secondary market by the original primary market investors was also important.

Fourth, Rajan and Zingales argue that vested-interest groups and social classes that capture the state may block the development of a stock market. It is clear in our case that the Dutch Republic was dominated by merchants. This was the case not only because of their absolute political power compared to the landowning classes. It was also because of the political and constitutional structure of the Republic, a federation in which the aristocracy was divided throughout the various provinces, while merchants were concentrated in several key-positioned cities. In England, the Crown and Parliament were dominated by the landowning classes. What can be learned from this is that it is not sufficient to view the state as an independent player representing the preferences of the sovereign. While Rajan and Zingales are right in identifying the breaking up of opposition to the stock market in England, they miss a similar and earlier process in the Dutch Republic. By adding their state-capture perspective to North and Weingast's credible-commitment perspective, one may explain the earlier timing of the rise of the stock market in the Dutch Republic. The institutional knowledge needed for conveying credible commitment was available in both the Dutch Republic and in England. But it could be applied in the Dutch Republic because of political support that would be lacking in England for another century.

Can we draw any policy recommendations from the encounter between the theories and the historical case study? Not directly implementable ones. The above conclusions are based on an early modern European case, not on a case located in a modern emerging market or LDC. The contexts are quite different. But we can gain some useful insights. The law matters for the development of business organizations and stock markets. But law reform is constrained by preexisting institutions and by social and interest groups. Reform in legal rules, say investor protection laws, cannot be fully effective without careful design of organizations that would enhance information flows and transparent governance structure. As the English example shows, it is not essential for a secondary share market to develop simultaneously with widely held business corporations. When designing policy recommendations there are often several possibilities that are not necessarily better or worse. They often present different tradeoffs, between the long term and the short term, between smaller-scale voluntary cooperation and larger-scale coerced investment, between institutions that offer easy exit and institutions that allow more voice. Because political and social environments and institutional baselines are often different in different LDCs and emerging economies, the same size cannot fit all. It is wise to recognize that conditions are different and that preferences in tradeoffs are different in different localities, and accordingly there should be plurality in policy recommendations.

Notes

1 I would like to acknowledge the research assistance of Kobi Ben-Zvi and Eyal Yaacoby and the financial support of the Cegla Center, Tel Aviv University. I would like to thank Lee Cabatingan, Robert Cooter, John Drew, Jesse Fried, Yarida Gonzales de Lara, Avner Greif, Santhi Hejeebu, Ella Jager, Bruce Johnsen, Lynne Kiesling, Dan Klerman, Timur Kuran, Naomi Lamoreaux, Walter Licht, Joel Mokyr, Robert Nelson, Dan Raff, Jean-Laurent Rosenthal, Harry Scheiber, Kenneth Sokoloff, Gianni Toniolo, Daniel Waldenstrom, Dean Williamson, Bill Whitney, Gavin Wright, and participants in seminars at George Mason and UC Berkeley, UCLA, Northwestern University, Stanford University, the Wharton Business School, Tel Aviv University, Harvard Business School, Hebrew University, USC, Duke, and World Justice Forum for their helpful comments and suggestions on earlier versions of this chapter and on the related paper on the formation of the EIC.

2 For good surveys of this literature see Dam (2006), Beck and Levine (2005).

3 I will focus here on equity investment in corporations, leaving aside corporate bonds.

4 In this chapter I will use the term "bond market" to refer to the market in government bonds, "share market" to refer to the market in corporate shares, and "stock market" and "stock exchange" to refer to the market in both government bonds and corporate shares. These terms are somewhat more consistent with the contemporary terms as they were developed in the seventeenth century, and better suit the exposition of my argument, than the modern terms in which "stock market" refers to corporate equity market.

5 There is also a secondary concern for expropriation by the state.

6 Later version of the LLSV thesis shifted the timing of divergence from the early years of the common law to the era of the French Revolution.

7 The chapter deals only with the first decade in the history of the companies. It focuses on finance and governance aspects, touches only indirectly upon trade, and does not deal at all with colonial and military consequences of the activities of the two companies.

8 For LLSV, see, for example, Berkowitz *et al.* (2003a, 2003b); Pistor *et al.* (2003); Beck *et al.* (2003); Beck and Levine (2005). For North and Weingast, see Sussman and Yafeh (2006); Clark (1996).

9 For the Amsterdam stock market of the late-seventeenth century, see Neal (1990).

10 Some scholars place its timing in the 1570s, others at around 1600. Some call attention to the fact that municipal borrowing began in the fifteenth century. Some stress the introduction of public borrowing while others view the reorganization of taxation as equally important. Some argue that the fundamental change was achieved by a shift to the level of the province while others believe that it was accomplished on the city level. Several scholars argue that on the debt side, it was the shift from short-term debt to long-term debt in the form of annuities that allowed more creditworthiness and increased borrowing, while others argued that transferable short-term obligations were in higher demand. Some argue that the liquidity of the market was limited due to the variation in bond types among various issuers and the resulting lack of standardization. Some argue that the suppliers of credit were mostly *rentiers*, while others claim that they were primarily merchants in search of liquid investment. See Tracy (1985); 't Hart (1993); Fritschy (2003).

11 The Bank of Amsterdam (Amsterdamsche Wisselbank) was founded in 1609. The Bank of England was founded in 1694.

12 This depends on which part of the company's assets would be subjected to the risks in Asia and on the ocean and on whether the company offered their shareholders

limited liability. Though some scholars claim that the VOC was a limited liability company, others do not find evidence for this. The debate about the legal nature of EIC is not developed. I side with those who do not find support for the limitation of liability of members in either of the corporations.

13 According to one version, they were associations of limited partnerships each of which was composed of an active merchant and his passive investors. According to another version, the pre-company was an association of several active partners and several passive partners.

14 More accurately *bewindhebbers* were required to hold a minimum amount of shares, 1,000 Flemish pounds (500 for Hoorn and Enkhuizen) to qualify for their status. They could not sell in the market their status as *bewindhebbers*. That status was hereditary. They were allowed to buy a larger share in the profits but they could not by this gain more voting power.

15 Subscription books for the other chambers did not survive.

16 The goods offered to club members, a share in the voyage's profit, was non-rivalrous because there was in fact no upper bound to investment in a voyage. When more capital was raised, more ships could be fitted or more goods (mainly silver) could be loaded on the given ships.

17 It can be argued, however, that the Dutch Republic was not a typical continental state. It was not an absolute monarchy. For this reason, LLSV's prediction may not apply to the Dutch Republic but can still apply to France or Germany.

Part IV

Rule of law and political development

Chapter 8

The politics of courts in democratization

Tom Ginsburg[1]

Introduction

My topic is the relationship of law to democratic transition. Much of the literature on this issue is normative in character, celebrating the role of courts in constraining or eliminating authoritarianism. The literature seems to assume that the rule-of-law and democracy go together like the proverbial motherhood and apple pie. I wish to take a more cautious view, trying to identify the conditions under which courts can play a positive role in facilitating democratization.

To undertake this inquiry, we need to understand how courts are viewed in different political regimes. Thus far the literature has tended to treat the politics of courts in authoritarian regimes differently from the politics of courts in democratic regimes. This chapter seeks to point out the similarities, and to treat the two in a unified framework. Only by doing so, I believe, can we both understand variation in the roles law plays in different phases and trajectories of democratization. More concretely, we need to understand the *legacies* of law in the authoritarian period before we can truly understand the *functions* of law in a democratic one.

My approach is interdisciplinary in character in that I draw on a tradition of scholarship that treats courts as political actors (Shapiro 1964, 1981; Maravall and Przeworski 2003b). My focus is not on the rule-of-law as an ideal, but on the rule-of-lawyers that populate real-world governmental institutions. Treating courts as governing institutions means that courts are likely to reflect, at a very broad level, policies of a governing regime. This should not be mistaken as seeing courts as pure agents of politicians and their immediate policy preferences, but rather to recognize that there must be some support for the broad policies that courts pursue in order for these policies to be sustainable. More generally, I seek to understand the roles of law at different phases of the democratization sequence. Courts are called on to play different functions in different societies and are given genuine independence and discretion over certain areas of policy to accomplish these functions. These roles are likely to vary with the needs and powers of other regime actors.

The chapter is organized as follows. I start by considering the role of courts in authoritarian regimes. I then develop four ideal types of the role of courts in democratization. This is followed by application of the framework to several recent cases. I conclude with some speculation on the links between authoritarian legacies and democratic roles of judicial institutions.

The politics of courts in autocracy

Political analysts of courts tend to treat judicial independence as a continuous variable, and to recognize that the degree to which judges exercise real power is always limited by the preferences of powerful actors who use various formal and informal techniques to discipline courts. These formal and informal techniques are well known. Regimes can impact the courts through controlling composition, such as by purging old members, appointing new ones and expanding or contracting the size of courts. They can manipulate career incentives to encourage judicial conformity. They can also focus on the design of the judicial arena, manipulating jurisdiction and creating special courts for categories of cases that are especially politically salient. They can pass new laws to overturn errant judicial interpretations. And in extreme cases, regimes can intimidate judges directly.[2]

Because use of any of these techniques for influencing judges requires coordination among elements of the regime, they are generally easier to utilize in autocracies than in democracies. In other words, judges are likely as a general matter to have a greater scope and depth of independence in democracies than in autocracies. But each particular regime is different. Structural factors, such as the cohesion of the governing elite and the constitutional ease of overruling courts, operate in both democracies and dictatorships. One might even imagine an authoritarian regime in which, for reasons to be discussed below, the scope of legality is greater than it is in some democracies. Singapore is a good example: the country regularly receives top scores on rule-of-law surveys and has a high quality legal system, yet according to some cannot be called a democracy (Silverstein 2003, 2008). Democracies in which the governing elite is cohesive and the process of disciplining judges easy may exhibit less scope for judicial independence (Ramseyer and Rasmusen 2003).

Not every authoritarian regime empowers courts. But we should expect that when they do so, it will affect the role of courts in democratization. If courts are seen as mere instruments of the authoritarian regime, and have not built up a stock of legitimacy by playing important social functions, it is unlikely that they will be empowered in the post-authoritarian period. In such circumstances, we should expect to see the creation of new bodies, such as designated constitutional courts, to take on important functions in the democratic era, because old judges will not be trusted. On the other hand, if judges exercised genuine independence in the authoritarian period, they may retain autonomy and power in the democratic era.

We thus need to understand the use of courts in authoritarianism to accomplish certain governance tasks. Judicial independence is everywhere limited in scope and this is easily apparent in authoritarian polities. At the same time we do see some empowerment of judges in polities as diverse as Marcos' Philippines; Pinochet's Chile; contemporary China; Islamist Iran; neo-czarist Russia, and many other examples (see generally Ginsburg and Moustafa 2008). These examples demonstrate that courts are useful for an incredibly broad range of regimes, whether nominally capitalist or socialist, religious or secular, ruled by a military or party-based regime.

A regime subtype particularly prone to using courts may be what Levitsky and Way (2002) call "competitive authoritarianism." These are regimes that have formal democratic institutions, but also violate the rules so often that they cannot be characterized as meeting minimal standards of democracy. Competitive authoritarians allow elections but rig the rules, control the media, and utilize the state security apparatus to ensure that no effective challenge arises to their rule. Courts may exist in competitive authoritarian regimes but are unlikely to develop the capacity to truly constrain the regime on core issues. They may become one of the instruments of governance, used to marginalize political opponents and interfere with institutions that show a modicum of independence, so that the role of courts increases as democracy declines (Trochev 2004). However, such courts may also have autonomy in some realms and may become a site of some substantive constraint on regimes.

In a recent volume, Tamir Moustafa and I (2008: Moustafa 2007b) focus on several functions courts serve for authoritarian regimes. *First*, they can serve as an effective instrument of social control. That is, courts can serve as part of the apparatus of repression in which they serve to intimidate, harass, or even eliminate opponents. *Second*, courts can provide credible commitments in the economic sphere (North and Weingast 1989). The key is to convince private actors and investors that the state will not interfere with the private economy for political purposes. Relatively independent courts with the ability to police government takings provide one mechanism to signal state restraint. More generally, by providing a forum for resolution of ordinary disputes, courts provide a service that facilitates economic development. *Third*, courts can serve as a vehicle for the control of lower-level bureaucrats. Authoritarian regimes, like democratic ones need to hire expert administrators to accomplish certain state functions and there is a risk that these agents may in fact not implement instructions. By providing a forum for the challenge of lower-level bureaucratic decisions, courts can help reduce corruption and increase discipline within the state apparatus. This function of administrative discipline is typically played by administrative law systems. *Fourth*, courts can provide a vehicle for resolving internal disputes among elements of the regime itself (Barros 2003). *Finally*, in some circumstances courts provide a legitimating device for the regime, masking the brute forces of power that are operating.

We now can see why regimes, both democratic and authoritarian, might delegate independent power and discretion to judicial systems. Some of the problems to which courts respond are in fact more severe in autocracies than democracies. Arguably, for example, stronger states may need more effective commitment devices in the economic sphere because they are less constrained by structural forces. And controlling lower-level administrators can be very tough for dictators, even though they have powerful tools to punish wayward employees. This is because information flows are not always good within dictatorships. Thus we can, in some circumstances, conceive of greater levels of "judicialization" in dictatorships as compared with democracies.

Against this motive, however, must be weighed the probability that courts will act as a "double-edged sword." For even as they help authoritarians accomplish certain tasks, the courts also provide formally neutral venues, in which clever activists can use the law to advance claims, embarrass the government, and call attention to important issues, even if they lose the particular cases in question. This quality results from the institutional structure of courts as transparent fora that apply publicly available rules. Judges may serve the regime most of the time. But there is the possibility of providing some political benefits to the opposition, or at least failing to uphold regime policies. Even in Stalin's USSR, judges would sometimes fail to fully implement laws they found excessive (Solomon 1996). In Brazil under dictatorship, ordinary courts had a role in security cases and acquitted an astonishingly high percentage of their defendants (averaging 55 percent over fifteen years) (Pereira 2005). Writing about Egypt, Moustafa (2007b) describes how a court system that was empowered to promote economic development gradually began providing victories to civil society groups that challenged regime policies, prompting a crackdown from the government. This suggests that there are risks for the authoritarian ruler in empowering courts and that, under certain circumstances, courts can be a vehicle for pressures to liberalize.

In some cases, the benefits provided to the opposition may not be all that apparent at the time the decision is made. Nevertheless, by changing the structure of political competition and guaranteeing the state plays by the nominal rules, they can provide downstream openings that can only be taken advantage of some years later. Minor rulings on jurisdiction and standing can help to encourage litigants to bring their cases to courts, which then provide a means of publicizing regime policies. Even court cases that involve pure repression can become rallying cries for the opposition. In Taiwan, for example, the regime tried virtually the entire leadership of the nascent opposition in trials following the 1979 Kaohsiung Incident (Roy 2003). These trials had a galvanizing effect on Taiwanese opposition to the KMT even though all the defendants lost their cases.[3] Individual leaders gained notoriety and experience through the trials that became an asset some years later.

To summarize the argument so far, the position of the courts in the predemocratic period is largely a product of decisions undertaken by the authoritarian regime. This provides the framework within which courts must operate during early phases of democratization. The key factors seem to be the extent to which courts are able to preserve a realm of independence, which in turn depends on how much the authoritarians need them to play crucial governance functions.

The politics of courts in democratization

What then is the role of courts in democratization? At this point we need to distinguish three alternative scenarios: courts as upstream triggers for democratization; courts as downstream guarantors of authoritarian position; and courts as downstream democratic consolidators, in which courts follow the initial decision to democratize and facilitate the process. A fourth possibility is judicial irrelevance, in which courts play no discernible role, either as guarantors, triggers, or consolidators.

Upstream triggers of democracy

In very rare instances, courts play a central role triggering democratization when the autocrat is *not* seeking to withdraw, and opposition arises. In these situations, courts are in fact at the center of the transition decision, providing *focal points* for mobilization. These are situations of conflict and contingency, in which democratization has not yet been embarked upon.

To understand how a court decision can play such a role, I draw from recent work by Weingast (1997). In his model, a ruler conspires with some citizens to dominate other citizens, using a combination of repression and selective incentives for regime insiders. The dominated group can be very large, but can only limit the ruler if it can coordinate to overturn the narrow ruling coalition. Coordination is very difficult to achieve. The difficulty is that citizens may not agree on what exactly constitutes a violation of the rules, and may not know whether other citizens will join in an effort to take power. Any subset of citizens thinking of rising up to challenge the regime can only succeed if others join them. Otherwise the opponent ends up in jail or worse and the regime maintains power (as the recent tragic events in Myanmar illustrated). Being uncertain as to what other citizens will do, the prospective mobilizers will likely stay quiescent and authoritarianism will be sustained. Only when there is agreement on what constitutes a violation and mutual expectations that citizens will in fact enforce the rules will democracy emerge and be sustained.

To achieve coordination requires focal points (Schelling 1960: 57). The particular focal points that will allow citizens to find ways to coordinate and to overcome their collective action problem are not obvious ex ante, and are not uniform across all times and places. My argument is that, in some limited conditions, court decisions can play a role in helping citizens to coordinate, and force the autocracy to liberalize. The court decision serves as a focal point for citizens to coordinate their efforts against the regime.

Why might citizens focus on a court decision? First a court decision can provide clarity as to what constitutes a violation of the rules by the government. Lacking an authoritative pronouncement, regime opponents might disagree about whether a violation occurred and may thus fail to coordinate to enforce the rules. By creating common knowledge that a violation of the rules has in fact occurred, a court decision can help citizens to overcome the collective action problem.

Second, a court decision against the government is an information transmission device. It communicates the view that the government apparatus is not completely unified on policy. It also indicates, at a minimum, that judges do not believe their personal safety is in jeopardy from challenging regime rules, and so may allow opponents to update their own assessments of the risks of challenge.

Third, a court decision raises the cost of repression and is a resource that can be used by activists to rally supporters to their cause. The court decision legitimates regime opposition and raises the costs of repression. A regime that arrests citizens after an unfavorable court decision will suffer greater reputational loss than it would before that decision. This is not to say that the court decision guarantees implementation – only that it can facilitate mobilization.

The incentives for courts to produce "trigger" decisions are not obvious ex ante. Courts have an institutional incentive in ensuring that their decisions are implemented rather than ignored, which requires predicting that citizens will actually respond to calls for change. Attempting to provide a focal point for regime opposition carries grave institutional risks in the event that the citizenry does not enforce the decision. The regime can respond in myriad ways to punish the courts. We should expect, then, that courts will engage in providing focal points only when they have strong institutional and political links to outside institutions that can defend them from punishment, or are sufficiently confident for other reasons that their decisions will be implemented. These conditions are not always present.

Gretchen Helmke's (2005) notion of "strategic defection" provides one set of conditions in which we might see the courts being willing to provide such focal points. Helmke focuses on highly unstable institutional environments (Argentina in particular), where new governments come in with some frequency and typically change the composition of the high courts when they do. In such places, argues Helmke,

> the relevant inter-temporal conflict of interest shifts from the standard scenario of a judge appointed by a past government who is primarily constrained by a current government, to a more uncertain situation in which a judge appointed by the current government faces potential constraints at the hands of a future opposition government.
>
> (ibid.: 13)

Under such circumstances, judges may start to rule against the current government as soon as it begins to weaken so as to preserve their position under a future regime. Judicial decisions in such circumstances provide information to the opposition about the imminence of decline, and thus can help to facilitate anti-regime coordination.

In very rare cases, then, courts may make crucial decisions that turn out to be focal points for broader oppositional coalitions to mobilize. That is, court decisions can become the crucial moment at which regime change coalesces. But court decisions are neither necessary nor sufficient for democratic transition to occur. And a historical review suggests such moments do not often occur.

Downstream guarantors

A more common scenario occurs when the authoritarian regime seeks to withdraw from active involvement in politics rather than maintain power indefinitely. This may be typical of some coup-makers, or a regime which relied on a short-term emergency to justify repressive policies. It may also be a rational decision once a regime realizes it cannot survive. In such cases, the autocrat faces the problem of guaranteeing that his or her core policies will not be overturned after a transition back to majoritarian rule. The autocrat may also be concerned with the property and liberty of his supporters, who are likely threatened by a change in power.

In this type of situation, the autocrat may seek to empower courts to act as downstream guarantors of the bargain for exit, providing policy security after the dictator goes. Hirschl (2004), writing in the context of industrial democracies, calls this function "hegemonic preservation" in which a declining powerful group uses courts to secure its policies and limit downstream actors. My version of this argument (Ginsburg 2003) focuses on minorities in general (which can include departing autocrats) and suggests that courts provide political insurance to prevent policy reversal and minimize the risks of the future. This should not strictly speaking be seen as an anti-democratic function – sometimes it can be necessary to induce the autocrat to give up power in the first place. But the court plays a basically conservative role of preserving a bargain against future disruption.

This scenario is only likely for certain kinds of transitions, typically gradual ones in which the autocrat is able to write the rules of the game and negotiate the terms of exit. Perhaps the paradigm example is modern-day South Africa, in which the National Party negotiated an extensive set of judicially enforceable rights as a condition of turning over power to majoritarian institutions. Some accounts of Chile's negotiated transition under Pinochet also appear to fit this account (but see further discussion below). The strategy of using courts to entrench policies is effective in a wide variety of settings, but there is also no guarantee that it will be fully effective, particularly if courts are tainted as instruments of the earlier regime. The classic account of French judicial politics traces fear of *government du juges* back to the French Revolution, in which the Magistrates served as a reactionary force and thus could not guarantee even their own heads. One can imagine, however, an alternative French history in which the judges induced the king to step down through guarantees that his property would remain intact. Whether the particular story here is credible or not, the basic point is that judges can serve democracy by upholding the rights of the former dictators, because such institutional guarantees can induce resignation without revolution.

Downstream democratic consolidators

In other times and places, courts may serve as instruments of the newly democratic regime, becoming central to the process *after* the crucial moment occurs. In these scenarios, the change from autocracy to democracy involves a removal of constraints on the legal system, or in some cases affirmative empowerment of legal actors. In these instances, the courts can become important sites of contestation between elements of the old regime and new, devices for facilitating transitional justice, allies of the new order, or systematic dismantlers of the legal infrastructure of the old regime. For example, in post-World War II Italy, the transition from fascism was ambiguous, in that the Italian position was that they had won the war and hence there was no push for a complete institutional overhaul. This left many of the old fascist statutes on the books (Volcansek 1994). It became the task of the Constitutional Court to work through challenges to these statutes one at a time, cleaning the legal system of its fascist legacy. The Court's role was essentially one of building up its own power through cleaning up the legacies of authoritarian rule. But the timing was one of follower rather than leader in democratization.

To state the matter this way is not to assert that judges and law are unimportant to transition. On the contrary, courts become crucial to structuring an environment of open political competition, free exchange of ideas and limited government. The legal system plays an essential role. It is only to point out that in most instances, legal actors are not at the very center of the transition decision, but rather are involved in the phase of consolidation.

Often (though not in the Italian case, since the Court was a new institution) this scenario results from a reinvention of the judicial role post-democratization. Formerly quiescent institutions can become more powerful and capable should they choose to do so, and skillful judges can adjust to the new era. Furthermore, as judicial personnel change, they are likely to become more daring and to serve as the expression of a new era.[4]

One area in which one sees particularly intense judicial involvement is criminal procedure, which constitutes the legal apparatus of social control. Democracies and dictatorships differ in their use of legal tools in this regard.

Typically, judges have a much greater role in democracies than they do in dictatorships, in which prosecutors and police operate with less judicial scrutiny. Judges asserting the need for greater judicial oversight of criminal procedure are at once advancing their institutional self-interest while ensuring conformity of the new regime with international standards.

Another zone of frequent judicial activity in new democracies involves administrative law. In many authoritarian regimes, administrative law is relatively underdeveloped as a discipline on bureaucratic discretion. Because dictators have lots of other tools for controlling bureaucrats, they do not always need to rely on courts to do so. A typical configuration involves loosely drafted statutes, under which bureaucrats exercise a good deal of discretion, subject to political rather than legal oversight. When new democratic governments take over, they are frequently stuck with the bureaucrats appointed by the authoritarian regime, and may lack sufficient personnel with technical expertise capable of running the government. In such circumstances, it is imperative to find ways to control bureaucrats, and courts can play a useful role in this regard. We often see increased use of "delegation" doctrines, requiring a tight linkage between legislative command and bureaucratic action, in the early years of new democracy (see Ginsburg 2003: chs 5 and 7).

Yet another "consolidation" function, quite particular to new democracies, involves dealing with the legacy of the past. Where the old forces are not totally defeated but retain a powerful position in politics, demands for transitional justice are likely to be suppressed (and appropriately so, since pushing too hard can undo the democratic turn). On the other hand, if the old forces are defeated, there will be significant demands for coming to terms with the past, and this frequently, though not always, involves the legal system.

There is a vast literature on lustration, judicial rehabilitation, truth commissions, and retroactive justice. When courts and the legal process are involved, complex technical issues arise involving, *inter alia*, the proscription on *ex post facto* law, statutes of limitations, and command responsibility. Frequently the rule-of-law, as classically defined, suffers when courts ignore legal formalities to hold accountable elements from the past regime. Nevertheless, from a political rather than formalist perspective, such a role can be helpful in furthering democratic consolidation and legitimation of the new regime in the eyes of the victims of the past one.

Judicial irrelevance

A fourth possibility can also be observed. This is where the courts, for whatever reason, remain on the sidelines without either supporting or hindering democratization. Hilbink's (2007a) account of Chilean judges during and after the Pinochet dictatorship seems to fit this story. The courts in Chile had internalized an ideology of "apoliticism" along with a hierarchical, self-reproducing institutional structure that rendered judges unequipped and disinclined to take stands in defense of liberal democratic principles before, during, and after the authoritarian interlude. Nor have courts been particularly effective enforcers of the policies put in place at the end of the Pinochet regime, failing to strike infringements on property rights as well (Couso 2003). This seems to be a case where the courts were agents neither of the past nor the future. To be sure, after two decades they began to play a role in transitional justice, indicting General Pinochet before his death in 2006, but overall, the story seems to be one of general irrelevance.

Summary

We have identified four different roles that courts can play in democratic transition. Sometimes they serve as agents of the past, policing a transition or even preserving policies of the authoritarian regime. Sometimes they act as agents of the future, helping to transform the political process and encouraging the consolidation of democracy. In some rare instances, courts themselves trigger the democratization process itself, encouraging mobilization and tipping the regime into transformation. Finally, courts can be simply marginal players who neither facilitate nor hinder a transition to democracy.

The legacy of the authoritarian period is likely to shape the role courts play in any particular situation, and to shape the politics of judicial involvement. It is also important to note that law plays multiple roles in any given transition. Courts may be called on to act as downstream guarantors in some areas – such as protecting an economic bargain, or enforcing immunities from prosecution granted to members of the old regime – while acting as consolidators in other areas, such as dismantling the apparatus of repression. Indeed, it is possible that playing a range of roles can maximize the institutional power of courts, since there will be a wide range of social forces with a stake in the courts as viable institutions, even if they are not happy with every decision the courts make.

The next section uses this framework to understand particular political scenarios of democratic transition in several prominent cases. The spirit of the inquiry is exploratory, and I expect that a more in-depth treatment of the cases will help to refine the framework.

Case studies of courts and democratic transition

South Africa: downstream guarantor

An example of courts serving as *downstream guarantor* comes from South Africa under the African National Congress (ANC). As Hirschl argues, there was a "near-miraculous conversion to constitutionalism and judicial review among South Africa's white political and business elites during the late 1980s and early 1990s, when it became clear that the days of apartheid were numbered and an ANC-controlled government became inevitable" (2005: 269). For much of South Africa's history, the white elites had opposed the creation of judicially created bills of rights. But when it became clear that the regime could not be maintained by repression, the regime shifted views and drafted its own version of a bill of rights. This was designed not only to preserve the rights of prospective minority in the face of near certain electoral loss (Ginsburg 2003) but also, crucially, to preserve the economic leverage of the elite. At the time of transition, the white minority had average incomes of eight times the black majority, and four conglomerates controlled 95 percent of productive capital (Hirschl 2000: 136). There would be inevitable pressures for redistribution after the new majority took over; drafting a new constitution securing property rights, and establishing a court to monitor violations, was a way of entrenching the power and wealth of the old elite (as well as ensuring credibility for the new ANC majority).

The new Constitutional Court oversaw the transition, even demanding changes in the final draft constitution to meet the requirements of the Interim Constitution. To be sure, the Constitutional Court has played many other roles in democratic transition (Klug 2000), helping to define the new order and to incorporate global human rights discourse into the country. In this sense, it has also been a vehicle of democratic consolidation. But it would arguably not have been created without its ability to serve as a downstream guarantor of the bargain ending apartheid. The core elements of this bargain – democratic rule in exchange for security of property rights and limited transitional justice – have remained intact against great political pressure, and the country's courts have been part of the reason. This has led to criticisms, to be sure, but all in all has garnered respect for the Court.

Ukraine: upstream trigger

Ukraine presents an environment in which the structure of the post-Soviet regime – the moderate dictatorship of Leonid Kuchma – allowed some space for institutionalization of courts and the development of some levels of judicial independence. There was significant institutional investment in the court system by European and American actors, even though Kuchma's corrupt regime embodied "competitive authoritarianism."

A dramatic moment in which courts appeared to play a triggering role occurred during the "Orange Revolution" of 2004–5. Kuchma had sought to use his position to promote the candidacy of his chosen successor, Viktor Yanukovych. Using a variety of methods, including seeking to poison the opposition candidate, Viktor Yushchenko, the government rigged the results of a run-off election in November 2004. Yushchenko's supporters refused to accept the results, and he held a symbolic inauguration. He also gathered a set of resolutions from local governments promising support. His supporters initiated widespread protests and demonstrations, as well as a court case seeking to annul the election results. In addition, the parliament voted no confidence in Yanukovych, who was serving as prime minister. Dramatically, on 3 December 2004, the Supreme Court resolved the immediate political deadlock when it ordered a re-vote for the presidential election later that month. The second election, held under intense international scrutiny, was handily won by Yushchenko, and the court dismissed Yanukovych's various legal challenges. The court was thus at the center of forcing a change in power, providing the capstone to a broad movement and turning back continued dictatorship.

The decision served as a trigger because of its temporal proximity to broader efforts at social mobilization. In this sense it differed from the decision of Chile's constitutional tribunal discussed above. The Ukrainian decision emboldened the opposition and buried the regime. Like the Chilean decision, though, the court did not pick the leader directly, but was involved in structuring political competition to ensure that the choice was made in a transparent manner, providing an opportunity for the opposition forces to exploit. This illustrates, again, one of the themes of how courts can assist with democratization: holding the regime to its nominal promises and providing fora for political forces to pursue their agendas.

Finally, note that the legacy of the authoritarian regime was apparent there. Had the post-Soviet regime gone a different route – say the totalitarian approach taken in Turkmenistan, for example – there is virtually no chance that democratization could have played out as it has. By structuring itself as a "competitive authoritarian" regime with the outer trappings of democracy, Kuchma's Ukraine allowed the opposition organizational openings that were eventually exploited.

Pakistan: trigger or guarantor?

Over the past two years, a fascinating drama involving the courts has taken place in Pakistan, leading ultimately to the fall of the regime of General Pervez Musharaf (Ghias 2008). In March of 2007, Musharaf attempted to suspend the Chief Justice of the Supreme Court, Iftikhar Mohammad Chaudhry, for "abuse of power and nepotism." Chaudhry had himself been appointed by Musharaf, but had not always been compliant with the General's policies. Some analysts tied the decision to Chaudhry's resistance to the establishment of military rule in the restive Northwest Frontier Province. The timing was also related to a series of cases in which Musharaf's rule was challenged in courts. Pakistan's courts have a long history of dealing with the legality of exceptional rule, generally being supportive but also trying to limit the temporal length of states of emergency (Mahmud 1993; Newberg 1995; Ghias 2008).

Chaudhry responded by resisting the attack and framing it as directed against the judiciary as a whole (Sanchez Urribarri 2007). The attack prompted broad demonstrations from the bar, which took to the streets to protest the decision and was joined by a broad coalition of supporters of the civilian political parties. The legal controversy ended in the courts, and featured the remarkable spectacle of the Supreme Court reinstating Chaudhry. Pressure continued to build on Musharaf's regime, and he was forced to allow former Prime Minister Benazir Bhutto to return to the country through a combination of judicial decision and pressure from his most important ally, the United States. The Supreme Court found that Ms Bhutto and former prime minister Nawaz Sharif had, as citizens, an inalienable right to return to the country. Sharif, however, who had been in exile in Saudi Arabia after fleeing corruption charges, was not initially permitted to re-enter the country (*Economist* 2007).

In late September, however, the Court surprised observers by holding that Musharaf himself could run for office, by a vote of six to three. This decision prompted protests from the bar association. Without getting into the legal merits of the decision, the effect was certainly to signal to Musharaf that the court was not inexorably opposed to him. The decision seemed to again confirm that the role of the court was *not* to pick winners and losers, but to structure, to the extent possible, a fair contest for leadership of the country, and to serve as the final arbiter. Musharaf's candidacy was again challenged before the courts.

On 3 November 2007, before the Supreme Court could rule, Musharaf declared a state of emergency, and arrested thousands of activists, lawyers, and political party workers. Taking a page from his American counterparts, he decried judicial activism and terrorism in the same breath. Bhutto and other political leaders were put under house arrest; a Provisional Constitutional Order (PCO) was issued prohibiting any court issuing an order against the president, prime minister, or any person exercising powers under their authority. The PCO further put the Constitution in abeyance, saying that the country would be governed "as nearly as may be by the Constitution" (Provisional Constitutional Order No. 1 (2007) Art. 2.1, Pakistan 2007). Only the five Supreme Court justices who took an oath to uphold the PCO would be allowed to remain; the other 12 were placed under house arrest, along with a number of Provincial High Court justices. Chaudhry called for resistance, from his house arrest.

On 12 November, the new Supreme Court announced that it would hear two petitions related to challenges to the PCO, including a call for immediate release of the detained lawyers and justices. Deposed justices asserted that any decision upholding the PCO would be unconstitutional. Lawyers further asserted that, despite Musharaf's assertion that it was only a state of emergency, in fact the Constitution has been suspended and martial law effected.

Musharaf won the battle, but lost the war. Under intense American pressure, Musharaf gave up his military post in accordance with constitutional requirements, and his political party was subsequently crushed in elections held shortly after Bhutto's assassination in late December 2007. The civilian political parties then, after some months, decided to reinstate the deposed judges in May 2008. This was not uncontroversial, as the leading political party, Bhutto's Pakistan People's Party, continues to resist implementing the reinstatement (as some of the figures in the judiciary had aggressively prosecuted corruption cases against party leaders).

In short, Pakistan appears to be a case of judges acting as a trigger for a return to democracy. The judges became a focal point for popular protest, which led to pressure on the regime. Ultimately, enforcement of Pakistan's constitutional order and the return to democracy required significant pressure from an external actor, but the judiciary was, in the mid-term, able to outwit the general, and return to power in a democratic era.

Taiwan and Korea: downstream consolidators

The role of downstream consolidator, which I believe to be most common of the various roles identified here, is illustrated by the cases of Taiwan and Korea (Ginsburg 2003: chs 5 and 7). In both countries, the authoritarian regimes empowered courts to a very limited degree, and exercised political constraint over them. Park Chung Hee's Yushin Republic involved downgrading of the Supreme Court after it had decided an important case against the regime. The Kuomintang in Taiwan put severe limitations on the jurisdiction of the Grand Justices in the 1950s. As time went on, however, the regimes did allow a bit more space for law even during the authoritarian period. In particular they used courts as ways of legitimating their rule.

In my view, *domestic* legitimation through legal mechanisms was minimal. The Chiangs and Park provided strongman rule, bound up in their charismatic authority, and sometimes drawing self consciously on Confucian notions of rule by the wise. These were, domestically, regimes that relied on the rule of man rather than rule-of-law for legitimation. The more important audience for legitimation was *international*. As cold war clients locked in existential struggles with communist adversaries who claimed to be the true representatives of the nation, Korea and Taiwan had relatively little room to maneuver ideologically. The regime's adoption of the label "Free China" meant that there had to be a distinction with unfree China. A nominally independent legal system of fairly genuine quality made a lot of sense from this perspective, and was designed to play as much back in Washington as in Seoul or Taipei.

Even though courts provided some outlet for contesting regime policies during the authoritarian period, they never acted as triggers. For the most part, the courts in these countries served as what I have called downstream consolidators rather than upstream triggers of democracy. The crucial decisions to embark on democratization were not taken in courtrooms. Rather, they were taken in the backroom discussions in 1987 in Seoul and 1985 in Taipei. Only once the direction of democratization was absolutely clear did the courts begin to act, around 1989 in both cases.

In Taiwan, much attention has been given to a dramatic decision in the democratization process, Interpretation No. 261 of the Council of Grand

Justices. In this case, the Council was called on to determine whether the "Old Thieves" (legislators who had been elected on mainland China some forty years previously) could be forced to retire in 1990. This was certainly a watershed moment, but as I explore at length in *Judicial Review in New Democracies* (2003), the decision cannot be seen as having been *independently* determined by judges. Rather the Council served as part of Lee Teng-hui's faction with the KMT, helping reform to proceed over the objections of an intra-party obstacle. Judges were not the triggers.

Once democratization occurred, however, the courts played an absolutely crucial role (see generally Ginsburg 2003). In Taipei, the Council of Grand Justices systematically removed many of the barriers to participation set up by the KMT, accelerating after the Council became majority Taiwan-born in 1994. The Court began a pattern of deciding cases against administrative agencies, using a non-delegation doctrine to require tighter links between a reinvigorated political process and administrative action. Leninist institutions that had been used to ensure ideological conformity of teachers and the media were cast aside as unconstitutional. The Council also instituted a total reform of criminal procedure, ensuring that police and prosecutors were henceforth under greater judicial scrutiny.

In Korea, the courts served as fora for the trials of former strongmen Chun Doo Hwan and Roh Tae-woo, and a number of other "transitional justice" cases. The courts also modified the National Security Act, which had been used to jail regime opponents. This was a bold step in a state that remains technically at war with its northern neighbor. Finally, the courts oversaw a complete reform of criminal procedure. Courts thus played an important role as downstream democratizers.

Linking legacy and role

We now seek to bring together the two parts of this chapter. Is there a link between the role of courts in the *ancien regime* and the role it plays in democratization?

The implicit argument laid out above is that some legacy of independence heightens the possibility that courts can play a role as a guarantor, consolidator, or trigger, rather than simply sit on the sidelines. But which role? I do not here seek to articulate a complete theory, and my sense is that individual trajectories will be determined in large part through the choices of judges themselves. That is, there is a significant role for judicial agency in accounting for variation across cases.

Nevertheless, I can offer some speculative thoughts. My sense is that the greater the role of courts in the authoritarian regime, the more likely they are to serve as guarantors or triggers. In apartheid South Africa, for example, the courts operated with a long tradition of strict positivism, applying the law neutrally notwithstanding its immoral character (Dyzenhaus 1991).[5] This stance no doubt served the institutional interest of the judiciary, and also made it a more trustworthy body to play the role of downstream guarantor. Weak courts will be less likely to serve as credible guarantors of policies against downstream reversals.

On the other hand, a set of courts that is empowered is also more able to play the role of upstream trigger for the democratization process. Courts that are perceived as being independent are more likely to generate compliance with anti-regime decisions. They also might be more willing to do so, as they are less likely to be controlled by elements of the regime. Furthermore, in instances when regime change is frequent (as in Helmke's analysis of Argentina) the court may be eager to do so to maximize their power in the next iteration of a repeated game.

Perhaps the most common configuration, however, is that of courts serving as downstream consolidators. This role requires no great courage on the part of judges. Rather. it seems to call only for an adjustment of their institutional role to fit a new political reality, in which the courts are serving a new democratic master instead of the old authoritarian one. We have many examples of courts set up to achieve one task adjusting to accomplish another as the political environment changes. To be sure, role transformation is sometimes difficult, and personnel can either retard or facilitate it. But the political perspective on judicial power suggests that such role transformation is necessary. As "one government agency among many" (Shapiro 1964: 15) courts need to ensure that their overall position in the political system is one that is relevant to the current environment.

There are numerous other variables that might contribute to judges' decisions to play one role or another in the democratization process. The type of democratic transition certainly makes a difference. The role of guarantor implies a deal to guarantee, and so we should expect that courts will more frequently play this role in pacted transitions as opposed to more ruptured transitions.

Another factor may be the extent to which the court seeks legitimacy through mass as opposed to elite coalitions. All courts need institutional allies, be they other government agencies, civil society, or political parties. The role of guarantor suggests courts working on behalf of a specific set of elites associated with the moment of transition. The role of consolidator, in contrast, admits of a broader range of potential allies, in civil society, mass organizations, and elite groups. Indeed, simply by playing a fluid role in facilitating the claims of different groups at different times, courts can encourage civil society. The availability of judicial remedies can also transform the strategies of interest groups in ways that contribute to both democratic consolidation and judicial power. For example, Javier Couso (2006) traces the emergence of a rights-oriented strategy among certain left-oriented groups in Latin America that would have earlier relied on mass action to advance their claims. Such mass-oriented coalitions are not served by courts who have taken on the role of guarantor, a point illustrated by many of the critics of the South African

Constitutional Court for its alleged failure to more aggressively enforce social and economic rights (Dugard and Roix 2006).

Conclusion

This chapter has provided a framework for thinking about the political role of courts and law in democratization. As the first part of this chapter showed, law should not be viewed exclusively as a product of democracy, and we have many examples of relatively empowered court systems even in authoritarian regimes. Such courts find themselves in myriad relationships with demands for democracy, often dictated by their position within the authoritarian setting.

Once the demands for liberalization arise, courts find themselves in one of four positions: they can seek to galvanize the demands and trigger a democratic transition; they can serve to ensure order in the transition process and guarantee the interests of declining hegemons; they can help to play a role in transforming the legal system to one that underpins the new democratic order, as consolidators; or they can seek to sit on the sidelines. The greater the role of law and courts in the previous regime, the more likely courts are to be called on to serve as downstream guarantors, and the more able they are to serve as upstream triggers. But the much more common role for courts is to serve as second-order actors in democratization, in which they facilitate democratic consolidation.

Which role they play, and at what times, depends ultimately on the decisions of individual judges, a variable about which we still have little systematic knowledge.

Notes

1 Many thanks to Lee Cabatingan, T.J. Cheng, Javier Couso, and Michael Dowdle for comments.

2 A recent example is the endgame regime of Robert Mugabe in Zimbabwe, which resorted to physical intimidation to undermine what was once one of Africa's best judiciaries. See Widner 2008.

3 Indeed, virtually the entire leadership of the current Democratic Progressive Party was involved as defendants or attorneys in those trials, including former president Chen, former vice president Lu, and former premiers Su and Frank Hsieh.

4 It is not surprising that the South African negotiations called on the creation of a *new* constitutional court, rather than relying on institutions affiliated with apartheid. But in general, new elites lack the breadth and depth of personnel to staff a full judiciary after transition, so that of necessity low-level judicial staff may remain who have been appointed by the previous regime. This can have significant downstream effects at low levels of policy conflict, in which judges can hamper the new regime.

5 This mattered during the authoritarian period, as certain crucial cases against ANC leaders ended in imprisonment rather than crude death sentences at the hands of state security personnel. This allowed them to survive to a democratic era.

Chapter 9

Principled principals in the founding moments of the rule-of-law[1]

Margaret Levi and Brad Epperly

Institutionally, the rule-of-law consists of the laws that protect personal security and private property and the means for monitoring and enforcing obedience with those laws. When coercion is the only or even primary means to achieve compliance, laws may exist but not the rule-of-law. The rule-of-law requires legitimacy, at least if legitimacy means reasoned deference to authority (Tyler 2006; Levi *et al.* forthcoming). When legitimacy exists, rule-of-law can create a virtuous circle of increasing levels of voluntary compliance (Levi and Sacks 2007). The expectation that others, including government officials and elites, should obey the law, followed by the observation that they are indeed obeying the law, increases the willingness of the populous to comply. Wide-scale compliance with the law then enhances the ability of government to provide law and other public goods that rule-of-law facilitates. Rule-of-law institutions are only effective to the extent that the general public believes in the value of being law-abiding and that the powerful of the society believe they, too, are subject to the law. If officeholders and the privileged act as if they are above the law, the rule-of-law becomes fragile or non-existent. And the virtuous circle is ruptured.

There is good reason to believe that rule-of-law enhances the processes of both democratization and economic development, as other research and other chapter in this volume attest. Social scientists and policymakers are fairly confident that the rule-of-law is essential to effective state building but are considerably less certain about how to bring it about (*Economist* 2008). We suggest there are three factors that need to come together for the establishment of rule-of-law and its maintenance.

The first is the right kind of leadership. Leaders able to establish rule-of-law institutions are those capable of obtaining the cooperation of elites and administrators who might prefer to free ride through defection, opposition, or theft. They must also be able to convince state agents and members of the polity that they are in a situation where corruption is unacceptable and laws likely to be upheld. Key to such leadership is the development of an organizational culture based upon leaders' credible commitments to principles that they will uphold even in unforeseen contingencies and even when it is against their personal interest to do so.

The second requirement, largely dependent on the first, is the existence of a bureaucracy that is itself law-abiding, that implements the laws of the state in a way that is both relatively honest and procedurally just. This is where the organizational culture established by leadership plays a significant role. Once the appropriate organizational culture is in place, the rule of law possible. It is still, however, fragile. When the first mover dies, is replaced, or experiences a motivational change, the rule of law may fall apart. To establish the rule-of-law as a stable equilibrium requires the establishment of an incentive structure that encourages enough of the state agents to uphold the law and, in addition, to report and punish those who break it. Only then will citizens have good reasons to believe that they are in a state of the world where the rule of law exists, and only then will they calculate that it makes sense to comply and ensure that others do.

The third requirement is the existence of citizen beliefs that they should be subject to the law and do their best to uphold it. Levi models popular compliance with government demands as a problem of quasi-voluntary compliance (Levi 1988, 1997). Compliance with and obedience to the law is contingent upon citizen (or subject) perceptions that government is meeting its obligations to them, has the capacity to locate and punish free riders, and is acting according to prevalent standards of fairness and procedural justice. To the extent citizens (or subjects) believe their government is trustworthy, fair, and capable of delivering on its promises, the more voluntary compliance it is likely to elicit. Coercion is always a requirement and a backdrop to quasi-voluntary compliance, providing assurances that lawbreakers will be compelled to obey or be punished. But an effective rule of law relies on consent as much or more than coercion.

Quasi-voluntary compliance is essential for maintaining the rule of law, but it is not the first step in the process of building an effective rule-of-law regime. The basis for quasi-voluntary compliance has to be constructed. The emergence of the rule of law requires the right set of institutions, yes, but it also entails beliefs – among leaders, bureaucrats, and citizens – that the rule-of-law exists, will continue to exist, and is of sufficient benefit to deserve their compliance, consent, and active support.

Achieving legitimacy and with it a relatively high degree of voluntary compliance with the law is neither simple to achieve in the first place nor easy to sustain over time. Without shared consensus on what the basic outlines of what the law should be, competing conceptions of law undermine the rule-of-law even in what appear to be stable societies. As groups previously excluded from or even harmed by the laws gain power, they may unsettle the status quo, particularly if the legal changes require major restructuring of valued privileges. Whether such rifts tear a society apart depends partially on whether the laws can easily be reformed to become universally fair and nondiscriminatory and if a generalized belief exists that the rule of law is worth having and preserving. Both of these beliefs often have their source in the founding moments of a society, during the process of constitution-making, institutional design, and articulation of national principals through laws and nation-building rituals.

Suffice to say, important structural and institutional factors must inform a complete analysis. Our emphasis here, however, is on those founding – and refounding – moments when the requisite factors exist that make possible the design and maintenance of the rule of law. Well-designed institutions are necessary but not sufficient. The rule of law also requires leaders who can credibly commit to self-constraint, agents who can be trusted to abide by the law as well as enforce it, and reasons for most of the population, both the powerful elites and the general mass, to believe they will benefit from the existence of the rule-of-law.

Once established, the rule of law can become a self-enforcing equilibrium in which social actors are able and willing to defend against transgressions of their rights by the state (Weingast 1997). This is a Madisonian model in which it is necessary to build in protections against the knaves but in which most people prefer to maintain the rule-of-law if possible. No one, save for some few outliers, desires to deviate from the equilibrium. A situation in which the state is rife with corruption, favoritism, and other activities anathema to the rule-of-law will be one in which few have any incentive to act in a manner supportive of its development. This lawbreaking equilibrium is one in which cooperation and compliance produce sucker payments. Both equilibria are stable, and the critical issue is how to transform a lawbreaking into a rule-of-law equilibrium.

The conception of law as equilibrium captures a significant but static reality. It fails to sufficiently credit the efforts put into the reproduction and maintenance of the rule of law. Yet, once established, an effective rule of law should produce the incentives for relevant actors to continue to uphold it. However, as definitions of rights change, and as new actors become part of the polity, reproduction becomes both more problematic and more important.

We know something about what maintains the rule-of-law once it is in place, albeit not enough. We know far less about how to create it initially, but in countries throughout the world that is the pressing question. We are increasingly learning that citizens will give their voluntary compliance to government if government is stable, relatively effective in providing social welfare, and relatively fair and procedurally just (Levi *et al.* forthcoming; Levi 1997; Tyler 1990). What we know considerably less about is how to produce such governments in the first place (Levi 2006).

We model this process in five stages (see Figure 9.1). At time 1 a leader (or leadership cadre) appears who has won a war, led a revolution, or otherwise successfully established a basis for governing the society and, potentially, reforming its institutions. In game theoretic language, nature moves to provide the leader, but nature here is historical contingency. If this leader possesses a principled commitment to developing the rule-of-law – for whatever reason, be it normative or strategic – and to making herself subject to it, then the rule-of-

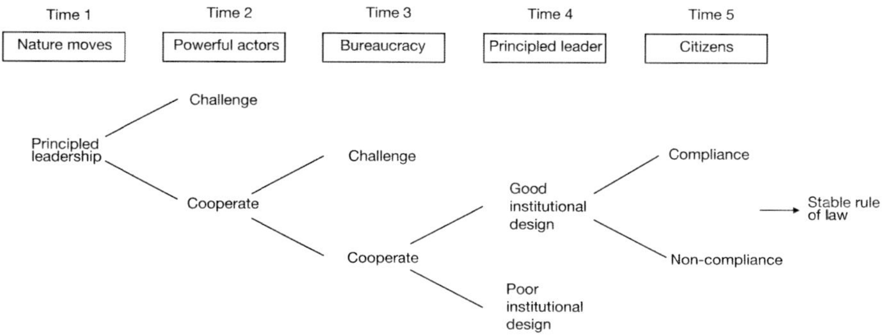

Figure 9.1 A model of the process of establishing the rule of law, given a principled first mover.

law stands some chance of developing. Unprincipled leaders or leaders with the wrong kinds of principles (i.e. those with ideologies that discount the importance of the rule of law) abound; those with the right principles are far scarcer. However, for discussion of the rule of law, principled leaders of the right sort are the ones that matter. We know from history that such people exist and can be used as models for other leaders trying to decide the path to take.

At time 2, the principled leader faces powerful elites who choose to cooperate with the leader's efforts to establish the rule of law – or not. If not, the game is over (although, in fact, the leader and constituents may continue to interact in an effort to realize cooperation). The first task of the leader is to obtain the cooperation of elite societal actors, those with significant relative bargaining power based in wealth, armies, or administrative resources (Levi 1988; Greif 2007). Then the role of those who staff the state and implement her policies and procedures becomes critical. At time 3 of a founding moment, a leader attempting reform faces the state bureaucracy, and, if able to obtain their cooperation, is able to move forward with desired policies.[2]

The defining moment, then, is when the leadership achieves sufficient cooperation to engage in institutional design for the future. At time 4, the leader, with the cooperation of powerful elite allies and the bureaucracy, chooses an institutional design. If the design involves *credible constraints on both the leader and on others with power*, the rule-of-law becomes possible. The combination of the institutional design, principled leadership, and appropriately functioning bureaucracy should, at time 5, produce legitimating beliefs and, therefore, compliance among the population served by the state. A rule-of-law equilibrium results. If the design is poor or poorly implemented, the rule of law is unlikely or, at best, exceedingly fragile. No equilibrium obtains unless the institutions are redesigned to constrain powerful societal actors and government officials.

Many analyses of the emergence of the rule-of-law start from the point at which society is already in one or another equilibrium state. The key actors have coordinated or failed to. This analysis starts with the foundational moments for institutional redesign. It begins to theorize rather than simply assume the leadership type and the interaction of leaders with powerful others. It emphasizes the importance of constraining all those who could undermine the rule-of-law, including societal actors, government leadership, and the officials who staff government. It makes clear where external agencies can intervene and make a difference, for better or worse. They can do more than help write the constitution. They may train or even install leadership. Their influence may also be felt at times 2 and 3 when those in society are deciding whether to cooperate with leadership; external agents may provide resources that will affect the incentives of those considering defection.

Founding and refounding moments

The founding moments of states, indeed of any organization, are critical to the beliefs and culture that will develop over time. Culture here refers not to the ethnographic, religious, racial, or ideological features of a society – although they can play a role. It refers to the defining norms and consensual values that influence the way members of the organization interact with each other. It refers to both the horizontal relationships among citizens and the vertical relationships with those who govern. It is culture in the sense David Kreps used the term in his seminal discussion of "corporate culture" (Kreps 1990): a set of principles that constitute the identity of the organization and establish the rules to guide the behavior of its members. In his model, and in ours, leadership is key.

This is not the moment to rehearse the debate about the relative influence of religion, geography, natural endowments, what the colonizing power did and when, or other structural features of a society that can influence the nature of its laws and the inclination of its people to support them.[3] While important, these large structural factors are the backdrop to the founding moments of institutions and constitutions.

Founding moments self-evidently occur at the birth of states and other organizations. More frequent, however, are those moments in which organizations rebuild themselves and thus experience renewed founding moments. Firms often do this. So do voluntary organizations.[4] Much can be learned from the behavior of such organizations, and much of what follows draws on arguments and findings concerning these founding or, more accurately, refounding moments, particularly in those instances when leaders design new – or adapt existing – institutions that constrain themselves as well as constituents and officials.[5]

Foundational moments of the rule-of-law are not those moments from which polities and institutions emerge from a Hobbesian state of nature. The Hobbesian moment is past; authority and enforcement of that authority's decrees exist at least in principle albeit they may have broken down. What concerns us is when a leader is able, for whatever reason, to affect change in the institutional makeup of government and society. Few, if any, truly foundational moments for institutions or society exist. Prior institutions, both formal and informal, constrain ever radical breaks from the past (as even a cursory glance at the histories of post-revolution states reveals).

Among states, few examples exist of a national government and organizational culture arising totally *de novo*: the United States is an exception, not the rule. And even the US possessed a vast number of institutions, formal and informal, at its birth. Furthermore, it had a wholly redefining moment as a consequence of the Civil War, as well as numerous redefining moments as women and African-Americans gained the suffrage and as the conception of protected civil rights changed. Older states went through major transformations: France as a result of its Revolution; Britain in the aftermath of centuries of traumatic wars, internal and external; Germany and Japan following World War II. India's founding moments came with its independence from Britain and the legacy of institutions and values from which the Indian constitution-makers could pick and choose while adding something of their own. South Africa very clearly had to revise and then recommit to what it meant by the rule-of-law in the process of abolishing Apartheid. At this very moment, Nepal is struggling with what it will become with the abolition of the monarchy and the election of the former Maoists to power, while Pakistan tries yet one more time to establish a constitutional basis for governance and the rule-of-law. Throughout the world countries are experiencing moments that could, in retrospect, be foundational.

They are also struggling to incorporate multiple bases for law and authority. Malaysia, Singapore, and many Islamic countries are searching for ways to combine what they value from the colonial legacy with sharia and other forms of both codified and customary practice (Hussin 2007). Countries throughout Africa, both sub-Saharan and northern, are still in conflict over the standing of traditional practices, such as female circumcision. The battle over headscarves is a battle over what the rule-of-law means in countries with histories as different as Turkey and France. Sweden, Denmark, and the Netherlands must incorporate new laws along with new immigrants.

These conflicts vary in their likelihood of tearing governments apart. At least part of the explanation for variable effects has to do with how the governing constitution emerged as much as with what it contains. Certain features of these foundational – or refoundational – moments appear to be crucial to the emergence and survival of the rule-of-law. Their presence does not ensure a stable equilibrium. Their absence appears to ensure a return to chaos.

Principled leadership

Charismatic leaders, traditional authorities, and strongmen abound, but how often does a Nelson Mandela appear or a cadre of political elites similar to the

Founding Fathers of the US or the constitution-makers of independent India? Motivations that encapsulate the interests of the general public,[6] the possibility of long-term survival, and the capacity for intelligent lawmaking are rare in combination. Does this reduce the probability of locating principled leadership to near zero? It does if moral motivation is essential, but morality is not the issue. The goal is not to locate a new Solon. It is to create an environment in which leaders – whatever the initial source of their authority – find it in their strategic interest to establish a set of operating principles that inform the organizational culture of the society,[7] signaling what the leader will do in a variety of circumstances and how elites, administrators, and the populace should behave. The leader must recognize it as in his interest to establish a reputation as a principled leader who stays true to those principles even in unforeseen circumstances that require actions in violation of their short-term interests.

The source of the principles may be simply strategic, or they may involve evoking meta-preferences for legal processes as the means for leaders to advance their preferences for power or wealth (Sen 1977; Hirschman 1984; Sanchez-Cuenca in progress). For some leaders, ideology and morality are the source of principles. Principles per se are not sufficient, however, only those that encompass commitments to the rule-of-law, of course. Marxist and nationalist credos motivate revolutions but may oppose private property rights or equal protection under the law. Hitler certainly devised an organizational culture based on principles and a reputation for upholding those principles. His regime was full of laws but had no rule-of-law.

Coase (1937) initiated the argument that the nature of firms and other forms of hierarchy involve a contracting problem between a principal (usually an employer) and an agent (worker, staff, or contractor).[8] Much of this literature focuses on how optimal levels of effort (from the principal's perspective) can be elicited from agents under different information structures, levels of risk aversion, and more or less complicated organizational structures. A specialized version of the collective action/public goods problem, generally referred to as the "moral hazard in teams" or team production problem, is instructive of why firm leadership establishes certain kinds of institutional arrangements and why they continue to uphold them. The basic set up is like so:

1 There is a team consisting of N individuals.
2 Each individual can contribute some *effort* to the group project. Effort is costly and each person decides noncooperatively how much effort to supply.
3 Each individual's effort level is *unobservable* and *unverifiable*. This effectively means that it is impossible to write a contract stipulating how much effort each person will supply. A related and usually implicit assumption is that agents cannot be coerced into supplying effort.
4 There is some function that determines what the total team output is, given the cumulative effort. This team output is observable and can be contracted upon.

5 There is a stochastic component to the team production function that causes the productivity of team effort to vary according to some distribution. Agents must choose their level of effort before they learn the true value of the stochastic productivity component. It is therefore impossible to write a contract conditional on the realized value of this random variable. It is possible, however, to write a contract on an ex ante announcement by one of the team members as to the true value of the stochastic parameter.
6 A contract, then, is a series of payments to each individual member. These payments can be made contingent on the team-level outcome and/or the announced value of the stochastic component.
7 The final output of the team efforts must be completely divided up, i.e. the sum of the payments to the team members cannot be more or less than total output. This condition is referred to as the *budget balancing* constraint.

Holmstrom (1982) shows that, where there is a team production problem, there is no Nash equilibrium incentive contract that is both budget balancing and Pareto efficient. The intuition behind this result is that individuals will only contribute to the group project up to the point that their individual marginal gain is equal to their individual marginal cost even if their marginal cost of effort is far lower than the marginal team-level output.

Hermalin (1998, 2007) looks to the role of a leader to improve the situation. What happens if there is some member of the team that can learn the value of this stochastic productivity factor?[9] Clearly this information is valuable to everyone. The problem arises because this agent (referred to as the leader) has an incentive to lie. Hermalin considers two possible avenues the leader can pursue for credibly transmitting her valuable knowledge: "sacrifice" and "leadership by example." In the first, the leader makes a gift to the members out of her pocket. In the second, the leader exerts effort in order to influence others to follow suit. Both, if successful, motivate members to exert themselves on behalf of the organization's project. However, "sacrifice" contributes nothing to the overall level of team production while "leading by example" contributes to and increases it.

The "sacrifice" solution is really just a mechanism design problem: is there a contract that will induce the leader to tell the truth and that makes the leader better off than the situation in which her knowledge is not utilized? Hermalin proves that there is. The gist of the result is that the optimal contract stipulates that in the high-productivity state, the leader distributes some fixed amount to the other team members. This amount is just big enough such that a leader in the low-productivity state has no incentive to copy. This solution relies on the enforceability of this contract and only allows the team to take advantage of the leader's superior knowledge; it does not overcome the team production problem. In this way, the "sacrifice" option is second best.

In the "lead by example" solution, Hermalin allows the leader to expend her effort before the rest of the team decides how much effort to contribute. By doing so, the leader signals to the team whether they are in a high- or low-productivity state based on her effort levels. Since this action is costly, it is credible, and a separating Bayesian equilibrium exists. The "leading by example" outcome is superior to the "sacrifice" option since the leader's action directly contributes to the overall level of team production.

The critical component underlying Hermalin's solutions is the transmission of information within the group, especially when leaders pursue the lead-by-example option. Members must be able to observe the leader's actions at low cost. Through repeat interactions between members and their leaders, leaders can build up reputations for credibility over time (Hermalin 2007). Those who begin their leadership roles already embedded in a network of the organization's members are more likely to have the trust of members at the start (Ganz 2000). Those who make themselves regularly available to membership or make their decisions transparent are more likely to retain that trust.

By institutionalizing constraints on themselves, principled leaders exemplify the behaviors they want of others and provide information as to their type. Ceding final determination of budgets to legislators, constitutional term limits, and establishing an independent judiciary with enforcement capacity are among the institutional arrangements that both delimit the power of leaders and signal their accountability. The willingness of the leadership to bind its own hands and ensure transparency of actions can gain them credibility with both staffs and publics.[10] While the "sacrifice" option may be a second-best solution to the team production problem, in the case of the development of the rule-of-law in states, it may be far from any sort of solution. Beyond the fact that the ability to make side-payments to crucial actors to induce compliance sooner or later reaches a ceiling, it is fundamentally in tension with attempts to establish the rule-of-law; individualized side-payments are antithetical to generalized rules applied universally.

Earlier work on the firm (Barnard 1938) as well as more recent research that builds on Coasian insights emphasize that it is "impossible for managers to realize the full efficiency potential of team production processes through the manipulation of short-term economic incentives alone" (Miller 1992: 198). They must inspire, and they must gain the confidence of those they are trying to motivate. The team production literature makes clear that the critical component is credible information and communication. Information transmission is crucial to the formation and modification of individual beliefs and affects the willingness of the staff to support leaders' policies (Arrow 1974; Levi 1997). Effective communication between the leader and those whose effort he is trying to elicit is critical for persuasion (Lupia and McCubbins 1998).

A demonstrated willingness to suffer for one's principles enables a leader to offer a costly signal of intentions to establish and then be bound by the rule-of-law. George Washington fought a war. Gandhi lived in poverty. Nehru and Mandela went to prison. Suu Kyi lives under house arrest. Others have suffered exile or torture for their cause. It is important to note, however, that a demonstrated commitment to principles does not in any way assure a commitment to the rule-of-law. Hitler spent time in prison, and Lenin lived in exile. Both were committed to their principles, which doubtless aided them in signaling to their agents what precisely their principles were, but those same principles were explicitly antithetical to the rule of law. Equally important to the commitment demonstrated by the Gandhis and Washingtons of history is the fact that, when the founding moment came, they discernibly worked hard to translate their ideals into constitutions, laws, and governance practices. Most subjected themselves to elections and term limits or left office willingly. Their principled action embodied and conveyed the norms they hoped would underpin the governance structures they helped create.

Principled leadership does not necessarily have to be democratic, however. While a thick description of rule-of-law embodies democratic institutions, laws promoting economic development neither depend on nor ensure democracy. It is the thin description that interests us here; the rule of law implies predictability and nondiscriminatory applicability to those considered subject to the rule of law. Perhaps most important is that the leadership and elites are willing to be bound by the laws and made to obey them even when they are not so willing. Singapore offers a contemporary case in point. Its leadership is autocratic, and its violations of democratic rights and processes mean that it falls outside some broad definitions of the rule of law. Nonetheless, it is a country famously governed by rules that are obeyed. Its prosperity and stability are among the consequences.

Nor do all the founders who begin as principled leaders survive with their principles intact. Power does, after all, corrupt. A recent example of such a phenomenon is the presidency of Mikheil Saakashvili in Georgia. Coming into office in 2003 on a wave of popular support during the Rose Revolution, he instituted a number of reforms, including cracking down on corruption in many branches of the civil service, earning Georgia accolades by the World Bank (World Bank 2006). However, when substantial political opposition appeared and protests similar to those led by Saakashvili in 2003 occurred, the principles evaporated, and Saakashvili declared a state of emergency, cracking down on protestors and curtailing media independence. The recent war with Russia over South Ossetia has to a large degree unified the elite and citizens around Saakashvili again, but it remains to be seen whether the longer-term effects will support or undermine the development of the rule-of-law in Georgia. A more extreme example is Robert Mugabe in Zimbabwe, vaunted as a principled leader during the 1980s and by the end of another decade considered one of Africa's worst authoritarians (Kohli 1987: 233–5).

Principled leadership is often grounded in moral and ideological motivation, but it can also have sources in more instrumental stimuli. Membership in a group creates dependencies that lead individuals to conform to the group norm, even coming to believe it over time (Hechter 1987). It also creates networks of obligation and reciprocity in which reputation is key for achievement of further goals (Cook *et al.* 2005). Membership has this effect as much for a privileged elite as for the participants in a commune. The process of winning independence or toppling a previous regime further forges and enforces a common worldview. The founding moment for establishing the rule-of-law then institutionalizes that worldview and its concurrent norms.

A leader can abide by principles and use them as a basis for rule even if that leader is instrumental. That is what Machiavelli advocated in *The Discourses* (Machiavelli 1950) and what Machiavellian has come to mean. Augustus Caesar offers a classical case in point. Hardly a saint and most certainly personally ambitious, the desire to create a dynasty, maintain peace, and nurture economic growth that would make himself, his followers, and his people better off and more loyal led him to encourage the establishment of laws that would govern his officials as well as the people. The aim was to ensure the predictability required for investment and trade.

Augustus initially stayed true to the principles he laid out, but before too long he strayed. Without effective constraints that operate over time, it is not surprising that an Augustus would deviate. Even the principles of the most principled of first movers are susceptible to corrosion, as the previous examples of Saakashvili and Mugabe demonstrate. Many of the famous "principled" leaders mentioned here, successful in developing or deepening the commitment to the rule-of-law in their polities, have come to be viewed as principled in a moral sense, but that is not what is critical for a discussion of principled leadership and the rule-of-law. Whether or not leaders such as Washington or Mandela operated with the best intentions is almost beside the point; the road to statehood may be paved similarly as the road to hell. What is critical is that a leader crafts institutions that constrain substantial deviation from the rules. This could as likely be done for strategic reasons as for ideational. Competition, dependency, and countervailing power are what constrain a leader. They are in part a consequence of institutional arrangements that enhance or delimit ruler power, but they are also determined by the resources available to the ruler and to those with whom she must bargain (Levi 1988). In the founding moments, when institutions, even if they exist, are fragile, who has and who uses their bargaining power can make the difference as to whether the rule-of-law is even a viable option.

The bureaucracy and rule-of-law reforms

Regardless of the level of commitment by principled leaders to establish the rule-of-law, they will have to make it worthwhile for other powerful actors in the society to cooperate. Political and economic elites – through action or inaction – can spur, hamper, or torpedo moves towards the rule-of-law, but critical to creating the rule-of-law is leadership's success of obtaining the cooperation of those whose interests are competitive or conflictual with the leadership's. Many have written on this (Weingast 1997, 2004; Sachs and Pistor

1997; Ginsburg *et al.* 2008). Creating a trustworthy and independent judiciary is also essential (Widner 2001; Helmke 2005; Moustafa 2007b; Guarnieri 2003). Our emphasis here, however, is on those who staff the state (Levi, under review) and whose task it is to implement the law. The influence of the bureaucracy has been inadequately explored, but its impact on reforms can be determinative.

Bureaucrats and officials throughout state administrative agencies can engage in corruption, shirk their mandates, and selectively enforce laws. They have the capability to openly sabotage attempts by a leader or leadership cadre in moving to a rule of law equilibrium. The strategic interaction between leaders and staff has consequences for the preferences of the state leadership with regard to pursuing rule-of-law reforms. Greif (2007) explores this aspect of what he labels administrative power, conceived as "the extent to which the ruler's choices and outcomes are influenced by potential defiance by those with administrative capacity."[11] A leader facing agents with high levels of administrative power may decide reform is hopeless and make no attempt to pursue it. A leader, no matter how principled, who lacks the courage or capacity to transform the bureaucracy, may instead be bowed by it.

Presuming, however, that leadership has pushed ahead, the founding moment provides an opportunity to reestablish the administrative practices of the state. The choice of institutional design and the content of the organizational culture not only ensure the emergence of the rule-of-law but also facilitate its survival over the *longue durée*. The moment of founding provides a strategic opportunity for leadership. Having solved certain problems of establishing a state and the peace that makes state building possible, a ruler has the confidence – however briefly – of the population and can undertake institutional design (or redesign). How she uses this window in which her charisma and potential are high can make all the difference for the possibility of an enduring rule-of-law.

The foundational leadership has to be alert to the bureaucratic question. It cannot simply establish the laws and institutions; it must also provide proper incentives for the staff. This involves leadership transparency and credibility based upon principles that are widely known and demonstrably enacted. Max Weber famously documented the structural conditions for the emergence of different kinds of bureaucratic structures (1968), and Herbert Simon provided an account of the individual decision-making processes within the organization, given the cognitive limits of agents (1947). The emergence of the rule-of-law definitely depends on factors they identified, but the interactions between the founding leadership and their staff is what concerns us here. It is to the models economists have devised to explain the role of leadership in firms that we now turn for guidance.

The level of signaling and the specific types of information exchange needed to demonstrate to those staffing the state that the leadership is committed to the rule-of-law is an area of empirical inquiry that deserves sustained research.

There is reason to believe that what may often be critical is not the level of information sustained over a period of time, but rather the leader signaling her intentions when it matters. George W. Bush's indifference to the rights of the Guantanamo prisoners signaled how little he values rule-of-law under conditions that he arbitrarily determined as pertaining to national security. It also signaled that the Justice Department need not be bound by the rule-of-law as it had previously been defined. The commitments of leaders throughout the world to various forms of transitional justice demonstrated their commitment to be bound to the law as it was emerging as well as the expectation that the bureaucracy would follow its prescriptions. Of course, there is no guarantee that agents will be able to correctly read the intentions signaled by principals, especially if habituated to cheap talk by the leadership of the polity.

Principal-agent problems, beyond those of signaling mentioned above, are at the heart of the difficulties principled leaders face in establishing the rule-of-law. Agency theory clarifies how asymmetric information and divergence of interests between the agent and the principal can affect bureaucratic behavior. If leaders are unable to solve their agency problems and motivate government staff to implement the law and to do so fairly, then the rule-of-law is non-existent. Bureaucratic recalcitrance through underperformance can make it impossible to establish a rule-of-law equilibrium or upset it once established. Whether it is simply by shirking job duties and failing to implement policies, or by the selective enforcement of laws, underperformance has detrimental effects on the diffusion of the new organizational culture the founders are attempting to create. Moreover, bureaucratic failure to implement laws fairly undermines citizen beliefs that the rule-of-law actually exists.

Even for a leader who credibly signals a commitment to the rule-of-law, obtaining the explicit cooperation of the myriad officials and bureaucrats who compose the staff is highly unlikely but, thankfully, unnecessary. If leaders are able to constrain the discretion of staff and prevent them from obstructing reforms, the bureaucrats are effectively "cooperating" with such reforms and unable to meaningfully challenge the establishment of the rule-of-law.

Mechanisms for constraining government officials and bureaucrats are of two general types: vertical accountability; and horizontal control. Elections are the archetypical form of vertical accountability in democratic politics. Retrospective voting provides citizens with the opportunity to "toss the bums out" when state officials are viewed as underperforming or abusing the positions to which they were elected (O'Donnell 2004). Electoral mechanisms function effectively for officials whose positions are contingent on the party or legislators in office, but it has little impact when there is a civil service or other system that insulates bureaucratic jobs from electoral changes. Another form of vertical accountability, similar to what some have called "societal accountability" (Smulovitz 2003), depends on interest group lobbying, grassroots campaigns, and watchdog groups as the monitors. This may be more effective than elections in controlling bureaucratic behavior.

To produce societal accountability principled leadership must foster an environment in which public associations, the media, and nongovernmental organizations are able to function freely, with a minimal number of regulations allowing for bureaucrats (at any level) to interfere with their activities. Contemporary Russia offers an exemplary negative case, where recent changes in the statutes governing nongovernmental organizations have created a situation of ambiguous rules and wide latitude in enforcement, and the state control of media has hobbled the ability of society to monitor the agents of the state (Blitt 2007; Fish 2005). The unprincipled leadership of Russia produces policies aimed at dismantling, rather than building, those institutions that might, in the right circumstances, help sustain a rule-of-law equilibrium.

Principled leaders possess a larger number of available mechanisms for constructing effective means of horizontal control, that is, the use of state institutions to monitor and sanction other arms of the state and hold other state actors accountable. Competing arms of the state bureaucracy, oversight agencies, and offices designed to elicit citizen reports of abuses are all mechanisms of horizontal accountability, in which some institutional feature of the state is used to check another.

Many of the findings of agency theory are more applicable to firms than to states. Moreover, the literature generally assumes features of advanced industrial economies – such as effective communications, transportation, and record-keeping – that ease information transfer and effective monitoring and sanctioning, assumptions that do not necessarily hold in analyses of less-developed countries (Kiser and Sacks 2008; Kiser 1994). The wholesale transfer of institutions of accountability from the developed to the developing world will not work without also transferring the infrastructure that supports the institutions.

Efforts at judicial reform in post-Soviet Estonia and Latvia are illustrative. The two countries inherited identical institutions and highly similar economies at the collapse of communism, and both sought to bring their judicial systems into line with European Union standards. A decade after the collapse of communism, the Estonian judicial system worked relatively well, but Latvia's was corrupt and performing poorly. Estonia's leadership devoted resources to modernize its judicial infrastructure and to enhance effective communication and information-sharing across the population. Latvia's courts were still operating largely with Soviet-era technologies and practices (Open Society Institute 2002).

Winning the cooperation of bureaucrats at time 3 partially depends on, among other factors, the design of institutional arrangements and signaling that elicit staff effort, reduce shirking and corruption, and at the same time signal the leader's type as principled. Ensuring the maintenance of that cooperation as well as achieving citizen compliance requires, at time 4, the further institutionalization of arrangements that facilitate the rule of law. If institutions are designed properly, future bureaucratic obstruction is minimized. Moreover, the bureaucracy itself can then serve as a constraint against potential defection by the leadership.

Bureaucratic corruption

Team production improves the capacity of leadership to elicit effort and increase the loyalty of the staff to it, but it does not necessarily eliminate predation by the staff on citizens and subjects of the state. Corruption is the bête noire of the rule-of-law. Without its elimination, there cannot be a stable rule-of-law equilibrium. It signals to citizens considering obedience that significant others are failing to comply and, moreover, reducing the quality of public goods that are part of the return to general law-abidingness. Overcoming the prevalence of corruption among nineteenth-century English tax collectors made it possible for the English state to win parliamentary approval and relatively widespread popular compliance with the income tax (Levi 1988; Brewer 1988). Similarly, in Hong Kong the ability of the government to establish effective anticorruption efforts resulted in much higher levels of confidence in government (Manion 2004).

There are, of course, multiple reasons for corruption, and not all corruption is equal. As Merton pointed out long ago, some forms of corruption may actually grease the wheels of government in ways that better serve the public (Merton 1968 [1957]). He was talking about ward heeling and not the rent seeking or extortion detrimental to state effectiveness and trustworthiness. Devastating to the rule-of-law is high-level corruption involving huge sums of money *à la* Bangladesh or the hidden bank accounts of the Papa Docs of the world. But perhaps as important, particularly in the developing world, are the police and other local officials who form protection rackets, who threaten and thieve from those they are supposed to safeguard.

Solutions to high-level corruption require powerful actors within the polity who possess the political will and resources to make a change, often with the support of international NGOs such as Transparency International or the World Bank.[12] Elimination of predatory actions by local officials often requires an appropriate structure of payment to street-level bureaucrats so that they depend on the state, rather than other sources, for their incomes, advancement, and well-being. They can then come to calculate that they are better off serving their clients than robbing them. At a minimum, they must receive a sufficient salary from the state (Bates 2008). In post-communist contexts corruption tends to be more prevalent when bureaucrats believe that their pay is below the cost of living, which leads them to feel that corruption is a justifiable necessity, even when they also consider it a social ill (Miller *et al.* 2001).[13]

Corruption at every level of the bureaucratic ladder remains a serious barrier to the establishment of a self-enforcing rule-of-law equilibrium. While corruption exists to some degree in any state, the effects of systematic corruption are qualitatively different, structuring interactions among state agents and between such agents and the populace (Manion 2004). For higher-level bureaucrats, widespread corruption can be seen as a signaling device, demonstrating to those at the same level of the hierarchy, as well as those below, that any commitment expressed by a principled leader is at best quixotic, and at worst fraudulent.

Again, the experiences of Estonia and Latvia are illustrative, demonstrating the important role of well-defined and well-enforced sanctions on state officials and staff. In the first years of independence, Estonia adopted some of the most extensive regulations on corruption of any of the Eastern European countries seeking European Union (EU) membership. A series of high-profile prosecutions of bureaucrats for the abuse of office took place throughout the 1990s. Consequently, during the EU accession process, Estonia was widely regarded as being the least corrupt of all new member countries (Open Society Institute 2002). Latvia, on the other hand, half-heartedly embraced anticorruption efforts, waiting a decade to enact real civil service reform and pursuing anti-corruption cases less than vigorously. Both high- and low-level corruption remains widespread. Without clear and credible sanctions, even well-monitored bureaucrats may be prone to deviant behavior. The benefits of corruption outweigh the costs if the costs are ill-defined or rarely imposed.

Perceptions of widespread corruption signal to each bureaucrat a low return from honest practices and from nondiscriminatory enforcement of law. In such contexts, the honest bureaucrat will end up being a sucker, shouldering the burdens and receiving none of the benefits. Corruption also reduces citizen confidence in government whether it is practiced by visible high-level bureaucrats whose behavior citizens learn about in media accounts or the accessible low-level bureaucrats with whom they interact regularly (Miller *et al.* 2001). Citizen perceptions of shirking, preferential treatment, and venality also negatively affect beliefs about the realization of the rule-of-law and undermine the possibility of a rule-of-law equilibrium.

Principled leadership is not sufficient to obtain the rule-of-law, but it is an important component. By publicly shaming and punishing corrupt officials, principled leaders provide information about their own principles as well as their commitment to creating a rule-of-law.

Without principled leadership, the probability of obtaining bureaucratic respect for the rule of law is minimal.[14] Without principled leadership committed to rule of law reforms, the threat of sanctions for transgressions against the dictates of the rule-of-law will not be credible. Why would bureaucratic agents believe that the principal will expend the resources required to effectively monitor and sanction the bureaucrats for not complying with policies that the principal herself is clearly not committed to implementing?

Achieving legitimacy and quasi-voluntary compliance

Legitimating beliefs about the state and the quasi-voluntary compliance that follows are essential to the successful establishment of the rule-of-law and to its maintenance over time. Public support and conviction that it is normatively appropriate to obey the law, *ceteris paribus*, transforms a coercive into a rule-of-law regime. But legitimating beliefs are a consequence of other prior factors, most importantly the credible commitments of principled leadership, bureaucratic performance and integrity, and institutional arrangements that ensure the continued observance by leaders and bureaucrats to the principles of the culture of law they are trying to realize.

How populations develop such perceptions and beliefs is not always straightforward, however, particularly when there are multiple groups within the polity. Again, leadership plays a critical role in establishing a common set of values – or not. Shared social norms of a group offer guidance to members about whether to consider deference or resistance to authority. The group also creates a setting in which its members develop a sense of reciprocity towards each other, making them more likely to conform with each other and less likely to free ride on the others' efforts. When a group perceives the leaders and bureaucrats of a state as unfair and discriminatory – or worse – it is likely to develop a normative stance of defiance. Shirking obligations, vandalism, and even armed struggle can result, and the rule-of-law becomes far more difficult. The Francophones in Canada, the Irish Catholics in Northern Ireland, the Basques of Spain are recent examples from the developed world. India still experiences communal riots, sixty years after Partition. Ethnic, religious, linguistic, and racial conflicts are constantly tearing apart countries with less governance capacity.

Those countries that can both experience strong tensions and maintain the rule-of-law have several features in common. First, they have constitutions and constitutional histories in which actual negotiations took place to ensure that all participating parties had protection under the law.[15] In India, this involved granting special rights to Dalits and others who had previously enjoyed no civil rights. In Canada and the United States, it produced forms of federalism to protect sectional and regional interests. Second, they had leadership that produced organizational cultures based on principles of relative equity and fairness. Such leadership facilitated the original constitutional negotiations, acted to obtain the initial cooperation of powerful elites, and then designed institutions that ensured that cooperation over time. Finally, these are countries whose institutions and leadership continue to exhibit the capacity to reform institutions to incorporate new actors and new understandings of appropriate law while, simultaneously, maintaining a commitment to the core values that initially stimulated building the rule of law (Ginsburg *et al.* 2008). The combination of principled leadership and reasonably well-designed institutions give citizens confidence they are dealing with a trustworthy and legitimate government whose authority they feel obligated to obey.

Institutions are not sufficient on their own. It is principled principals who design, transform, and breathe life into them, and it is bureaucrats and citizens who uphold them. It is principled principals whose leadership by example signals to the elites, the staff, and the populace the nature of the world they inhabit and the reasons for complying with the rule of law.

Notes

1 We have received many helpful comments on this chapter. We are particularly grateful to Robert Nelson, Avner Greif, Barry Weingast, Steve Pfaff, Trey Causey, and the participants in the Seminar in Institutional Analysis, University of Washington.
2 Times 2 and 3 are reversed in some cases. That is, we can imagine a leader who uses the cooperation of the state bureaucracy in obtaining the cooperation/compliance of otherwise recalcitrant elites.
3 The literature is long and getting longer. Important contributions include Acemoglu *et al.* (2001, 2002); Lipset (1959); Przeworski (2004); Engerman *et al.* (1997); Engerman and Sokoloff (2008); and North, Wallis, and Weingast (2009). James Mahoney and Steven Wilkinson have manuscripts in process.
4 Notable examples include the transformation of the dockworkers' union on the West Coast of the US after its Big Strike of 1934 (Levi 2005) or the reinvention of itself by the Young Men's Christian Association when its traditional base was replaced by a very different demographic group (Zald 1970).
5 This is research on the reasons for variation in the organizational cultures of unions, supported by grants from the National Science Foundation SES-0717454 and SES-0517735 and from the Harry Bridges Center for Labor Studies, University of Washington.
6 This draws on Hardin's conception of "encapsulated self-interest" (Hardin 2002).
7 This builds on Kreps' (1990) conception of a corporate culture.
8 This section draws from John Ahlquist and Margaret Levi's ongoing work (Ahlquist and Levi 2008).
9 Whether this agent learns the true value with certainty or simply has better information as to the distribution is irrelevant for the substance of his results.
10 This follows a line of reasoning developed by Ferejohn (1999) and then by Alt (2002). Also see Levi (2005).
11 Greif suggests a number of potential equilibria that develop given the combination of the costs of replacement and of technological, environmental, and cultural factors. He offers the beginnings of a useful model that fits well with our purposes here.
12 This is the current strategy in Bangladesh.
13 Interestingly, such opinions were also reported by many respondents who were themselves not bureaucrats, suggesting that little (or in some cases no) pay has an effect on attitudes toward corruption throughout the populace.
14 Manion (2004) discusses this with regard to anticorruption efforts in Hong Kong and the People's Republic of China.
15 This is an empirical claim we need to explore further. But see Ginsburg *et al.* (2008).

Chapter 10

The fight for basic legal freedoms

Mobilization by the legal complex[1]

Terence C. Halliday

Rights discourse is now global discourse (Hajjar 2004). International organizations such as the United Nations propagate universal human rights (Boyle 2002; Merry 2003, 2005). International courts prosecute military personnel and political leaders for the abrogation of basic human rights (Hagan 2003, 2005; Hagan *et al.* 2005). International financial institutions champion property rights and a rule-of-law that will uphold them (La Porta *et al.* 1997). National governments appraise other governments against the standard of their fealty to human rights. Citizens claim rights, not only in countries where they are well institutionalized, but in countries where they are regularly abrogated. Indeed, one of the principal ways that citizens or residents of a country now hold their government accountable is by alleging the government's breach of a right thoroughly institutionalized in global normative scripts, such as the UN Universal Declaration of Human Rights.

This chapter focuses on those foundational rights of western political liberalism, variously referred to as core civil rights, basic legal freedoms, or first generation rights. Frequently these rights, which emerged in the seventeenth and eighteenth centuries, are taken for granted as the frontier of rights has successively pushed forward to social, economic, and political rights. Nevertheless, in countries where core civil rights have been long established, their persistence cannot be taken for granted (Halliday and Karpik 1998b). And in countries where they have never been institutionalized, struggles remain immanent and widespread.

Understanding how core legal rights are institutionalized, how they are maintained and defended, warrants careful sociological inquiry. Who are the primary bearers of rights, their advocates and defenders? What are the conditions under which they are established, consolidated, and protected? These questions have been broached in an international collective project on lawyers and the fates of political liberalism. For the past 15 years, a collaborative of social scientists, historians, and legal academics has examined some 20–30 cases of transitions towards and away from political liberalism. These cases range from Continental and North American states in the eighteenth to nineteenth centuries to countries in Latin America, the Middle East, Asia, and Europe in the twentieth century (Halliday and Karpik 1998a; Halliday *et al.* 2007a).

The national case studies establish, first, that in widely varying times and places lawyers mobilize frequently on behalf of political liberalism; second, that in various configurations lawyers are often but not invariably joined by other legal professions, including judges and legal academics, and occasionally prosecutors and state lawyers; and third, that on many occasions this mobilization is associated with the obtaining, consolidating, or protecting of basic legal freedoms. In other words, evidence indicates that the presence or absence of the legal complex in the politics of rights frequently accompany movements towards or away from this aspect of the rule-of-law.

To identify the reoccurrence of a social phenomenon, however, is not to explain it. Advance towards a theory requires the identification of conditions and factors that distinguish instances of (successful) mobilization from a failure to mobilize (successfully) and that situate the role of the legal complex in a wider matrix of factors that are likely to have causal significance. This chapter provides a reanalysis of case studies from the Americas, East Asia, Europe, and the Middle East, principally in the twentieth century, to isolate factors that recur across cases and will be integral to a theory of lawyers' mobilization for those basic legal freedoms constitutive of the rule-of-law.

After a brief review of the principal concepts, and an equally succinct overview of mobilization by the legal complex, the chapter identifies sets of factors and some of the observed relations among them that are salient for a comparative and historical theory of the legal complex, political liberalism, and the rule-of-law.

Basic concepts

Transitions to politically liberal regimes that institutionalize some version of the rule-of-law have been amongst the most notable macro-sociological changes in western countries over the past three centuries. The struggles over liberal politics can be freshly approached from a distinctive angle – the agency of the legal complex.

We define "political liberalism" as a cluster of three attributes (Halliday and Karpik 1998b; Halliday *et al.* 2007b).[2] First, at its core lie civil rights or *basic legal freedoms*, expressions we use interchangeably. These core rights of citizenship include (a) negative freedoms from arbitrary and unrestrained state power, such as habeas corpus, due process, representation by counsel, and freedom from arbitrary arrest, detention, torture, and death; (b) positive rights, including freedoms of speech, religion, association, and movement, and (c) property rights. Second, the matrix of political liberalism core rights is nested within a *moderate state* which we define both in terms of a fragmenting of internal state power and some counterbalance to the state from outside it. Third, core civil rights and the moderate state are sustained by *civil society*, which comprises both voluntary associations and a public sphere.

Because many of the core civil rights are basic *legal* freedoms, and have a strongly juridical flavor, it is not surprising that lawyers are heavily implicated in their creation, reproduction, and defense. Earlier historical research demonstrates that in eighteenth- and nineteenth-century Britain (Pue 1998), nineteenth-century Germany (Rueschemeyer 1998), seventeenth- and eighteenth-century France (Bell 1998; Karpik 1998), and nineteenth- and twentieth-century United States (Halliday 1987), individual lawyers and often their collective associations fought for rights which are now part of the civil rights canon. The historical case studies produced what should not have been an unexpected finding. The likelihood that lawyers would mobilize on behalf of rights, and their efficacy in doing so, frequently depended on their relationships with the judiciary. This opens up the proposition that lawyers' relationships with other legally trained occupations might offer more complete explanations of the rise and fall of political liberalism, with civil rights at its core. The concept of the *legal complex* therefore seeks to capture the set of relationships among all legally trained occupations that are practicing law.[3] These may include (a) private lawyers, (b) public lawyers, who serve in ministries of justice or regulatory agencies of government, (c) judges, (d) prosecutors, a particular genus of public lawyers, and (e) legal academics (Halliday *et al.* 2007b).

When the legal complex fights for political liberalism, it is also fighting for elements of the rule of law. It will be seen that the specification of one aspect of political liberalism, basic legal freedoms, as a combination of negative rights against state tyranny, positive rights to political speech and expression, and property rights coincides with narrow formal and substantive renderings of the rule of law where (a) law is applied equally, with certainty, and prospectively, and (b) where individual rights to privacy, property, and protection of a person's dignity are maintained against arbitrary state incursions (Tamanaha 2004). For purposes of this chapter, therefore, reference to basic legal freedoms, core civil rights, or first general rights should also be understood as constitutive of basic substantive rights in philosophical renderings of the rule of law.

Three moments in struggles for basic legal freedoms

The fight for core civil rights reveals itself in three moments across a diverse array of circumstances (Table 10.1).

Obtaining freedom

The first involves the legal complex in fights to *obtain* freedom. These struggles sometimes are to advance towards a political society that has never existed before (e.g. China, Egypt, Korea, Taiwan);[4] at other times they are to regain a political society that has been lost to illiberal politics in an intermission of fascism (e.g. Nazi Germany, 1933–45), military dictatorship (Chile, 1973–80s), or totalitarianism (e.g. Poland, Hungary, 1945–89), among others.

Table 10.1 Actions of legal complex and rights in play by moments of transition and country/episode

Moments of Transition	*Country (source)*	*Episode*	*Action of Legal Complex*	*Actions on Behalf of Basic Legal Freedoms/Legal Rights*
Obtaining Basic Legal Freedoms	Egypt (Moustafa 2007a)	1990s–2000s	Against Mubarak's assault on human rights, suppression of civil society, and freedoms of speech	Legal rights: Human rights groups documenting abuses, bringing cases, monitoring detention, torture, prison conditions. Problem of recurrent detention. Championing right of defense by lawyers Political freedoms: Supreme Constitutional Court (SCC) enabling political life, legalization of opposition parties; SCC striking down provisions in criminal law that limited freedom of press and ability of press to unmask government corruption and inefficiency; limiting prosecutions of opposition leaders via libel law; championing right of defense. SCC acting as a "shield" for opposition parties, human rights groups, etc.
	Hong Kong (Jones 2007)	1970s–1980s	Against colonial arbitrariness	Legal rights: legal accountability of government, legal redress for citizens, legal transparency. Bill of Rights. Full political rights excluded but political rights advocated
	Korea (Ginsburg 2007)	1980s–1990s	Against military dictatorship	Political rights: formation of initially secret, later public lawyers' association (Minbyeon).
	Spain (Hilbink 2007b)	1960s–1970s	Against Franco's authoritarianism	Legal rights: *Judicia Democratica* rights for detainees, against extended preventive detention, for due process and habeas corpus. Political rights: *Judicia Democratica* fights for liberty of expression, assembly
	Taiwan (Ginsburg 2007)	1970s–1990s	Against Kuomingtang one-party rule	Political rights: lawyers' struggles for freedom of speech & association; defense of detainees against treason charges; monitoring of treatment in detention; advocacy for aboriginal rights.

(continued on next page)

Table 10.1 (continued)

Moments of Transition	*Country (source)*	*Episode*	*Action of Legal Complex*	*Actions on Behalf of Basic Legal Freedoms/Legal Rights*
	China (Halliday and Liu 2007)	2002–2006	Against arbitrary repression in criminal justice system	Legal rights: criminal defense lawyers providing lawyer representation (meeting suspects, collecting evidence, protection from prosecution), defending due process (extended detention, confession by torture, sentence before trial) Political rights: lawyer advocacy for autonomous lawyers' associations
	Japan (Feeley and Miyazawa 2007)	1886-1920s	Against arbitrary state administration	Legal rights: lawyer defense of labor and party leaders; challenges to illegal land seizures; human rights protection Political rights: e.g., Japan Civil Liberties Union established in 1946 to defend freedom of speech and other basic rights
Maintaining Basic Legal Freedoms	United States (Abel 2007)	2000-2006	Against executive assaults on international conventions, basic legal freedoms	Legal rights: lawyer representation, access to civil courts, protection from torture, habeas corpus, against extended detention
	Brazil (Brinks 2007)	1990s-2000s	Against police killings	Legal rights: lawyer representation; prosecution of unlawful police homicides
	Argentina (Brinks 2007)	1990s-2000s	Against police killings	Legal rights: lawyer representation; prosecution of unlawful police homicides
	Italy (Guarnieri 2007)	1970s	Against domestic terrorism & organized crime	Legal rights: representation by lawyers, due process
Losing Basic Legal Freedoms	Argentina (Brinks 2007)	1990s	Failure to mobilize against police killings	Legal rights: due process, arbitrary police power, police killings

(continued on next page)

Table 10.1 (continued)

Moments of Transition	*Country (source)*	*Episode*	*Action of Legal Complex*	*Actions on Behalf of Basic Legal Freedoms/Legal Rights*
	Brazil (Brinks 2007)	1990s	Failure to mobilize against police killings	Legal rights: due process, arbitrary police power, police killings
	Israel (Barzilai 2007)	1990s–2000s	Failure to mobilize against torture, arbitrary arrests & killings of Palestinians	Legal rights: extra-judicial targeted killings; torture; extended detention Political rights: freedom of movement by Palestinians
	Chile (Couso 2007)	1980s	Complicity with Pinochet's military Junta and loss of basic legal freedoms	Legal rights: arbitrary detention, torture, extra-judicial killings, due process, legal representation Political rights: freedom of speech, association, movement
	Fascist Italy (Guarnieri 2007)	1920s–1930s	Complicity with fascist domestication of the judiciary and attacks on basic legal freedoms	Legal rights: arbitrary detention, torture, extra-judicial killings, due process, legal representation Political rights: freedom of speech, association, movement
	Militaristic Japan (Feeley and Miyazawa 2007)	1920s–1930s	Complicity with national repression of legal rights and civil society	Legal rights: arbitrary detention, torture, extra-judicial killings, due process, legal representation Political rights: freedom of speech, association, movement
	Venezuela (Perdomo 2007)	2000s	Failure to forestall retreat from political liberalism	Legal rights: due process; legal representation Political rights: freedom of political expression
	Hong Kong (Jones 2007)	1998–2000s	Limits to defense of rule of law	Legal rights: legal accountability of government, legal redress, legal transparency, Bill of Rights. Political rights: freedom of political expression, association.

Consolidating and maintaining freedom

The inception of a politically liberal regime protective of the rule-of-law does not ensure its continuity. The consolidation and maintenance of core civil rights occur in the face of challenges to one or more of its elements – challenges to narrow the gap between constitutional aspirations and everyday defense of basic liberties (e.g. Brazil, Argentina), challenges from internationally sponsored threats to security (e.g. US), challenges from domestic threats to security (e.g. Italy, Brazil, Argentina), challenges from threats to territorial integrity (e.g. Turkey), challenges that result from the conflict of one set of freedoms (e.g. religious expression, political speech) with sanctified principles of state constitutionalism (e.g. secularism, national integrity in Turkey), challenges from the expansiveness or entrenchment of an administrative state (e.g. Japan).

Losing freedom

A third moment of transition concerns the readiness or ability of the legal complex to fight against a dramatic *loss* of basic legal freedoms. This takes many forms, such as a military coup (Chile, 1973), the systematic dismantling of liberalism's institutions (Venezuela, 2005), or the progressive consolidation of a one-party state (e.g. Zimbabwe), among others. Freedom can be lost decisively across all dimensions of political liberalism. Assaults upon freedom come from military takeovers and civil war (Brazil, Argentina, Chile, China, Spain), or a regressive slide into authoritarianism or totalitarianism by an elected government (Italy, Venezuela, Japan), or by the consolidation of a one-party regime by a dominant leader (Kenya), among others. Ultimately, in all cases, the legal complex is compelled to surrender most or all of its defensive powers. We are compelled to ask, however, could it have been different? How do the attributes of the legal complex result in capitulation with a fight or without?

Conditions of mobilization

To identify explanatory factors from the great diversity of case studies I isolate factors that recur across cases, consider relations among these, and thereby begin to explicate what appear as conditions under which the legal complex may be causally and constitutively implicated in those conditions.

Elements of the legal complex

The politics within the legal complex itself, its structure and dynamics, clearly affect the probability that the legal complex as a whole or in part will mobilize, just as they affect the probable effectiveness of that action.

Private bar

Considerable evidence supports the proposition that the development of an autonomous bar in recent decades depends upon the emergence of a private market for legal services (China, Venezuela, Kenya, Israel, Korea, Spain) or, relatedly, the construction of a legal system that will at least deliver the minima of the rule-of-law for legal certainty in the market. While I return to the politics of lawyers and markets in more detail below, the significance of the market for the politics of lawyers contrasts contemporary bases of lawyers' mobilization from the early modern period where, for instance, in France, Karpik finds that a decision to define themselves against the market permitted lawyers to lead movements for political/legal reform (Karpik 1988). The size and resources of the private bar also determine the depth of the pool from which lawyer activists can be drawn, the financial independence of individual lawyers from state control, and the potential financial resources available for their collective action.

Collective action in turn varies markedly across countries: by the type of association that can collectively aggregate professional interests; by internal divisions within the profession; and by the differential powers of regulatory organizations to monopolize public expression of professional interests.

Typically, lawyers organize themselves in three ways. Most commonly, every profession has official associations, sometimes local (e.g. US, Venezuela, Turkey), usually national (e.g. Egypt, Turkey, Israel, Korea, Taiwan, Italy) that purport to represent and sometimes regulate the profession as a whole. Less commonly, but integral to mobilization, many professions also form voluntary, alternative, or even clandestine associations that are sharply focused on advocacy or defense of political freedom (e.g. Japan, Korea, Taiwan, US, Spain). Not infrequently, informal networks of lawyers or invisible groupings come together around a shared cause although repression requires them to maintain a low organizational profile (e.g. Spain, China, Korea).

Structural and temporal permutations of these three forms of organization provide the infrastructures around which mobilization can occur. In cases of severe repression, the informal relationships grow outside (e.g. Spain, Korea) and occasionally inside (e.g. China) formal structures which provide infrastructures for dissident lawyers; some subsequently formalize as interest groups on behalf of political liberalism (e.g. Spain, Korea, Taiwan, Japan); and, on occasion, the rump groups come to overtake the formal associations that represent the entire profession (e.g. Taiwan). In many countries (e.g. Chile, Venezuela, Italy, China), the official associations seek to choke off any appearance of potential rivals. In these settings the official associations are more susceptible to state incursions on their autonomy.

Moreover, in the later twentieth and twenty-first centuries, leadership on behalf of core legal rights more often arises not from the center of the profession, which can be co-opted or controlled by the state, but from the periphery of the organized bar. Hence the organized bar finds itself in a quandary: as a national entity of all practitioners its associational strength might better ward off incursions on lawyers' responsibilities but at the risk of co-optation by the state, or inertia and divisiveness from within; by taking the route of organizing as marginal rump groups of lawyers dedicated to well-defined causes, ideological purity and focused energy may render the group more vulnerable to state attacks and to opposition from professional peers less convinced or less committed.

An explanatory theory must therefore incorporate the following factors: (1) size of the private market for legal services, (2) the unity or diversity of bar associations, (3) the degree of assimilation of bar associations by the state, (4) opportunities for professional organization outside state-approved or mandated associations, and (5) the prospect of a progressive movement of political lawyers from the margins to the center of the profession. Several national studies support the hypotheses that (a) the greater the number of private lawyers with financial resources independent of the state, the greater the pool of potential activists for restraint of arbitrary state power; (b) the more freely lawyers can organize, the more likely that a minority of political lawyers[5] will form informal or formal associations potentially committed to activism on behalf of basic legal freedoms; and (c) if repression prevents the national organization of private lawyers from acting on behalf of basic legal freedoms, then rump lawyers will find clandestine means to meet and mobilize.

Judiciary

Judges bear an ambivalent relationship to political liberalism. In numbers of cases judges aligned themselves with the state apparatus, sometimes aiding and abetting their repression (e.g. Chile), and sometimes defining their calling so narrowly that they carried on business as usual while turning a blind eye to incursions on liberal ideals (e.g. Chile, Italy, Egypt). The cases of Egypt, Spain, and Italy support the hypothesis that courts are less likely to defend basic legal freedoms when: a positivist jurisprudence insulates courts from substantive standards of justice and rights; and a hierarchical structure of organization rigidifies this insulation through the court system such that dissident judges obtain few degrees of freedom to deviate from the "apoliticism" of positivist jurisprudence.[6] Ironically, some of the most complicit courts were also the most independent. Autonomy of courts does not guarantee either the ability or willingness to act as a check on executive power.

Ironically, in many situations, the cause of political liberalism advances only when judges in a regular court system are prepared to coexist with special courts that lie outside the jurisdiction of conventional courts. Special courts contrast sharply in their significance for political liberalism. On the one hand, repressive regimes regularly create security courts to remove troublesome political agitators from the public view, suspend or abrogate procedural rights, substitute regular judges by military officers, and insulate their detainees from the jurisdiction of regular appellate courts (cf. Italy, Spain, Egypt, Chile, China) (Ginsburg and Moustafa 2008). This enables these countries to project from their regular courts a patina of legalism to their populations and the world while engaging in arbitrary, brutal, cruel, and often murderous treatment far from the public eye. On the other hand, the protection of basic legal freedoms frequently relies on the existence of a constitutional court. As Egypt in the 1990s dramatically exemplified (cf. also Korea, Taiwan, Italy), the formation of a powerful constitutional court with a capacity to hold state actions accountable to the local formulation of universal standards can constructively unsettle a reactionary established judicial system. It offers a forum in which grievances can be aired; it permits styled argumentation that might otherwise be censored; it provides a counterpoint to the executive; and thus offers a stage for lawyer-leaders to address and even crystallize publics. Its disruptive functions can extend to the lower courts in the regular judiciary insofar as it sends signals about cases and arguments that it will accept on appeal (cf. Korea, Taiwan, Egypt). Nevertheless, constitutional courts within repressive regimes are particularly vulnerable. Their viability depends upon an acute sensitivity about the balance between their perceived legitimacy and support in relation to the scope and expansiveness of their powers. Excessively muscular decisions (cf. Egypt) or premature overreaching (e.g. Mongolia) can lead to sudden dismemberment or partial dismantlement (Ginsburg 2003). Constitutional courts, themselves, also rely on political and market demand for legal institutions that facilitate investment and economic growth.

Repeatedly, the case studies show that the potential of judiciaries for political liberalism depends upon their social embeddedness. In relation to the executive arms of the state, too few benefits to state administration or reputation render them dispensable; too great an affinity with state politics renders them impotent. In relation to political parties, too distant a position from the policy ideals of parties renders courts irrelevant; too deep an immersion of judges in party politics converts courts into yet another arena of politics and subverts justice from within. In relation to the bar, too attenuated a relationship leaves courts vulnerable; too integral a relationship with lawyers diminishes courts' authority. In relation to the public, too little public support denies judiciaries a primary source of legitimation; too much sensitivity to public opinion makes courts manipulable. In these respects, courts face a threefold problem of autonomy: from the state, from markets (e.g. corruption), from publics.

An explanatory theory of the legal complex and political liberalism will more often include the following factors related to judiciaries: (1) the jurisprudence and ideology of the judiciary vis-à-vis basic legal freedoms; (2) the extent of control over lower courts exerted by higher courts and the judicial administration; (3) the extent of court differentiation or autonomy from the state; (4) relations of general courts with special or parallel security courts; (5)

the prestige of judges in the legal complex and social order; (6) the methods and terms of judicial appointment; (7) financing of the judiciary, and (8) the extent of legitimacy and support accorded the courts by the public.

We can hypothesize that judiciaries are not likely to fight for basic legal freedoms when (a) the judiciary subscribes to a positivist jurisprudence which restricts its authority to positive law, (b) is recruited for its political fealty, (c) is controlled hierarchically by judicial elites that eschew engagement on behalf of universal juridical rights, and (d) historically is regarded as an arm of state administration.

Legal academics

We can observe three stances of the *legal academy* in fights for political liberalism. First, when not fully professionalized, when steeped in a positivist jurisprudence, and when riven by partisan political factionalism, a legal academy, even if quite prestigious, offers no leadership for political liberalism (cf. Chile, 1973; Italy during fascism). Second, a professionalized and prestigious legal academy whose jurisprudence is responsive to juridical, religious and philosophical ideals celebratory of political liberalism, and institutionalized within a university, will frequently obtain some autonomy from the state. Many of its members will craft the ideologies for mobilization of the legal complex, academics will provide intellectual legitimacy and support for reformist courts and lawyers, and the legal academy can offer a cosmopolitanism and internationalism less pervasive in other parts of the legal complex (cf. China, Spain, Korea, Venezuela, Hong Kong). Third, the legal academy appears never to act as a collectivity. It mobilizes through congeries of like-minded individuals who share networks or orientations (cf. Deans in Venezuela). In this respect it is the least susceptible to collective mobilization as a social organization.

Whether legal academics will mobilize on behalf of basic legal freedoms will therefore depend on: (1) whether there is a full-time professionalized legal academy, (2) whether the dominant jurisprudence of legal academics is conducive to mobilization for core rights beyond the limits of positive law, (3) whether the legal academy is permeated and riven by party politics, (4) whether the academy is exposed and integrated into international liberal legal networks, and (5) whether legal academics have the opportunity and willingness to act as leaders of professional and public opinion.

Prosecutors

In principle, state prosecutors stand closest to the exercise of executive power by the state. Their natural allies are the police – who frequently are subversive of basic legal freedoms (cf. China, Brazil, Argentina, Hong Kong, Italy). Most commonly they are the unspoken or designated agents of repression either through zealous prosecution on behalf of repressive states (cf. China, Chile,

Venezuela) or through failure to hold accountable actors in a justice system that threaten basic rights (e.g. Brazil, Argentina). On occasion, some prosecutors did align themselves eventually with the forces for liberalism, as Hilbink (2007b) shows in Francoist Spain, and Ginsburg (2007) discovers in democratizing Korea. Or they may be seen in the guise of protecting the state and society from threats to the social and political fabric without abrogating core rights. Guarnieri (2007) demonstrates that examining prosecutors took leadership in the legal complex in the fights against terror, organized crime, and political corruption, thus strengthening the power and legitimacy of the judicial-prosecutorial system.

But in many countries, the story of prosecutors is caught up in the dynamics of differentiation and coordination. In China, it is the differentiation of prosecutors from the Party, police, and courts that marks a current struggle for a re-equilibration of power in criminal defense (Halliday and Liu 2007). In Brazil and Spain, it is the differentiation of the prosecutors from police. In Korea, it was the differentiation of prosecutors from administrative guidance by an imperative state (Ginsburg 2007). For liberalism, differentiation must be complemented by coordination, not least with the practicing bar where liberalism usually finds its natural affinity. Effective societal response to threats requires sufficient coordination to protect social order within the ideals of core rights but sufficient differentiation from a sometimes brutal arm of state enforcement.

Hence a theory of political liberalism will attend to attributes of public prosecutors that includes: (1) their ideology (e.g. a broader commitment to the rule-of-law versus a narrower focus on striking crime); (2) the professionalization and differentiation of prosecutors from political control, and (3) the proclivity of prosecutors to align with liberal segments of the legal complex.

A distinctive variant of prosecutors can be found in the Latin American *private prosecutor*. Here the corrective for a failure of state prosecutors to differentiate themselves appropriately from the police, courts, or demagogic politicians comes from private lawyers whose clients are the victims of police brutality and homicides. This straddling of the private/public divide, or the legal complex and civil society, has the effect of compelling a retributive justice system to conform to the constitutional ideals of political liberalism. The necessity for this kind of mobilization on behalf of justice suggests that the re-equilibration of power within the legal complex, thereby moderating the state, will not infrequently result from a common cause being found between the margins of the legal complex and the margins of civil society against the inertia of the state apparatus (Brinks 2007, 2008).

Government lawyers

Three studies yield intriguing results about government officials whose commitment to ideals of legality result in the championing of the rule-of-law. Hilbink (2007b) finds that in the last years of Franco's rule, as he opened Spain to Europe's market by invigorating the economy, a group of conservative technocrats (lawyers and economists) decided that a rule-of-law regime, complete with courts independent of political interference, would provide the institutional preconditions for market development. They advocated an *Estato de Derecho* with a reinvigorated Council of State and revitalized administrative courts.

Jones (2007) makes the unexpected discovery that the hidden heroes of Hong Kong's political development were "in-house" legal and political advisors whose interventions ranged from the restraints on highly repressive anti-Chinese regulations in the mid-nineteenth century through the exercise of leadership in moderating the government's repressive tendencies in the 1950s and 1960s. When Hong Kong took its rapid strides towards political liberalism in the 1970s, it was the government lawyers who were integral to its design and implementation, though by now they were joined by individuals from various other fragments of the legal complex.

Abel (2007) also shows that much resistance to the Bush Administration's cavalier disregard for rights of detainees came from inside the military – from the judge advocate's corps, and from other lawyers farther removed from the ideological heights of the Justice Department and Pentagon. In this resistance they were joined by distinguished retired military lawyers who can now speak with less restraint about the abrogation of fundamental protections. These three instances indicate that the structure of the legal complex may embrace government lawyers and that explanations of activism by the legal complex require investigation of their mobilization.

Factors salient for theory construction therefore include: (1) whether government lawyers are professionalized as lawyers qua lawyers; (2) whether they subscribe to principles of the rule-of-law that transcend bureaucratic loyalties, and (3) whether they maintain a professional identity independent of their bureaucratic positions.

Properties of the legal complex

The more capable the legal complex of mobilizing collectively across its various segments, the greater its probable impact for legal and political liberalism. To understand the capacity of the legal complex to produce and protect judicial power, it is critical to know when and how the legal complex itself divides and combines.

Eighteenth- and nineteenth-century reforms towards political liberalism support the proposition that an alliance between the bar and courts significantly increases the willingness and impact of either the bar or courts on basic legal freedoms (Halliday and Karpik 1998a). The case studies indicate that the obverse also follows – when the bench and bar join forces in reactionary support of a repressive state, or indeed, both independently decline to uphold basic legal freedoms, state moderation is doomed, as Argentina and Chile demonstrate during their military dictatorships and as Korea, Taiwan, and Japan experienced during their respective years of illiberal politics. Nonetheless, in several instances neither the entire bar nor the entire bench is necessary to enable a liberal opening: in Egypt, a vanguard of human-rights lawyers appearing before the Constitutional Court was sufficient to arrest and even reverse some of the government's authoritarian actions; in Korea and Taiwan, small voluntary cause-oriented associations found that a responsive constitutional court sufficed to add momentum towards liberalization. Here there is a sense of powerful human agency from groups whose formation came from the edges of the profession.

In fact, actual patterns of alliance and division across the legal complex are quite complex. A cohesive autonomous bar joining forces with a unified independent judiciary is rare in the case studies. Rather, the legal complex mobilizes for political liberalism in fragmentary patchworks of association, at least in the earlier phases of obtaining freedom. Later, as the pace quickens, a transition occurs, and consolidation begins, the bar and bench as a whole may coalesce around the ascendant standards of liberalism. And later still, if regression from political liberalism begins, it will again be a concomitant or coordinated coalition of fragments rather than entire segments of the profession that join forces. We are therefore confronted with a formidable explanatory task for predicting which course of action is likely in varying circumstances.

Hints of that explanation occurs in several places as scholars trace the historical institutionalization of their respective legal complexes. In one development sequence, both Chile and Venezuela exemplify cases in which historically separate fragments of the legal complex, founded at different historical moments and following distinctive historical trajectories, have begun to cohere in the last several decades. In a second developmental sequence, a contrary dynamic may be in motion – historically fused fractions of the legal complex in China (judges, prosecutors, lawyers) are beginning to differentiate. In a third developmental sequence, there has been a moving equilibrium in the North East Asian legal complex in which a small, independent bar and independent but constrained judiciary, both under the shadow of a powerful state administration, are transformed over two decades into larger, more activist legal professions which find receptive and bolder courts ready to hold state bureaucracies accountable. In a fourth developmental sequence, the US legal complex has grown up together, with lawyers, judges, and legal academics merging and mixing for the past century. This presents many opportunities for parts of each fragment to combine with others for and against basic legal freedoms. Other patterns will also emerge as research depends. It can be hypothesized that the more historically entrenched are patterns of differentiation and integration, the more fraught will be transitions towards mutually supportive mobilization on behalf of political liberalism.

The probability of coordinated mobilization will also turn on the education of legally trained professions, their mobility among different branches of practice, and the inclusiveness of their professional associations.

Hence intra-structural and dynamic factors that affect mobilization by the legal complex include: (1) whether professionals in different segments of the legal complex are recruited from similar social classes and educational and professional pools; (2) the frequency of career mobility that takes place among segments of the legal complex (e.g. from private practice or academia to the bench); (3) whether professionals across the legal complex share a legal ideology; (4) whether that ideology is conducive to the defense of core rights; (5) whether segments of the legal complex have a history or precedent for alliances for mutual protection or mobilization; (6) whether the legal complex has a heroic tradition or a collective memory on which it can draw in situations of crisis, siege or repression; (7) whether one or more segments of the legal complex obtain foreign or international support for advocacy of core rights.

Civil society

At once lawyers themselves partially constitute civil society and have an unusual capacity to lead it. In the case studies no account of lawyers, the legal complex, and hence of judicial activism, proceeds without relying on the mutual reliance among the legal complex and civil society.

We distinguish between organized civil society, and its manifestation in associations and networks, and unorganized civil society, and its expression in amorphous publics (Halliday *et al.* 2007b). In country after country, at each moment of transition, nongovernment organizations (NGOs) feature as partners of the legal complex. Most common are justice-related NGOs, such as generalist human-rights groups (e.g. Egypt, Venezuela, Israel) or indigenous NGOs that are focused on a specific problem within the justice system, such as CORREPI in Argentina on the victims of police homicides. NGOs monitor judicial decisions and prisons (cf. Egypt), monitor the police (cf. Brazil, Argentina), mount demonstrations and hunger strikes (cf. Egypt), formulate legal reform manifestoes (cf. Korea), mobilize the public for vocal criticism of deficiencies in the justice system (cf. Brazil, Argentina), submit amicus briefs to courts (cf. US), and create links with international organizations. Most justice-related NGOs straddle the legal complex/society divide for they are led by lawyers or depend heavily on lawyers for advice and expertise. Not infrequently, lawyers exasperated with the inertia of their colleagues reach into civil society to form associations that will lend force and sometimes protections for their advocacy (cf. Korea).

The importance of NGOs relates to the phase of political liberalism. Where they are banned or rigidly controlled, as in authoritarian countries, then loose informal networks or underground groups function in their stead (cf. China). As authoritarianism begins to break down, civil associations accompany the political spring and quicken the thaw. A consolidated politically liberal regime opens the terrain for an increasing density of associational life, although, as Japan demonstrates, strictures on the formation of NGOs can retard their growth even in a supposedly mature democracy. When a slide begins away from political freedom, an indicator of its danger can be found in the volume of protest generated from outside the state. In 1930s Japan, 1970s Chile, and 1990s Venezuela, the quietude from organized groups outside the state indicates the limited brakes on regressive momentum. In Hong Kong since 1997, however, the success of civil society groups, often led by lawyers, to bring hundreds of thousands of citizens into the streets, signaled to the Hong Kong government, and even more to Beijing, that the retraction of rights will be a very public, very contested, and very vocal enterprise, with hefty political cost.

Karpik (1998) showed that the political force of the eighteenth-century French bar relied upon its ability to convince the Crown that it spoke on behalf of a public, at that time more fictive than real. In twentieth and twenty-first century struggles for freedom, the public, as a diffuse force outside the state, appears in numbers of our cases. But its currents flow in contradictory tides. From one vantage point the public is a latent ally that can be mobilized by organized civil society and the legal complex. In Uruguay it demands that police function within constitutional limits; in Brazil and Argentina sections of the public can pressure prosecutors and judges to check police homicides; in Hong Kong its vast numbers forced Beijing to back down; in Italy it supported the magistracy's bold steps to strike aggressively against organized crime and to root out political corruption (Brinks 2007; Guarnieri 2007; Jones 2007). From another vantage point the public is a fickle force easily manipulated by demagogic leaders or aroused to hysteria by fear and threat. Police killings of suspects occur with impunity in Brazil and Argentina because the public at large permits its fears to be intensified by law-and-order politicians. Confession by torture and attacks on criminal defense lawyers continue unchecked in China because the masses fear disorder more than they fear apparently mild abrogations of unfamiliar rights. Brinks is surely correct, however, that the rule-of-law, institutionalized in a moderate state and defended by an active bar, cannot be sustained without a broad-based public belief that arbitrary and excessive state action must be checked by procedural and substantive rights (Brinks 2007). Political liberalism cannot be institutionalized on the basis of leadership by the legal complex alone.

In sum, civil society's capacity to ally with the legal complex on behalf of basic legal freedoms will depend upon: (1) the ability and willingness of civil society groups to form within a country; (2) the resources available to civil society groups – material, ideal and organizational; (3) the ideological inclinations of civil society groups to tackle basic rights; (4) the openness of civil society groups to legal complex leadership, membership, or alliance; (5) the availability and opening of public spaces for public discourse on rights; and (6) the availability of lawyers, judges or legal academics as spokesmen for the public and interlocutors with the publics.

What evidence do the case studies provide for a causal relationship between the legal complex and civil society? In fact, they appear synergistic, feeding off each other in potential virtuous or vicious cycles. Almost always lawyers and judges precede civil society: whether or not any space exists for association and discourse outside the state, there will always be lawyers and judges in service of the state or market, except in the most rare of cases, such as Mao's Cultural Revolution. In one sense lawyers may constitute civil society, often because lawyers are accustomed to representing others, because they have an affinity with the formalization of association, and because their use of rules to constitute social groups is a natural lawyerly adaptation to a collective expression of interest. Indeed, lawyers' associations themselves, when formed outside the state, express an impulse of civil society and thus emblemize it. Moreover, lawyers have a special capacity to lead publics even if publics themselves are not aggregated or congealed in continuing associations. When the French bar in the eighteenth century took advantage of the stage offered by the courtroom, it spoke and published *memoires* designed to reach the ears of listeners open to persuasion and eventually concertation. Moreover, lawyers' groups occasionally are among the few or only survivors when repressive regimes crush associations outside the state. Instances as dispersed as the eighteenth-century Paris bar, the Brazilian bar association in the 1980s, the Kenyan Law Society under Moi's authoritarian one-party regime, and the Malaysian bar in the 1980s and 1990s all survived, albeit under siege, when all other groups, excepting on occasion the church, are crushed.

Yet the Paris bar did not invent the salons of Parisian intellectuals. Civil society emerges from other impetuses, sometimes led by intellectuals. Most frequently in the west and many of its former colonies, it is the church that has a resilience possibly exceeding the bar itself. While religious groups are not invariably supporters of liberal legal ideals, when they do they are among the most critical potential allies of the bar, as lawyers' groups discovered in Brazil and Kenya.

There appears, then, a reciprocal causality in which civil society groups and publics offer places of association, arenas of discourse, and potential alliances for liberal segments of the legal complex. Yet at the same time the very existence, leadership and survival of those groups relies upon the machinery of law and its practitioners.

Civil society: media

The media offer great potential to spearhead and to amplify the campaigns of other groups for the rule-of-law. In principle, they can broadcast points of view, call to arms, mobilize publics and mediate public exchanges among the legal complex, civil society and publics. In the case studies media can be observed aiding the push to obtain freedom in Spain, where Madrid's nationally circulated *El País* eventually took the bold step to publicize *Judicia Democratica*'s reports. In Mubarak's Egypt during the 1990s NGOs and lawyers gained much media leverage through publicity over their fights to keep the

Supreme Constitutional Court's powers of judicial review, not to mention attention to public demonstrations and hunger strikes. Even in the heavily censored Chinese media, some papers and some journalists take risks in the "gray zone" of journalism (Lin 2008) to publicize egregious abuses of lawyers, such as arresting and harassing defense attorneys, and suspects, such as use of "confession by torture," by the police and procuracy. In the struggles over the loss of liberalism in Venezuela, those fragments of the legal complex that have taken a stand have leveraged their impact through public statements to media outlets, opinion/editorial articles, press conferences, and invitations of journalists to notable trials.

Yet the media may be compromised. When the state controls the media, the selective permission to publicize certain events amounts to systematic bias of news by state authorities. When the media must survive in a market, they are subject to manipulation by large corporate advertisers, by vocal reader groups, or by the consumption habits of readers. Moreover, the media themselves are often associated with a particular political party, religious group, or similar source of systematic bias. While a powerful potential channel for the legal complex to reach its public constituencies, therefore, the media is a vulnerable and scarcely neutral conduit into the public arena.

The proliferation of electronic media may herald new opportunities and capabilities for insurgent groups on behalf of rule-of-law. In contemporary China the Internet, public bulletin boards, and "private" electronic forums are often given much more freedom by government censors than public print or electronic newspapers and magazines. They also have more opportunities to evade censors. This new technological capability, for example, has enabled activist lawyers across China to find each other by means that otherwise would have been impossible before the electronic age (Halliday and Liu 2007). It also provides lawyers the capacity to lead publics and to amplify the impact of civil society groups.

A theory of mobilization of the legal complex must take account of: (1) the varieties of media available for political speech; (2) the type of control exercised directly (e.g. through ownership of state or private media) or indirectly (e.g. through regulation) over the media (state, commercial, party); (3) the access of the public to media; (4) the access of the legal complex to the media; and (5) the affinity of media for the causes and campaigns of the legal complex.

Again a reciprocal causal relationship appears between the media and the legal complex. On the one hand, the print and electronic media *precede* the mobilization. Their existence can leverage the impact of the legal complex, even help protect legal activism on behalf of basic legal freedoms. On the other hand, it is the legal complex itself – lawyers and judges – who are primary actors in securing the freedom of speech required for the media to be effective allies of legal actors. As fights demonstrate in the Egyptian courts during the 1990s, the ability of some newspapers to advocate the cause of political liberalism depended on the efficacy of political liberals to secure that latitude through law. Again, therefore, the legal complex and media exist in a mutually constructive or destructive relationship, each ratcheting up or down the capacity of the other to press liberal causes.

Civil society: religion

The impact of religious beliefs and organizations recurs repeatedly in struggles for political liberalism. Variation across circumstances, religions and historical moments is not sufficient as yet to disentangle when and in what circumstances religious groups will press for defense of basic legal freedoms on their account, or when they will join with segments of the legal complex in common cause. Yet there are enough instances to begin identifying patterns that require more intensive research (Halliday 2008).[7]

In several cases the alliance of progressive elements of the legal complex and with Christian churches are decisive for the obtaining or defending of basic rights. Hilbink (2007b) shows that the liberal wing of the Catholic Church in Spain provided shelter, infrastructure, and even protection for dissident churches and lawyers, the famous monastery at Montserrat at one point being the meeting place for clandestine councils and the printing press for its manifestoes. Brinks finds that it is an NGO formed by the Roman Catholic diocese of São Paolo that is most effective in bringing private prosecutions against homicidal police. Halliday points to the alliance between the Law Society of Kenya and a mainline church coalition that led the move away from Moi's authoritarian rule. Abel (2007) shows that some Christian and Jewish groups stood with those members of the legal complex who resisted the Bush Administration's cavalier attitudes to the rule-of-law, although these were in the distinct minority. Other research, most especially on Brazil during the military dictatorship, reveals that the Roman Catholic Church and the Brazilian Bar Association were the only powerful civil society groups left standing in the face of military repression. They drew support from each other (Falcao 1988).

Yet there are numerous cases where the church was either silent or complicit in retreats from defense of core civil rights. In Spain, Chile, and Argentina the Roman Catholic Church hierarchies overwhelmingly supported regimes that were hostile to "Communist," "socialist," or left-wing threats purportedly to religion as well as politics. The Chilean Catholic hierarchy greeted Pinochet's coup with a celebratory mass (Couso 2007). Nonetheless, even in Spain and Chile the Roman Catholic Church was a broad tent that contained much dissent. The Cardinal of Santiago, Chile, used his cathedral as a refuge for persecuted dissidents and founded the *Vicariate* to document human rights abuses by security forces. Catalonian and Basque priests found common cause with those lawyers and magistrates brave enough to build resistance against Franco's security measures. In Turkey, Islamic institutions were kept well away from political power by secularist Kemalists. The rise of a moderate, Islamic politics in recent years, however, has embraced many, if not all, aspects of legal liberalism, even if religious values and the differentiation of state and religion continue as issues of fierce debate inside Turkey (Arslan 2007; Karpik 2007). In Israel, Barzilai (2007) shows that at the point where an otherwise liberal legal complex confronts Palestinian issues its unaccustomed silence on issues of law and justice effectively concurs with conservative Judaism's differential standards of justice for Jews and Palestinians.

Furthermore, religion can transform the bar from within, both for and against political liberalism. Karpik (1988, 1998) shows that it was Jansenist lawyers within the Paris bar that led a fierce assault on the illiberal expression of power by an absolute monarchy which relied upon the authority of the Catholic hierarchy which itself was hostile to the "Protestant" leanings of Jansenist clergy and laity alike. Jansenists inside the church and inside the bar used the Paris Order of Barristers and the courts themselves as stages on which to fight concomitantly religious and legal battles. By contrast, the permeation in the 1990s of the Egyptian bar, as thousands of conservative Muslims poured into a previously secular-leaning Lawyers Syndicate, gave Mubarak's government precisely the excuse it wanted to put the entire troublesome lawyers' organization into receivership as part of its crackdown against the Muslim Brotherhood (Moustafa 2007a, 2007b).

What is common to all these episodes is that Protestant and Roman Catholic Christians, Muslims, and Orthodox Jews influenced the trajectory of liberalism and its particular expression at critical historical junctures. While we cannot yet explain when religious groups will align with a liberalizing legal complex and when they will be complicit with the forces against political liberalism, we can identify factors that must be part of any explanation of the rise and defense of political liberalism: (1) whether religious groups exist in a society and how well they are organized; (2) whether religious groups have some autonomy from the state or are subjugated to or co-opted by state power; (3) whether religious groups embrace doctrines that emphasize human dignity and articulate theological affinities with basic legal freedoms; and (4) the proximity of religious groups supportive of legal liberalism to the legal complex, either through (a) the religious views of lawyers, judges, and others, or (b) the readiness of religious organizations to ally or to align themselves with an activist legal complex for political liberalism.

In a causal theory, the religious and legal streams of advocacy for basic legal freedoms are not readily distinguished, not least because law and religion are fused in Judaism, Christianity, and Islam for much of their histories. When law begins to differentiate itself from religion in the west, it brings certain core religious values with it, values emphasized even more strongly in and after the Protestant Reformation. In this sense religion precedes and infuses law with values, even when law itself appears to have secularized and is differentiated structurally from religious institutions. Moreover, religious groups usually can draw upon a longer and visceral basis of organization that has a resilience seldom matched by any other in civil society. Religion penetrates to the edges of society more completely and comprehensively than law. Thus its entailment in political liberalism cannot be gainsaid. In a sense religion also precedes mobilization by the legal complex as lawyers, judges, and others import their religious commitments and affiliations into legal institutions. A structural differentiation of law and religion, in other words, elides within the person of a religious lawyer. Nevertheless, where religion has been co-opted by the state, then secular segments of the legal complex, such as parts of the bar and legal academy, may take the leadership in the defense of rights, knowing that the support from religious institutions will be marginal at best. Yet again there are enough cases – Brazil, Kenya, France – where religious groups and the legal complex have joined forces simultaneously, where the priority of one or another in their respective mobilizations cannot be readily distinguished, to show that an affinity of values and resilience of organization, not to mention an inter-penetration of members, drives both.

Civil society: politics

The legal complex bears an ambiguous relationship to partisan party politics. On the one hand, a mutuality can coexist between the two. In several countries where oppositional parties are banned, parts of the legal complex served as a shadow opposition in lieu of a developed party system (e.g. Spain, Egypt, Korea, Taiwan). Furthermore, the legal complex has often been a primary agent in the breaking open of a formal competitive party system, breaking bans on previously banned opposition parties (e.g. Egypt, Taiwan). Not infrequently lawyers emerge as the leaders of the new parties, which sometimes go on to assume political power (e.g. Korea, Taiwan). Yet the legal complex can also be co-opted by state partisanship when repressive regimes directly or indirectly ensure that the leadership of parts of the legal complex, especially the organized bar, maintains the line of the ruling party.

On the other hand, in many civil law countries the relationship between the legal complex and political parties appears to diminish the capacity of the organized bar in particular to assert a distinguished authority that is not irreducible to party politics. Where the institutions of the legal complex – bar, bench, legal academy – are themselves internally divided by partisan political affiliations, and leadership contests or orientations to issues of the day follow partisan lines, then the political complex has effectively colonized the legal complex (cf. Chile, Venezuela, Italy, Spain). This forecloses the prospect of a professional solidarity that transcends other social cleavages and it inhibits the emergence of a legal "class." Put another way, the permeation of the legal complex by political parties potentially subverts the capacity of lawyers and other parts of the legal complex to act on singularly legal grounds above the political fray. The effect of close party alliances is to link the fortunes of fractions of the legal complex to the fortunes of the parties. Thus the legal complex follows the rise and fall of dominant parties and thereby cannot easily act as a counterweight to parties-in-power (e.g. Chile, Italy, Spain). It is not surprising, then, that a legal complex dominated by a political party supportive of Pinochet did not resist his attacks on liberalism. It is perfectly consistent that when an opposition party came to dominate the *Collegio*, lawyers began to speak out against political repression. Even in the case of bar associations acting in lieu of opposition parties a similar danger exists – a potentially distinctive lawyers' voice becomes susceptible to attack on grounds it is another political voice in lawyerly disguise.

It follows that an added protection that the legal complex can offer political liberalism, particularly that part located in civil society (lawyers, legal academy), depends upon lawyers' capacity to find a commonality that transcends political partisanship. That commonality rests upon an ideology of legality or constitutionalism that cannot readily be attacked on grounds of its partisanship or reduced to party politics. Procedural justice in a narrow, formal, and substantive version of the rule-of-law offers one such option. Lawyers who might otherwise be divided on distributive politics can often find common ground on procedural protections through basic legal rights. This stance elevates lawyers above the arena of interest politics in which the rest of society may be configured. Thereby it provides an ideological basis on which organizational resistance can be mobilized to the programs of any political party when it attains power.

A difficult case is presented by Turkey where Arslan (2007) shows that the secularized legal complex has steadfastly opposed the authorization of religious political parties or Kurdish political parties on grounds that the former would threaten Turkey's commitment to secularism and the latter would potentially foster separatism and ultimately secession. Here fundamental values of political liberalism clash: freedom of speech, association, and religion. Arlsan finds the legal complex on the wrong (illiberal) side: a legal order resists both civil society and the legislative will.

Hence a theory of political liberalism must incorporate factors concerning party politics: (1) the existence of single versus multiple political parties; (2) if a one-party state, the degree to which the ruling party permits freedom of political speech, especially at the margins (e.g. inside "private" associations); (3) the capacity of courts to protect the right and ability of multiple and oppositional political parties to exist; (4) the extent to which lawyers' strategies of mobilization proceed through lawyers' associations or via professional politics; and (5) the degree of penetration of party politics into the legal complex at the expense of a trans-professional unifying *legal* basis of mobilization.

In historical developments of political liberalism the causal sequence runs more often from lawyers to parties than vice versa. Lawyers' organizations can exist in an absolutist, authoritarian, or one-party state, albeit often with narrowly circumscribed activities. By definition, multiple parties do not, at least formally. Frequently therefore the advocacy of the legal complex for core political rights – speech, association, movement – is a condition of the emergence of liberal party politics. The legal complex, especially the bar, often has acted as a party in exile or opposition, in part because courts and the law provide protections that lawyer/oppositionists could not otherwise obtain. Moreover, the legal complex in some situations, notably Egypt, but in numbers of African countries, has been an advocate for the establishment and maintenance of parties, not least in the politics of constitutionalism. To a point, therefore, defenders of multi-party politics and the legal complex have an affinity of beliefs (i.e. freedoms of speech, negative rights) and a commonality of interests. Thus a curvilinear relationship can be hypothesized between the multiplicity of parties and the activism of the legal complex for political liberalism: too little political expression and institutionalized political debate inhibits mobilization by the legal complex, although it may provoke the legal complex to champion the cause of political speech and a multiparty political regime; too much party-political infusion of professional politics may destroy the very distinctiveness of a liberal-legal politics within the legal complex that gives it a singular authority in the defense of a narrow version of the rule-of-law. When the legal complex helps produce and sustain competitive party politics without those politics producing conflicts within the legal complex itself, then the legal complex has an enhanced capacity to champion political liberalism.

Markets

On the basis of our first wave of studies we initially hypothesized (Halliday and Karpik 1998c) that an orientation towards the market might distract lawyers from politics. Subsequent findings do not permit such a broad conclusion. Several authors (Halliday *et al.* 2007a) offer evidence that the expansion of the market for legal services has positive consequences for lawyers and politics. In Venezuela, the opening up of legal services in the market gave lawyers a foothold outside the state and thus some capacity to stand against the regime. It also multiplied the number of lawyers (Perdomo 2007). In Taiwan and Korea, Ginsburg (2007) similarly maintains that liberalization of the market increased numbers of lawyers. This gave them some independence and moved legal professionals out from under the government umbrella into the private sphere. This autonomy at work makes it easier for professionals to brace the government, a view that also appears in Feeley and Miyasawa's (2007) interpretation of legal development in Japan. In the case of Egypt, Moustafa (2007a) goes further to argue that lawyers' relationship to the market significantly affects the numbers, quality, and ultimate influence of practitioners drawn into the profession who may subsequently exercise leadership against a repressive government. The Egyptian legal complex was most effective in expanding its liberal project when the free market provided an economic base for an independent legal profession, placed some pressure on the regime to enable courts to protect property rights, diffused centers of power and reduced regime levers of control, and impelled groups to mobilize if their interests would be threatened by undermining of the judiciary. In a similar vein, Hilbink (2007b) suggests that government technocrats, although politically conservative, believed that a legal regime protective of property rights and committed to the rule-of-law was a necessary condition for Spain's economic development, a belief that was translated into the building or renovation of legal institutions and the march of administrative law as a protection for business. Brinks (2007) recognizes that the capacity of private prosecutors in Latin America to compel the state to live up to its constitutional commitments depended upon the ability of lawyers to make a living while engaging this kind of law. For many reasons, therefore, the market nurtures capacities for political lawyering.

But markets may also divert lawyers from political engagement and, indeed, may actively dampen activist sentiments in the bar. The overwhelming majority of solicitors in Hong Kong are entirely absorbed with market activities and express some disgruntlement with barristers who stir up trouble on behalf of the rights of workers, or protections of basic rights, or express reservations about intrusive police surveillance and powers (Jones 2007). The shape of the market has affected the nature of representation in China. In the 1980s, before the major expansion of the market, all lawyers had to do some criminal work and therefore were available as counsel. Now many can avoid it, and do. Most of the best lawyers find extraordinary rewards in commercial practice and they distance themselves from the "dirt" of criminal practice. They present mobilization of the profession as a whole for "political" causes rather than allowing business lawyers to keep on making money. Even in criminal law there can be a market distortion as defense lawyers gravitate to those areas of practice that are lucrative, such as corruption cases against officials, rather than those areas where repression is more pronounced, if less well remunerated (Michelson 2003).

Finally, the situation in Singapore demonstrates that it is a hollow hope to suppose that the entrenchment of an independent judiciary for the market, and the establishment of the rule-of-law in commercial dispute resolution, will spill over into issues that threaten the discretionary powers of the state. It is entirely possible for a liberal market and legal system to exist side by side with an illiberal polity and a legal system that insulates itself from "political" engagement (Silverstein 2008).

Hence the theory of the legal complex and political liberalism requires attention to: (1) the legal conditions that rulers decide are necessary to stimulate their national economy and the course of economic development; (2) the size of the private market for legal services and hence the degree of autonomy this gives at least some lawyers from control by the state; and (3) the willingness and ability of the private bar, together with other segments of the legal complex, to withstand a Singaporean-type assault on any expression of legal liberalism that steps outside market transactions.

In a historically contingent theory of rule-of-law development, it will be necessary to disentangle the relative priority of law and economic activity. On the one hand, it is clear that many markets have thrived without a sophisticated legal apparatus, without reliance on law, and without a developed legal complex, as several of the Asian Tigers (Thailand, Indonesia, Korea) illustrate (Ginsburg 2007; Halliday and Carruthers 2009). Markets, in short, can be antecedent to law. On the other hand, it is commonly believed that large, dispersed markets rely on the rational-legal apparatus of a formal legal system that will permit predictability, certainty, and fair treatment of all market players. This may be particularly necessary the further trade expands beyond national boundaries in globalizing markets. Moreover, lawyers and law firms that stand at the apex of professional prestige as commercial lawyers are frequently also vigorous advocates of rights (Dezalay and Garth 2002)

In virtually all cases, success in transitions towards political liberalism was accompanied by a shift of command to market economies or some loosening of national markets from state direction. A theory of political mobilization by the legal complex must test the hypotheses that expanding markets (1) provide more independence and resources for lawyers, (2) attract higher quality, higher prestige classes to legal professions, (3) compel governments to increase the size of the legal profession, (4) increase protection for property rights, and thus (5) strengthen rule-of-law institutions such as constitutional, administrative, and regular courts. But markets can also divert lawyers from "political" activity (cf. France, Hong Kong). And the mere existence of an advanced economy with superb commercial courts does not guarantee full civil rights (cf. Singapore). It is thus a fallacy to imagine that economic development necessarily leads to the institutionalization of basic legal freedoms and political liberalism as a whole. Indeed, the contrary may be so. The conditions under which market professionals turn their back on political mobilization must be a key problem for research.

The state

By definition, political liberalism involves a restructuring of the state. The moderate state is internally divided or counterbalanced by forces outside the state. Civil society exists in counterpoint to the state in its own sphere. First-generation rights frequently are described as rights citizens hold against the state, even if inscribed within it. To get from a politically illiberal state to a state that tolerates or institutionalizes political liberalism must also be a story of state reconstruction.

Although the diverse case studies from four continents do not attempt any typology of states, nor do they focus primarily on attributes of the state itself, nevertheless implicit and sometimes explicit hypotheses arise. A continuing condition that crosses virtually all types of illiberal states requires that rulers provide justice of some sort. No matter how that justice is defined, the demands on rulers require that forums exist in which citizens or residents can have disputes resolved, where state mechanisms for enforcement of social order can be regularized, and where residents within a state may be assured that rule is not entirely arbitrary, especially as it has an impact on their own survival. The legitimacy of rule depends in no small part on the presence of a justice system.

In short, all states, with very few exceptions (cf. Mao's cultural revolution), require systems of justice and those in turn usually involve lawyers, judges, officials, and those who educate them. From this universal of "state-ness" it follows that a legal complex is incipient, however illiberal or segmented it may be. Hence the functional demands of states invariably are accompanied by the structural existence, albeit with many variants, of roles and organizations that valorize law.

To put it more strongly, modern authoritarian rulers require functioning courts to maintain power (Ginsburg and Moustafa 2008), and they adopt strategies to ensure they work sufficiently well to underwrite a legitimacy that cannot be tested in an open vote of the citizenry. In this sense, some differentiation of legal functions already exists in illiberal polities. Hence authoritarian states carry seeds of their own destruction.

The defeat of illiberalism may be hastened by state fragmentation and state incapacity. If rulers cannot control internal divisions between government ministries, within ministries, or across levels of government (e.g. from the capital to the provinces, counties and towns), then competing centers of power can emerge within the state. Such fragmentation can include the justice system which itself can be divided internally and from higher to lower organizational entities. Actors outside the state will act strategically to strengthen those elements of government that best match their interests and where their influence is likely to be most effective. Since private lawyers have a close affinity with courts – in many systems they are also "officers of the court" – a synergistic relationship readily can be nurtured between a vanguard of sympathetic judges and like-minded attorneys. Fragmentation within the justice system therefore potentially facilitates a bridgehead for liberally oriented lawyers and judges who draw sustenance from each other.

State fragmentation may produce state incapacity. Authoritarian state centers may have limited ability to control their cadres at the grassroots level. One solution is to give citizens law and courts in which to bring complaints against administrative failures, corruption, or arbitrariness, as the Chinese government is haphazardly trying. State incapacity can provide openings for new state actors, such as courts, to step into the breach and assert their power. The judicialization of politics is substantially premised on the inadequacies of legislatures and executives to cope with policy issues that produce political deadlock or dangerous disharmony.

States also vary in their dependence on other states and supra-national institutions. Where states, such as Korea and Taiwan during the 1980s

(Ginsburg 2007), shelter underneath a security umbrella, the power providing the security will influence domestic politics, initially in those cases towards authoritarian anti-Communist regimes, but later indirectly and directly through the diffusion of rights discourses and claims. Where states depend on foreign investment and trade, they are likely to be more susceptible to adopt the legal frameworks that purportedly are institutional foundations for both, as Egypt and Spain both demonstrated. Moreover to legitimate themselves in the wider international community, states may be compelled to adopt international norms, such as UN conventions on rights, initially with no expectation that they will be enforced domestically but subsequently with the discovery that rights-conscious domestic constituencies, frequently led by lawyers, will seize what was intended as a symbolic gesture and make it real.

International influences

National developmental sequences are affected by the international milieux of national legal complexes. A quickening of activism and changing relations between the courts, administrative state, and legal profession occurred in Korea and Taiwan in part because their security relationship with the United States brought large numbers of lawyers and judges into contact with their US counterparts who variously valorized separation of powers, use of litigation for social change, and rights consciousness. Spanish judges and lawyers in the frontline of reforms under Franco drew intellectual and moral support from their counterparts in Europe once the borders were opened for the freer flow of people and ideas.

In several countries (cf. Egypt) justice-related NGOs depend heavily on foreign resources – money, advice, access to foreign media, visibility and protection. But the Egyptian case also shows the paradoxical impact of external funding. On the one hand, the vibrancy of the human rights and NGO sector within Egypt depended heavily on overseas funding. On the other hand, when the government became increasingly upset by the success of local NGOs in the SCC, it found it relatively easy to cut them down to size. It painted groups receiving outside money as unpatriotic or even treasonous. On those grounds, it was able to cut overseas funding to a trickle and cut the heart out of the NGO and HRs leadership of civil society. It is a technique well understood by many other repressive regimes or those that are headed in an authoritarian direction, such as Venezuela.

Hence, a theory of political mobilization must treat (1) the type of dependency relationships a nation-state has with other states supportive of political liberalism; (2) the impact of international markets on legal development within a nation-state; and (3) the direct resources from nonstate and state actors that flow to a liberal legal complex or groups allied with a liberal legal complex.

Ideational forces

States and civil societies exist in a world of discourses, ideologies, and beliefs, all of which permeate national orientations to varying degrees and structure domestic politics, including those of the legal complex. The case studies show that political ideologies heavily influence the openness of national elites to liberal politics, whether they take the form of the illiberal manifestations of nationalism (e.g. Japan and Germany, 1930s, China 2000s), fascism (e.g. Germany in the Third Reich, Italy under Mussolini) and Communism (e.g. the former Soviet Union, China), or illiberal responses, such as anti-Communist authoritarian regimes supported by the US and manifested in Latin America and Asia during the Cold War. By contrast, argue world society scholars, in the twentieth century, and especially after World War II, there has emerged a universal culture of individualism, rationality, and modernity that has been institutionalized in transnational institutions from the UN to the European Court of Human Rights and that advances a particular version of the rule-of-law which threatens illiberal politics. This discourse and its claims to universality is conveyed and reinforced by ideologies of professionalism, with its amalgam of commitments to science, neutrality, universals, and autonomy from political control (Boyle and Meyer 2002; Silbey 1997).

The politics of the legal complex, however, also are permeated by juridical theories. Although these are not extensively developed in the national case studies, a contrast is drawn between positivist jurisprudence, which insists upon the fealty of judges to the ascendancy of state-based law, and a liberal legal jurisprudence, which argues for the primacy of rights that transcend the constitutions or statutes of any state. The former, it is argued, enables judges and lawyers to lend support to authoritarian regimes so long as those regimes adhere to certain formal modes of lawmaking; the latter, it is maintained, hold rulers and lawmaking of all sorts accountable to higher values than those formalized in statutes or executive orders.

The intersection of legal and economic theory provides a salient ideational context for political liberalism. The extant theory of law and finance currently advocated by international financial institutions directly links rule-of-law-type regimes with the probability that developing and transitional nations will obtain adequate foreign investment for domestic economic growth. Whether or not national leaders believe that stronger and independent courts, expanded private legal professions, and a raft of new statutes and regulatory regimes will stimulate the in-bound flow of capital, they are compelled by a global consensus, and occasionally coerced by IFIs, to conform their domestic institutions to the global models. Even if there is a substantial decoupling between symbolic compliance and implementation, activists in an enhanced legal complex may obtain legitimacy and structural facilities to transform symbolic into actual institutions.

A theory of mobilization by the legal complex, therefore, will integrate three sets of ideational factors: (1) the force of prevailing regional and global ideologies that champion basic legal freedoms, (2) the pervasiveness of jurisprudential theory that valorizes fundamental rights of citizenship over positive law; and (3) the content of market ideology, especially in the ways it links law to economic behavior.

Precipitating factors

While international and national cultural and social institutions may be variably conducive to a move towards or away from the rule-of-law components of political liberalism, a decisive move frequently is associated with a trigger or *cause célèbre* or precipitating event that stimulates a legal complex and states to act.

Repeatedly we observe that threats to nation-states and their ruling classes trigger a restriction of basic legal freedoms. The threat can be external (Korea, Taiwan, US, Israel, Japan) or internal (e.g. Communism in Spain and Chile, Islamic fundamentalism in Egypt, lawlessness in Argentina, Brazil). Whether the threat is "real" or made to seem real may be immaterial. If publics can be persuaded they are under threat, then leaders obtain support for repression. An exception is Hong Kong in the 1960s and 1970s: the rule-of-law was expanded by Hong Kong authorities precisely as a counterpoint to the ideology of Communist China.

Events can also trigger a sudden surge in demands for a strengthening of the rule-of-law, not infrequently led by the legal complex. An especially egregious abrogation of rights by security forces, arbitrary killings, an excessive response to public protests, the sudden collapse or defeat of a repressive government, a severing of foreign aid in response to rights abuses, the public disclosure of torture and assassinations, an obviously rigged election, an assault on the judiciary or attacks on lawyers – each of these in propitious circumstances has been the match that has lit a fire.

Nevertheless, a mutual contingency exists between facilitating factors and precipitating events. A slowly developing conduciveness to basic legal freedoms, inside the legal complex, the state, civil society, and the market, may not crystallize until a trigger compels recognition of the incipient developments that are then institutionalized in visible form. Conversely, a spark may stimulate outrage, riots, public statements, foreign condemnations, and activism, but without the groundwork, without structures already in place, without templates for action and alliances in place, an opportunity for the assertion of core rights will be lost.

Conclusion

From a large variety of case studies this chapter has extracted sets of factors that are integral to a theory of mobilization by the legal complex on behalf of political liberalism. It has shown where research finds interactions among those factors that transcend a single historical instance. And it has proceeded inductively towards a causal and constitutive theory of the role of the legal complex in the construction of a liberal politics that protects fundamental freedoms integral to the rule-of-law.

The limits of this exercise point to further questions and subsequent steps in theory development. First, it has not yet been shown whether the factors that influence mobilization are constant across different types of political transition. For instance, the role of the legal complex, and the significance of factors that shape it, might differ markedly when the legal complex is fighting for a transition to a rule-of-law society, rather than when it is consolidating such a regime, or defending it against attack or the threat of dissolution. The capacity for mobilization by the legal complex and the conduciveness of civil society, political parties, and market-based groups may be much greater in consolidation and defense of the rule-of-law than in the struggle for its establishment. Correlatively, the impact of international political and juridical ideology, and the influence of international associations, may be proportionately much greater when lawyers and judges are fighting against authoritarian regimes than when a breakthrough to a rule-of-law regime has already occurred. Hence it is necessary to examine whether the structure and dynamics of the legal complex, and the social forces that influence it, require a theory contingent on type of political transition.

Second, mobilization by the legal complex is not to be confused with success. The case studies are replete with examples of unsuccessful mobilization – when fragments of the legal complex or its coalitions act to obtain or defend the rule-of-law but are impaired, frustrated, or repudiated. Indeed, in country after country the fight for an initial transition from an illiberal to liberal regime may go on for decades, if not centuries, before any breakthrough occurs – and in many cases such a transition never occurs decisively. In the case of state attributes, for instance, there is evidence that success by the legal complex will be associated with a change in state policy to encourage international capital, increased international trade, or international legitimacy (e.g. Spain 1950s, Egypt 1970s, China 1990s), and by a state's establishment or extension of rule-of-law institutions, such as constitutional and administrative courts, to comply with international pressures. By contrast, in many instances failure has been associated with imperative state-led models of economic development, rampant nationalism, and international conflict.

Third, there are limits to a causal analysis which compound the theoretical problem. The factors we have identified do not array in a simple line of antecedent and subsequent causes. Because the legal complex is partially constitutive of the state and partially constitutive of civil society, at most there is a recursive dynamic of reciprocal cycles of reinforcement or retreat, and at least there is a mutual constitutiveness that renders the parsing out of effects seemingly intractable.

In conclusion, a historical and comparative inductively generated theory of the legal complex, political liberalism, and the rule-of-law remains a significant challenge. We have shown that the legal complex frequently is implicated in mobilization for basic freedoms in many regions and historical instances. We can parse out structural and dynamic attributes of that mobilization and identify many factors that recur. It remains to develop theory through complementary efforts at intensive case studies and refined comparative research.

Notes

1 This chapter builds upon a collaborative project whose principal results were published in Halliday *et al.* (2007a). I am particularly grateful to my colleagues, Lucien Karpik and Malcolm Feeley, for their comments on earlier fragments of this chapter. This research was supported by the American Bar Foundation and two grants from the National Science Foundation (SES-9213156; SES-0452250) for which I express appreciation.
2 For details on the logic of using this concept and the explication of its elements, see Halliday and Karpik (1998b) and Halliday *et al.* (2007b).
3 The stipulation of "practicing law" excludes those large numbers of legally trained graduates of universities in Europe and Latin America who never practice law but go into business, politics, or government bureaucracies.
4 Bracketed references to case studies can be cross-referenced to their authors in Table 10.1. It should be emphasized that the references are to studies of specific events, limited by time and territory, and not to any generalized typification of a country or period.
5 By "political lawyers" we refer to those who self-consciously mobilize on behalf of political liberalism in pursuit of the rule-of-law (Halliday and Karpik 2001; Karpik 2007).
6 Just the contrary argument has been made for the bureaucratic integration of courts – that by coordinating all courts in one coordinated structure that is administered by a court administration, this provides some protection for the incursions on local courts by local politics. See Halliday (1987).
7 For another perspective on the play of religion, see Karpik (2007).

Chapter 11

Social norms, rule of law, and gender reality

An essay on the limits of the dominant rule-of-law paradigm[1]

Katharina Pistor, Antara Haldar, and Amrit Amirapu

Introduction

The rule-of-law is a powerful concept that has inspired political theorists over the centuries. More recently it has become one of the dominant paradigms for social and economic reforms and policy agendas at multilateral institutions, such as the World Bank,[2] or for interest group organizations, like the American Bar Association.[3] The enthusiasm for the rule-of-law as a remedy for a range of social and economic ills is supported by empirical data showing a strong positive association between measures of the rule-of-law and a host of desirable outcome variables, ranging from levels of GDP, foreign direct investment, and trade flows, all the way to human rights and child mortality data.[4] Rule of law proponents are not, however, without their critics. Some of the most forcefully voiced critiques focus on measurement issues (Voigt 2008); others on the interpretation of the data and their translation into policy prescriptions (Arndt and Oman 2006); while still others have questioned whether the observed empirical affinity between rule-of-law and different outcome variables has been sufficiently theorized to generate meaningful insights (Thomas 2007).

In this chapter we raise a different issue, namely the limited ability of "rule-of-law" to explain observable differences *within* a given country. More specifically, we focus on minorities that either do not share in whatever benefits are commonly associated with rule-of-law reforms or else share in the benefits only indirectly in ways that are insufficiently understood. We analyze these "minorities" by focusing on women as an example. Our claim is that the basic insights this chapter generates could be applied to other disadvantaged social groups as well.

Technically speaking, women are not a minority. In principle the numbers of men and women in any given society should be roughly equal. Nonetheless, in many countries males outnumber women by a significant margin – a phenomenon Amartya Sen has famously described as the "missing women" (Sen 1989).[5] This gender gap has been attributed to both sex selective foeticide and female infanticide, but also, crucially, neglect of girl children, which substantially lowers life expectancy for infant girls. Further, in some countries the ratio of women to men has worsened recently, suggesting that this phenomenon cannot be traced to historical legacies or rates of poverty alone.[6] This includes countries with impressive recent economic growth achievements, such as China and India. But mortality rates are, of course, only the crudest way of measuring the status of women in society. Indeed, over the past decade a number of indices have been created that seek to measure women's "capabilities" more broadly (the UN's Gender Development and Gender Empowerment Indices, GDI and GEM), women's achievements or status in relation to men (the World Economic Forum's Gender Gap Index, GAP), as well as the legal and social institutions that determine the status of women (the OECD's Gender Institutions and Development Index, GID). In order to provide a fuller account of the status and well-being of women in a society, we will discuss these various indices in the paper and will explore their relationship with widely recognized rule-of-law indicators. In addition, we will analyze specific legal interventions at the international and national levels aimed at affecting the status of women in society and assess their results.

At the very outset, we would like to emphasize that this chapter does not purport to explain the status of women in society. Instead, it uses a gendered approach to expose the limits of the dominant rule-of-law paradigm and to suggest new avenues for future research and policy considerations.

The chapter is divided into three parts. Part A explores the relation between the rule-of-law and the status of women in society using existing data sets. Part B assesses the impact of specific legal policy interventions on gender reality at the international and the national levels. Part C uses the findings of Parts A and B as the basis for a critique of the dominant rule-of-law paradigm. In the conclusion, we make suggestions for future research and policy design.

Part A: Rule of law and gender reality

The current fascination with the rule-of-law is closely associated with the forays that economics and political science have made into the field of law and legal institutions and the technologies they have brought to this field – including, although not limited to, the ability to quantify institutions and use statistical tools to assess their impact. The importance of the rule-of-law for economic development was first documented in quantitative terms by Knack and Keefer (1994), as well as Mauro (1995). These early studies relied heavily on single surveys primarily of foreign investors and their perception of the rule of law in the host countries in which they were investing.[7] In these studies, rule of law was a component variable based on several questions that asked about the dominance of formal legal devices over others, including violence, politics, or personal relations, for resolving disputes primarily in the realm of contracts and property. Over the past 15 years, both survey techniques, and the construction of indices have improved. The most comprehensive indices related to the rule-of-law currently available are the World Bank's governance indicators, also referred to as the WGI (Kaufmann *et al.* 2007b). The WGI measure various dimensions of governance such as the "rule of law" and "government effectiveness." The indices are based on surveys and combine the results from a variety of different sources. By averaging information from multiple data sources, the WGI seek to mitigate the idiosyncrasies of individual survey instruments in an attempt to enhance their informational content.[8] The WGI have been widely used in the literature to assert the importance of the rule of law.

Nevertheless, using survey instruments to measure the quality of institutions remains highly problematic. Sampling issues loom large, as well as concerns about the familiarity of respondents with the institutions they are queried about, and the implicit benchmark they might be using when ranking the institutions of a particular country on a scale. To avoid these problems, other indices have sought to measure the rule-of-law in a more objective fashion. The most comprehensive index based on close readings of constitutions and legal statutes is the "Political Constraints Index" (PolCon) developed by Witold Henisz (2000).[9] The primary purpose of the PolCon index is to measure the formal constraints on state power by recording the number of institutionalized vetoes in a given political system. Interestingly, the two indices seem to capture different aspects of the rule-of-law, indicated by the less than perfect correlation between them (see Table 11.1). In the empirical tests that follow, we use both PolCon and the "rule of law" (ROL) index from the WGI in order to show that our results are robust for at least two fairly dissimilar measures of the rule of law, both of which are used widely in the literature.

Against the backdrop of numerous empirical studies that show a positive correlation between rule-of-law (ROL) or Political Constraints (PolCon) and a host of desirable outcome variables, one might expect that a similar relationship would also hold between rule-of-law and the status of women in society. But as per a new worldwide survey instrument by the Economic Forum in Davos measuring the "gender gap," equality between men and women – in the sense of equal access to political, economic, and social positions of power – has not been achieved in *any* society. According to the 2007 Gender GAP data, Sweden, is the highest-ranking country, with a score of 0.8146 on the Gender Gap index, where a ratio of 1.0 would indicate full equality. Thus, even in Sweden there is still a substantial gap between men and women (Hausmann *et al.* 2007: 7).

Table 11.1 Two measures of the rule of law: ROL correlated with PolCon (including number of observations; unit: countries)

	rol2006
polconiii	0.440**
(# of obs)	182

Note: ** significant at .05 level.

Nonetheless, there is evidence that in many countries the status of women has improved substantially over the past decades. Further, it is not unreasonable to believe that legal mechanisms have played an important role in supporting this change. It is certainly the case that the observed change in the socioeconomic status of women, especially in countries of the West, coincides with important legal change – including universal suffrage, changes in family law, as well as legally enshrined affirmative action programs. Yet, there is little evidence beyond these observations to show that legal change has indeed brought about greater gender equality. In fact, there are good reasons to be skeptical about the ability of formal legal change to have an immediate impact on social outcomes. Social change tends to be a long-term process and social engineering by way of legal reform has not been wildly successful.[10] Even in the realm of civil and commercial law, transplanting legal institutions from one society has required more than simply supplying "good" institutions. Instead, the process of transplanting law, or the "demand" side of legal reform has proved to be critical for new institutions to make an imprint in the host environment (See Berkowitz and Clay 2005; Berkowitz *et al.* 2003a).

To investigate the relationship between the rule-of-law and the status of women more systematically, we analyze the correlations between "rule-of-law" (ROL) – probably the most widely used of the of the six components of WGI – as well as PolCon, and several proximate measures of the status of women in society.[11] Among the possible proxies, we select three indices that explicitly aim to measure the status of women in society. Two of these indices have been around for a while, although to our knowledge they have not been widely used in studies related to the rule-of-law. These are the gender-related development index, or GDI, and the gender empowerment measure, or GEM, both developed under the auspices of the UNDP. Conceptually, they are subsets of the Human Development Index (HDI). Based on Amartya Sen's seminal work on the importance of human capabilities, HDI codes three aspects of human development: "a long and healthy life" (measured by life expectancy at birth), "knowledge" (i.e. educational attainment captured by adult literacy rates and gross enrollment ratios), and a "decent standard of living" (measured by GDP per capita). Specifically, GDI compares how males and females score on the HDI subindices and on this basis constructs "equally distributed indices" for each of these subindices. GEM measures more directly the political, economic and social status of women by constructing indices for "political participation and decision-making," "economic participation and decision-making," and "power over economic resources." The differential between males and females is used to construct three "equally distributed equivalent percentage" (EDEP) subindices, which comprise GEM.

The Economic Forum's GAP index, referred to above, has strong similarities with the GDI and GEM indices – measuring inequality in the domains of politics, economics, health, and education – but differs in two important respects. First, it does not include income directly as a component.[12] Second, it measures only the ratio of women's values on certain outcome variables (school enrolment, life expectancy, etc.) to men's values on those variables. It therefore ranks countries by the size of the gender difference (or "gap") in social achievements and does not penalize countries for having low base levels of outcome variables to begin with. For example, a country is not penalized if it has low school-enrollment rates. Rather, it receives a low score only if the ratio between female and male school-enrollment rates is low.

Meanwhile the OECD has constructed yet another index, the Gender, Institutions and Development (GID) Index. Unlike GDI, GEM, and GAP, GID focuses on institutions that affect gender equality in society including the prevailing family code, women's physical integrity, women's civil liberties, and women's ownership rights. Therefore, GID measures "input" variables of women's status, while GAP, GEM, and GDI attempt to measure "outcome" variables, or the status of women itself. Mindful of the relevance of both formal and informal institutions to the status of women, most of the sub-indices of the GID index measure both formal and informal institutions. We will return to the important distinction between formal and informal institutions in Part C, but for now we are only interested in the relationship between *formal* legal institutions and the status of women. Thus we cannot use the GID index as it exists as a measure of either legal institutions, informal institutions, or the status of women, because the index measures all three concepts at once.[13] Table 11.2 below reports simple correlations between the four gender-related indices discussed above, as well as correlations between these indices and our chosen measures of the rule-of-law (ROL and PolCon).

As can be seen, the gender indices are all positively correlated. Of particular note is the high correlation between GDI and HDI (more than 0.99), and the correspondingly high correlation between GDI and GDP.[14] This figure may not be so surprising given that GDP is an important subcomponent of HDI – and therefore GDI – but it does make GDI less valuable as an outcome measure of the status of women. Although income is likely to be correlated with the status of women in society, we would like to avoid measuring income directly if possible. GEM, on the other hand, has a lower correlation with income levels but it also has the smallest sample size, making it less suitable for use in statistical tests. The best index for our purposes of measuring the status of women, from a theoretical as well as an empirical standpoint, seems to be the Gender Gap index. This index contains data for more than 100 countries, measures only outcome variables, does not measure income, culture, or policies directly, and measures only the presence of gender-based inequality via female-to-male ratios rather than overall poor development. Therefore, it is this index that will be the focal point of most of our subsequent analysis, although we will also provide tests using other outcome measures when suitable, to strengthen our claims for robustness.

Also of interest in Table 11.2 are the correlations between the gender indices and the rule-of-law indices (in bold type). The correlations between rule-of-law and the status of women are moderate to strong for all indices, though the

Table 11.2 Gender related indices correlated against rule of law indices (including number of observations; unit: countries)

	gid	gap07	*gdi*	gem	*hdi*	*rol2006*	*polconiii*
gid	1.0000 117						
gap07	0.7039 102	1.0000 128					
gdi	0.7545 105	0.5855 115	1.0000 131				
gem	0.6450 62	0.8170 73	0.7166 69	1.0000 73			
hdi	0.7157 116	0.5688 123	0.9995 131	0.7128 73	1.0000 153		
rol2006	**0.4862** 117	**0.4616** 128	**0.7482** 131	**0.7361** 73	**0.7213** 153	1.0000 211	
polconiii	**0.4800** 117	**0.3542** 127	**0.4127** 131	**0.5446** 73	**0.3745** 150	0.4404 182	1.0000 182
lngdp2005	0.6133 116	0.4952 128	0.9303 131	0.7139 73	0.9292 150	0.8156 174	0.3247 169

Note: All correlations significant at .05 level.

correlation is lowest for those indices that do not explicitly include income as a component (i.e. GAP and GID). This finding is, so far, consistent with the dominant Rule of Law (ROL) paradigm referred to above. Given the assumptions of the ROL paradigm, we would expect countries with better levels of the rule of law to have higher levels of women's status, and, from the correlations above, there appears to be at least some preliminary support for this hypothesis. The results of the correlations are displayed graphically in Figures 11.1a and 11.1b.

Before we proceed any further, let us pause to look at the variables we are examining more closely. Table 11.3 reports descriptive statistics for our main indicators of the status of women and the rule-of-law: GAP, ROL, and PolCon. For each variable, statistics are given for the full sample of countries for which there is data on the variable, as well as for two smaller groups of countries: a restricted sample of about 60 countries for which we have household-level data on social norms about gender equality, and another subset consisting of the countries of the EU and North America (EU/NA), which we offer as a benchmark group for purposes of regional comparisons. All three variables, GAP, ROL, and PolCon, are treated as continuous variables whose

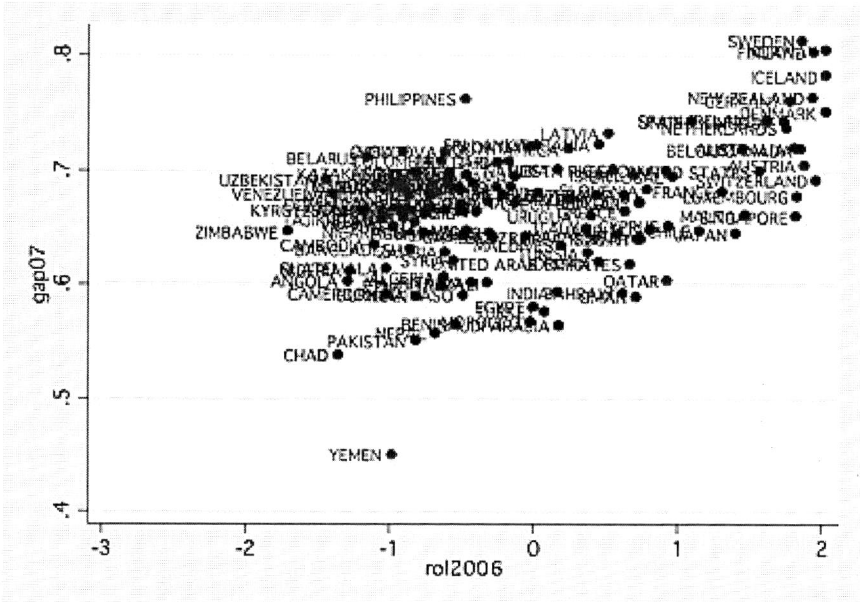

Figure 11.1a Women's status vs rule of law: GAP vs ROL.

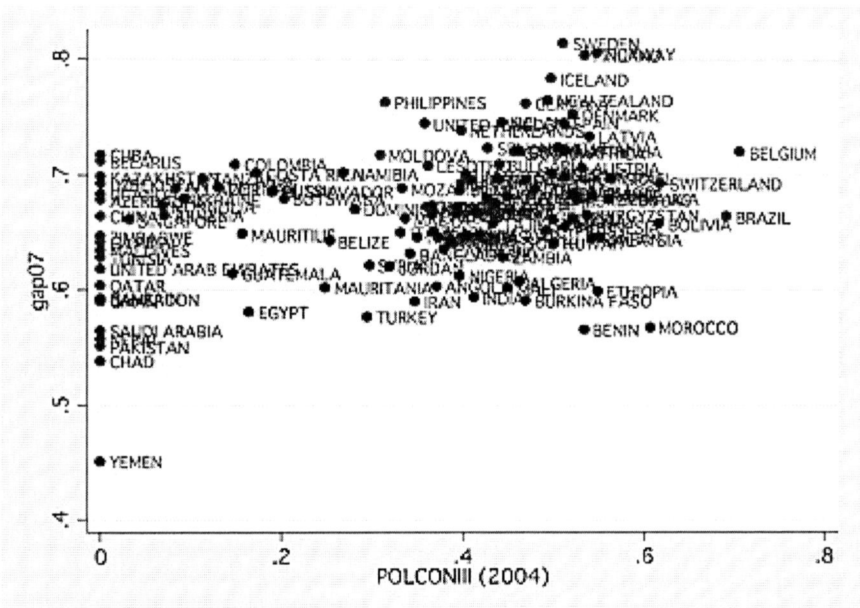

Figure 11.1b Women's status vs rule of law: GAP vs PolCon.

Table 11.3 Descriptive statistics on GAP, ROL, and PolCon

	gap07			*rol2006*			*polconiii*		
	full sample	*restricted sample*	*EU/ NA*	*full sample*	*restricted sample*	*EU/ NA*	*full sample*	*restricted sample*	*EU/ NA*
mean	.667	.680	.727	.000	.281	1.539	.280	.366	.477
median	.671	.681	.720	−.174	.207	1.471	.345	.410	.498
st. dev.	.057	.056	.049	1	1.064	.492	.211	.184	.095
variance	.003	.003	.002	1	1.132	.242	.045	.034	.009
min	.451	.551	.650	−2.530	−1.949	.372	0	0	.332
max	.815	.815	.815	2.030	2.030	2.030	.706	.706	.706
skew	−.309	−.129	.266	.207	.079	−1.047	−.176	−.891	.351
kurtosis	4.233	3.057	2.085	2.169	1.938	2.938	1.605	2.753	2.901
obs	128	64	21	211	68	22	182	66	21

values may theoretically range between 0 and 1 (for GAP and PolCon) or about -2.5 to 2.5 (in the case of ROL), with higher scores indicating higher levels of either women's status or the rule-of-law, as the case may be.

So far, the conventional wisdom appears justified – higher levels of rule-of-law tend to correlate with better status of women. But closer examination reveals that by dividing countries up by income bracket, a very different picture starts to emerge. We do this in Table 11.4, and depict the results

Table 11.4 The Gender Puzzle: GAP correlated against ROL and PolCon by income brackets (including significance and number of observations; unit: countries)

		gap06
	rol2006	0.7030**
HIC		36
	polconiii	0.6110**
		36
	rol2006	-0.0682
UMC		23
	polconiii	0.0960
		23
	rol2006	0.1065
LMC		31
	polconiii	0.0685
		31
	rol2006	0.0963
LIC		25
	polconiii	0.1155
		25

graphically in scatter plots below (Figures 11.2a and 11.2b). In both the correlation results and the scatter plots, we see that the positive correlation between GAP and ROL/PolCon is limited *exclusively* to the group of high-income countries. *In no other income group does there appear to be a correlation between rule-of-law and the status of women.* It is this rather vexing "Gender Puzzle" that will be the central focus of our subsequent discussion.

What could be the explanation for this anomalous result? The positive relationship between rule-of-law and the status of women in high-income countries does not, in itself, tell us much. And it is certainly not clear why the correlation exists only for high-income countries and not for other income brackets. Why is it that a sufficient level of economic development seems to be necessary before higher values of the rule-of-law are translated into higher levels of the status of minority groups such as women? Indeed, this perplexing role of income in the rule-of-law–women's status relationship is complicated even further by recent data from China and India suggesting that economic growth may be correlated with a decline, rather than an improvement, in the status of women, as suggested by the increase in female mortality rates during the high-growth period in both countries (Klasen and Wink 2003). Is the problem essentially one of "transplanting" foreign institutions to "unreceptive" soil? Or could it also be the case that both our conception of the rule-of-law and gender equality is socially and culturally constructed, i.e. a construct of

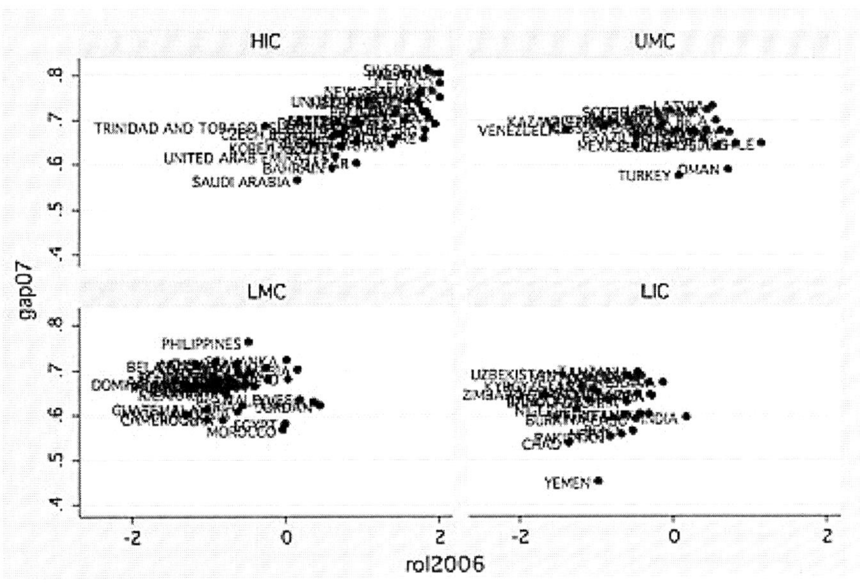

Figure 11.2a The Gender Puzzle: GAP vs ROL by income bracket.

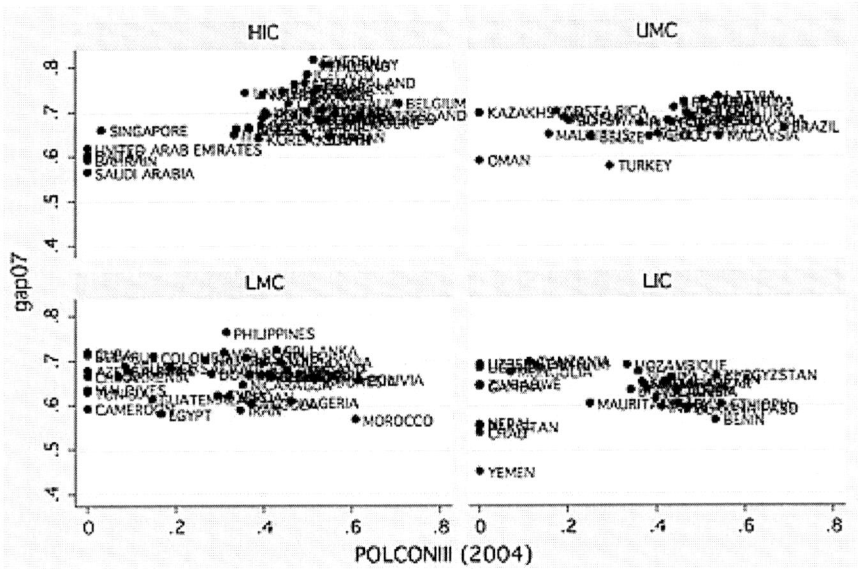

Figure 11.2b The Gender Puzzle: GAP vs PolCon by income bracket.

Western preferences or historical experiences, but neither replicable nor as universal as usually claimed?

Probing these questions further will be the main task of Part B of this chapter. At this juncture, however, we attempt to develop a better sense of the regional variation of the status of women in society by dividing the world by region and reporting correlations of GAP with ROL and PolCon accordingly (see Table 11.5 and Figures 11.3a and 11.3b).

These results are much more ambiguous – although in part this may be due to low numbers of observations in each regional category. There appears to be a strong linear relationship between GAP and ROL in Europe and North America, i.e. predominantly high-income countries, while the relationships between women's status and rule-of-law in other regions are less clear, if they exist at all.

We find statistically significant levels of correlation across the different indices used only in the Middle East and North Africa and in sub-Saharan Africa. These results suggest that the relationship between the rule-of-law and the status of women is not uniform around the globe. Nevertheless, our results in Table 11.4 and Figures 11.2a and 11.2b do seem to suggest that, within income brackets, the strong positive correlations expected between women's status and rule-of-law do seem to be glaringly absent from all but the richest group of countries. To put it more provocatively, if we were to consider the share of the female world population for which we can establish a positive correlation and for which we cannot, we are confronted with a ratio of 15 to 85 percent.[15]

Table 11.5 The Gender Puzzle: GAP correlated against ROL and PolCon by region (including significance and number of observations; unit: countries)

Region		*gap07*
CAS	rol2006	0.0665
		25
	polconiii	0.0776
		25
EAP	rol2006	0.2489
		13
	polconiii	0.0612
		13
MENA	rol2006	0.5954**
		16
	polconiii	0.4515*
		16
SA	rol2006	0.4954
		6
	polconiii	0.6169
		6
SSA	rol2006	0.5068**
		24
	polconiii	-0.0590
		24
LAC	rol2006	-0.0337
		23
	polconiii	-0.2530
		22
EU&NA	rol2006	0.6288**
		21
	polconiii	0.3291
		21

Part B: The dominant rule-of-law paradigm in light of social theories

One possible explanation of the observed breakdown in the relationship between rule-of-law and the status of women may be the "transplant" hypothesis mentioned briefly above. If a legal system is imposed on a country from without, we might expect the rule-of-law to have less traction in that country when compared to another country that had either originated its own legal system or adapted another legal system to its own particular needs and

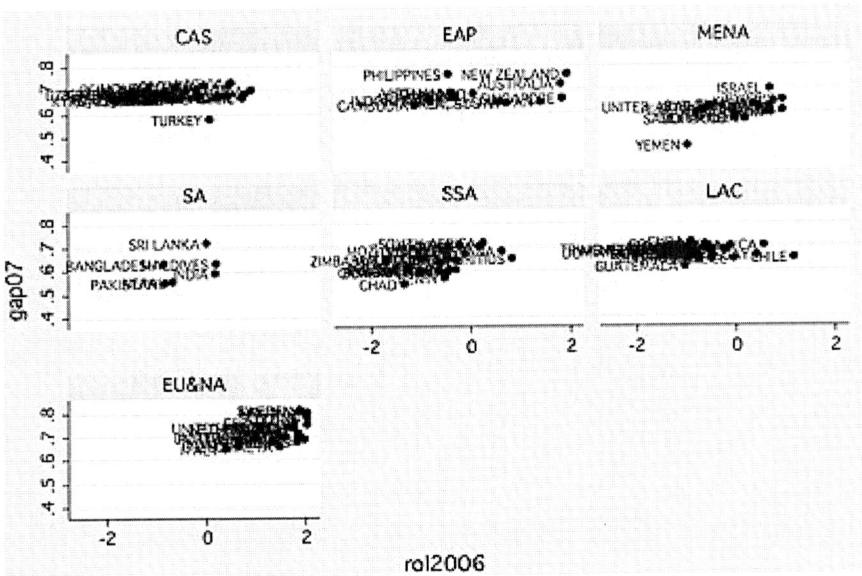

Figure 11.3a GAP vs ROL by region.

circumstances. If this is the case, and assuming that the rule-of-law – in ideal circumstances – has a positive effect on the status of women, we would expect the correlation between the status of women and the rule-of-law to be higher in those countries that were originators of legal systems or "receptive transplants," when compared to the group of countries that had foreign legal systems imposed upon them ("unreceptive transplants"). This is indeed what we observe in Table 11.6. Because the group of "origin/receptive" countries is, in essence, a subset of the high-income countries,[16] this might explain why there

Table 11.6 The Transplant Explanation: GAP correlated against ROL/PolCon by transplant status (including significance and numbers of observations; unit: countries)

Region		*gap07*
Origin/Receptive Countries	rol2006	.536**
		21
	polconiii	0.120
		21
Unreceptive Countries	rol2006	0.131
		26
	polconiii	0.277
		26

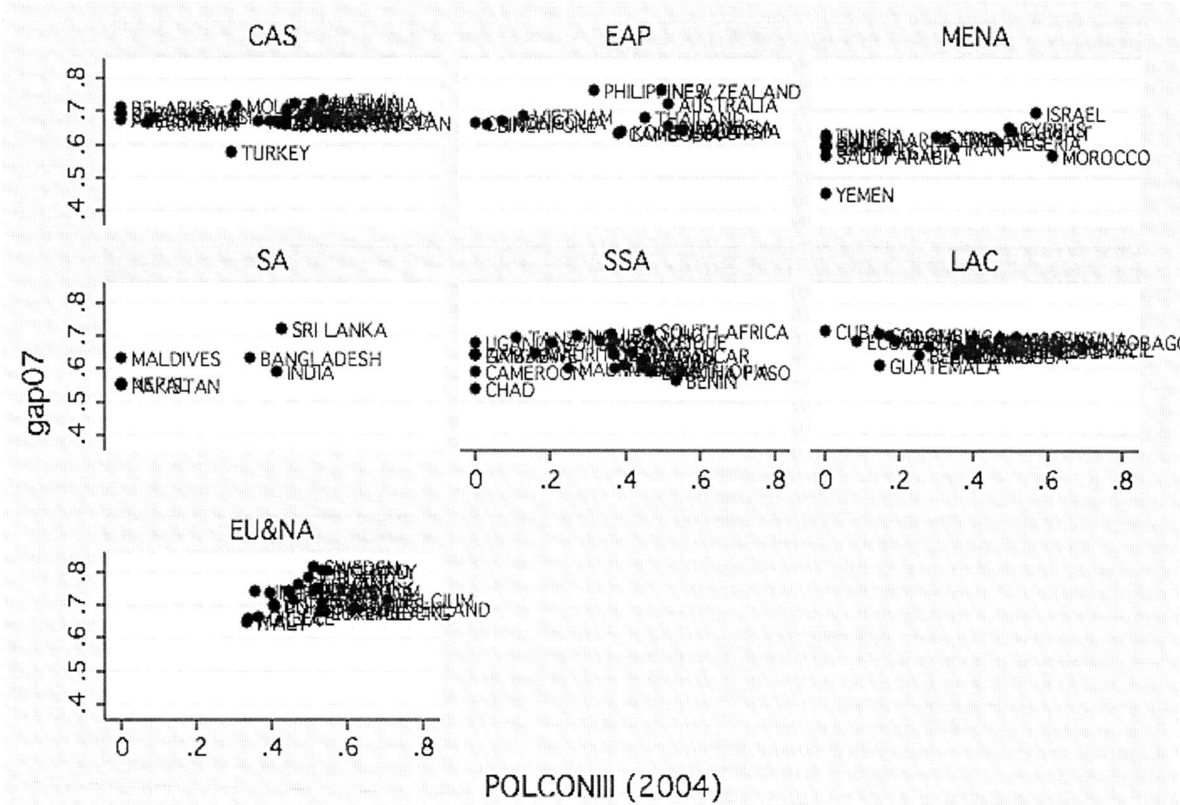

Figure 11.3b GAP vs PolCon by region.

is a correlation between the status of women and the rule-of-law only for high-income countries.

But this insight may reveal deeper misunderstandings underlying the current rule-of-law paradigm. Indeed, there is currently a lively debate over measuring and interpretation problems of the rule-of-law. Some authors have critiqued the WGI, because they are based entirely on perception-based indicators generated by survey instruments rather than objective indicators (Voigt 2008; Kurtz and Schrank 2007b). Others have argued that measurements of the rule-of-law lack concept validity as they are not well grounded in existing theoretical literatures (Thomas 2007). Yet others have pointed out that existing theories about the impact of certain concepts on policy outcomes (i.e. the rule-of-law on economic growth) require better theoretical foundations and greater issue specificity than the current governance indicators have (Kurtz and Schrank 2007a).

We share many of these critiques. Yet our main point is a different one. Rather than suggesting that the rule-of-law paradigm is under-theorized, we suggest that it is based implicitly on a social theory which is deeply flawed. In a nutshell, the implicit social theory of the rule-of-law paradigm assumes that law is authoritative and capable of changing outcomes irrespective of pre-existing conditions; it assumes that legal institutions once in place will be used in a bottom-up process of social ordering where, in principle, everyone can mobilize the law to further their ends; and that the major cleavage in every society is between the state and individuals. To illustrate how these assumptions affect the conceptualization of the rule-of-law, we analyze key elements of the dominant rule-of-law paradigm and compare it with other accounts. As our point of departure we take the definition of the rule-of-law as proposed by the World Justice Project (WJP), a new initiative sponsored by the American Bar Association. The WJP uses a working definition for its public forums and the construction of a new rule-of-law index, which comprises four allegedly "universal" principles (see column 1 in Table 11.7).[17] The WJP's definition has certain advantages over the WGI's conceptualization of the rule-of-law. It is more precise, and unlike the WGI the concept has not shifted over time,[18] which is not surprising given its recent vintage. Moreover, arguably there is a better overlap with prevailing theories of the rule-of-law as those summarized by Fallon (1997) (see column 2 of Table 11.7).[19] Fallon identifies five elements of the rule-of-law, which are listed in column 2.

Nonetheless, there are also important differences in the two definitions, which are worth examining more closely.[20] As compared to Fallon's summary of the key ingredients for the rule-of-law, the WJP's indicators are not only more "wordy" (creating the possibility of multiple interpretations), but they also include substantive policy preferences.[21] Thus, while Fallon adopts a largely formal or procedural concept of the rule-of-law, the WJP mixes it with specific normative goals. Examples include the emphasis on fundamental rights and in particular on "security of persons and property" where Fallon's definition is limited to the stability of legal rules. "Fairness" is another term that appears

Table 11.7 Competing rule of law concepts

World Justice Project (2007) "rule of law"	*Fallon (1997) "rule of law"*
	The capacity of legal rules, standards or principles to guide people in the conduct of their affairs
The government and its officials and agents are accountable under the law	The supremacy of legal authority *for citizens* and government actors
The laws are clear, publicized, stable, and *fair, and protect fundamental rights, including the security of persons and property*	The stability of legal rules
The process by which the laws are enacted, administered, and enforced is accessible, *fair*, and efficient	The efficacy of legal rules
The laws are upheld, and access to justice is provided, by competent, independent, and ethical law enforcement officials, attorneys or representatives, *and judges, who are of sufficient number, have adequate resources, and reflect the makeup of the communities they serve*	The availability of impartial institutions of enforcement

twice in the WJP definition without further explanation (i.e. fairness in procedural or substantive terms; according to whose judgment, etc.), but is missing in Fallon's definition.

It should be noted that Fallon's concept is not completely devoid of normative principles. However, they are stated quite differently. The first principle of the rule-of-law according to his definition requires that legal rules, standards or principles have the capacity to guide people in the conduct of their affairs. How this capacity is generated is a core question of social theories many of which emphasize the importance of social norms and of legitimacy.

The failure to raise the question of when law and legal institutions are capable of guiding people is, in our view, a major flaw in the WJP's rule-of-law concept – as well as related concepts, such as the World Bank's ill-specified rule-of-law definitions, but also Henisz's exclusive focus on veto powers within the formal constitutional order. Substituting a serious inquiry about the conditions under which compliance with law is generated across different societies with a claim about the superiority of certain normative goals assumes that these goals – i.e. property rights, the security of the person, and fairness – are universal norms and that their priority over other normative claims is uncontested. It must, further, assume (at least if the claim is that this rule-of-law concept has any predictive power for social outcomes) that because these are universal and uncontested norms their endorsement by law will generate respect for the law and, thus, compliance. This conjecture assumes what should be proven.

Analyzing the relation between the status of women in society and the rule-of-law can help illustrate this point. Gender relations – as most social relations – in any society are governed by multiple sets of overlapping systems of norms.[22] The formal legal system is only one of them and may not be the dominant one. In fact, as the evidence discussed in the previous sections suggest, formal law is often not outcome determinative for the de facto status of women in society. Thus, it is reasonable to assume that in many contexts the formal legal system and prevailing social norms on gender equality are not mutually reinforcing, but that they conflict with each other.

To demonstrate this point we have collected data from the World Value Survey (WVS), which surveys thousands of individuals around the world to find out how they value certain aspects of social and political life (European Values Study Foundation and World Values Survey Association 2006). The WVS is not without problems. Many of the questions designed to capture attitudes about gender equality are culturally rooted in Western societies, so that questions about the "right to work outside the home" or the "right to have an abortion" might have very different interpretations in other countries. Specifically, these questions are likely to gain a very different meaning in contexts where the survival of the family requires not only women but even children to work, or where forced abortion is a means of state-enforced policies of birth control. Still, in the absence of better data, we present some evidence on the relation between social norms and the rule-of-law and their relative importance in determining the status of women in society. From among the questions in the WVS that address gender issues we selected one that, at face value, seems to be less affected by economic or political differences. This question asks whether in times of job scarcity men should be given preference in obtaining jobs over women. Respondents' answers are given on a binary scale, which we then average over countries to yield a continuous country-level variable, termed simply "jobs." We use the resulting variable as a proxy for social norms or attitudes towards women in different countries. In countries where a large proportion of respondents answered, "Yes, men should be given preference in obtaining jobs over women during times of job scarcity," their score on "jobs" is low, and we interpret this to imply the existence of adverse or discriminatory social attitudes towards women. In countries where most respondents answered, "No, men should not be given jobs over women," we take this to imply the relative absence of social norms against women.

Admittedly, interpretations for this question are also bound to vary depending on the political and cultural context. Nevertheless, in our opinion, "jobs" avoids some of the more blatant pitfalls that surround interpretation of the other gender-related questions in the WVS, such as the ones mentioned above. This variable also has the advantage that it gives the greatest country coverage – many of the other gender-related questions in the WVS were administered only in a smaller subset of thirty-odd countries. "Jobs" is available for 68 countries, and it is this group of countries which we referred to earlier as the "restricted sample" when presenting descriptive statistics on GAP, ROL and PolCon (Table 11.3). Figure 11.4a presents scatter plots between our proxy for values about gender equality ("jobs") and the rule-of-law for two groups of countries: high-income countries and non high-income countries. As can be seen, there is hardly any meaningful correlation in either group,[23] implying that the quality of governance as measured by ROL tells you little about a country's social norms/attitudes towards women once you hold income-level constant.

The correlation between social norms and the status of women, on the other hand, is striking. Consider Figure 11.4b, which plots GAP against "jobs," revealing an almost perfectly linear relationship.[24]

With the motivation provided by this graph in mind, we turn to the task of comparing the relative significance of the rule-of-law versus social norms in predicting the status of women in a society. Table 11.8a, 11.8b, and 11.8c present the results of regressing three measures of the status of women against our two measures of the rule-of-law. In Table 11.8a we regress our primary measure of the status of women, GAP, against ROL. In the very first iteration (model 1), GAP is regressed against ROL alone and there is a small but significant coefficient on ROL. In model 3 GAP is regressed against both ROL and "jobs," and we see that the coefficient on "jobs" is both practically and statistically very significant, while the coefficient on ROL drops to zero. The coefficient on "jobs" is 0.167, implying that a country with a value on "jobs"

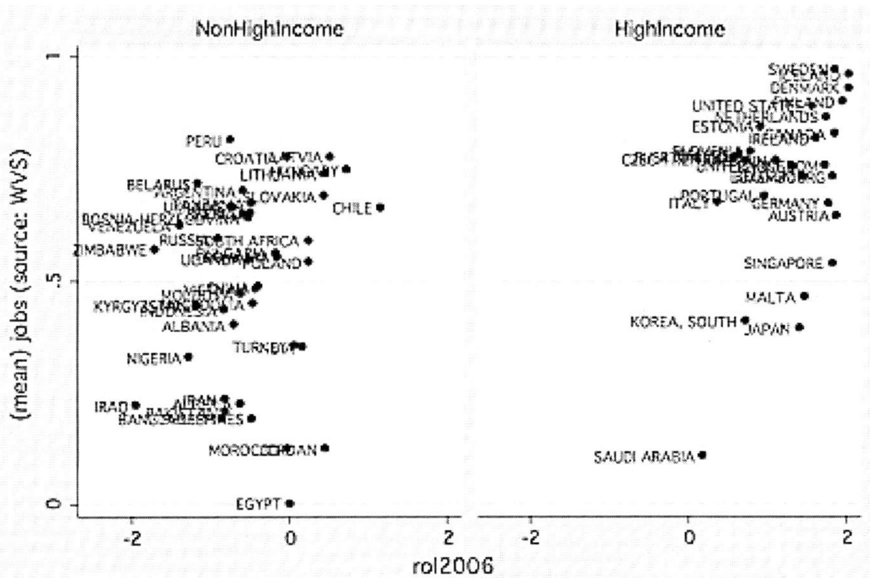

Figure 11.4a Social norms (jobs) plotted against rule of law (ROL) by high-income status.

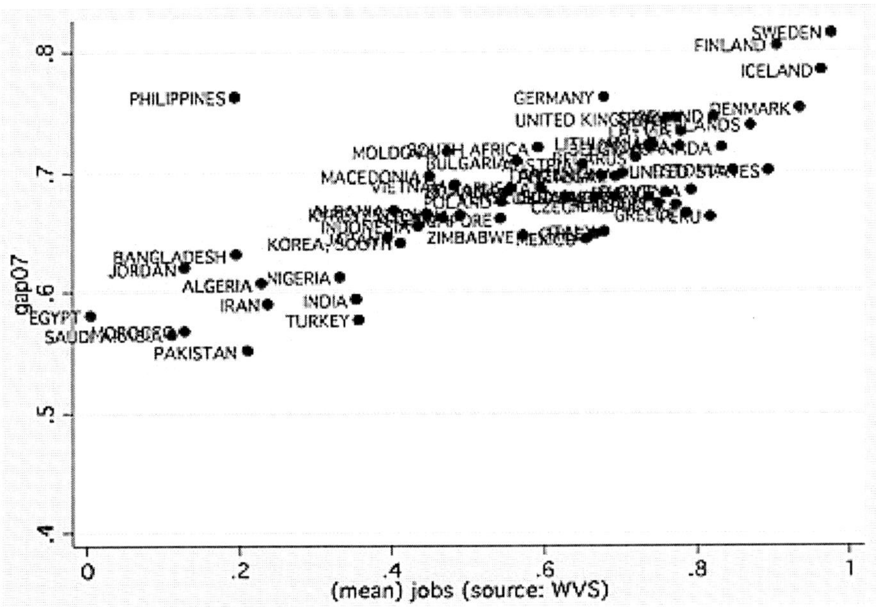

Figure 11.4b The status of women (GAP07) plotted against social norms (jobs).

of 1 ought to have a GAP score higher by 0.167 than a country with a value on "jobs" of 0 that is otherwise similar. This is quite a large difference, given that GAP only ranges from 0.451 to 0.815. The inclusion of "jobs" in model 3 moves the "adjusted R-squared" from about 0.2 to 0.56, further bolstering the claim that social norms are highly predictive of the status of women. Notice, however, that the number of observations in model 3 drops by a factor of two from model 1. This is because there is only data on "jobs" for a small subsample of countries, and it implies that the sample of countries in model 1 may be very different from the countries in model 2. To check that the relative significance of "jobs" over ROL is not caused by peculiar sample selection, we rerun the regression from model 1 on the same countries we use in model 3, namely, the countries for which there is data on "jobs." The results for this regression on the "restricted sample" are given under model 2, and they are identical to the results of model 1. In further models, we simply add controlling factors: first income in model 4 and then regional dummies in model 7. In each case we first look at the regression without "jobs" (models 1, 4, 7), then we redo the regression for the restricted sample (models 2, 5, 8) and then finally we add "jobs" as a covariate (models 3, 6, 9). In every case, we see that "jobs" is highly significant while ROL is made insignificant when the other covariates (particularly "jobs") are included.

Table 11.8a GAP regressed against ROL with restricted samples

	Dependent Variable (gap07)								
	Model (1)	*(2) restr.* sample	*(3)*	*(4)*	*(5) restr. sample*	*(6)*	*(7)*	*(8) restr. sample*	*(9)*
rol2006	0.027***	0.025***	0.006	0.008	0.005	0.016	0.017*	0.016	0.014
	(0.005)	(0.006)	(0.005)	(0.010)	(0.014)	(0.010)	(0.009)	(0.011)	(0.010)
gdppc				0.003*	0.004	–0.002	0.001	–0.001	–0.003*
				(0.002)	(0.002)	(0.002)	(0.001)	(0.002)	(0.002)
gdppcsq				–0.000	–0.000	0.000	–0.000	0.000	0.000
				(0.000)	(0.000)	(0.000)	(0.000)	(0.000)	(0.000)
CASdum							–0.005	–0.035*	–0.035*
							(0.018)	(0.020)	(0.018)
EAPdum							–0.022	–0.050**	–0.014
							(0.018)	(0.022)	(0.021)
MENAdum							–0.098***	–0.137***	–0.065**
							(0.017)	(0.026)	(0.029)
SAdum							–0.068***	–0.134***	–0.089***
							(0.024)	(0.034)	(0.032)
SSAdum							–0.039**	–0.049	–0.051*
							(0.020)	(0.030)	(0.027)
LACdum							–0.012	–0.051*	–0.065***
							(0.019)	(0.026)	(0.023)
jobs			0.167***			0.180***			0.161***
			(0.023)			(0.027)			(0.041)
Constant	0.665***	0.672***	0.580***	0.640***	0.638***	0.590***	0.684***	0.737***	0.657***
	(0.004)	(0.007)	(0.014)	(0.013)	(0.020)	(0.017)	(0.021)	(0.030)	(0.034)
Obs	128	64	64	128	64	64	128	64	64
Adjusted R-squared	0.207	0.211	0.562	0.221	0.224	0.557	0.491	0.519	0.619

Note: *** $p<0.01$, ** $p<0.05$, * $p<0.1$. Standard errors in parenthesis.

Table 11.8b GAP regressed against PolCon with restricted samples

	Dependent Variable (gap07)								
	Model(1)	*(2) restr. sample*	*(3)*	*(4)*	*(5) restr. sample*	*(6)*	*(7)*	*(8) restr. sample*	*(9)*
polconiii	0.102***	0.108***	0.028	0.063***	0.048	0.027	0.023	0.041	0.046
	(0.024)	(0.039)	(0.029)	(0.024)	(0.039)	(0.030)	(0.020)	(0.033)	(0.030)
gdppc				0.003***	0.004**	0.000	0.003***	0.000	–0.002
				(0.001)	(0.001)	(0.001)	(0.001)	(0.001)	(0.001)
gdppcsq				–0.000	–0.000	–0.000	–0.000**	–0.000	0.000
				(0.000)	(0.000)	(0.000)	(0.000)	(0.000)	(0.000)
CASdum							–0.010	–0.039*	–0.039**
							(0.018)	(0.020)	(0.017)
EAPdum							–0.020	–0.046**	–0.008
							(0.018)	(0.022)	(0.022)
MENAdum							–0.098***	–0.134***	–0.060**
							(0.018)	(0.026)	(0.029)
SAdum							–0.061**	–0.126***	–0.081**
							(0.025)	(0.034)	(0.032)
SSAdum							–0.037*	–0.044	–0.046*
							(0.020)	(0.030)	(0.027)
LACdum							–0.018	–0.062**	–0.075***
							(0.019)	(0.026)	(0.023)
jobs			0.173***			0.171***			0.166***
			(0.021)			(0.027)			(0.041)
Constant	0.633***	0.639***	0.568***	0.615***	0.621***	0.568***	0.661***	0.707***	0.624***
	(0.009)	(0.016)	(0.014)	(0.010)	(0.016)	(0.015)	(0.021)	(0.030)	(0.033)
Obs	127	64	64	127	64	64	127	64	64
Adjusted R-squared	0.118	0.098	0.560	0.260	0.241	0.546	0.481	0.514	0.621

Note: *** $p<0.01$, ** $p<0.05$, * $p<0.1$. Standard errors in parenthesis.

Table 11.8c Alternate measures of the status of women against ROL and PolCon

	Dependent Variable							
	genital mutilation				*missing women*			
	Model (1)	*(2) full controls*	*(3)*	*(4) full controls*	*(5)*	*(6) full controls*	*(7)*	*(8) full controls*
rol2006	–0.003	–0.039			–0.003	–0.018		
	(0.020)	(0.041)			(0.024)	(0.036)		
polconiii			0.104	0.068			0.373***	0.318***
			(0.112)	(0.131)			(0.130)	(0.107)
gdppc		0.009		0.004		0.011		0.003
		(0.008)		(0.006)		(0.007)		(0.005)
gdppcsq		–0.000		–0.000		–0.000		–0.000
		(0.000)		(0.000)		(0.000)		(0.000)
CASdum		0.048		0.055		0.063		0.038
		(0.076)		(0.076)		(0.061)		(0.057)
EAPdum		0.081		0.086		–0.132		–0.136*
		(0.095)		(0.096)		(0.081)		(0.074)
MENAdum		–0.001		–0.007		–0.234**		–0.246**
		(0.125)		(0.125)		(0.111)		(0.102)
SAdum		0.143		0.136		–0.572***		–0.590***
		(0.135)		(0.136)		(0.111)		(0.101)
SSAdum		–0.045		–0.032		–0.013		–0.012
		(0.113)		(0.114)		(0.094)		(0.087)
LACdum		0.027		0.040		0.085		0.037
		(0.095)		(0.094)		(0.080)		(0.075)
jobs	0.202**	0.191	0.167**	0.179	0.605***	–0.020	0.495***	0.009
	(0.087)	(0.168)	(0.077)	(0.168)	(0.116)	(0.146)	(0.098)	(0.134)
Constant	0.852***	0.750***	0.831***	0.775***	0.537***	0.828***	0.457***	0.786***
	(0.050)	(0.149)	(0.052)	(0.147)	(0.071)	(0.119)	(0.066)	(0.106)
Obs	55	55	55	55	59	57	57	57
Adj. R^2	0.089	0.075	0.103	0.062	0.389	0.692	0.467	0.741

Note: ***p<0.01, **p<0.05, *p<0.1. Standard errors in parenthesis.

To show that the results above are robust to different measures of the rule-of-law, we redo the regressions with PolCon instead of ROL (Table 11.8b). The results are indeed similar: without the other covariates, the coefficient on PolCon is statistically (and practically) significant. Including "jobs," however, reduces the magnitude of the coefficient on PolCon in addition to making it statistically insignificant. The coefficient on "jobs," on the other hand, is still large and significant (at about 0.17).

In Table 11.8c, we consider two alternative measures of the status of women in order to make sure that our results are not peculiar to the particular variable we have chosen to represent the status of women, GAP. These two measures are "missing women" and "genital mutilation." The variable "genital mutilation" is a subcomponent of the GID index which measures "estimated prevalence of female genital mutilation (in %)" (Jütting *et al.* 2006). We have recoded the variable so that higher values imply lower levels of genital mutilation. The variable "missing women" is also taken from the GID database but it is not a component of the GID index. It is based on Amartya Sen's concept and ranks countries according to the percentage of missing women relative to the total number of women in each country. Countries with very high proportions of missing women are given low values (close to 0) while countries with low proportions of missing women are given high values on this variable.[25]

In model 1 of Table 11.8c, we see that when "genital mutilation" is regressed against only ROL and "jobs," the coefficient on ROL is insignificant while the coefficient on "jobs" is very large and significant at 0.202. The coefficient on "jobs" stays large although it loses statistical significance when income and regional dummies are added (model 2). Models 3 and 4 replicate 1 and 2 – substituting PolCon for ROL – with more or less identical results. Models 5–8 in Table 11.8c use "missing women" as the dependent variable but are otherwise identical to models 1–4. In models 5 and 7, "missing women" is first regressed against ROL and "jobs" and then PolCon and "jobs." The coefficient on "jobs" is significant (and extremely large) in both cases, while, for the first time, ROL and PolCon behave quite differently: ROL is insignificant while PolCon seems to bear a strong relationship with the dependent variable. Controlling for income and region makes the coefficient on "jobs" shrink to zero – also for the first time.

What do these results tell us? In summary, the state of social norms and attitudes towards women, as measured by "jobs," seems to be a very strong and consistent predictor of the status of women. Our two measures of the rule-of-law, on the other hand, seem to play a relatively minimal role in determining the status of women in a country. In fact the only exceptions to this pattern are found in models 6 and 8 of Table 11.8c, where "missing women" is regressed against ROL/PolCon and "jobs" while controlling for income and region. In both models, the coefficient on "jobs" is insignificant. In addition, in model 8, the coefficient on PolCon is significant and large, a fact that we find interesting and difficult to explain.[26] However, there are some likely explanations for the apparent insignificance of "jobs" in predicting "missing women." The most likely of these is that the erratic behavior of the coefficient on "jobs" is due to multicollinearity in the model: "jobs" is highly correlated with the regional dummies, which are in turn extremely highly correlated with the dependent variable itself. The phenomenon of missing women is largely a South Asian problem, as evidenced by the large coefficients on MENAdum and SAdum. But the lack of significance might also be a function of statistical power (or lack thereof): there are only three South Asian countries for which there is data on "jobs." A similar regional explanation might account for the loss of statistical significance (though not practical significance) in the coefficients on "jobs" is in models 2 and 4 of Table 11.8c. "Genital mutilation" is largely an African problem, and, again, "jobs" is highly correlated with the regional dummies.

While we caution against relying too heavily on these quantitative results, they are consistent with insights from social theory that the status of women in society is determined by competing norm systems, and that by and large social norms trump the formal legal system when it comes to affecting the status of women in a society.

Part C: Targeted legislative interventions

A possible argument against our above analysis is that the rule of law is too broad a concept to even expect it to have a measurable impact on the status of women in society. Therefore, in this part we focus instead on more specific legal interventions deemed to be consistent with the rule-of-law paradigm but more specifically targeted at improving the status of women. In particular, we focus on the possible impact that legislation aimed at preventing and punishing violence against women might have on the status of women. The measure we use to analyze such legislation is a variable termed "violaw," which is another subcomponent of the GID database. "Violaw" measures the existence of specific legislation addressing three types of gender-related violence, where countries with higher scores have more concrete legislation on the books compared to countries with lower scores (Jütting *et al.* 2006). We use this measure as a covariate (in place of ROL or PolCon) in regressions of the various measures of the status of women. Table 11.9 displays the results of these regressions.

The results of Table 11.9 might seem familiar by now. In the first three models where our three measures of the status of women are regressed against "violaw" and "jobs" only, the coefficient on "jobs" is always significant and larger than the coefficient on "violaw," which is insignificant except in model 1. The introduction of regional covariates induces the same complications (again, probably due to multicollinearity between jobs and the regional dummies) but most of the general conclusions from these regressions are the same as those of the previous ones: "jobs" is generally significant, except when the dependent variable is "missing women" and regional covariates are included.

Table 11.9 The impact of targeted legislation: status of women against "violaw"

	Dependent Variable					
	gap07	*missing women*	*genital mutilation*	*gap07*	*missing women*	*genital mutilation*
	Model (1)	*(2)*	*(3)*	*(4)*	*(5)*	*(6)*
violaw	0.044**	-0.006	0.085	0.054**	0.138	0.036
	(0.022)	(0.103)	(0.084)	(0.023)	(0.091)	(0.095)
gdppc				-0.002	0.008	0.004
				(0.001)	(0.005)	(0.006)
gdppcsq				0.000	-0.000	-0.000
				(0.000)	(0.000)	(0.000)
CASdum				-0.027	0.090	0.062
				(0.017)	(0.062)	(0.077)
EAPdum				-0.003	-0.105	0.091
				(0.021)	(0.080)	(0.097)
MENAdum				-0.043	-0.155	0.004
				(0.030)	(0.120)	(0.129)
SAdum				-0.085***	-0.577***	0.133
				(0.031)	(0.108)	(0.136)
SSAdum				-0.038	0.024	-0.029
				(0.026)	(0.095)	(0.115)
LACdum				-0.068***	0.100	0.050
				(0.022)	(0.077)	(0.093)
jobs	0.165***	0.599***	0.160**	0.162***	-0.016	0.175
	(0.021)	(0.102)	(0.079)	(0.040)	(0.143)	(0.169)
Constant	0.558***	0.542***	0.825***	0.603***	0.751***	0.771***
	(0.015)	(0.073)	(0.054)	(0.034)	(0.127)	(0.154)
Observations	64	59	55	64	57	55
Adj. R^2	0.581	0.389	0.825***	0.643	0.706	0.059

Note: ***p<0.01, **p<0.05, *p<0.1. Standard errors in parenthesis.

Perhaps the only difference is that now our measure of formal targeted legislation is significant in the case where the dependent variable is GAP, although the coefficient on "violaw" is still weaker than the coefficient on "jobs." We are left with the impression that, even when legislation is specifically targeted towards gender-related ends, social norms are more significant than formal law in determining the status of women in a society.

India: the limited impact of legislative change

To illustrate the difficulties of using law as a means of changing social practices, consider the experience of India – a country with a long history of deep-rooted gender inequality. India has adopted a long list of legislation aimed at improving the status of women in society. Many of these legislative interventions have been accompanied by establishing committees or organizations charged with complementing these reforms. However, a brief survey of these reform-attempts suggests that they have not dislodged persisting gender inequality.

Indeed, on paper, India has one of the most progressive legal systems in the world. Indian women have had the right to vote since 1950. Article 14 of the Indian constitution explicitly guarantees "equality before the law," Article 15 prohibits discrimination on the grounds of sex, while Article 16–1 provides for equality of opportunity in matters of public employment.

Legislation exists to prohibit violence against women, guaranteeing far-reaching negative rights: for example, the Commission of Sati (Prevention) Act 1987 outlaws the practice of burning the widow at the funeral pyre of the dead husband, whilst the Medical Termination of Pregnancy Act of 1971, and the Pre-Natal Diagnostic Techniques (Regulation and Prevention of Misuse) Act of 1994 deal with the problem of selective foeticide and infanticide.[27] In addition, the Indian Penal Code criminalizes a wide range of sexual and matrimonial offenses.[28] Obstacles to the liberty and equality of women are also addressed by legislation including the Dowry Prohibition Act 1961, the Child Marriage Restraint Act of 1929, the Suppression of Immoral Traffic in Women and Girls Act of 1986 (criminalizing trafficking in women and children) and the Indecent Representation of Women (Prohibition) Act of 1986 (on pornography and other related offenses).

Positive socioeconomic rights for women in India further ensure that they have the legal protection they need to lead a modern life on par with their male counterparts. Women are equal beneficiaries of gender-neutral socio-economic rights, guaranteed by, for example, the Minimum Wages Act of 1948; by legislation protecting the rights of children, such as the Juvenile Justice (Care and Protection of Children) Act of 2000; and by the prohibition of child labor in certain dangerous occupations through, for instance, the Child Labor (Prohibition and Regulation) Act of 1986 and the Employment of Children Act 1938. In addition, the Right to Education Bill – which currently is at the draft stage – will guarantee universal access to primary and secondary education. In fact, although these statutes apply universally, they often contain specific provisions protecting the rights of women.

In addition, socioeconomic rights guaranteed by the Indian legal system also include a host of measures enacted specifically to guarantee the equal treatment of women. Thus, women's right to equal pay is guaranteed not only by the Constitution (Article 39.d), but reinforced by the Equal Remuneration Act of 1975; women have the right to maternity leave under the Maternity Benefit Act of 1961; women's property rights are protected by legislation like the Hindu Women's Right to Property Act and the Hindu Succession Act; and all Indian, including Muslim, women have the right to divorce, as reaffirmed by the Muslim Women (Protection of Rights of Divorce) Act of 1986.[29]

Moreover, there exist institutions whose specific purpose is to implement this substantive law. Apart from an elaborate apparatus of courts and a wide police network, commissions with special mandates in priority areas have been set up. These include the National Commission for Women, set up to review and supervise "all matters relating to safeguards provided for women under the Constitution as well as other Acts" (India 1990) and the National Human Rights Commission with analogous powers. Lastly, India is a signatory to most major international human-rights conventions including those pertaining particularly to women, such as the Convention on the Elimination of All Forms of Discrimination Against Women 1979 (CEDAW).[30]

Gender reality is another story altogether. Indeed, perhaps nothing indexes the reality of women's lives in India as graphically as the "missing" Indian women – all 30 million of them. As mentioned above, this describes the phenomenon that – contrary to the biological fact that more girls are born than boys everywhere and that, given equal care, women are significantly more likely to survive than men – the Indian population shows a substantial deficit in women. And, indeed, one that has increased in the recent period of economic growth (Klasen and Wink 2003; see also Dubey and Verschoor 2007). Part of the problem is caused by the fact that despite legislative prohibitions on sex-selective abortion and infanticide, their practice continues unabated. But given the number of "missing women," this can only be a partial explanation. It appears, therefore, that "the comparative neglect of female health and nutrition, especially ... during childhood" is the major factor at play (Sen 1999a: 106; see also Bhadra 1999 and Saha 2003). It is striking that extensive constitutional guarantees of nondiscrimination coexist with discrimination so pervasive and fundamental that it results in the death of more women than the entire population of a country the size of Canada.[31]

But the violence goes further still. According to a study done by the World Health Organization, a woman is raped in India every 54 minutes.[32] The National Crime Reports Bureau recorded 16,496 rape cases in the year 2000 (as quoted by Vasudev and Renuka 2002) – which would translate into a ratio of 1.6 rapes per 100,000 inhabitants. While this would be relatively low in international comparison,[33] Iyer (1999: 1–8) writes that a large proportion of sexual abuse occurs within the family home, often perpetrated by fathers.[34] This is to say nothing of the gross under-reporting of these incidents. Contrary to the stringent law on child marriage, Bhadra (1999) estimates that 40 percent of rural girls are married off before the legal age, a large proportion at an age as young as 14 (ibid.: 6). Despite the prohibitions on dowry, these marriages almost universally take place at enormous cost to the bride's family. And, indeed, the price of not paying is high: there were "officially" 7,026 dowry deaths in India in 2004, a 13.2 percent increase over the previous year (India, National Crime Records Bureau 2006).[35] Rhoodie (1989) writes that as late as 1987, a Rajisthani woman was burnt along with her dead husband as thousands of people watched, despite sati having been banned by the British over 160 years ago. The ritual lasted 12 days – uninterrupted by the authorities. In addition, since girls are considered the most dispensable members of the family, they are typically the ones made to work as underage domestic help, or even sold as prostitutes, in order to support the family (see Sen, S. 2004).

Finally, in spite of the wide range of guarantees of socioeconomic equality, women's achievement indices consistently fall short of men's. Despite both a constitutional and a statutory guarantee of equality in working conditions,[36] there exists a pay differential between men and women of more than 250 percent, while the employment participation rate for women is estimated at 50 percent that of men.[37] Moreover, 90 percent of the female labor force in India is estimated to be working in the "unorganized sector" – sectors of the economy recognized as being economically productive but considered too diffused to be brought under the ambit of legislation (India 2005). Finally, in the context of education, arguably the major battleground in the fight for gender equality, female adult literacy is 65 percent of the male rate at 47.8 percent compared with 73.4 percent (United Nations Development Program 2005, percentage of population over 15). As one might imagine from the information compiled from various sources, India scores near the bottom on all the indicators used to measure women's status (see Table 11.10). In Figure 11.5, India's average rating on the "Rule of Law" index is contrasted with its extremely poor score (15th from the bottom) on the GAP index.

It is evident from the account provided that law on gender issues in India is honored more in the breach than in the observance. Despite an elaborate array of legal guarantees, women's rights in India have consistently and blatantly been violated, suggesting that the mere existence of law tells us little about its impact.

Determinants of the status of women in society

The empirical quantitative and qualitative evidence presented in this chapter suggest that the rule-of-law is not a miracle cure for societal discrimination against women. This leaves us with the question whether existing social theories, in particular theories that have motivated many of the rule-of-law studies that we have referred to, have specified the determinants for the status of women in society and how law may affect their status. We use this final section to briefly review the implied social theories of the dominant rule-of-law paradigm. Any such theory will need to address the determinants of legal authority and the determinants of social change more broadly.

Table 11.10 India's rank on women's status indicators

	Indicator of Women's Status				*Social Norms*
	gap07	*gem*	*gdi*	*gid*	*jobs*
India's Rank/ Total Countries	113/128	N/A	92/131	106/117	57/68

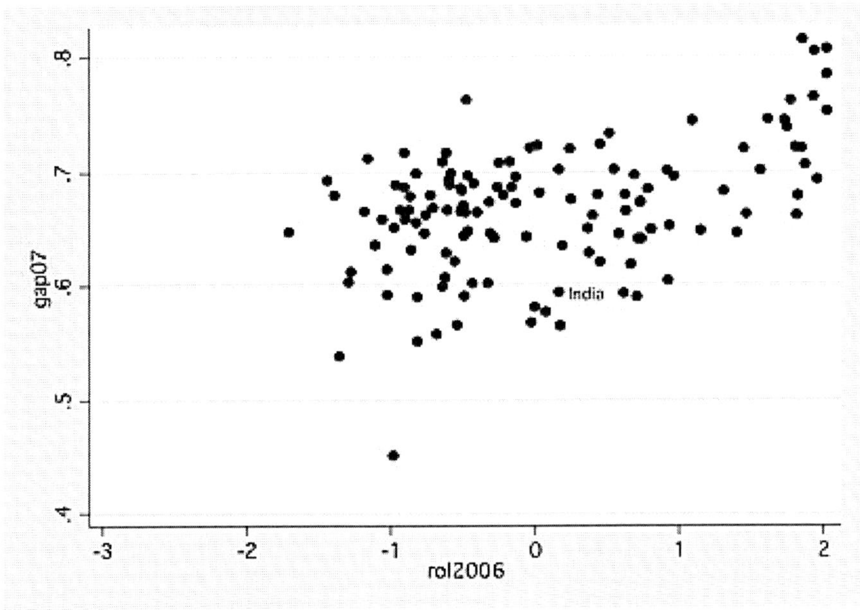

Figure 11.5 GAP vs ROL (with the position of India labeled).

On the authority of law

The dominant rule-of-law paradigm claims that authority of the rule-of-law as a concept is universal and, by implication, the supremacy of law in all spheres of social life. Arguably, the WJP's conceptualization of the rule-of-law is less far-reaching in this respect, as it postulates the supremacy of law only for government actors, not for citizens as well, as does Fallon's definition. Thus, one might interpret the WJP's rule-of-law concept as a means to constrain government actors, but to leave society to 'spontaneous ordering' – to use Hayek's term.[38] Such a limited rule-of-law concept would make it indifferent as to social norms that condone the supremacy of males over females – or any other power relations within society that does not involve government actors. Nonetheless, the breadth of social issues the ABA's World Justice Project (and similar development programs in recent years) has brought under the umbrella of their rule-of-law agenda (including eliminating poverty, public health, business and finance, all the way to gender issues) suggests that the claim is in fact broader than the rule-of-law criteria suggest. It is therefore worthwhile to examine the theoretical foundations for such a claim.

Max Weber has laid the foundations for a social theory of the supremacy of law (see Weber 1980: 122–76). He argues that every authority is rooted in legitimacy, i.e. a widely shared belief among members of society that they ought to respect the authority. Weber dismisses a simple cost–benefit calculation that focuses on material interests as the foundation of legitimacy as inherently unstable and therefore insufficient. Legitimacy, or the willingness to obey an authority can have different reasons. Weber distinguishes three types of authority, each based on different legitimacy-creating mechanisms. Rational authority is founded on the belief in the legality of the established order. The rationality of procedures for making and implementing laws and the expertise of government officials takes precedent over any substantive conflicts between the norms (or interests) condoned by formal law and those held by members of society. Weber contrasts rational authority with traditional and charismatic authority. Traditional authority is founded on the belief in the divinity of the existing order, while a charismatic order is based on the extraordinary abilities of a leader as a warrior or person of high moral standing.

There are important affinities between the dominant rule-of-law paradigm and Weber's characterization of a rational legal order. The emphasis on clarity and predictability of the law and the supremacy of law vis-à-vis government actors are among them. However, there are also important differences, in particular the different emphasis placed on the perception of authority and its foundations in the eyes of the ruled. Weber stresses society's belief in the legitimacy of an order (*Legitimitätsglaube*) and distinguishes it from an authority's legitimacy claim (*Legitimitätsanspruch*). This distinction gets lost in today's conceptualization of the rule-of-law and the indicators used to measure it. Instead, it is widely assumed that formal law is inherently legitimate, indeed that a state that endorses key elements of the rule-of-law has a legitimacy claim.

The question whether the peoples' belief in the legitimacy of an order or the claim of an authority to be legitimate is more important for ensuring substantial compliance with the formal legal order is ultimately an empirical question. Several studies have investigated this question empirically, with some focusing on the famous gap between the law on the books and law in action, and others investigating the cultural predisposition for endorsing an order based on the rule-of-law. While the results are far from conclusive, the findings tend to support the notion that the efficacy of a governance system depends to a large extent on the perspective of the norm addressee.

The gap between the law on the books and law in action is a common phenomenon in legal systems. Yet, in some societies, the gap seems more substantial in that law is largely ignored and few investments are made to ensure the operation of legal institutions. This systemic irrelevance of law has been termed the "transplant effect" (Berkowitz *et al.* 2003b). In a cross-sectional study of 49 countries around the world, Berkowitz *et al.* show that similar laws on the books have little predictive power for the effectiveness of law and legal institutions as measured by a range of indicators, including rule-of-law or government effectiveness captured by WGI. Instead, the process by which formal law was introduced to countries around the world is associated with effectiveness of law in these countries today. In countries, where formal law and legal institutions were imposed without regard to local conditions or the familiarity of people living in these countries with the norms on which the transplanted law rested, the effectiveness of law is significantly lower today than in countries that developed their formal legal order internally, or that transplanted law in a manner that ensured that local conditions were taken into account.[39] Similarly, Berkowitz and Clay (2005) suggest that differences in the effectiveness of legal institutions across the states in the US can be largely attributed to the transplant effect. Of the 50 states of the union, at least ten started off with a legal order formed on the basis of Spanish, French, or German civil law. These states later switched to the common-law system (with the exception of Louisiana). Yet, to this day they diverge from other states in the effectiveness of legal institutions – the perceived effectiveness (based on survey results) and the resources they invest in the legal system (based on budget allocations to the judiciary), among others.

Berkowitz *et al.* (2003b) argue that the failure of a legal order transplanted from one place to another to take hold in different soil may result from the failure to generate legitimacy of the new order. Viewed in this light, the transplantation of law from the West to different parts of the world during the period of imperialism was destined to undermine the legitimacy of these institutions in the eyes of the people subjected to this rule.[40] Still, the focus on the process of legal transplantation does suggest that if done "right" legal transplants might work and might even engender legitimacy in the transplanted institutions.

In contrast, some scholars suggest that the attributes of the rule-of-law are culturally grounded and may not take root in cultures with very different presuppositions. Licht *et al.* (2007) use data compiled by cultural psychologists to assess preferences for organizing social relations. Key indicators for differences are preference for autonomy versus embeddedness; mastery versus harmony; and hierarchy versus egalitarianism. When correlating cultural traits with rule-of-law indicators (WGI), they find that the rule-of-law (as conceived by WGI) fits well with cultures that tend towards individualism and egalitarianism rather than social embeddedness and hierarchy; not however with those that display a preference for embeddedness, hierarchy, and harmony. Similar results are obtained when regressing cultural traits against rule-of-law while controlling for a host of other variables, including distribution of income (Gini coefficient); colonial legacy; legal origin; and ethnolingual fractionalization (Licht *et al.* 2007: 671, Table 2). This study suggests that as long as these cultural traits persist – and they do seem to be sticky – policy reforms that mobilize law as conceived in the West are inherently limited. Once again, this does not necessarily imply that social change is impossible, but that the role law can play in this context should be reconsidered.

The studies by Berkowitz *et al.* and Licht *et al.* do not focus on gender. Yet they have implications for the possible role law can play in altering gender relations. There are several predictions that follow from these studies for the authority of law to influence the status of women in society.

First, in societies where the process by which formal law was transplanted undermined its legitimacy, law has limited authority in general, and even less for social relations governed by powerful competing norm systems, such as gender relations.

Second, societies that suffer from the transplant effect under-invest in formal law and legal institutions. As a result, even for those who may, at present, be unaffected by the legacy (i.e. a "bad process") of legal transplants, the infrastructure for mobilizing law may simply not be available.

Third, in societies with deeply rooted cultural preferences for hierarchy and embeddedness, introducing institutions designed to enhance autonomy and other challenges to existing norms and authorities are unlikely to affect change.

Fourth, societies with preferences for hierarchy and embeddedness tend to endorse gender inequality.

These are essentially testable propositions. In fact, we find some support for the fourth proposition. Using data from the World Value Survey, we analyzed the correlation between values related to gender equality (i.e. "jobs") and preferences for the organization and particular branches of government. Countries whose populations place a higher value on inequality tend to display strong confidence in hierarchical forms of government (army rule or a strong leader) (see Table 11.11).

Even if we regard existing studies as inconclusive and the data sets they use as problematic,[41] they do have the benefit that they are grounded in social theories that would caution against over-simplistic efforts of social engineering – and lend them at least tacit support. One may, of course, challenge these theories and propose that formal law and legal institutions do have authority that transcends differences in culture or legacies of colonialism. This, however, would require more than stating the claim or the construction of an index, but the development of a theory capable of generating predictions as to when and why the rule-of-law can engender authority to achieve social change.

Table 11.11 WVS Governance variables correlated with 'social norms' at country level (including significance and number of observation; unit: countries)

	confpolice	*confparl*	*confciv*	polsysgov	*strongleader*	*armyrule*	*respectHR*	*bribe*
jobs	–0.038	–0.256**	–0.397**	–0.022	0.210*	0.520**	0.145	–0.166
# of obs	65	65	66	50	67	66	67	68

Note: * =significant at .10 level; ** = significant at .05 level

Determinants for changes in social norms

References to social norms or culture are often taken to suggest that these are neither capable of change nor do they in fact change within time periods that might be relevant for policymakers. These conjectures are supported by some of the classical thinkers, such as Montesquieu who have pointed to differences in culture as a reason for being skeptical about the likelihood that institutions transplanted from one soil will work at all, or at least similarly in different soil.[42] Yet cultural anthropologists acknowledge the mutability of culture and social norms even within relatively short periods of time. This is not the place to revisit the debate about what culture is and how it affects behavior. We therefore adopt a simple definition of what we mean by social norms and survey literatures that speaks to this issue.

Social norms, as used in this chapter, are norms that determine social behavior. The literature on new institutional economics tends to differentiate between formal and informal institutions – where institutions are defined as man-made constraints on human actions (North 1990). Formal institutions are those established in formal processes, in particular laws and regulations. Informal institutions are those that lack such formal endorsement. This definition of institutions and the distinction between formal and informal institutions has been criticized. Aoki (2001), for example, argues that a formal law is not an institution. It only becomes one once it is part of the collective expectations that shape social behavior. Similarly, Greif defines institutions as regularized patterns of behavior (2006). Like Aoki, he abandons the distinction between formal and informal and focuses on observable outcomes. We tend to agree that observable outcome is critical in determining whether normative claims are in fact realized in practice. The normative claim can come from formal law – if and to the extent that it exerts authority to govern relevant relations – or from social norms. For the purpose of the current analysis we are primarily interested in factors that trigger change in observable behavior outcomes. Moreover, given that our previous analysis has suggested that law on its own is not a powerful motor of change, we focus on changes in outcome that have causes other than legal change.

The major triggers of behavior change identified in the social-science literatures are exogenous shocks as well as defection by key actors from established patterns of behavior, which in turn trigger a broader shift in social conduct. Several economists have argued that a crisis may be necessary in order to effectively alter entrenched patterns of behavior. The case has been made for behavioral patterns associated with hyperinflation, but even more generally, for the organization of the economy and in particular for the influence by entrenched interest groups that prevent change.[43] Examples for exogenous shocks include major economic or financial crises that destroy interest groups or their ability to organize and gain broader influence or war and revolutions that undermine the quest of a ruling class to hold on to power. It is, however, important to note that these examples demonstrate only how entrenched interests are destroyed by exogenous shocks. But they say little about what interests will be able to regroup and exert influence over others in the aftermath of such a shock. Moreover, they focus entirely on the impact of crises on elites – not, however, on the large parts of the population we are interested in, namely minorities. In fact, there is substantial evidence that minorities have been heavily victimized in many crises, both economic crises and war.

Even if we accept that social elites play a critical role in bringing about important institutional change, closer scrutiny suggests that existing theories are also incomplete. It is widely accepted that the first constitutional power sharing was triggered by major political crisis that forced the reallocation of allegiances among the Tories, the Whigs, and the monarch in early modern England (see Weingast 1997). The constitution itself was designed to uphold this power-sharing arrangement. To accomplish this goal it already incorporated important features that have become the hallmark of constitutional orders, including the supremacy of law – and perhaps even more importantly, the neutrality of the legal order. In order to engender legitimacy in the eyes of all concerned parties, the new constitutional order had to be neutral. It offered procedures for resolving future disagreements among the parties, but it refrained from any attempts to reallocate control rights or favor one of the parties in any other way. The logic of this arrangement is impeccable as long as one assumes that the power struggle that resulted in this neutral arrangement lies in the past and has – at least for a historical moment – created an opportunity to overcome a stalemate by creating institutional power-sharing arrangements. Suppose, a similar arrangement had been put in place prior to the realignment of political forces. Under such conditions, it is far less likely that the new order would have been sustainable. Not surprisingly, many institutional arrangements that either ignored power relations or underestimate their possible impact on the formal institutions have proved to be unsustainable.[44]

Not all theories on changes in social norms insist that a shake-up is required for social norms to change. Some argue that institutions may also change in a more incremental fashion. Thus, Greif (2006) suggests institutional change – i.e. changes in regularized patterns of behavior can result from individual actors defecting from existing regularized patterns of behavior. This is the case in particular for actors that have some standing among others, i.e. whose example is likely to be followed. To put it differently, the defection of key actors can trigger a mass defection.[45] The more actors change their behavior – whether by responding individually to changes in the environment or by following a leader – the greater the likelihood that a new pattern of regularized behavior will emerge – i.e. that a new pattern becomes institutionalized.

This model of endogenous institutional change suggests that all institutions can change in principle – as long as some actors with authority are willing to defect. However, it says little about the conditions that will trigger defection. Moreover, just as with the crisis model, the theory focuses on elites and has little to say about how norms that negatively affect minorities are likely to change – as in these cases it is far less likely that members of the elites will alter their behavior. The critical question then is when and why elites may alter behavior that seems to benefit them, but comes at the expense of minorities within their societies. Greif does not really provide an answer to this. In his account of the failure of the Maghribi traders to adapt their trading patterns, he instead reverts to cultural preferences. Thus, when comparing the institutions governing long-distance trade in the Mediterranean in the Middle Ages, Greif finds that after a long hiatus, merchants of the city of Genova come to rely on impersonal formal institutions of contract enforcement. By contrast, the Maghribi traders from the Middle East who relied on a network of ethnically related middlemen prove incapable of making that change and ultimately fail to adapt their institutions to a changing environment. Greif attributes these differences to culture, in particular to preference for what Licht *et al.* following Hofstätter would term autonomy in the case of the Genova traders, and embeddedness in the case of the Maghribi traders. As a result, this theory of endogenous institutional change offers few insights in how norms and patterns of behavior vis-à-vis women would change over time. The only exception might be the rise of a charismatic leader, but the current literature offers few insights as to how such a change would come about.

In sum, we seem to lack theoretical constructs and empirical evidence to develop a broader analytical framework for identifying critical determinants for changing the status of women in society. Promoting the rule-of-law will do little to deepen our understanding, and is more likely to be met with disappointment that typically sets in once a "one-fits-all" policy has been tried and failed.[46]

Concluding comments

Traditionally, empirical studies were a means to an end – they used data to test theories. Established, or newly developed, theories are used to generate predictions and to identify relevant data for testing, i.e. for falsifying or verifying the hypotheses that follow from them (see King *et al.* 1994). In recent years, however, data construction has become an end in itself, taking precedent over theory development, and even over theory testing. Once data are available they are tested even when both data and predictions lack deeper grounding in existing social theory.

This chapter, by contrast, uses available data to demonstrate that the assumptions used to construct them are inconsistent with underlying theories (implying that a deconstruction of the data is almost beside the point);[47] and to show where social theories are lacking to predict social outcomes in the field of gender equality. To make our case we use the very data that we critique (and some, such as the WVS, that may be deemed even worse) – a move that some may deem a fatal flaw of our approach. Yet we use the data to show something most other studies have overlooked, namely that the core claim of the rule-of-law's universal impact does not hold – even on the rule-of-law advocates' own terms. Once we break down the population of every country by gender and group countries by region and income brackets, a far more complex picture emerges than the widely reported simple regression results about the benefits of the rule-of-law suggest. Indeed, for all but high-income countries, we see no correlation at all between rule-of-law and the status of women. In fact, our proxy for social norms turns out be a better predictor of women's status than rule-of-law. We buttress our empirical analysis by presenting our own case study of India – a representative example of a well-intentioned, but failed, effort at changing women's status through legal interventions.

The combination of data analysis and case studies leads us to conclude that there is a substantial mismatch between the predictions that inform data construction and data analysis and available social theories from which such predictions should have been generated in the first place. To illustrate this, we summarize several social theories relevant for our inquiry – in particular Weber's analysis of the origins of social order and the importance of legitimacy belief, not only legitimacy claim in the authorities; as well as more recent theories about institutional development and institutional change. We conclude that neither existing theories nor empirical data support the claim that the authority of law is universally perceived as legitimate irrespective of earlier experiences with Western legal transplants or social norms. In addition, we point to a major lacuna in existing theories of institutions and institutional change and policies based on them – namely an account for when and how the status of social minorities might change over time. Existing theories rely heavily on behavioral change by the elites. Yet the fundamental developmental challenge for societies around the world is to address the fate of those Collier (2007) has called "the bottom billion." While Collier locates them in a set of countries, we suggest that the majority of those left behind by well-meaning policy strategies are disadvantaged groups within almost all developing states – including those that may be in the medium-income range and have average or better rule-of-law indices.

Notes

1 Funding for this project by the American Bar Foundation is gratefully acknowledged.
2 Since the mid-1990s the World Bank has increasingly focused on "governance." It has created a World Bank Institute (WBI) on corruption and governance, which has compiled data sets and created aggregate measurements for ranking countries around the globe on governance. See WBI (2008) for details.
3 The ABA launched an International Rule of Law Symposium, which convened in Washington, DC in 2006 and has followed up with a meeting of the "World Justice Forum" in Vienna in the summer of 2008.
4 Among the early studies, see Knack and Keefer (1994) and Mauro (1995). Many of the subsequent studies have been produced by Kaufmann *et al.* See, for example, Kaufmann *et al.* (1999, 2005, 2007b).

5 The methodology Sen used to compute these numbers has not been undisputed. Nonetheless, subsequent studies have confirmed the existence of the missing-women syndrome even if their account of the size of the problem differs somewhat. For a recent assessment of the literature, see Klasen and Wink (2003).
6 In fact, a recent study on the missing-women syndrome in India suggests that the syndrome is most pronounced in middle-class families and not amongst the very poor. See Dubey and Verschoor (2007).
7 In fact, the data they used had originally been compiled by companies selling information about country risk to prospective investors.
8 Critics have pointed out, however, that this has muddied the waters and thus does not enhance their explanatory value. See Kurtz and Schrank (2007b).
9 The construction of the PolCon data is detailed in Henisz (2000) and in the downloadable version of the database available online at the Political Constraint Index (PolCon) Dataset (Henisz 2005). Critical variables are the number of institutional players in a given political system; data on partisan alignment (including coalitions); and data on party composition of the legislature. In the absence of reliable objective data on an independent judiciary, a later version of PolCon uses survey data from ICRG. We have not used that version, as for our purposes the focus on objective measures was critical for comparative purposes with the World Bank's WGI.
10 For an early critique of the under-conceptualization and naiveté of rule-of-law movements, see Trubek and Galanter (1974). For a more nuanced account, however, see Tamanaha (1995). See also Cooter and Rubenfeld (1990) for a critique of studies comparing courts and litigation rates.
11 The six components of the WGI are (1) voice and accountability; (2) political stability and absence of violence; (3) government effectiveness; (4) regulatory quality, (5) rule-of-law; and (6) control of corruption.
12 This can be observed in the relatively low correlation between GAP and GDP in Table 11.2.
13 However, we do use one of the purely formal subcomponents of the GID index ("violaw": the existence of legislation that addresses violence against women) when analyzing the impact of a specific legal intervention targeted at improving the status of women.
14 Actually the log of GDP per capita, in 2005, adjusted for purchasing-power parity.
15 This is simply the ratio of the population in high-income countries versus all other countries, assuming a share of 50 percent females.
16 Out of 21 origin/receptive countries, 19 are in the high-income bracket, compared to only 7 out of 28 unreceptive countries, which are more or less evenly split between all income brackets.
17 See the World Justice Project (2007) for further details.
18 The WGI 1999 define rule-of-law as "citizen respect for the state and its rules," WGI 2005 as the "quality of contract enforcement, the police, and the courts *and* the likelihood of crime and violence," WGI 2006 as the "extent to which agents have confidence in and abide by the rule of society *and* the above," and Kaufmann *et al.* (2007b) refer to the rule-of-law as "norms of limited governance." See Kurtz and Schrank (2007b: 2).
19 See Thomas (2007: 18) for a summary of Fallon's rule-of-law definition.
20 For a critique of the WJP's rule-of-law definition, and more broadly the enthusiasm for the rule-of-law in Washington policy circles, see also Carothers (1998).
21 For a similar critique of the WGI indicators, see Kurtz and Schrank (2007a).
22 Social theories widely acknowledge the coexistence of normative systems in any society. Thus, Max Weber distinguishes different types of authority, including one based on a rational legal system, but points out that they hardly ever exist in pure

form. See Weber (1980: 122). In other words, the phenomenon is not limited to less-developed countries or those that received formal law in the process of colonization. For a general discussion of legal pluralism see Merry (1988); for a critique of this concept see Tamanaha (1993).

23 There is actually a moderately strong correlation between "jobs" and ROL for high-income countries. However, this correlation becomes weak and statistically insignificant when excluding a single outlier: Saudi Arabia.

24 Although we did not include the following result, the relationship between GAP and "jobs" survives intact when splitting up countries by income bracket, as we did for GAP vs ROL/PolCon.

25 On the GID Database website, the variable is described as follows:

> Missing women describes the difference between the number of women that should be alive (assuming gender equality) and the actual number of women in a country. A value of 1 was assigned to the country with the highest percentage of missing women relative to the total number of women (i.e. Afghanistan with a share of 9.3 percent). All other countries are assigned values between 0 (no women are missing) and 1 accordingly. [In our use of the variable, we reverse the scale so that higher values denote fewer missing women.]
>
> (OECD 2008)

26 Indeed, we will not even attempt to explain it.

27 On sati and for an excellent, if dated, overview of women's rights in India see Rhoodie (1989: 395–401).

28 For a compendious overview of the Indian law on offenses against women see Dewan (2000) and Kaushal (2000).

29 For an overview of legislation and caselaw in this area see Kant (2003).

30 See India, Ministry of Home Affairs (2008) for a complete list.

31 According to Statistics Canada (2008) the population of Canada was estimated to be 33,311,389 on 1 July 2008.

32 The accuracy of these data is questionable. Estimates for the US suggest that a rape occurs every two minutes.

33 Data of this sort are notoriously problematic, as they may be affected both by under-reporting and by over-reporting. This also makes cross-country comparisons extremely problematic. The United Nations Office on Drugs and Crimes documents crime statistics for a number of countries – India not being one of them. The ratio of rapes in 2002 per 100,000 people ranges from a high of 151 in South Africa to a low 0.27 reported for Saudi Arabia. The ratio for the US is 32.99 (United Nations, Office on Drugs and Crime 2002: Table 2.8).

34 Iyer (1999) notes further that the fear of sexual abuse within the home is a fundamental impetus to get girls married off as early as possible.

35 Dowry deaths refer to the killing of women by husbands and in-laws when the material demands made of their parents are not met. On this subject, see further Joga Rao (2002) and Menski (1998).

36 Section 4 of India's Equal Remuneration Act (1976) expressly states that "it is the duty of the employer to pay equal remuneration to men and women for the same work or work of a similar nature;" section 5 further guarantees that "no discrimination is to be made while recruiting men and women workers."

37 Estimates based on statistics in the UNDP's Human Development Report (HDR) (United Nations Development Program 2005).

38 For his theory of spontaneous or "grown" order, which he contrasts with a government imposed or "made" order, see Hayek (1973).

39 This interpretation of the results is based on classifying countries as "origins" and "transplants" respectively and by subdividing transplants into "receptive" transplants (i.e. those that made changes to the transplanted law or had a population in place that was familiar with the underlying norms) and "unreceptive ones." For details, compare Berkowitz *et al.* (2003b).

40 There is a different interpretation in the literature on how the process of colonization may have impacted the quality of institutions. Acemoglu *et al.* (2001) argue that institutional choices made at the time of colonization, which in turn were determined by the hospitality of the local environment to foreign settlers was critical. Thus, in environments with high settler mortality, institutions were established that facilitated extraction, whereas in environments with low settler mortality, institutions were more benign. It should, however, be noted that "settler mortality" in this context serves primarily statistical purposes as an instrumental variable and that there is little substantive evidence to support a broader theory about the relation between institutional choice and settler mortality. See also Rodrik (2004).

41 Note, for example, that Berkowitz *et al.* (2003b) and Licht *et al.* (2007) rely heavily on WGI data. See also our criticisms of the World Value Survey earlier in the chapter.

42 In his "L'Esprit de Loi," Montesquieu (1977) famously stated that because of cultural differences, the success of such transplants would be a matter of luck. For a restatement of this proposition with a greater focus on politics rather than culture, see, however, Kahn-Freund (1974).

43 For a general account of collective action theory and the risk of petrification, see Olson (1971).

44 See, for example, Doyle and Sambanis (2006) for the importance of power-sharing arrangements as a condition for the reestablishment of political order in failed states.

45 Unfortunately, the theory is not very explicit about the sources of authority.

46 For a recent critical report by the World Bank on the failures of the Washington Consensus, see World Bank (2005).

47 For this reason we do not go into an extensive analysis of the possibility that existing rule-of-law indices are gender biased. Others have already pointed out that they are pro-business. See, for example, Kurtz and Schrank (2007b).

Chapter 12

Constitutionalism and the challenge of ethnic diversity

Yash Ghai[1]

Argument

This chapter examines how traditional notions of constitutionalism are challenged by the rise of ethnic identity in numerous parts of the globe. In their origin, the rule-of-law and constitutionalism, closely connected, paid little attention to diversities among the people of the state. They were based on the assumption of the homogeneity of the people, in part by the exclusion of specific communities, religious or ethnic, from rights and participation in public life. After the Westphalian settlement, political and legal concepts, developed under the sovereignty of the state, reflected the essential principles of the modern state. Gradually the concept of citizenship, based on the rights and duties of the individual, became central to membership in the political community constituted by the state. With growth of the notion of human rights and democracy, members of excluded communities were given the right to citizenship. This did not imply the political incorporation of these communities, as such; instead citizenship became a means towards their assimilation in the wider political community.

From the eighteenth century onwards, as the political map of Europe came to be redrawn, the homogeneity of the people (defined by their cultural, particularly linguistic, affiliation) became the basis of the creation of new states. Congruence between a cultural community and the boundaries of the state became the major principle of the reorganization of states ("nation state"). This approach was justified on the grounds of the preservation of both culture and democracy, and subsequently social welfare (arguing that redistribution of resources implicit in welfare programs was possible only if there is social solidarity, dependent on a common history and culture). The rise of ethnic consciousness and its political mobilization (for which phenomenon I use the term "ethnicity") has challenged many of these assumptions, including the concept of a homogenous people. I examine reasons for the rise of ethnicity, the form its challenge has taken, and the implications for the rule-of-law and constitutionalism. Ethnicity presents its claims as imperatives of identity. Under its impact, some key principles and components of the liberal state (which came to personify the rule of law and constitutionalism in its "highest" form) have been critically examined and are being redefined: sovereignty as vested in the entire people as a collectivity and manifested in the centralization of the state; common citizenship with equal rights and obligations; equality; uniformity of law and legal institutions; majoritarian democracy; the nature of rights; and the distinction between the public and the private.

Constitutionalism

There is a close connection between constitutionalism and the rule-of-law. Both are premised on the importance of limits on the power of the state, with law as the principal means of defining and ensuring the limits. Charles Howard McIlwain said that "in all its successive phases, constitutionalism has one essential quality: it is a legal limitation on government; it is the anti-thesis of arbitrary rule; its opposite is despotic government, the government of will instead of law" (1947: 21–2). The rise of the notion of limits on power can be traced to disputes about the prerogatives of the monarch; in England at least, the limitations were introduced through decisions of courts. The democratic element of constitutionalism came later, with the end of royal rule, and the supremacy of parliament. Courts, which were in the forefront of the struggle for the limitation of state power, were now subordinated to parliament (in terms of jurisdiction and the degree of the scrutiny of the executive) – justified by the democratic imperative. For a while the courts tried to introduce limitations by invoking the common law,[2] but could not long resist the superiority of legislation. Subsequently parliamentary sovereignty itself came to be seen as a threat to the rule-of-law.

However, in most countries which adopted formal constitutions, led by the US and France, the powers of the legislature were also limited; the constitution, not parliament, was supreme, establishing close connections between constitutionalism and the rule-of-law. Both were concerned with the limits on state power, but unlike the origins of the rule of law, constitutionalism also emphasized the political mandate and accountability of the government, which placed a greater responsibility, and importance, on the legislature. In fact, increasingly the constitution became the foundations of the state, the social contract among the people – even though the constitution often did little more than reflect the balance of social and economic forces in society.[3] The constitution became an act of deliberation, not necessarily organic growth – a notion which marked earlier understandings of a constitution – "that assemblage of laws, institutions and customs, derived from certain fixed principles of reason, directed to certain fixed objects of public good, that compose the general system, according to which the community hath agreed to be governed" (ibid.: 3, quoting Bolingbroke).[4] As I shall argue later, the role of the constitution, and the process of making it, in contemporary multiethnic states is fundamentally different; nation building is as important, if not more, than state building.[5]

Frequently commentators have seen a contradiction between the rule-of-law and democracy.[6] Democracy, as the will of the people and their rulers, tended towards the expansion of state power, and was seen to threaten the rule-of-law. The notion of people's power implied restrictions on the jurisdiction of judges, so as not to subvert its sovereignty. The rule of law began to be seen as a conservative ideology, blocking social and economic reform.

Various attempts have been made to bridge the gap between democracy and the rule-of-law, particularly by the common acceptance of the centrality of human rights. The concept of the rule of law has been broadened, from absolute fidelity to any law, to the notion of just law made through the democratic process. The rule of law now also focuses on institutional arrangements of the state, including the separation of powers, and the franchise. This broader concern first appeared in the Delhi Declaration on the Rule of Law in the 1950s (and is now extensively elaborated in the American Bar Association Index on the Rule of Law). On the other hand, the notion of democracy became more substantive than procedural, emphasizing the rights of citizens and the protection of minorities.

Traditionally neither the rule-of-law nor constitutionalism paid much heed to ethnic differences. The states in which constitutionalism arose did not acknowledge this kind of diversity. The Virginia Declaration of the Rights of Man ignored not only women but also slaves and aboriginal people, as did the Philadelphia Convention (where slaves were acknowledged only in determining the size of representation of states in the Senate, for which they did not themselves vote – and were deemed as the property of others). The French Revolution was explicitly about developing a common national identity; and Shakespeare's dramas played their role in the formation of English nationalism. The political reorganization of Europe after each major war increasingly took the form of the "nation state," determined primarily by linguistic homogeneity. Elsewhere "national" languages displaced "local dialectics." The king's religion became the religion of the region (until, after the scourge of centuries of religious wars, secularism was discovered as the remedy to peace). There were many advocates of the "nation state" (like John Stuart Mill), but the high priest was undoubtedly the German philosopher Herder. He invoked the authority of God in his revelation that the "best political arrangement obtains when each nation forms a state of its own" (Kedourie 1993: 52). He also described as "unnatural" states in which there is more than one nation; "they become oppressive, and finally doomed to decay" (ibid.).

This framework of constitutionalism is now under threat from the rise of identity politics, which forces us to re-examine the foundations of constitutionalism as we have understood the term, including the relationship between territory and political power, and to explore its relevance in an increasingly multiethnic and multicultural world.

Foundations of constitutionalism

Constitutionalism is based on the notion of a supreme law which governs the jurisdiction and powers of state institutions and determines the limits and mode of their exercise. In England this supreme law was effectively created and enforced by the courts, defining the restrictions on kingly powers, in the face of countervailing authority and doctrines of the royal prerogative (and confirmed by the Glorious Revolution). In many other places it is the constitution which established the supreme law (the US and France). An understanding of certain principles, rules, and procedures developed around the concept of the rule-of-law associated with the supremacy of the law: the importance of law (written or otherwise) and its non-retrospectivity, especially as regards criminal liability, the independence of the judiciary, certain presumptions (like that of the innocence of the accused), open trials, and access to lawyers and courts. Courts became central to making law and maintaining its supremacy; some of the most distinguished names and heroes of the movement, at least in its home, England, were lawyers and judges (Glanvill, Bracton, Coke, Mansfield).

The focus of much legal activity was the powers and privileges of the executive in the form of the monarchy. Subsequently, attention shifted to the lawmaking process, particularly the powers of the legislature which began to monopolize lawmaking. Limits on the powers of the legislature were most clearly enunciated in the form of the protection of fundamental rights. In England itself, the supremacy of parliament prevented the notion of the supremacy of the constitution. Even to this day there are doctrinal, although no serious practical, problems with parliamentary supremacy as the UK joined the EU, granted autonomy to Scotland, and adopted the European Convention on Human Rights. Much of this took place without full attention to democracy; there were wide restrictions on the right to vote and to stand for elections.

The introduction of democracy introduced new understandings of the responsibilities of the executive and the legislature, and diminished the importance of the judiciary, raising key theoretical dilemmas about the relative importance of legality and democracy. The recognition of the sovereignty of the people to replace the sovereignty of the monarch (which was used in England to overcome precedents tending towards supreme monarchical powers) marks the turning point in the rule of law and constitutionalism. From the more technical aspects of jurisdiction in which the debate about the rule-of-law was conducted, fundamental questions of political representation, franchise, political processes, including accountability, became more central concerns. Much thought was given to how people's sovereignty should be reflected in the state, and limited (e.g. the Madison representative government and fundamental human rights). The constitutionalization of the emerging principles of democracy, checks and balances, and in time political relations between classes, came to the fore (the notion of "people" being more complex than "monarchy"). Questions of political theory superseded those of legality. In the fullness of time constitutionalism or the rule-of-law came to encompass a number of components, values, institutions, and procedures, including criteria for procedure and substance that determined whether a rule purporting to be law would in fact enjoy the status of binding rule. States in which these principles were central came to be known as liberal states.

Another dominant influence on the structures of state and the importance of law was the emerging market principles of organization of the economy. The case in which the courts questioned the authority of the monarch to grant monopolies of commerce and trade in restraint of the ability of others to engage in these areas was one of the first decisions to limit the power of the monarch – and in the typical English way, the monarch, without conceding the restriction, promised not to grant monopolies by prerogative. The market requires much more than restriction on monopolies – it requires clear rules defining the nature and uses of, and transactions in, property; the framework for, and the sanctity of, contracts; and guarantees of state enforcement of agreements made by private parties (and yet limiting the direct role of the state in the economy). Underlying the development of the infrastructure of constitutionalism has been the imperative of the market, not seriously challenged until the rise of the welfare state, which infused new values in our understanding of the rule-of-law.

The liberal vision of a multiethnic society is that of tolerance and pluralism, and in which all cultures may flourish and members of minorities may freely pursue their goals. An extensive bill of rights, concentrating on civil and political rights, is central to this protective framework, guaranteeing various rights, such as the right to association, the freedom of expression, the use of languages, the freedom of conscience, protections of due process, freedom from discrimination and torture, etc. The liberal state achieves these goals by relegating a large sector of life and society to the private domain, the scope of which is expansively defined, in part by the protections of rights and the definition of the polity (and its ultimate goal of individual freedom). In the civil or private domain, communities may organize their own social, religious, educational, and economic life. They may converse with others in their own language, and may cultivate cultural and social links with members of their own ethnic or kin communities in other lands, such as through vernacular newspapers, visits, and other exchanges. At the same time they are protected from the imposition of the norms, culture, institutions, and symbols of the majority communities. Thus a sharp distinction between the public and private, which underlies the liberal state, is essential to the protection of minorities.

This self-image of the liberal society has come under considerable criticism, in recent years, by those who argue that it does not respond to the circumstances of a multiethnic society. Bhikhu Parekh, for example, describes various institutional and structural features of the modern state which in his view impose uniformity and ignore diversity. The organizing principle is state sovereignty, which justifies the centralization of power and displaces local and group sites of power. This sovereignty operates on a territorial basis, with hard boundaries. Rules for the exercise of this sovereignty are biased towards majoritarianism, stifling the voices of minorities (Parekh 1997). People relate to the state through the concept of citizenship, based rigidly on equal rights and obligations of all persons, premised on loyalty to the state, and acknowledging no distinctions of culture or tradition. Citizens have rights but these are rights of individuals, based on an abstract and uniform view of the human person. The state operates through the medium of the law, but it is the law created by the state, rather than preexisting bodies of customs or local law. The state favors the uniformity of structures and seeks to achieve the homogenization of culture and ideology, propagating them as universal values. The domain of the state is the public space, with an ever-shrinking area of private space, which alone allows some expression of cultural diversity.

Another critic, James Tully, writes that the modern constitution, based on the assumption of a homogenous culture, was designed to exclude or assimilate other cultures and thus deny diversity (1995: 58). Noting different communities or groups who are seeking constitutional recognition of their cultural or social specificity – immigrants, women, indigenous peoples, religious or linguistic minorities – he concludes that what they seek is participation in existing institutions of the dominant society, but in ways that recognize and affirm, rather than denigrate, exclude, and assimilate their culturally diverse ways of thinking, speaking, and acting. They share a longing for self-rule: to rule themselves in accordance with their customs and ways (ibid.: 4). Symmetries of power, institutions, and laws which define the modern state are inconsistent with the diversity of forms of self-government that Tully considers necessary for a just order in multiethnic states. Such a constitution should be "a form of accommodation" of cultural diversity, of intercultural dialogue in which the culturally diverse sovereign citizens of contemporary societies negotiate agreements on their forms of association over time (ibid.: 30).

The nature of ethnicity

I use the term "ethnicity" to refer to a situation when a community goes beyond a mere consciousness of what binds the community together (such as language, religion, race) and what distinguishes it from other communities, to claims that these differences are politically significant, and constitute the community as a "people" or "nation" which is entitled to special recognition as such. The process of the rise of political consciousness is not dissimilar to that of the stimulation and promotion of "nationalism," which in earlier periods formed the basis of the "nation state." It generally begins with intellectuals or persons with political ambitions, who begin to give symbolic, emotional, and material significance to their differences from other communities in the state (cementing internal cohesion and distancing from other communities). This therefore involves the presence of some objective factors like language or religion, but which increasingly take on a symbolic or political meaning. This subjective factor can rise from a consciousness of discrimination against, or social or economic exclusion of, the community, a rediscovery of history when the community existed as a political entity, and increasingly of demands and insurgencies happening in other places.

The political claims that it makes vary from a constitutional or legal recognition of some aspects of its culture (such as relations within the family or dispute settlement mechanisms), special measures to improve its social and economic situation, inclusion through representation, and state support for its religion or culture. Sometimes (especially when their claims are denied) there is progression from modest to the more substantial demands, including a fundamental redesign of the state or even secession (arguing that only through this radical reform can its legitimate demands be met). Increasingly, these claims are justified by reference to international norms of human rights.

There are a number of reasons why in recent decades there has been such a resurgence of ethnicity, such a ready response to those who would mobilize on the basis of ethnic differences. There are many multiethnic states now. Unlike the policy of "self-determination" which led to the establishment of "nation states" in empires vanquished in wars in Europe in nineteenth and twentieth centuries, in Asia and Africa the territorial principle took priority over the cultural, except in the prominent case of India – a partition which led to terrible carnage and massive transfers of people, which event may have dissuaded the international community from the cultural/linguistic basis of the decolonized state. States that have customarily thought of their populations as distinctively singular, particularly in the West, have become diverse. Globalization has intensified interstate transfers of peoples, as has the suppression of some communities in their homelands. In many states that emerged out of the dissolution of states after the Second World War, the diversity produced severe political conflicts.

The presence of diverse people does not necessarily lead to ethnicity. A distinguished Indian political scientist, Rajni Kothari, has argued that rise of ethnicity is due to the consequences of the centralization and monopolization of the state (comparing the modern state to precolonial polities in Asia which did not aim at centralization of all authority, recognized diverse communities with their religion and customary practices, and whose borders were porous) (1988). The growth of market relations and globalization led to the marginalization, and subsequent disruption of the cohesion of communities, causing insecurities produced by economic changes over which they have no control. This also affects the nature of ethnic consciousness, turning it from a positive and inclusive form to negativity, exclusion, and violence.

In the West, it is more fashionable to talk of the resurgence of ethnicity in terms of the imperatives of identity, based on Kant's emphasis on the autonomy of the individual (particularly the work of Charles Taylor[7] and Will Kymlicka[8]). The antecedents of this approach can be traced to the influential work of the anthropologist, Clifford Geertz, who argued that ethnicity flows from "primordial" affiliations in the context of a state. Primordial links were based on what he called "givens," the accidents of birth in a community, to which one may be connected by ties of religion, language, descent, history. "These congruities of blood, speech, custom and so on, are seen to have an ineffable, and at times overpowering, coerciveness in and of themselves" (Geertz 1963: 109). In new states, these primordial attachments are particularly strong and are in frequent tension with the affiliation with, and expectation from, the state – and deeply destabilizing.

Charles Taylor defines identity as "a person's understanding of who they are, of their fundamental characteristics as a human being" (Taylor 1994: 25). Identity is achieved through a person's search for their inner soul. At another point, he says, "There is a certain way of being that is *my* way. I am called upon to live my life in this way ... If am not true [to myself], I miss the point of my life" (ibid.: 30). According to Taylor, this consciousness of the uniqueness of one's identity is the result of the breakdown of social hierarchies, which had defined our roles and gave us the understanding of our place in society. But with democracy and the reordering of society, our identity comes from self-reflection and contemplation. Identity has become essential to the sense of our own dignity, as an attribute of our being human. Thus dignity is closely related to equality. And equality in turn depends on recognition by others, in the form of demands for the equal status of cultures and gender.

Although identity understood in this sense is an intensely personal affair, achieving a satisfactory understanding of oneself and one's potential, and of orienting oneself, depends on our contacts with others. Kymlicka says that our orientation, the way we negotiate values and make choices, comes from our membership of a cultural community. Thus in their different ways, Taylor and Kymlicka place the individual securely within a cultural context, and interactions within a community. In an earlier period, Herder and other German philosophers had claimed uniqueness for these communities, a unique, historically, even ethnically derived identity for each community, the nation. Thus Kant's emphasis on individual autonomy was given firm roots in the community. The politics of recognition, in public and private spheres, has become central to our quest for just political and social orders.

Although there is now wide acceptance of the recognition of identity, and its corollary of social and cultural diversity, there are acute controversies about the nature of identity and the forms of its recognition.[9] If in the West identity is a matter of psychic satisfaction, in Asia identity politics are important as a means to resources, although just as in the West material benefits are not irrelevant, in Asia pride in one's community is also an important factor (although Taylor's explanation of the importance of individual identity due to the disappearance of social hierarchy does not apply equally in Asia). Identity is more a matter of political mobilization than a precise delineation of a community's characteristics or beliefs. Ethnicity has become a way of dealing and bargaining with the state. Because electoral politics and government interventions respond to ethnic pressures, economic issues are transformed into issues of cultural survival. For example, in most cases, ethnic fighting is not about religion, but about jobs; religion is used as a pretext, emptying religion of its sacred and ritual aspects.

A community's entitlements may depend on how it and others perceive it. A self-conscious ethnic group can place itself in different categories, deriving from political science or legal discourse – it can be a cultural, religious, or linguistic group, or it can be a minority, or a nation, or a "people" or "indigenous peoples." Each of these categories is associated with a specific set of claims – participation, representation, recognition of language, religion, education, land, autonomy, etc. How does one establish a claim to one or the other category? They are in part derived from political theory or practice, such as a "nation," with a clear notion of the right to self-determination, including separatism or secession, or a minority or indigenous peoples, which derives more from legal norms or rules (e.g. article 27 of the ICCPR, or the Declaration on the Rights of Minorities, or the ILO Conventions on Indigenous Peoples). Perhaps the most significant of these are the concept of "nation" and "indigenous peoples" as they carry a large or high set of entitlements. To this extent a community's self-definition is determined or at least influenced by international political or legal norms, and sometimes the characterization or classification under national law (as in Spain).

Minorities have an interest in bringing themselves under the category of "people," for in this case they are entitled to self-determination. Although the political understanding of self-determination is still associated with the "nation state" (and has political resonances as such), its contemporary legal meaning is for the most part restricted to the internal organization of the state, and the right of all citizens and communities to participate in decisions on that organization, including the drafting of the constitution. The right of minorities to participate in public affairs and in state institutions as well as to enjoy their culture now ranks high in the lexicon of self-determination. This much is clear from the way the UN Human Rights Committee has interpreted article 1 of the two covenants and linked it to article 25 ("public participation") and article 27 ("minorities") of the Covenant on Civil and Political Rights. Self-determination in this sense has become the framework for negotiations between the state and insurgents, denied the option of independence by internal and external forces.

Constitutionalism for diversity

The critical claims of ethnic groups concern the orientation and structure of the state. We have already noted critiques of the liberal state (embedded in the philosophy of the rule-of-law) as failing to meet these claims. There is now a wide variety of principles and institutions that seek to accommodate ethnicity. The recognition of ethnicity as a politically relevant category yields different results, paradoxically a "neutral," "liberal," secular state (in an attempt to be fair to all groups), a federal-type solution where each group has significant autonomy, a corporate-autonomy-based state (Belgium), or perversely, a state which privileges one ethnicity over others (Israel, apartheid South Africa, and Fiji). "Schizophrenia" is also possible: torn between the liberal and the cultural or ethnic; a state with the formal features of a liberal state but the practices of ethnic hegemony.

For present purposes, two distinct approaches are identified. One seeks to respond to the concerns of minorities within a broadly traditional liberal framework, avoiding the political recognition of communities, but providing electoral and other incentives for different communities to work together. This approach, relying on rights of individual citizenship, and seeking political integration, can be accommodated within traditional understandings of constitutionalism and the rule-of-law. The other major approach (which is the focus of this chapter) proceeds from the political recognition of communities, and their participation in the affairs of the state. Individual citizenship is combined with rights of communities, producing a complex set of relationships regarding entitlements. There is a particular emphasis on power sharing as well as autonomy of communities, and proportionate share in state institutions.

There are clear implications for the design of the state for diversity following from this last approach. The traditional notion of state sovereignty that tends towards its centralization needs to be revised, perhaps through a notion of sovereignty shared by communities and regions, as, for example, in federalism. The "nation state" theory with its exclusive cultural underpinnings must give way to the concept of a multicultural or multinational state in which all cultures will be equally respected (and diversity of regimes of personal and family laws will be applied in place of a unified code). The excessive emphasis on human rights as (a) individual rights and (b) civil and political rights has to be balanced by group rights and economic and social rights (the latter being especially important to minorities who tend to be socially and economically disadvantaged). Democracy has to be reconceptualized, moving away from the majoritarian model, as a compact not so much between citizens as between communities. New forms of representation and electoral systems must be established. More participatory and collaborative forms of the exercise of power must be devised. Citizenship itself has to be reconceptualized, establishing legal links not only to the state but to communities.

Some of these developments may require the reconsideration of the distinction between private and public spheres – ethnicity pushes into the public domain what has largely been seen, at least in modern state forms, as belonging to the private domain. This results in part from the emergence of human rights which recognize private rights in the public sphere, and because of the demands for public recognition of communities with their relationships and practices. Yet at another level, communities (which may not have a distinction between the public and private such as Hinduism and Islam) get more control over community affairs – what might otherwise be state functions or responsibilities – creating different spheres of the public. It is possible here to consider only a few of these directions.

Nature of constitutions and constitution-making process

Traditionally the role of the constitution was to establish institutions of the state and define their jurisdiction, based on the assumption that, because of common history and underlying cultural understandings, there is substantial agreement on values, aspirations, and identity. It is indeed these understandings (and joint commitment to live together) which makes it possible for the people to form a state. It is claimed that Britain did not need a written constitution because of the great agreement among its people ("a nation") on values and procedures of government. James Madison thought that the underlying assumption on which the Philadelphia Convention could proceed to make a constitution was that the people of the 13 colonies had already agreed to "form one society" – as with Rousseau, he considered that the agreement among the people to form one nation was necessary (but "nowhere reduced to writing"), before they could proceed to establish a system of government (Berns 1988: 121–2).

When there is not this commonality, the constitution must provide it. Thus there are at least two roles of the constitution in multiethnic societies faced with identity crisis: to fashion or consolidate a compact among the people, defining a new identity, and to establish and maintain political and legal systems for its different communities, with very fine balances (inherently subject to continuing contestation) (Tully and Chambers 1998). The first compact is usually negotiated around the principles of the constitution since differences among the communities are about the organization of the public space – and their share in and control of it. This is primarily a process which involves communities (or at least is conducted in the name of communities). In its idealized form, it would resemble the framework that the Supreme Court of Canada sets out in its decision on whether Quebec has a unilateral right to secede from Canada (*Reference re the Secession of Quebec* (1998)).

The court held that there was no right under Canadian or international law which entitled Quebec to secede unilaterally. But that was not the end of the matter, for if in a democratic and pluralistic society as Canada, a member wished to secede, the central and other governments were obliged to negotiate with it to solve the problem, even if by secession.[10] An interesting aspect of the framework is that before a community is entitled to negotiate with the state, it must prove that there is a significant support within the community for secession or some other adjustment in its relations with the rest (in this case to be manifested through a referendum ("clear support on a clear question")). On the one hand, this results in the communalization of politics; and on the other, it excludes from negotiations those members of communities who support a more cosmopolitan or national approach.

The Court also implies that the negotiations must be conducted in good faith, which means that each side must try to understand the concerns of the others, and search for ways in which differences can be resolved. The decision therefore has particular relevance to constitutional discourses and the making of constitutions. A common identity is a matter of negotiations. Negotiations must involve not just a few "leaders" but communities and the people generally. A settlement reached after such negotiations will be the more stable and will strengthen the sense of belonging to the new political identity so fashioned.

Redefining sovereignty

In practice it is unlikely that negotiations will be conducted in this form: the negotiators do not often have the mandate of their communities or of the state (being commanders of warring factions); they have interests which may not reflect the true wishes of the community; the circumstances of armed conflict are such that the Supreme Court's formula for "clear support on a clear question" may be impossible to test (Sri Lanka is a classic example). There is considerable disagreement as to which communities are entitled to a seat at the table – perhaps a combination of success at reinventing a group as a "nation," "a nationality," "a distinctive people," and the possession of a sufficient number of AK47s. If a constitution is achieved, it is proclaimed not in the name of "We the People" but "We the Nations, Nationalities and Peoples of [Ethiopia]" or in the name of "Bosniacs, Croats, and Serbs, as constituent peoples (along with Others), and citizens of Bosnia and Herzegovina." Or there are other indications that the true bearers of sovereignty are not the people but "constituent peoples." Progress in the making of the Spanish constitution of 1978 became possible only when the question of sovereignty was resolved, enabling a move away from Franco's unitary and centralized state, through an ambiguity that both recognized Spaniards as a sovereign people and gave its communities considerable sovereignty through autonomy.

Sovereignty is compromised in another way. Internal conflicts almost always bring about the intervention of the international community, which attempts to play a critical role in resolving them (although this was not the case in Spain). Constitution-making is then less an exercise of people's sovereignty than dictates of outsiders (for example, the peace process in the Sudan, Bosnia-Herzegovina, and Kosovo). The current EU fashion is to convert diversity into apartheid, in the name of peace (as discussed below).

Here it is appropriate to give a brief account of the ways in which communities are incorporated in constitutions, as necessary background to understand specific constitutional devices discussed below. There is no single model for the recognition of communities (for example, though the constitutions of Northern Ireland, Bosnia-Herzegovina, and Fiji recognize communities, the entitlements which are connected to community membership are significantly different). For an overview it suffices to say that preambles celebrate diversity of communities, and some specifically and more significantly, constitute them as political entities. Rights are vested not only in individual citizens, but also in communities. Some of these rights are exercised by the community collectively (such as linguistic or religious, of ancient lineage, or ownership of land) but some by individuals through membership of a community (such as affirmative action or residence in a locality). Regimes of personal laws, based on religion or culture, seem to fall in between. Communities may be entitled to autonomy, territorial or cultural, giving it a degree of self-government.

Recent developments have emphasized political rights of, or relating to, communities. In some extreme cases, as in Bosnia-Herzegovina, political representation in legislative and executive bodies is distributed by community, as are certain state offices. Members of a community elect their own representatives, and in the legislature and the executive these representatives share power (as, for example, in collective presidency and rotation in other important offices). Complex rules of decision-making are based on a high degree of consensus, and some times give a community veto over laws or policy deemed to be prejudicial to its interests. This often has the effect of privileging some communities over others (as in Bosnia-Herzegovina). Much of the system of government is designed for intercommunity negotiations. Because of the centrality of communal interests, some constitutions provide, as part of the state structure, for umpiring by outsiders (as administrators, judges, and peace keepers) to ensure the prescribed ethnic balance and procedures.

The incorporation of communities as political entities makes the constitutional and political systems complex, dependent on continuing negotiations. Thus the constitution is important not only for defining political identities but also setting up complex and delicate balancing between them, vulnerable to the dynamics of communal politics. The fragmentation of sovereignty compels toward the consensus principle, introducing considerable rigidity. Thus, unlike constitutions in "nation states" which operate for the most part smoothly due to common understanding of the national interest, the constitution of multiethnic states requires constant support and nourishment, often with outside intervention.

Sovereignty is not only fragmented internally, but it seems to be conditional. The incipient doctrine of "earned sovereignty" is a threat, but for the moment the more critical is international supervision (especially now with another incipient doctrine, the duty to protect, requiring international intervention in national politics). The United Kingdom suspended the "sovereignty" of Northern Ireland for nonconformity with the Good Friday Agreement, and in Bosnia-Herzegovina there is an international component which exercises important aspects of its sovereignty (particularly in the appointment and powers of the High Commissioner and to a lesser extent external presence in the Constitutional Court). Apart from fragmented sovereignty, the complexity arises from the changed concept of citizenship to which I now turn.

Citizenship

What might seem at first sight as the strength of the liberal state from the perspectives of minorities, that is equal rights and obligations of citizenship, is seen as problematic from identity point of view. The primary political relationship in liberalism is that between the individual, as citizen, and the state. But if citizenship with plenitude of rights, is a means to inclusion, it can also be the means of limited or extensive exclusion – by the denial of citizenship. Certain categories of persons will be entitled to citizenship (e.g. those born in the country or born of parents at least one of whom is a citizen). But the prospects of others to citizenship depend on the discretion of the government within rules which define eligibility rather than entitlement. In most states there are restrictions on the acquisition of citizenship (sometimes on racial or cultural criteria), and in some there are rules for the deprivation of citizenship. Even liberal states vary in this respect, some with greater bias towards territory, some towards "culture/nation."[11]

Citizenship rules produce anxiety among long-term residents or migrants at the prospects of expulsion and make it difficult for them to integrate in the "host community" or to protect their legitimate interests (Amartya Sen notes that the generous British rules of political participation granted to all members of the Commonwealth have facilitated their integration). The application of the rules can also result in some members of a "foreign" community becoming citizens and others not, and yet the community has social and cultural cohesion, and common interests.

Even when members of minorities have equal citizenship, the critique of liberalism advanced earlier says that this equality is superficial; that it hides the reality that the values and mores of the majority in fact suffuse the state, to the great economic, social, and political disadvantage of minorities and their culture. Because the public space in which many of these rights are exercised may not be culture- or religion-neutral (for example, holidays based on the dominant group's major religious ritual or festivities, its language the official language, and laws, for example on marriage or inheritance grounded in the social or religious traditions of the majority, and electoral laws favoring the majority), minorities may feel alienated and insufficiently recognized. Consequently they demand what has come to be called "differentiated" citizenship which, by recognizing their cultural, linguistic, or religions differences, provides them with effective equality and participation. There are many ways in which "differences" can be recognized, as I have tried to show.

Some, perhaps most, of these rights can be secured only through political and constitutional recognition of ethnic communities, as collective or communal rights. What happens when communities are so recognized? We have seen how they can affect the understanding of sovereignty. How do they bear on the understanding of citizenship? The following sections on democracy, human rights, and autonomy spell out the structural and procedural aspects of the recognition of special rights. Here it is sufficient to note that the consequent recognition of communities introduces a key factor in citizenship: some rights can only be exercised through membership of the prescribed community, when certain voting, economic, or land rights, for example, are restricted to the community. Thus the rules defining membership of the community can take a significance no less critical than the rules defining citizenship. As part of the autonomy of the community, rules whereby a person acquires and loses membership of the community, and the differential consequences of membership, are left to the community itself. While on the whole this kind of scheme is intended for the benefit of members of the community, it is possible that some of them may be disadvantaged, such as women or persons belonging to lower castes within the community.

How then are their citizenship rights to be protected? And as under autonomy regimes, authority structures of the community are vested with functions of government and regulation (e.g. the allocation of resources, or rule making), how can equal political and participatory rights of all its members be protected (when traditionally a key characteristic of the community may have been age, gender or caste discrimination – sometimes sanctioned by sacred texts)? So here we are concerned not only with relations of the members the community with citizens outside the community, especially as the exercise of special rights impact on the latter (for example, as land historically vested in the community) but also the equality of rights between different members of the community. Obligations also vary among different categories of citizens, not only because of duties owed to the community, but also because there may be exemptions for certain citizens from duties owed to the state (e.g. the wearing of helmets when riding a motorbike which is extended to Sikhs who wear turbans, or the consumption of liquors, otherwise prohibited, often extended to indigenous communities). Thus the relationship of some citizens to the state is defined through membership and mores of the community. It is then easy to see how fundamental principles and values of citizenship under liberalism can come under severe strain through this kind of mosaic, in the spheres of rights and democracy.

There is a further dimension to the constitutional recognition of communities. Communities compete with the state for jurisdiction and moral authority – and loyalty. Sometimes the relationship of the community to the state is set out in the law, and in any case it is deeply influenced by politics. And then there is the relationship between communities. For example, in Pakistan, an Islamic state, the religious status of a community will affect not only its relationship with the state but also with other communities (as the Ahmediyyas have learned to their cost). And in a place like Fiji with communal forms of representation and voting, the state is forced to mediate between competing claims of communities. Distinctions between the public and the private are difficult to maintain, especially in multiethnic societies, where consciously or unconsciously there is the desire for the political recognition of the fundamental values or symbols of the community, as well as dominance of even the private domain by the politically and economically powerful. The state is inevitably drawn into the affairs of the community – something a liberal state professes to avoid.

Human rights[12]

Ethnicity both invokes and undermines human rights. The fundamental dilemma of rights and diversity is well captured by Charles Taylor when he writes,

> Now underlying the demand [for recognition of diversity] is a principle of universal equality. The politics of difference is full of denunciations of discrimination and refusals of second class citizenship. This gives the principle of universal equality a point of entry within the politics of dignity. But once inside, as it were, its demands are hard to assimilate to that politics. For it asks we give acknowledgement and status to something that is not universally shared. Or, otherwise put, we give due acknowledgment only what is universally present – every one has an identity – through recognizing what is peculiar to each. The universal demand powers and acknowledgement of specificity.
>
> (Taylor 1994: 39)

The post-Second World War development of the regime of human rights was based on individual rights, with minimum explicit recognition of community rights. Undoubtedly many of these rights (such as equality, freedom of conscience, rights to and of family, freedom of movement, freedom of expression, and the right of association, assembly and demonstration) benefit minorities. But until recently international instruments were parsimonious about cultural or minority rights. Little serious attention was paid to economic and social rights. This was undoubtedly due to the hostility of supporters of the market economy, as distorting the economy and increasing the role of the state. But the resistance to economic and social rights has been expressed in term of their inconsistency with the rule-of-law. A distinction is made between law and policy; civil rights, with clear rules, are compatible with law but economic and social rights, dependent on the availability of resources and open-ended in scope, are policy. The emphasis on individual rights came under considerable attack from the proponents of cultural relativism, who stressed links between a society and its culture. The subordination of economic and social rights upset the marginalized communities as it deprived them of means of redress, and deprived society of possibility of balancing communal interests.

These attacks highlighted what seem to be various contradictions between human rights and ethnicity. Human rights seek to be color-blind, aloof from religious or other affiliations; ethnicity makes these affiliations basic to identity and human existence. Human rights empower the individual; ethnicity the group. Human rights are the framework for relations between citizens *inter se* and between citizens and the state; ethnicity compels attention to and regulation of interethnic relations, and the relations of the group to the state. Human rights aim to be inclusive, ethnicity exclusive. Thus ethnicity has posed problems for human rights in a way that nationalism did not. Nationalism did not seek accommodation of rights within an existing state, but sought its own state; ethnicity seeks accommodation within an existing state. It internalizes to the state problems that would otherwise dissipate on the formation of a new state; it brings problems of cultural relativism not as concerns between distant societies, but as basic to the very definition and existence of a state. Ethnicity seeks to reconfigure the state as the principal framework for the formulation and enforcement of rights, with fundamental implications for how the scope and nature of rights are perceived (in the ways outlined above). If the quarter century after the end of the Second World War saw the rise of the ideology of individual-oriented human rights, the last quarter saw a major challenge, in the name of the community, to that approach. If in the first period, self-determination was the foundation of state sovereignty, in the second period it was mobilized to challenge that sovereignty.

For multicultural states, as people everywhere are finding new identities, human rights, as negotiated understanding of the acceptable framework for co-existence and the respect for each culture, are more important than for mono-cultural or mono-ethnic societies, where other forms of solidarity and identity can be invoked, to minimize or cope with conflicts. The conflict between human rights and cultural relativism cannot be treated simply as a philosophical or political discourse, but as a conflict which must be resolved concretely if some degree of order, stability, and mutual respect is to be achieved. In other words, precisely where the concept and conceptions of rights are most difficult, they are most needed. The task is difficult, but possible, even if it may not be always completely successful.

Here the Indian approach is of interest, and shows ways of balancing national identity and interests with the communal. In preparing the Bill of Rights, the Indian Constituent Assembly (sitting between 1947 and 1950) tried to balance rights as the means to unify the country and promote a common identity (just as Pierre Trudeau thought many years later for Canada when he promoted the Charter of Rights) and to deal with cultural diversity, social hierarchy, and poverty. The Assembly was anxious to protect minorities, wanted to move away from the divisive way the British had ruled India, abandoning the conferment of corporate identities to religious or cultural groups, and shifting towards a more liberal framework. Conscious of the cultural diversity of India, they were at the same time preoccupied by the imperative of "nation building," cultivation of a common identity and common loyalties. To an extent these opposing objectives were balanced by adopting the device of an enforceable Bill of Rights for, but not exclusively, civil and political rights, and a nonjusticiable charter of Directive Principles for measures of social and economic equality. Where the necessary social and economic reforms could only be achieved by qualifying civil or political rights, such as those of equality and property, the authority for this was clearly stated in the Bill of Rights.

Notwithstanding that India was a deeply religious society, with many beliefs between which there was tension, the Constituent Assembly decided that the Bill of Rights was to be the principal agency of social reform. The Bill is strongly oriented towards universalism and social reform. Rights are used as a critique of culture, especially Hindu culture. "Untouchability" is abolished and its practice prohibited (art. 17). Traffic in human beings, servitude and similar practices of forced labor are abolished (art. 23). The freedom of conscience and religion was drawn carefully to ensure that practices like *purdah* or *sati* (widow-burning) were not indirectly entrenched (art. 25(2)). Hindu practices which prevent Dalits ("untouchables") from access to the use of public facilities, including wells, are prohibited. The imperative of social reform is evident also in Directive Principles, particularly in article 38(1) which requires the state to "strive to promote the welfare of the people by securing and protecting as effectively as it may a social order in which justice, social, economic and political, shall inform all the institutions of the national life."

The lesson perhaps is that in relation to most rights, the notion of absolutism is unhelpful; but qualifications on rights must be consistent with the core of the rights. The appropriate formulation and protection of social, economic, and cultural rights, emphasizing the "positive duties" of the state, is often fundamental to a settlement, both to acknowledge the importance of culture and of redress of ethnic inequalities. Thus for this (and other reasons of "ethnic" management) there arises the necessity for an activist state. Since interethnic relations are so crucial to an enduring settlement and past history may have been marked by discrimination or exploitation, a substantial part of the regime of rights has to be made binding on private parties.

Achieving this balancing involves the recognition of corporate identities as bearer of rights. To preserve their culture, some communities claim wide exemptions from the application of the Bill of Rights. This has a dual effect on possibilities of rights. One is internal to the community which seeks exemptions; cultural values may in many respects be hostile to rights and modern democratic thought, and this places groups within the community at risk, such as women and lower castes. The other can be discrimination against members of other communities, as with exclusive claims to certain resources. The discrimination is resented by groups both within and outside the community. The consequences spill over into the political domain, raising questions of national integration. Affirmative action in Malaysia and India for "indigenous" Malays or Dalits or tribals in India have caused much resentment among other communities. At the same time it reinforces ethnic and caste communities, particularly among the disadvantaged communities who would otherwise have an interest in national and social integration as an escape – for it is only through preserving those classifications that the preferential scheme can be sustained. And yet it is by redressing past or present injustices that a sense of national unity can be fostered.

Regimes of personal, cultural, or religious laws

Some of the dilemmas for the regime of human rights in the recognition of diversity can be illustrated by an examination of the schemes of personal laws (based on religion or custom), covering marriage and family. As has already been mentioned, the development of a common regime of family law was the consequence of the "nation state." The major remnants of separate personal laws today are the hangovers of colonies. Colonial powers, having an interest in preventing national consciousness among their subjects, devised separate communal systems to emphasize differences among them. Today, with assertions of identity and multiculturalism, the concept of religion-based personal laws has been revived (evidenced by intense debates on the subject in Britain, Canada, Kenya, France, India, and Malaysia).

Some members of a community, perhaps a minority, consider the application of personal laws critical for maintaining its culture and identity. Others, particularly members of the majority, may believe that common laws on these matters are essential for national integration. These divisions emerged between the Hindu majority and Muslim minority when the Indian Constituent Assembly wanted, in a reversal of colonial policy, to mandate a common civil code. The compromise was that the constitution prescribed a common code merely as an objective of state policy, and over time a convention emerged that the shariah would continue to apply so long as Muslims desired it (although in recent years this convention has become controversial, worsening communal relations). The debate has become more complex, adding to the integration issue the effect on the vulnerable members of the community due to its discriminatory rules. So differences arise not only between the majority and the minority, but primarily within members of the community (as is evident in the current Canadian controversy on whether and how the shariah should be applied).[13]

But the issue is also of general interest, as religious or customary personal laws affect women and children adversely. The experience of Israel, which has an extensive scheme of personal laws, is instructive (Edelman 1994). Israel has courts for 14 recognized religious communities, with exclusive jurisdiction over matters relating to marriage and divorce (there is no civil marriage or divorce in Israel). These courts also resolve other personal- and private-law issues. Since legislative authority over these matters is rarely exercised, courts have a profound effect on shaping the country's political culture, involving rights of women, contacts between members of different communities, and more generally the lives of Israelis (ibid.). Although linked to and supported by the state, these courts are administered independently of the state.

The presence of shariah courts has reinforced Muslims' sense of community and its values, and helped in the social reproduction of the community – an important factor for minorities, especially when under foreign occupation (ibid.). These conclusions corroborate an argument for cultural autonomy, namely, that it "supports political stability by providing nondominant (and unassimilable) groups with mechanisms that enable them to minimise the effects of their inferior position in the larger society" (Jacobsohn 1993: 30). But the separate regime of Muslim law has isolated Arabs from the mainstream of Israeli politics. For the Jews, the rabbinical courts have been deeply divisive, symbolizing the fundamental schism between orthodox and secular Jews. In both instances the courts give the clergy, committed to the preservation of orthodoxy, a specially privileged position. The law is slow to change in these circumstances, and can lag well behind social attitudes and social realities. Edelman concludes that while civil courts have sought to promote democratic political culture based upon the rule-of-law, religious courts and personal legal regimes have sharpened distinctions between Israel's communities, retarding the development of intercommunity social relations and a unifying political culture (1994: 119). He observes, "Yet without a shared political culture and the concomitant sense of a shared national identity, the prospects for a sustained, peaceful national existence are not bright" (ibid).

This view is not endorsed by Jacobsohn, who says that studies of Jewish public opinion in Israel reveal that shared ethnicity and a shared set of religious symbols are much more important than a shared set of values in providing unity for Israeli society. "Thus, the subordination of cultural aspects to individual liberties on the basis of the assertion that the latter are 'principles' has less justification in a polity where cultural imperatives may legitimately demand principled consideration" (Jacobsohn 1993: 37). Here it may be noted that the Indian majority wanted an integrated political society, while most governments in Israel did not.

One of the major problems with cultural/religious/legal autonomy of this kind is that it puts certain sections of the relevant community at a disadvantage. Edelman shows how both Jewish and Muslim women come off worse in their respective autonomous courts. In Canada (before reform impressed on it by the UN Human Rights Committee) a woman from a first nation who married a person outside that community lost all rights in the community (including access to land) – unlike a man who married an outsider. In this way the hierarchies and discriminations in the community are reinforced by state-sanctioned personal laws. In India, Muslim women are unable to benefit from the more liberal legal regime that has applied to other Indian women after the reforms of the 1960s. One aspect of their disadvantage was illustrated in 1985 by the famous Shah Banu case, where the Supreme Court held that the maintenance that a Muslim divorced woman could claim from her former husband was to be determined under the general national law, which provided a higher amount than she would get under the shariah. This decision, although favored by many Muslims, provoked a violent reaction from a section of the community, including the clergy, and, to preserve its political support, the government passed a bill to overrule the decision. The rise of Hindu nationalism is often ascribed to this "capitulation" by the government to Muslim minority demands. The irony is that the debate or law on personal laws can also tear up the community concerned, as the Indian and Israeli experience (and recent Canadian developments) shows.

Today, the question of special personal laws is inevitably controversial and politicized. It raises critical and difficult moral and technical issues (for which there is no space here). However, the dilemma for constitutionalism and the tensions between individual rights and community cohesion, are well captured in two quotes from Marion Boyd's report (2004). She criticizes the secular position excluding religious family law from the legal system for failing to "acknowledge that some people live their lives in a manner more closely aligned to their faiths than others" and that state laws themselves may be influenced by the dominant religion, "making their impact disproportionate on those who do not belong to the dominant culture" and serving "to alienate from the mainstream those who do not see themselves reflected" in these laws (Boyd 1994: 91). At the same time she is able to say,

> By placing primacy on the right of the minority group to protect itself from external influences, those individuals in the minority group whose rights may be violated must bear the burden of the protection of the culture within the dominant society. As a result, individual autonomy is sacrificed for the sake of group survival.
>
> (ibid.: 92)

Democracy

I have left till the last consideration of how the understanding of democracy, as the most comprehensive and complex concept of constitutionalism, has been affected by the rise of identity politics. Democracy is supposed to provide an overarching framework of values and procedures within which national decisions are made and citizens pursue their common and separate objectives. It is based on the representation of the people and the accountability of government. It is the liberal vision of nation building. Liberal democracy is often contrasted with the consociational, representing a partnership between ethnic communities. Constitutional devices for diversity described in this chapter affect the conception and functioning of democracy, critically the understandings of sovereignty, communities, and citizenship. There is no single model to which these devices conform, but there is a distinct bias towards the consociational, and thus on ethnicity, on which my discussion is largely based.

Ethnicity leads to great politicization of society. The issues it raises, based on sharp polarities, are emotional and uncomplicated for the ordinary person. The complexities of life and relationships, grounded on the multiplicity of identities of an individual, are obscured by the singularization of identity, which governs the world view of so many caught up in ethnic politics. Politics are less about policies than communal entitlements, which leads to the "invention" of new communities. Public discourses on social issues are impoverished. Social justice is viewed through a narrow perspective, often ignoring women, children, workers, the disabled, and the most disadvantaged. So ethnicity becomes the principal mode of mass mobilization. Political parties tend to rely on blocks of ethnic supporters (the "vote bank" as Indians call the system). Communities are given, in different forms, considerable powers of self-government, and become significant sites of powers.

Consociation, especially when legislative seats or executive posts are ethnically allocated, institutionalizes these "vote banks;" the logic of the system is ethnic parties. Within communities power passes to traditional or modern political elites – and this too affects the quality of participation and democracy. Normally the extreme factions outvote the more moderate (the experience of Northern Ireland and Bosnia-Herzegovina attest to this). When communities play such important roles in the political system, the quality of democracy is increasingly determined by their values and practices. As we have seen, it is due to the inegalitarian and discriminatory nature of many communities that there is resistance to their official recognition.

Constitutionally mandated coalitions affect participation, decision-making, and democracy. Key national decisions are made in negotiations between a small number of key ethnic politicians. In the legislative body, there is little space for formal opposition, and there is a strong tendency towards rubber-stamping decisions made by the ethnic leaders. In the executive, there is considerable horse trading, based on ethnic sharing of resources. There is also, as mentioned above, considerable narrowing of the distinction between the public and civic/private spheres, resulting in part from the politicization of communities. This degree of politicization of society is inimical to constitutionalism.

Concluding observations

There are very marked differences in the characteristics of "multiethnic" constitutions from the "liberal" constitutions that previously defined the rule of law and constitutionalism. In many instances the distinction between the public and private has become tenuous (although this has to some extent been happening in contemporary liberal systems). Citizenship now represents a complex set of relationships, and can be highly differentiated. Cultural communities have become political entities; sometimes the public sphere is carved among them. In Bosnia-Herzegovina the traditional principle of the separation of legislative and executive authorities has little relevance. Increasingly in multiethnic constitutions, the task of balancing power is achieved by powers vested in communities, through multiple membership of the presidency, as in Bosnia-Herzegovina and Iraq, or by the system of voting in the legislature when in addition to an overall majority, each community has a veto, at least on certain important issues.

Claims of community compete with claims of individuals. The concept of equality is redefined; it is based on the legal recognition of *difference*. And individual equality is not particularly valued, as we have seen in the case of schemes of cultural autonomies. Distinctions may be more principled and carefully circumscribed when related to social justice (as in affirmative action). An important function of the regime of rights is to accommodate diversities, with particular regard to definitions of religion and entitlements under it. There is a move away from thematic rights to group rights (indigenous peoples, women, and children).

The nature of state sovereignty is reconfigured, moving away from one central point. This diffusion of sovereignty fragments the political community and leads to legal pluralism undermining the uniformity of the legal system. There are new understandings of democracy, away from majoritarianism to the balancing of community interests. Rights of participation can depend even more on membership of communities than citizenship. Fundamental issues of public policy may be disregarded in the pursuit of ethnic balances, in the pursuit of singular rather than multiple identities. Accountability can become difficult when politics are dominated by alliances of ethnic leaders.

The constitution becomes more important because it is a register of negotiated identities and difficult compromises that must be sustained. But the constant interethnic negotiations that are required by the constitution deprive the law of some of its "autonomy," and certainly can weaken the institutions of the law. A framework constitution privileges negotiations over adjudication (although most ethnic constitutions are a detailed codification of a settlement, unlike the Canadian constitution which retains elements of the "framework," at least as far as the first nations are concerned, less so for Quebec).

I leave it at that and postpone to another occasion the important question: Do these developments represent merely differences of technique from traditional rule-of-law and constitutionalism practices or reflect fundamental shifts in values and policy? For now it suffices to say that the challenge is to reflect diversity and fairness to communities within a constitutional framework which encourages political integration and the building of a minimum core of common values.

Notes

1 Emeritus Professor, University of Hong Kong. I would like to acknowledge with thanks the Distinguished Researcher Award which has facilitated my research for this chapter.

2 McIlwain says that for some early

> 'liberal conservatives' the safeguarding of necessary liberties seems to have implied the preservation intact of the customary law of the nation in its entirety. Sir Edward Coke, for example, appears to have thought nothing less than the whole body of the English common law must be kept inviolate if the liberty of the subject was to be protected against arbitrary rule.
>
> (McIlwain 1947: 12)

He saw the common law as "fundamental law."

3 Soon after the Philadelphia Constitution, Thomas Paine said that constitutions "are to liberty, what a grammar is to language" and a government without a constitution is "power without right" (as quoted in McIlwain 1947: 2).

4 This is a major theme of McIlwain's book, and informs much of the criticism of modern constitutional approaches by James Tully (1995).

5 For the changing functions of constitutions, see Ghai (2005).

6 For recent perspectives, see Maravall and Przeworski (2003a).

7 This chapter relies largely on Taylor's, "The Politics of Recognition" (1994).

8 This chapter relies principally on Kymlicka's first, important book, *Liberalism, Community and Culture* (1989).

9 See the critiques of Amartya Sen (2006a) and Anthony Appiah (1994).

10 The Supreme Court of Canada said,

> Our democratic institutions necessarily accommodate a continuous process of discussion and evolution, which is reflected in the constitutional right of each participant in the federation to initiate constitutional change. This right implies a reciprocal duty on the other participants to engage in discussions to address any legitimate initiative to change the constitutional order.
>
> (*Reference re the Secession of Quebec* (1988), para. 150)

11 Rogers Brubaker (1996) compares and contrasts the attitudes towards citizenship and the rules for acquiring it, with France more generous but also more assimilationist, and Germany ethno-cultural and restrictive.

12 This and the next sections draw upon several of my publications, including *Public Participation and Minorities* (2001); "Constitutional Asymmetries: Communal Representation, Federalism, and Cultural Autonomy" (2002); *Human Rights and Governance: The Asia Debate* (1994); "Universalism and Relativism: Human Rights as a Framework for Negotiating Interethnic Claims" (2000); and "Understanding Human Rights in Asia" (forthcoming).

13 The arguments for and against are set out at length in the report by Marion Boyd to the Ontario's Attorney General and to the Minister Responsible for Women's Affairs, *Dispute Resolution in Family Law: Protecting Choice, Promoting Inclusion* (Boyd 2004). See also the controversial speech of the Archbishop of Canterbury supporting the application of the shariah in Islamic courts in the UK, and the flood of attack that followed (Williams 2008).

References

Abel, R.L. (2007) "Contesting Legality in the United States after September 11," in T.C. Halliday, L. Karpik, and M.M. Feeley (eds.) *Fighting for Political Freedom: Comparative Studies of the Legal Complex for Political Change*, Oxford: Hart Publishing.

Acemoglu, D. and Johnson, S. (2005) "Unbundling Institutions," *Journal of Political Economy*, 113 (5): 949–95.

Acemoglu, D., Johnson, S., and Robinson, J.A. (2001) "The Colonial Origins of Comparative Development: An Empirical Investigation," *American Economic Review*, 91: 1369–401.

——(2002) "Reversal of Fortune: Geography and Institutions in the Making of the Modern World Income Distribution," *The Quarterly Journal of Economics*, 117: 1231–94.

Adams, J. (2005) *The Familial State: Ruling Families and Merchant Capitalism in Early Modern Europe*, Ithaca, NY: Cornell University Press.

Agell, J. (1999) "On the Benefits from Rigid Labour Markets: Norms, Market Failures, and Social Insurance," *Economic Journal*, 109(453): F143–64.

Ahlquist, J. and Levi, M. (2008) "The Lenin Problem: How Some Organizations Transform Conceptions of Self-Interest," paper presented at University of California, Los Angeles, Department of Political Science, 12 November.

Al-Rasheed, M. (2002) *A History of Saudi Arabia*, New York: Cambridge University Press.

Allen, F. and Qian, J. (2008) "Corruption and Competition," working paper, Boston College, Boston.

Allen, F., Qian, J., and Qian, M. (2005) "Law, Finance, and Economic Growth in China," *Journal of Financial Economics*, 77(1): 57–116.

——(2008) "China's Financial System: Past, Present and Future," in L. Brandt and T. Rawski (eds) *China's Great Economic Transformation*, Cambridge: Cambridge University Press.

Allen, F., Chakrabarti, R., De, S., Qian, J., and Qian, M. (2008) "Financing Firms in India," working paper, Wharton Financial Institutions Center, Philadelphia.

Allouche, A. (1994) *Mamluk Economics: A Study and Translation of Al-Maqrīzī's Ighāthah*, Salt Lake City: University of Utah Press.

Alt, J.E. (2002) "Comparative Political Economy: Credibility, Transparency, Accountability and Institutions," in I. Katznelson and H. Milner (eds) *The State of the Discipline: Power, Choice, and the State*, New York: W.W. Norton.

American Bar Association (2008) *The World Justice Project*. Online. Available HTTP: http://www.worldjusticeproject.org/ (accessed 6 November 2008).

Aoki, M. (2001) *Toward a Comparative Institutional Analysis*, Cambridge, MA: Cambridge University Press.

Appiah, A. (1994) "Identity, Authenticity, Survival: Multicultural Societies and Social Reproduction," in A. Gutman (ed.) *Multiculturalism: Examining the Politics of Recognition*, Princeton: Princeton University Press.

Aristotle (1988) *The Politics*, ed. Stephen Everson, Cambridge: Cambridge University Press.

Arndt, C. and Oman, C. (2006) *Uses and Abuses of Governance Indicators*, Paris: OECD.

Arrow, K. (1951) *Social Choice and Individual Values*, New York: Wiley.

——(1974) *The Limits of Organization*, New York: W.W. Norton.

Arslan, Z. (2007) "Reluctantly Sailing Towards Political Liberalism: The Political Role of the Judiciary in Turkey," in T.C. Halliday, L. Karpik, and M.M. Feeley (eds) *Fighting for Political Freedom: Comparative Studies of the Legal Complex for Political Change*, Oxford: Hart Publishing.

Ashton, R. (1960) *The Crown and the Money Market, 1603–1640*, Oxford: Clarendon Press.

Ashtor, E. (1976) *A Social and Economic History of the Near East in the Middle Ages*, London: Collins.

Bank for International Settlements (2008) *Statistics on Payment and Settlement Systems in Selected Countries: Figures for 2006*. Online. Available HTTP: http://www.bis.org/publ/cpss82.pdf (accessed 23 November 2008).

Barnard, C.I. (1938) *The Functions of the Executive*, Cambridge, MA: Harvard University Press.

Barraclough, S. (1998) "Al-Azhar: Between the Government and the Islamists," *Middle East Journal*, 52: 236–49.

Barros, R. (2003) "Dictatorship and the Rule of Law: Rules and Military Power in Pinochet's Chile," in J.M. Maravall and A. Przeworski (eds) *Democracy and the Rule of Law*, New York: Cambridge University Press.

Barzilai, G. (2007) "The Ambivalent Language of Lawyers: Between Liberal Politics, Economic Liberalism, Silence, and Dissent," in T.C. Halliday, L. Karpik, and M.M. Feeley (eds) *Fighting for Political Freedom: Comparative Studies of the Legal Complex for Political Change*, Oxford: Hart Publishing.

Bates, R.H. (1983) "The Nature and Origins of Agricultural Policies in Africa," in Robert H. Bates (ed.) *Essays on the Political Economy of Rural Africa*, Cambridge: Cambridge University Press.

——(2008) *Why States Fail*, New York: Cambridge.

Bearak, B. (2000) "In India, the Wheels of Justice Hardly Move," *New York Times*, World section, A1 (1 June).

Beck, T. and Levine, R. (2005) "Legal Institutions and Financial Development," in C. Menard and M.M. Shirley (eds) *Handbook for New Institutional Economics*, Dordrecht: Springer.

Beck, T., Demirguc-Kunt, A. and Levine, R. (2003) "Law and Finance: Why Does Legal Origin Matter?" *Journal of Comparative Economics*, 31: 653–75.

Behdad, S. (1994) "A Disputed Utopia: Islamic Economics in Revolutionary Iran," *Comparative Studies in Society and History*, 36: 775–813.

Bell, D.A. (1998) "Barristers, Politics, and the Failure of Civil Society in Old Regime France," in T.C. Halliday and L. Karpik (eds) *Lawyers and the Rise of Western*

Political Liberalism: Europe and North America from the Eighteenth to Twentieth Centuries, Oxford: Oxford University Press.

Berkowitz, D. and Clay, K. (2005) "Initial Conditions, Institutional Dynamics and Economic Performance: Evidence from the American States," *American Law and Economics Review*, 7: 62–84.

Berkowitz, D., Pistor, K., and Richard, J.F. (2003a) "Economic Development, Legality, and the Transplant Effect," *European Economic Review*, 47: 165–95.

——(2003b) "The Transplant Effect," *American Journal of Comparative Law*, 51: 163–203.

Berman, S. (2007a) "Lessons from Europe," *Journal of Democracy*, 18(1): 28–41.

——(2007b) "The Vain Hope for 'Correct' Timing," *Journal of Democracy*, 18(3): 14–17.

Berns, W. (1988) "The Making of the Constitution of the United States," in R.A. Goodwin and A. Kaufman (eds) *Constitution Makers on Constitution Making*, Washington, DC: American Enterprise Institute.

Bernstein, L. (1992) "Opting Out of the Legal System: Extralegal Contractual Relations in the Diamond Industry," *Journal of Legal Studies*, 21: 115–57.

Bessen, J. and Meurer, M.J. (2008) *Patent Failure: How Judges, Bureaucrats, and Lawyers Put Innovators at Risk*, Princeton: Princeton University Press.

Bhadra, M. (ed.) (1999) *Girl Child in Indian Society*, Jaipur: Rawat Publications.

Blanchard, O. and Wolfers, J. (2000) "The Role of Shocks and Institutions in the Rise of European Unemployment: The Aggregate Evidence," *Economic Journal*, 110(462): C1–33.

Blitt, R.C. (2007) *Babushka Said Two Things – It Will Either Rain or Snow; It Either Will or Will Not: An Analysis of the Provisions and Human Rights Implications of Russia's New Law on Nongovernmental Organizations as Told Through Eleven Russian Proverbs*, University of Tennessee Legal Studies Research Paper No. 2. Online. Available HTTP: http://ssrn.com/abstract=1009400 (accessed 25 October 2008).

Board of Governors of the Federal Reserve System (2008) "94th Annual Report 2007," Washington, DC: The Federal Reserve Board.

Bolt, W., Humphrey, D., and Uittenbogaard, R. (2005) "The Effects of Transaction Pricing on the Adoption of Electronic Payments: A Cross-country Comparison," *International Journal of Central Banking*, 4(1): 89–123.

Bovenberg, A.L., Hansen, M.I., and Sørensen, P.B. (2008) "Individual Savings Accounts for Social Insurance: Rationale and Alternative Designs," *International Tax and Public Finance*, 15(1): 67–86.

Boyd, M. (2004) *Dispute Resolution in Family Law: Protecting Choice, Promoting Inclusion*. Online. Available HTTP: http://www.attorneygeneral.jus.gov.on.ca/english/about/pubs/boyd/ (accessed 19 October 2008).

Boyle, E.H. (2002) *Female Genital Cutting: Cultural Conflict in the Global Community*, Baltimore: Johns Hopkins University Press.

Boyle, E.H. and Meyer, J. (2002) "Modern Law as a Secularized and Global Model: Implications for the Sociology of Law," in Y. Dezalay and B. Garth (eds) *Global Prescriptions: The Production, Exportation, and Importation of a New Legal Orthodoxy*, Ann Arbor: University of Michigan Press.

Braddick, M. J. (1996) *The Nerves of State: Taxation and the Financing of the English State, 1558–1714*, New York: Manchester University Press.

Brandt, L. and Rawski, T. (2008) *China's Great Economic Transformation*, Cambridge: Cambridge University Press.

Braudel, F. (1982) *The Wheels of Commerce*, New York: Harper and Row.

Brewer, J. (1988) "The English State and Fiscal Appropriation: Taxes and Public Finance in England, 1688–1789," *Politics and Society*, 16: 335–85.

——(1990) *The Sinews of Power: War, Money and the English State, 1688–1783*, Cambridge, MA: Harvard University Press.

Brinks, D.M. (2007) "Of Gulliver and the State: The Legal Complex and the Response to Police Violence in South America," in T.C. Halliday, L. Karpik, and M.M. Feeley (eds) *Fighting for Political Freedom: Comparative Studies of the Legal Complex for Political Change*, Oxford: Hart Publishing.

——(2008) *The Judicial Response to Police Killings in Latin America*, New York: Cambridge University Press.

Brubaker, R. (1996) *Citizenship and Nationhood in France and Germany*, Cambridge, MA: Harvard University Press.

Carothers, T. (1998) "The Rule of Law Revival," *Foreign Affairs*, 77(2): 95–106.

——(2001) "The Many Agendas of Rule-of-Law Reform in Latin America," in P. Domingo and R. Sieder (eds) *Rule of Law in Latin America: The International Promotion of Judicial Reform*, London: Institute of Latin American Studies.

—— (2006) *Promoting the Rule of Law Aboard: The Search for Knowledge*, Washington, DC: Carnegie Endowment.

——(2007a) "The 'Sequencing' Fallacy," *Journal of Democracy*, 18(1): 12–27.

——(2007b) "Misunderstanding Gradualism," *Journal of Democracy*, 18(3): 18–22.

Chancellor, E. (1999) *Devil Take the Hindmost: A History of Financial Speculation*, Basingstoke: Macmillan.

Chaudhuri, K.N. (1965) *The English East India Company: The Study of an Early Joint-Stock Company, 1600–1640*, New York: A.M. Kelley.

Chaudhury, S. and Morineau, M. (1999) *Merchants, Companies, and Trade: Europe and Asia in the Early Modern Era*, New York: Cambridge University Press.

China, Government of (1904) Company Law.

China, People's Republic of (2007) Enterprise Bankruptcy Law of People's Republic of China.

Clark, G. (1996) "The Political Foundations of Modern Economic Growth," *Journal of Interdisciplinary History*, 26: 563–88.

Clarke, D., Murrell, P., and Whiting, S. (2008) "The Role of Law in China's Economic Development," in L. Brandt and T. Rawski (eds) *China's Great Economic Transformation*, Cambridge: Cambridge University Press.

Coase, R.H. (1937) "The Nature of the Firm," *Economica*, 4: 386–405.

Collier, P. (2007) *The Bottom Billion: Why the Poorest Countries are Failing and What Can be Done About It*, Oxford: Oxford University Press.

Cook, K.S., Hardin, R., and Levi, M. (2005) *Cooperation Without Trust?* New York: Russell Sage Foundation.

Cooter, R.D. and Rubenfeld, D.L. (1990) "Trial Courts: An Economic Perspective," *Law and Society Review*, 24: 533–46.

Coşgel, M., Ahmed, R., and Miceli, T. (2009) "Law, State Power, and Taxation in Islamic History," *Journal of Economic Behavior and Organization*, forthcoming.

Coulson, N.J. (1971) *Succession in the Muslim Family*, Cambridge: Cambridge University Press.

Couso, J. (2003) "The Politics of Judicial Review in Chile in the Era of Democratic Transition 1990–2002," *Democratization*, 10(4): 70–91.

——(2006) "The Changing Role of Law and Courts in Latin America: From an Obstacle to Social Change to a Tool of Social Inquiry," in R. Gargarella, P.

Domingo, and T. Roix (eds) *Courts and Social Transformation in New Democracies: An Institutional Voice for the Poor?* Aldershot: Ashgate Publishing.

——(2007) "When the 'Political Complex' Takes the Lead," in T.C. Halliday, L. Karpik, and M.M. Feeley (eds) *Fighting for Political Freedom: Comparative Studies of the Legal Complex for Political Change*, Oxford: Hart Publishing.

Creswell, J. (2006) "So Small a Town, So Many Patent Suits," *New York Times*, Technology section (24 September).

Dam, K.W. (2006) *The Law–Growth Nexus: The Rule of Law and Economic Development*, Washington, DC: Brookings Institution Press.

Darling, L. (1996) *Revenue-Raising and Legitimacy: Tax Collection and Finance in the Ottoman Empire, 1560–1660*, Leiden: E.J. Brill.

Davis, S.J. and Henrekson, M. (2006) "Economic Performance and Work Activity in Sweden After the Crisis of the Early 1990s," working paper 12768, National Bureau of Economic Research.

——(2008) "Economic Performance and Work Activity in Sweden after the Crisis of the Early 1990s," in R.B. Freeman, B. Swedenborg, and R. Topel (eds) *Reforming the Welfare State: Recovery and Beyond in Sweden*, Chicago: University of Chicago Press.

de Condorcet, M. (1785) *Essai sur l'Application de l'Analyse a la Probabilite des Decisions rendues a la Pluralite des Voix*, Paris: L'Imprimerie Royale.

de Vries, J. and van der Woude, A. (1997) *The First Modern Economy: Success, Failure, and Perseverance of the Dutch Economy, 1500–1815*, Cambridge: Cambridge University Press.

den Heijer, H.J. (2005) *De geoctrooieerde compagnie: De VOC en de WIC als voorlopers van de naamloze vennootschap*, Deventer, Netherlands: Kluwer Legal Publishers.

Dewan, V.K. (2000) *Law Relating to Offences Against Women*, New Delhi: Orient Law House.

Dewatripont, M. and Legros, P. (2007) "Essential Patents, FRAND Royalties and Technological Standards," working paper, European Center for Advanced Research in Economics and Statistics, Brussels.

Dezalay, Y. and Garth, B.G. (2002) *The Internationalization of Palace Wars: Lawyers, Economists, and the Contest to Transform Latin American States* (Chicago Series in Law and Society), Chicago: University of Chicago Press.

Diaz-Cayeros, A., Magaloni, B., and Weingast, B.R. (2008) "Tragic Brilliance: Equilibrium Party Hegemony in Mexico," working paper, Hoover Institution.

Dickson, P.G.M. (1967) *The Financial Revolution in England: A Study in the Development of Public Credit, 1688–1756*, London: Macmillan.

Dixit, A. (2004) *Lawlessness and Economics*, Princeton: Princeton University Press.

Djankov, S. and Murrell, P. (2002) "Enterprise Restructuring in Transition: A Quantitative Survey," *Journal of Economic Literature*, 40: 739–92.

Djankov, S., La Porta, R., Lopez-de-Silanes, F. and Shleifer, A. (2002) "The Regulation of Entry," *Quarterly Journal of Economics*, 117(1): 1–37.

Doyle, M.W. and Sambanis, N. (2006) *Making War and Building Peace*, Princeton: Princeton University Press.

Dubey, A. and Verschoor, A. (2007) "Does Intra-household Discrimination Account for the Bulk of India's 'Missing Women'?" *Journal of South Asian Development*, 2(1): 1–18.

Dugard, J. and Roix, T. (2006) "The Record of the South African Constitutional Court in Providing an Institutional Voice for the Poor: 1005–2004," in R. Gargarella, P. Domingo, and T. Roix (eds) *Courts and Social Transformation in New Democracies: An Institutional Voice for the Poor?* Aldershot: Ashgate Publishing.

Dyzenhaus, D. (1991) *Hard Cases in Wicked Legal Systems*, New York: Clarendon Press.

Easterly, W. (2001) *The Elusive Quest for Growth: Economists' Adventures and Misadventures in the Tropics*, Cambridge, MA: MIT Press.

Economist (2007) "Home and Away," 15 September: 31–3.

——(2008) "Order in the Jungle," 13 March 2008. Online. Available HTTP: http://www.economist.com/displaystory.cfm?story_id = 10849115 (accessed 11 May 2008).

Edelman, M. (1994) *Courts, Politics and Culture in Israel*, Charlottesville: University of Virginia Press.

EIC Charter (1600) reprinted in John Shaw (ed.) (1887) *Charters Relating to the East India Company from 1600 to 1761*, Madras: Government Press.

Engerman, S.L. and Sokoloff, K.L. (2008) "Debating the Role of Institutions in Political and Economic Development: Theory, History, and Findings," *Annual Review of Political Science*, 11: 119–35.

Engerman, S.L., Sokoloff, K.L., and Haber, S. (1997) "Factor Endowments, Institutions, and Differential Paths of Growth Among New World Economies: A View from Economic Historians of the United States," in S. Haber (ed.) *Economic Growth and Latin American Economic Historiography*, Cambridge, MA: MIT Press.

European Values Study Foundation and World Values Survey Association (2006) *European and World Values Surveys Four-Wave Integrated Data File, 1981–2004, v.20060423*. Online. Available HTTP: http://www.worldvaluessurvey.org/ (accessed 14 October 2008).

Falcao, J. (1988) "Lawyers in Brazil," in R.L. Abel and P.S.C. Lewis (eds) *Lawyers in Society: Civil Law Countries*, Berkeley: University of California Press.

Fallon, R.H. Jr (1997) "'The Rule of Law' as a Concept in Constitutional Discourse," *Columbia Law Review*, 97: 1–56.

Feeley, M.M. and Miyazawa, S. (2007) "The State, Civil Society, and the Legal Complex in Modern Japan: Continuity and Change," in T.C. Halliday, L. Karpik, and M. M. Feeley (eds) *Fighting for Political Freedom: Comparative Studies of the Legal Complex for Political Change*, Oxford: Hart Publishing.

Feldman, N. (2008) *The Fall and Rise of the Islamic State*, Princeton: Princeton University Press.

Ferejohn, J. (1999) "Accountability and Authority: Toward a Theory of Political Accountability," in A. Przeworski, S.C. Stokes, and B. Manin (eds) *Democracy, Accountability and Representation*, New York: Cambridge University Press.

Fish, M.S. (2005) *Democracy Derailed in Russia: the Failure of Open Politics*, New York: Cambridge University Press.

Fisher, M. (2007) "Download Uproar: Record Industry Goes After Personal Use," *Washington Post*, Sunday Arts: M5 (30 December).

Flinn, C.J. (2002) "Labour Market Structure and Inequality: A Comparison of Italy and the US," *Review of Economic Studies*, 69(3): 611–45.

Forslund, A. and Krueger, A.B. (2008) "Did Active Labour Market Policies Help Sweden Rebound from the Depression of the Early 1990s?" in R.B. Freeman, B. Swedenborg, and R. Topel (eds) *Reforming the Welfare State: Recovery and Beyond in Sweden*, Chicago: University of Chicago Press.

Freeman, R.B. (2002) "Institutional Differences and Economic Performance among OECD Countries," CEP discussion paper, Centre for Economic Performance, London School of Economics.

Freeman, R.B., Swedenborg, B., and Topel, R. (eds) (2006) *Att Reformera Välfärds-staten: Amerikanskt Perspektiv på den svenska modellen*, Stockholm. Studieförbundet Näringsliv och samhälle.

Fritschy, W. (2003) "A 'Financial Revolution' Reconsidered: Public Finance in Holland During the Dutch Revolt, 1568–1648," *Economic History Review*, 56: 57–89.

Fukuyama, F. (2007) "Liberalism Versus State-Building," *Journal of Democracy*, 18(3): 10–13.

Furber, H. (1976) *Rival Empires of Trade in the Orient, 1600–1800*, Minneapolis: University of Minnesota Press.

Fyzee, A.A.A. (1964) *Outlines of Muhammadan Law*, third edn, London: Oxford University Press.

Gaastra, F.S. (2008) *VOC – Organization*, Netherlands. Online. Available HTTP: http://www.tanap.net/content/voc/organization/organization_intro.htm (accessed 25 November 2008).

Ganz, M. (2000) "Resources and Resourcefulness: Strategic Capacity in the Unionization of California Agriculture, 1959–66," *American Journal of Sociology*, 105: 1003–62.

Garber, P.M. (2000) *Famous First Bubbles: The Fundamentals of Early Manias*, Cambridge, MA: MIT Press.

Geertz, C. (1963) *Old Societies and New States: The Quest for Modernity in Asia and Africa*, New York: Free Press.

Gelderblom, O. and Jonker, J. (2004) "Completing a Financial Revolution: The Finance of the Dutch East India Trade and the Rise of the Amsterdam Capital Market, 1595–1612," *Journal of Economic History*, 64: 641–72.

——(2005) "Amsterdam as the Cradle of Modern Futures and Options Trading, 1550–1650," in W.N. Goetzmann and K.G. Rouwenhorst (eds) *The Origins of Value: The Financial Innovations that Created Modern Capital Markets*, Oxford: Oxford University Press.

Gepken-Jager, E. (2005) "The Dutch East India Company (VOC)," in E. Gepken-Jager, G. Van Solinge, and L. Timmerman (eds) *VOC 1602–2002 – 400 Years of Company Law*, Deventer, Netherlands: Kluwer Legal Publishers.

Ghai, Y. (1994) *Human Rights and Governance: The Asia Debate*, San Francisco: The Asia Foundation.

——(2000) "Universalism and Relativism: Human Rights as a Framework for Negotiating Interethnic Claims," *Cardozo Law Review*, 21: 1095–140.

——(2001; rev. edn 2003) *Public Participation and Minorities*, London: Minority Rights Group.

——(2002) "Constitutional Asymmetries: Communal Representation, Federalism, and Cultural Autonomy," in A. Reynolds (ed.) *The Architecture of Democracy*, Oxford: Oxford University Press.

——(2005) "A Journey around Constitutions: Reflections on Contemporary Constitutions," *South African Law Journal*, 4: 804–31.

——(forthcoming) "Understanding Human Rights in Asia," in M. Scheinin and M. Suksi (eds) *Human Rights: A Textbook* (tentative title).

Ghai, Y. and Cottrell, J. (eds)(forthcoming) *Marginalized Communities and Access to Justice*, Abingdon: Routledge-Cavendish.

Ghias, S. (2008) "Miscarriage of Chief Justice: The Rise and Fall of Judicial Power in Pakistan," manuscript, University of California at Berkeley, JSP Program.

Ginsburg, T. (2003) *Judicial Review in New Democracies: Constitutional Courts in Asian Cases*, New York: Cambridge University Press.
——(2007) "Law and the Liberal Transformation of the Northeast Asian Legal Complex in Korea and Taiwan," in T.C. Halliday, L. Karpik, and M.M. Feeley (eds) *Fighting for Political Freedom: Comparative Studies of the Legal Complex for Political Change*, Oxford: Hart Publishing.
Ginsburg, T. and Moustafa, T. (eds) (2008) *Rule By Law: The Politics of Courts in Authoritarian Regimes*, New York: Cambridge University Press.
Ginsburg, T., Elkins, Z., and Melton, J. (2008) "The Lifespan of Written Constitutions," working paper. Online. Available HTTP: http://www.americanbarfoundation.org/research/World_Justice_Project0/Papers.html (accessed 21 October 2008).
Glaeser, E.L. and Shleifer, A. (2002) "Legal Origins," *Quarterly Journal of Economics*, 117(4): 1193–229.
Glaeser, E.L., La Porta, R., Lopez-de-Silanes, F., and Shleifer, A. (2004) "Do Institutions Cause Growth?" *Journal of Economic Growth*, 9(3): 271–303.
Greif, A. (1989) "Reputation and Coalitions in Medieval Trade: Evidence on the Maghribi Traders," *Journal of Economic History*, 49: 857–82.
——(1993) "Contract Enforceability and Economic Institutions in Early Trade: The Maghribi Traders' Coalition," *American Economic Review*, 83: 525–48.
——(2006) *Institutions and the Path to the Modern Economy: Lessons from Medieval Trade* (Political Economy of Institutions and Decisions), Cambridge: Cambridge University Press.
——(2007) *The Impact of Administrative Power on Political and Economic Development: Toward Political Economy of Implementation.* Online. Available HTTP: http://ssrn.com/abstract=1004394 (accessed 21 October 2008).
Guarnieri, C. (2003) "Courts as an Instrument of Horizontal Accountability: The Case of Latin Europe," in A. Przeworski and J.M. Maravall (eds) *Democracy and the Rule of Law*, New York: Cambridge University Press.
——(2007) "Lawyers and Statist Liberalisms in Italy," in T.C. Halliday, L. Karpik, and M.M. Feeley (eds) *Fighting for Political Freedom: Comparative Studies of the Legal Complex for Political Change*, Oxford: Hart Publishing.
Haber, S.H., Klein, H.S., Maurer, N., and Middlebrook, K.J. (2008) *The Second Mexican Revolution: Economic, Political, and Social Change in Mexico since 1980*, Cambridge: Cambridge University Press.
Hagan, J. (2003) *Justice in the Balkans: Prosecuting War Crimes in the Hague Tribunal*, Chicago: University of Chicago Press.
——(2005) "Crimes of War and the Force of Law," *Social Forces*, 83(4): 1499–534.
Hagan, J., Rymond-Richmond, W., and Parker, P. (2005) "The Criminology of Genocide: The Death and Rape of Darfur," *Criminology*, 43(3): 525–61.
Haggard, S., MacIntyre, A., and Tiede, L. (2008) "The Rule of Law and Economic Development," *Annual Review of Political Science*, 11: 205–34.
Hajjar, L. (2004) "Human Rights," in A. Sarat (ed.) *The Blackwell Companion to Law and Society*, Malden, MA: Blackwell Publishing.
Halliday, T.C. (1987) *Beyond Monopoly: Lawyers, State Crises, and Professional Empowerment*, Chicago: University of Chicago Press.
——(2008) "The Legal Complex, Religion, and the Fates of Political Liberalism," invited lecture presented to MacMillan Center Initiative on Religion, Politics and Society, Yale University, 11 February 2008.

Halliday, T.C. and Carruthers, B.G. (2009) *Bankrupt: Global Lawmaking and Systemic Financial Crisis*, Palo Alto: Stanford University Press.

Halliday, T.C. and Karpik, L. (eds) (1998a) *Lawyers and the Rise of Western Political Liberalism: Europe and North America from the Eighteenth to Twentieth Centuries*, Oxford: Oxford University Press.

——(1998b) "Politics Matter: A Comparative Theory of Lawyers in the Making of Political Liberalism," in T.C. Halliday and L. Karpik (eds) *Lawyers and the Rise of Western Political Liberalism: Europe and North America from the Eighteenth to Twentieth Centuries*, Oxford: Oxford University Press.

——(1998c) "Postscript: Lawyers and the Globalization of Liberal Politics," in T.C. Halliday and L. Karpik (eds) *Lawyers and the Rise of Western Political Liberalism: Legal Professions and the Constitution of Modern Politics*, Oxford: Oxford University Press.

——(2001) "Political Lawyering," in N.J. Smelser and P.B. Baltes (eds) *International Encyclopedia of Social and Behavioral Sciences*, Oxford: Elsevier.

Halliday, T.C. and Liu, S. (2007) "Birth of a Liberal Moment? Looking Through a One-Way Mirror at Lawyers' Defense of Criminal Defendants in China," in T.C. Halliday, L. Karpik, and M.M. Feeley (eds) *Fighting for Political Freedom: Comparative Studies of the Legal Complex for Political Change*, Oxford: Hart Publishing.

Halliday, T.C., Karpik, L., and Feeley, M.M. (eds) (2007a) *Fighting for Political Freedom: Comparative Studies of the Legal Complex for Political Change*, Oxford: Hart Publishing.

——(2007b) "The Legal Complex and Struggles for Political Liberalism," in T.C. Halliday, L. Karpik, and M.M. Feeley (eds) *Fighting for Political Freedom: Comparative Studies of the Legal Complex for Political Change,* Oxford: Hart Publishing.

Hamermesh, D.S. (2004) "Labor Demand in Latin America and the Caribbean: What Does It Tell Us?" in J.J. Heckman and C. Pagés (eds) *Law and Employment: Lessons from Latin America and the Caribbean*, Chicago: University of Chicago Press.

Haneef, M.A. (1995) *Contemporary Islamic Economic Thought: A Selected Comparative Analysis*, Petaling Jaya, Malaysia: Ikraq.

Hardin, R. (2002) *Trust and Trustworthiness*, New York: Russell Sage Foundation.

Harris, R. (2000) *Industrializing English Law: Entrepreneurship and Business Organization, 1720–1844*, New York: Cambridge University Press.

——(2004) "Government and the Economy, 1688–1850," *The Cambridge Economic History of Modern Britain*, 1: 204–37.

——(2005a) "The English East India Company and the History of Company Law," in E. Gepken-Jager, G. Van Solinge, and L. Timmerman (eds) *VOC 1602–2002 – 400 Years of Company Law*, Deventer, Netherlands: Kluwer Legal Publishers.

——(2005b) "The Formation of the East India Company as a Cooperation-Enhancing Institution," working paper, SSRN. Online. Available HTTP: http://papers.ssrn.com/sol3/papers.cfm?abstract_id = 874406 (accessed 25 November 2008).

Hart, H.L.A. (1973) "Rawls on Liberty and Its Priority," *University of Chicago Law Review*, 40: 534–55.

Hausmann, R., Tyson, L.D., and Zahidi, S. (2007) *The Global Gender Gap Report 2007*, Geneva: World Economic Forum. Online. Available HTTP: http://www.weforum.org/pdf/gendergap/report2007.pdf (accessed 14 November 2008).

Hayek, F.A. (1960) *The Constitution of Liberty*, Chicago: Chicago University Press.

——(1973) *Law, Legislation and Liberty – Rules and Order (Vol. 1)*, Chicago: University of Chicago Press.

——(1973–9) *Law, Legislation and Liberty*, 3 vols, Chicago: University of Chicago Press.

Hechter, M. (1987) *Principles of Group Solidarity*, Berkeley: University of California Press.

Heckman, J.J. and Pagés, C. (eds) (2004) *Law and Employment: Lessons from Latin America and the Caribbean*, Chicago: University of Chicago Press.

Heckman, J.J., LaLonde, R.J., and Smith, J.A. (1999) "The Economics and Econometrics of Active Labor Market Programs," in O. Ashenfelter and D. Card (eds) *Handbook of Labor Economics*, Volume 3A, New York: North-Holland.

Heckman, J.J., Ljunge, M., and Ragan, K. (2006) "What are the Key Employment Challenges and Policy Priorities for OECD Countries?" paper presented at "Boosting Jobs and Incomes", Toronto, Ontario, Canada, 15 June 2006.

Heckman, J.J., Nelson, R. and Neukom, W. (2007) "Relationship between the Rule of Law and Social and Economic Development," *The World Justice Project Research Program*. Online. Available HTTP: http://jenni.uchicago.edu/WJP/more.html (accessed 6 October 2008).

Helmke, G. (2005) *Courts under Constraints: Judges, Generals and Presidents in Argentina*, New York: Cambridge University Press.

Henisz, W.J. (2000) "The Institutional Environment for Economic Growth," *Economics and Politics*, 12: 1–31.

——(2005) *Political Constraint Index (PolCon) Dataset*, Philadelphia: The Wharton School of the University of Pennsylvania. Online. Available HTTP: http://www-management.wharton.upenn.edu/henisz/POLCON/ContactInfo.html (accessed 14 November 2008).

Hermalin, B.E. (1998) "Toward an Economic Theory of Leadership," *American Economic Review*, 88: 1188–206.

——(2007) "Leading for the Long Term," *Journal of Economic Behavior and Organization*, 62: 1–19.

Heston, A. (2008) "The 2005 Global Report on PPPs: A Preliminary Review," working paper, University of Pennsylvania, Philadelphia.

Hilbink, L. (2007a) *The Politics of Judicial Apoliticism: Chile in Comparative Perspective*, New York: Cambridge University Press.

——(2007b) "Politicising Law to Liberalise Politics: Anti-Francoist Judges and Prosecutors in Spain's Democratic Transition," in T.C. Halliday, L. Karpik, and M.M. Feeley (eds) *Fighting for Political Freedom: Comparative Studies of the Legal Complex for Political Change*, Oxford: Hart Publishing.

Hirschl, R. (2000) "The Political Origins of Judicial Empowerment through Constitutionalization: Lessons from Four Constitutional Revolutions," *Law and Social Inquiry*, 25: 91–147.

——(2004) *Towards Juristocracy*, Cambridge, MA: Harvard University Press.

——(2005) "Preserving Hegemony? Assessing the Political Origins of the EU Constitution," *International Journal of Constitutional Law*, 3: 269–91.

Hirschman, A. (1984) "Against Parsimony: Three Easy Ways of Complicating Some Categories of Economic Discourse," *American Economic Review*, 74: 89–96.

Hirst, D. (1986) *Authority and Conflict: England 1603–58*, New York: Cambridge University Press.

Hofstadter, R. (1969) *The Idea of a Party System*, Berkeley: University of California Press.

Holmstrom, B. (1982) "Moral Hazard in Teams," *Bell Journal of Economics*, 13: 324–40.

Hume, D. (1966) *An Enquiry Concerning the Principles of Morals*, La Salle, IL: Open Court.

Humphrey, D., Pulley, L., and Vesala, J. (1996) "Cash, Paper, and Electronic Payments: A Cross-country Analysis," *Journal of Money, Credit, and Banking*, 28: 914–39.

Hussin, I. (2007) "The Politics of Islamic Law: Local Elites and Colonial Authority in India, Malaya and Egypt," dissertation, Department of Political Science, University of Washington.

Ibn Khaldun (1359/1958) *The Muqaddimah: An Introduction to History*, 3 vols, trans. F. Rosenthal, New York: Pantheon.

Imber, C. (1997) *Ebu's-Su'ud: The Islamic Legal Tradition*, Stanford: Stanford University Press.

İnalcık, H. (1970) "The Ottoman Economic Mind and Aspects of the Ottoman Economy," in M.A. Cook (ed.) *Studies in the Economic History of the Middle East*, London: Oxford University Press.

——(1994) "The Ottoman State: Economy and Society, 1300–1600," in H. İnalcık with D. Quataert (ed.) *An Economic and Social History of the Ottoman Empire, 1300–1914*, New York: Cambridge University Press.

India, Government of (1976) "Equal Remuneration Act, No. 25 of 1976."

——(1990) "The National Commission for Women Act, 1990: No. 20 of 1990."

——(2005) "II and III Periodic Report on the Convention on the Elimination of All Forms of Discrimination Against Women."

India, Ministry of Home Affairs (2008) *Human Rights Division*. Online. Available HTTP: http://mha.gov.in/uniquepage.asp?ID_PK = 235 (accessed 14 November 2008).

India, National Crime Records Bureau (NCRB) (2006) *Annual Report (2004–5)*, New Delhi: National Crime Records Bureau.

International Monetary Fund (IMF) (2008) *World Economic Outlook Database*. Online. Available HTTP: http://www.imf.org/external/pubs/ft/weo/2008/01/weodata/index.aspx (accessed 23 November 2008).

Israel, J. (1989) *Dutch Primacy in World Trade, 1585–1740*, Oxford: Clarendon Press.

Iyer, S. (1999) *The Struggle to be Human: Women's Human Rights*, Bangalore: Books for Change.

Jacobsohn, J. (1993) *Apple of Gold: Constitutionalism in Israel*, Princeton, NJ: Princeton University Press.

Joga Rao, S.V. (ed.) (2002) *Dowry and the Law*, Bangalore: LexisNexis.

Jones, C. (2007) "'Dissolving the People': Capitalism, Law and Democracy in Hong Kong," in T.C. Halliday, L. Karpik, and M.M. Feeley (eds) *Fighting for Political Freedom: Comparative Studies of the Legal Complex for Political Change*, Oxford: Hart Publishing.

Jones, J.R. (1972) *The Revolution of 1688 in England*, New York: W.W. Norton.

Jütting, J.P., Morrison, C., Dayton-Johnson, J., and Dreschler, D. (2006) "Measuring Gender (In)Equality: Introducing the Gender, Institutions and Development Data Base (GID)," working paper, OECD, Paris.

Kahn-Freund, O. (1974) "On Uses and Misuses of Comparative Law," *Modern Law Review*, 37: 1–27.

Kant, A. (2003) *Women and the Law*, New Delhi: APH Publishing Corporation.

Karaman, K. (2009) "Decentralized Coercion and Self-Restraint in Provincial Taxation: The Ottoman Empire, 15th–16th Centuries," *Journal of Economic Behavior and Organization*.

Karpik, L. (1988) "Lawyers and Politics in France, 1814–1950: the State, the Market, and the Public," *Law and Social Inquiry*, 13(4): 707–36.

——(1998) "Builders of Liberal Society: French Lawyers and Politics," in T.C. Halliday and L. Karpik (eds) *Lawyers and the Rise of Western Political Liberalism: Europe and North America from the Eighteenth to Twentieth Centuries*, Oxford: Oxford University Press.

——(2007) "Postscript: Political Lawyering," in T.C. Halliday, L. Karpik, and M.M. Feeley (eds) *Fighting for Political Freedom: Comparative Studies of the Legal Complex for Political Change*, Oxford: Hart Publishing.

Kaufmann, D., Kraay, A., and Zoido-Lobaton, P. (1999) "Aggregating Governance Indicators," Washington DC: World Bank.

Kaufmann, D., Kraay, D., and Mastruzzi, M. (2005) "Governance Matters IV: Governance Indicators for 1996–2004," in World Bank (ed.) *Policy Research Working Papers*, Washington, DC: World Bank.

——(2007a) *Governance Matters VI: Governance Indicators for 1996–2006*, World Bank Policy Research Working Paper No. 4280. Online. Available HTTP: http://ssrn.com/abstract=999979.

——(2007b) *The Worldwide Governance Indicator's Project: Answering the Critics*, Washington, DC: World Bank.

Kaushal, R. (2000) *Women and Human Rights in India*, New Delhi: Kaveri Books.

Kedourie, E. (1993) *Nationalism*, Oxford: Blackwell.

Khadduri, M. (1984) *The Islamic Conception of Justice*, Baltimore: Johns Hopkins University Press.

Khan, Z. (2005) *The Democratization of Invention: Patents and Copyrights in American Economic Development, 1790–1920*, Cambridge: Cambridge University Press.

Kimes, M. (2008) "Cars: 6 Chinese Knock-offs," *CNNMoney.com*. Online. Available HTTP: http://money.cnn.com/galleries/2008/fortune/0810/gallery.china_cars.fortune/ (accessed 8 December 2008).

King, G., Keohane, R.O., and Verba, S. (1994) *Designing Social Inquiry*, Princeton: Princeton University Press.

Kirby, W. (1995) "China Unincorporated: Company Law and Business Enterprise in Twentieth-Century China," *Journal of Asian Studies*, 54: 43–63.

Kiser, E. (1994) "Markets and Hierarchies in Early Modern Tax Systems: A Principal-Agent Analysis," *Politics and Society*, 22: 285–316.

Kiser, E. and Sacks, A. (2008) "African Patrimonialism in Historical Perspective: Assessing Decentralized and Privatized Tax Administration," paper presented at Yale University, Center for Comparative Research Conference, "Lineages of Patrimonial Politics, Then and Now," New Haven, CT, May 2008; published in J. Adams and M.M. Charrad (eds) (forthcoming) *Patrimonialism: Then and Now*.

Klasen, S. and Wink, C. (2003) "'Missing Women': Revisiting the Debate," *Feminist Economics*, 9: 263–99.

Klerman, D. and Mahoney, P. (2005) "The Value of Judicial Independence: Evidence from Eighteenth-Century England," *American Law and Economics Review*, 7: 1–27.

Klug, H. (2000) *Constituting Democracy: Law, Globalism and South Africa's Political Reconstruction*, New York: Cambridge University Press.

Knack, S. and Keefer, P. (1994) "Institutions and Economic Performance: Cross-Country Tests Using Alternative Institutional Measures," *Economics and Politics*, 7: 207–27.

Kohli, A. (1987) *The State and Poverty in India: the Politics of Reform*, New York: Cambridge University Press.

Kohn, M. (1999) "The Capital Market before 1600," working paper, Department of Economics, Dartmouth College, Hanover, NH.

Kondo, J. (2007) "Self-Regulation and Enforcement: Evidence from Investor-Broker Disputes at NASD," working paper, MIT, Boston.

Kopf, E. (1929) "Notes on the Origin and Development of Reinsurance," *Proceedings of the Casualty Actuarial Society*, XVI(33–34): 22–92.

Kothari, R. (1988) "Ethnicity," in R. Kothari, *Rethinking Development: In Search of Humane Alternatives*, Delhi: Ajanta Publications.

Kreps, D.M. (1990) "Corporate Culture and Economic Theory," in J. Alt and K. Shepsle (eds) *Perspectives in Positive Political Economy*, New York: Cambridge University Press.

Kuran, T. (1995) *Private Truths, Public Lies: The Social Consequences of Preference Falsification*, Cambridge, MA: Harvard University Press.

——(2001) "The Provision of Public Goods under Islamic Law: Origins, Impact, and Limitations of the Waqf System," *Law and Society Review*, 35: 841–97.

——(2003) "Islamic Redistribution through *Zakat*: Historical Record and Modern Realities," in M. Bonner, M. Ener, and A. Singer (eds) *Poverty and Charity in Middle Eastern Contexts*, Albany: State University of New York Press.

——(2004) *Islam and Mammon: the Economic Predicaments of Islamism*, Princeton: Princeton University Press.

Kurtz, M.J. and Schrank, A. (2007a) "Growth and Governance: Models, Measures and Mechanisms," *Journal of Politics*, 69: 538–54.

——(2007b) "Conceptualizing and Measuring Institutions: A View from Political Science," paper presented at second workshop on "Measuring Law and Institutions," Paris, December 2007.

Kymlicka, W. (1989) *Liberalism, Community and Culture*, Oxford: Oxford University Press.

La Porta, R., Lopez-de-Silanes, F., Shleifer, A., and Vishny, R.W. (1997) "Legal Determinants of External Finance," *Journal of Finance*, 52: 1131–50.

——(1998) "Law and Finance," *Journal of Political Economy*, 106: 1113–55.

Landry, P. (2008) "How Weak Institutions Can Produce Strong Regimes: Patents, Lawyers, and the Improbable Creation of an Intellectual Property Regime in China (1985–2007)," paper presented at workshop on "Rule of Law," Yale University, 28–29 March.

Layard, R., Nickell, S., and Jackman, R. (1991) *Unemployment: Macroeconomic Performance and the Labour Market*, Oxford: Oxford University Press.

Lee, T.V. (1993) "Risky Business: Courts, Culture, and the Marketplace," *University of Miami Law Review*, 47: 1335–414.

LegalMetric (2008) *Eastern District of Texas Patent Litigation Study*. Online. Available HTTP: http://www.legalmetric.com/studies/txed_pat_study.html (accessed 23 November 2008).

Lerner, J. (2002) "150 Years of Patent Protection," *American Economic Review Papers and Proceedings*, 92: 221–5.

——(2005) "150 Years of Patent Office Practice," *American Law and Economics Review*, 7: 112–43.

Levi, M. (1988) *Of Rule and Revenue*, Berkeley: University of California Press.
——(1997) *Consent, Dissent and Patriotism*, New York: Cambridge University Press.
——(2005) "Inducing Preferences within Organizations," in I. Katznelson and B.R. Weingast (eds) *Preferences and Situations: Points of Intersection between Historical and Rational Choice Institutionalism*, New York: Russell Sage Foundation.
——(2006) "Why We Need a New Theory of Government," *Perspectives on Politics*, 4: 5–19.
——(under review) *Staffing the State: Handbook of Rational Choice*, New York: Russell Sage Foundation.
Levi, M. and Sacks, A. (2007) "Legitimating Beliefs: Concepts and Indicators," in *Afrobarometer* (Working Paper No. 74), East Lansing: Michigan State University
Levi, M., Sacks, A., and Tyler, T.R. (forthcoming) "Conceptualizing Legitimacy, Measuring Legitimating Beliefs," *American Behavioral Scientist*.
Levitsky, S. and Way, L. (2002) "The Rise of Competitive Authoritarianism," *Journal of Democracy*, 13(2): 51–65.
Lewis, B. (1988) *The Political Language of Islam*, Chicago: University of Chicago Press.
——(1990) *Race and Slavery in the Middle East: An Historical Enquiry*, New York: Oxford University Press.
Li, S. (2001) "Bankruptcy Law in China: Lessons of the Past Twelve Years," *Harvard Asia Quarterly*, V(1). Available HTTP: http://www.asiaquarterly.com/content/view/95/40/ (accessed 31 March 2009).
Licht, A., Goldschmidt, C., and Schwartz, S.H. (2007) "Culture Rules: The Foundations of the Rule of Law and Other Norms of Governance," *Journal of Comparative Economics*, 35: 659–88.
Lin, F. (2008) "Turning Gray: Transition of Political Communication in China, 1978–2008," PhD dissertation, Department of Sociology, University of Chicago.
Lindbeck, A. and Snower, D. (1989) *The Insider–Outsider Theory of Employment and Unemployment*, Cambridge, MA: MIT Press.
Lindert, P.H. (2005) *Growing Public: Social Spending and Economic Growth since the Eighteenth Century*, Cambridge: Cambridge University Press.
Lipset, S.M. (1959) "Some Social Requisites of Democracy," *American Political Science Review*, 53: 69–105.
Ljunge, M. (2006) "Half the Job Is Showing Up: Returns to Work, Taxes, and Sick Leave Choices," PhD thesis, University of Chicago.
Locke, J. (1980[1690]) *Second Treatise of Government*, ed. C.B. Macpherson, Indianapolis, IN: Hackett.
Løkkegaard, F. (1950) *Islamic Taxation in the Classic Period, with Special Reference to Circumstances in Iraq*, Copenhagen: Branner and Korch.
Lupia, A. and McCubbins, M.D. (1998) *The Democratic Dilemma: Can Citizens Learn What They Need to Know?* New York: Cambridge University Press.
Macaulay, S. (1963) "Non-contractual Relations in Business: A Preliminary Study," *American Sociological Review*, 28(1): 55–67.
McIlwain, C.H. (1947) *Constitutionalism: Ancient and Modern*, Ithaca, NY: Great Seal Books.
Machiavelli, N. (1950) *The Prince and the Discourses*, New York: The Modern Library.
Mahmud, T. (1993) "Praetorianism and Common Law in Post-Colonial Settings: Judicial Responses to Constitutional Breakdowns in Pakistan," *Utah Law Review*, 1225–305.

Manion, M. (2004) *Corruption by Design: Bribery in Chinese Enterprise Licensing*, Cambridge, MA: Harvard University Press.
Mansfield, E.D. and Snyder, J. (2005) *Electing to Fight: Why Emerging Democracies Go to War*, Cambridge, MA: MIT Press.
——(2007) "The Sequencing 'Fallacy,'" *Journal of Democracy*, 18(3): 5–10.
Mansvelt, W.M.F. (1922) *Rechtsvorm en geldelijk beheer bij de Oost-Indische Compagnie*, Amsterdam: Swets and Zeitlinger.
Maravall, J.M. and Przeworski, A. (eds) (2003a) *Democracy and the Rule of Law*, New York: Cambridge University Press.
——(2003b) "Introduction," in J.M. Maravall and A. Przeworski (eds), *Democracy and the Rule of Law*, New York: Cambridge University Press.
Marryat, F. (1830) *The King's Own*, London: H. Colburn and R. Bentley.
Martin, J.P. and Grubb, D. (2001) "What Works and for Whom: A Review of OECD Countries' Experiences with Active Labour Market Policies," *Swedish Economic Policy Review*, 8(2): 9–56.
Mathias, P. and O'Brien, P. (1976) "Taxation in Britain and France, 1715–1810. A Comparison of the Social and Economic Incidence of Taxes Collected for the Central Governments," *Journal of European Economic History*, 5: 601–40.
Mauro, P. (1995) "Corruption and Growth," *Quarterly Journal of Economics*, CX: 681–712.
Mayer, C. (2008) "Trust in Financial Markets," *European Financial Management*, 14: 617–32.
Menski, W. (1998) *South Asians and the Dowry Problem*, New Delhi: Vistaar Publications.
Merry, S.E. (1988) "Legal Pluralism," *Law and Society Review*, 22(5): 869–96.
——(2003) "Rights Talk and the Experience of Law: Implementing Women's Human Rights to Protection from Violence," *Human Rights Quarterly*, 25: 343–81.
——(2005) *Human Rights and Gender Violence: Translating International Law into Local Justice*, Chicago: University of Chicago Press.
Merton, R.K. (1968[1957]) *Social Theory and Social Structure*, Glencoe, IL: Free Press.
Messick, B. (1993) *The Calligraphic State: Textual Domination and History in a Muslim Society*, Berkeley: University of California Press.
Michelson, E. (2003) *Unhooking from the State: Chinese Lawyers in Transition*, PhD dissertation, Department of Sociology, University of Chicago.
Michie, R.C. (1999) *The London Stock Exchange: A History*, Oxford: Oxford University Press.
Miller, G. (1992) *Managerial Dilemmas*, New York: Cambridge University Press.
Miller, W.L., Grodeland, A.B., and Koshechkina, T.Y. (2001) *A Culture of Corruption? Coping with Government in Post-Communist Europe*, Budapest: Central European University Press.
Montesquieu, C.L. (1977) *The Spirit of Laws*, Berkeley: University of California Press.
Morgan, E.V. and Thomas, W.A. (1969) *The Stock Exchange: Its History and Function*, London: Elek.
Moustafa, T. (2007a) "Mobilising the Law in an Authoritarian State: The Legal Complex in Contemporary Egypt," in T.C. Halliday, L. Karpik, and M.M. Feeley (eds) *Fighting for Political Freedom: Comparative Studies of the Legal Complex for Political Change*, Oxford: Hart Publishing.
——(2007b) *The Struggle for Constitutional Power: Law, Politics and Economic Development in Egypt*, New York: Cambridge University Press.

Nagel, T. (2005) "The Problem of Global Justice," *Philosophy and Public Affairs*, 33: 113–47.

Nasr, S.V.R. (2001) *Islamic Leviathan: Islam and the Making of State Power*, New York: Oxford University Press.

Neal, L. (1990) *The Rise of Financial Capitalism: International Capital Markets in the Age of Reason*, New York: Cambridge University Press.

Newberg, P. (1995) *Judging the State: Courts and Constitutional Politics in Pakistan*, New York: Cambridge University Press.

Nickell, S., Wadhwani, S., and Wall, M. (1992) "Productivity Growth in UK Companies, 1975–86," *European Economic Review*, 36(5): 1055–85.

Nicoletti, G. and Scarpetta, S. (2001) "Interactions between Product and Labour Market Regulations: Do They Affect Employment? Evidence from OECD Countries," paper presented at the Banco de Portugal conference on "Labour Market Institutions and Economic Outcomes," Cascais, Portugal, 3–4 June.

—— (2003) "Regulation, Productivity, and Growth: OECD Evidence," *Economic Policy*, 18(36): 9–72.

North, D.C. (1981) *Structure and Change in Economic History*, New York: Norton.

——(1990) *Institutions, Institutional Change, and Economic Performance*, Cambridge: Cambridge University Press.

——(2005) *Understanding the Process of Economic Change*, Princeton: Princeton University Press.

North, D.C. and Weingast, B.R. (1989) "Constitutions and Commitment: The Evolution of Institutions Governing Public Choice in 17th Century England," *Journal of Economic History*, 49: 803–32.

North, D.C., Wallis, J.J., Webb, S.B., and Weingast, B.R. (2007) "Limited Access Orders in the Developing World: A New Approach to the Problems of Development," working paper, World Bank.

North, D.C., Wallis, J.J., and Weingast, B.R. (2009) *Violence and Social Orders: A Conceptual Framework for Understanding Recorded Human History*, Cambridge: Cambridge University Press.

Nussbaum, M.C. and Sen, A. (1993) *The Quality of Life*, Oxford: Clarendon Press.

Oberholzer-Gee, F. and Strumpf, K. (2007) "The Effect of File Sharing on Record Sales: An Empirical Analysis," *Journal of Political Economy*, 115: 1–42.

O'Brien, P.K. (1988) "The Political Economy of British Taxation, 1660–1815," *Economic History Review*, 41: 1–32.

O'Donnell, G.A. (2004) "Why the Rule of Law Matters," *Journal of Democracy*, 15: 32–46.

Olson, M. (1971) *The Logic of Collective Action: Public Goods and the Theory of Groups*, Cambridge, MA: Harvard University Press.

——(1993) "Democracy, Dictatorship, and Development," *American Political Science Review*, 87(3): 567–75.

Open Society Institute (2002) "Monitoring the EU Accession Process: Corruption and Anti-Corruption Policy," New York: Open Society Institute.

Organisation for Economic Co-operation and Development (OECD) (1994) *The OECD Jobs Study: Facts, Analysis, Strategies*, Washington, D.C.: OECD Publications and Information Centre.

——(2005a) *Education at a Glance: OECD Indicators 2005*, Paris: OECD Publishing.

——(2005b) *Society at a Glance: OECD Social Indicators*, Paris: OECD Publishing.

——(2006a) *OECD Economic Outlook*, Paris: OECD Publishing

——(2006b) *OECD Employment Outlook: Boosting Jobs and Incomes*, Paris: OECD Publishing.

——(2007a) *Labour Force Statistics 1986-2006*, Paris: OECD Publishing.

——(2007b) *OECD Factbook 2006*, Paris: OECD Publishing.

——(2008) "Gender, Institutions and Development Data Base (GID): Missing Women," on *OECD.StatExtracts*. Online. Available HTTP: http://stats.oecd.org/OECD-Stat_Metadata/ShowMetadata.ashx?Dataset = GID&Coords = %5BVARIABLE%5D.%5BPI_3%5D&ShowOnWeb = true&Lang = en (accessed 14 November 2008).

Organisation for Economic Co-operation and Development (OECD), Directorate for Financial and Enterprise Affairs of the Competition Committee (2005) "Policy Roundtables: Intellectual Property Rights 2004." Online. Available HTTP: http://www.oecd.org/dataoecd/61/48/34306055.pdf (accessed 23 November 2008).

Outhwaite, R.B. (1966) "The Trials of Foreign Borrowing: the English Crown and the Antwerp Money Market in the Mid-Sixteenth Century," *Economic History Review*, 19: 289–305.

——(1971) "Royal Borrowing in the Reign of Elizabeth I: The Aftermath of Antwerp," *English Historical Review*, 86: 251–63.

Pakistan, Government of (2007) *Provisional Constitutional Order No. 1*.

Parekh, B. (1997) "Cultural Diversity and the Modern State," in M. Doornbos and S. Kaviraj (eds) *Dynamics of State Formation*, New Delhi: Sage Publications.

Pencavel, J. (1999) "The Appropriate Design of Collective Bargaining Systems: Learning from the Experience of Britain, Australia and New Zealand," *Comparative Labor Law and Policy Journal*, 20(3): 447–82.

——(2004) "The Surprising Retreat of Union Britain," in D.E. Card, R. Blundell, and R.B. Freeman (eds) *Seeking a Premier Economy: The Economic Effects of British Economic Reforms, 1980–2000*, NBER Comparative Labor Markets Series, Chicago: University of Chicago Press.

Perdomo, R.P. (2007) "Lawyers and Political Liberalism in Venezuela," in T.C. Halliday, L. Karpik, and M.M. Feeley (eds) *Fighting for Political Freedom: Comparative Studies of the Legal Complex for Political Change*, Oxford: Hart Publishing.

Pereira, A.W. (2005) *Political (In)Justice: Authoritarianism and the Rule of Law in Brazil, Chile and Argentina*, Pittsburgh: University of Pittsburgh Press.

Pils, E. (2008) "Peasants Struggle for Land in China," paper presented at the meeting on "Access to Justice," American Bar Association, Washington, DC, 2–4 March.

Pistor, K., Keinan, Y., Kleinheisterkamp, J., and West, M.D. (2003) "Evolution of Corporate Law and the Transplant Effect: Lessons from Six Countries," *World Bank Research Observer*, 18: 89–112.

Prakash, O. (1985) *The Dutch East India Company and the Economy of Bengal 1630–1720*, Princeton: Princeton University Press.

Przeworski, A. (2004) "Institutions Matter?" *Government and Opposition*, 39: 527–40.

Pue, W.W. (1998) "Lawyers and Political Liberalism in Eighteenth- and Nineteenth-Century England," in T.C. Halliday and L. Karpik (eds) *Lawyers and the Rise of Western Political Liberalism: Europe and North America from the Eighteenth to Twentieth Centuries*, Oxford: Oxford University Press.

Qian, Y. and Weingast, B. (1997) "Federalism as a Commitment to Preserving Market Incentives," *Journal of Economic Perspectives*, 11: 83–92.

Rahman, F. (1979) *Islam*, second edn, Chicago: University of Chicago Press.

——(1982) *Islam and Modernity: Transformation of an Intellectual Tradition*, Chicago: University of Chicago Press.

Rahnema, A. and Nomani, F. (1990) *The Secular Miracle: Religion, Politics, and Economic Policy in Iran*, London: Zed Books.

Rajan, R. and Zingales, L. (2003a) "The Great Reversals: The Politics of Financial Development in the Twentieth Century," *Journal of Financial Economics*, 69: 5–50.

——(2003b) *Saving Capitalism from Capitalists: Unleashing the Power of Financial Markets to Create Wealth and Spread Opportunity*, New York: Random House.

Ramseyer, J.M. and Rasmusen, E. (2003) *Measuring Judicial Independence*, Chicago: University of Chicago Press.

Ravallion, M. and Chen, S. (2004) *China's (Uneven) Progress against Poverty*, World Bank Policy Research Working Paper 3408, Washington, DC: World Bank.

Rawls, J. (1971) *A Theory of Justice*, Cambridge, MA: Harvard University Press.

——(1993) *Political Liberalism*, New York: Columbia University Press.

——(1999) *The Law of Peoples*, Cambridge, MA: Harvard University Press.

Rhoodie, E.M. (1989) *Discrimination Against Women: A Global Survey of the Economic, Educational, Social and Political Status of Women*, Jefferson, NC: McFarland.

Riemersma, J.C. (1950) "Oceanic Expansion: Government Influence on Company Organization in Holland and England (1550–1650)," *Journal of Economic History*, 10: 31–9.

——(1952) "Trading and Shipping Associations in 16th Century Holland," *Tijdschrift voor Geschiedenis*, 65: 330–8.

Rodriguez, V.E. (1995) "Municipal Autonomy and the Politics of Inter governmental Finance: Is it Different for the Opposition?" in V.E. Rodriguez and P.M. Ward (eds) *Opposition Government in Mexico*, Albuquerque: University of New Mexico Press.

Rodrik, D. (2004) "Getting Institutions Right," unpublished mimeo, Harvard University. Online. Available HTTP: http://ksghome.harvard.edu/~drodrik/papers.html (accessed 14 October 2008).

Rosen, L. (1989) *The Anthropology of Justice: Law as Culture in Islamic Society*, Cambridge: Cambridge University Press.

Roy, D. (2003) *Taiwan: A Political History*, Ithaca: Cornell University Press.

Rueschemeyer, D. (1998) "State, Capitalism, and the Organization of Legal Counsel: Examining an Extreme Case – the Prussian Bar, 1700–1914," in T.C. Halliday and L. Karpik (eds) *Lawyers and the Rise of Western Political Liberalism: Europe and North America from the Eighteenth to Twentieth Centuries*, Oxford: Oxford University Press.

Saavedra, J. and Torero, M. (2004) "Labor Market Reforms and Their Impact Over Formal Labor Demand and Job Market Turnover: The Case of Peru," in J.J. Heckman and C. Pagés (eds) *Law and Employment: Lessons from Latin America and the Caribbean*, Chicago: University of Chicago Press.

Sachs, J.D. (2006) "Welfare States, Beyond Ideology," *Scientific American*, 295(5): 42.

Sachs, J.D. and Pistor, K. (eds) (1997) *The Rule of Law and Economic Reform in Russia*, Boulder, CO: Westview Press.

Saha, C. (2003) *Gender Equity and Equality: Study of Girl Child in Rajasthan*, Jaipur: Rawat Publications.

Samaniego, R.M. (2006) "Employment Protection and High-Tech Aversion," *Review of Economic Dynamics*, 9(2): 224–41.

Sanchez Urribarri, R. (2007) "News from the Comparative Realm," *Law and Courts Newsletter*, 11–13.

Sanchez-Cuenca, I. (in progress) "Preferences Over Choices," Juan March Institute, Madrid.

Sapir, A. (2006) "Globalization and the Reform of European Social Models," *Journal of Common Market Studies*, 44(2): 369–90.

Schelling, T. (1960) *The Strategy of Conflict*, Cambridge: Harvard University Press.

Schleifer, A. and Glaeser, E.L. (2002) "Legal Origins," *Quarterly Journal of Economics*, 117: 1191–229.

Scott, W.R. (1912) *The Constitution and Finance of English, Scottish, and Irish Joint-Stock Companies to 1720*, Cambridge: Cambridge University Press.

Sen, A. (1970) *Collective Choice and Social Welfare*, San Francisco: Holden-Day; (1979) Amsterdam: North-Holland.

——(1977) "Rational Fools," *Philosophy and Public Affairs*, 6: 317–44.

——(1980) "Equality of What?" in S.M. McMurrin (ed.) *The Tanner Lectures on Human Values*, Volume I, Cambridge: Cambridge University Press.

——(1985) *Commodities and Capabilities*, Amsterdam: North-Holland.

——(1989) "Women's Survival as a Development Problem," *Bulletin of the American Academy of Arts*, 43: 14–29.

——(1990a) "Global Justice: Beyond International Equity," in I. Kaul, I. Grunberg, and M.A. Stern (eds) *Global Public Goods: International Cooperation in the 21st Century*, Oxford: Oxford University Press.

——(1990b) "Justice: Means versus Freedoms," *Philosophy and Public Affairs*, 19(2): 111–21.

——(1993) "Capability and Well-being," in M. Nussbaum and A. Sen (eds) *The Quality of Life*, Oxford: Oxford University Press.

——(1997) "Maximization and the Act of Choice," *Econometrica*, 65: 745–79.

——(1999a) *Development as Freedom*, New York: Random House.

——(1999b) "The Possibility of Social Choice," *American Economic Review*, 89: 349–78.

——(2000) "Consequential Evaluation and Practical Reason," *Journal of Philosophy*, 97: 477–502.

——(2001) "The Many Faces of Gender Inequality," *The New Republic*, 17 September.

——(2002) "Justice across Borders," in P. De Greiff and C. Cronin (eds) *Global Justice and Transnational Politics*, Cambridge, MA: MIT Press.

——(2004a) "Elements of a Theory of Human Rights," *Philosophy and Public Affairs*, 32(4): 315–56.

——(2004b) "Incompleteness and Reasoned Choice," *Synthese*, 140: 43–60.

——(2006a) *Identity and Violence: The Illusion of Destiny*, London: Allen Lane.

——(2006b) "What Do We Want from a Theory of Justice?" *Journal of Philosophy*, 103: 215–38.

——(2009, forthcoming) *The Idea of Justice*, London: Penguin; and Cambridge, MA: Belknap Press.

Sen, S. (coordinator) (2004) *A Report on Trafficking in Women and Children in India, 2002–2003*, New Delhi: Institute of Social Sciences, National Human Rights Commission, and UNIFEM.

Shapiro, M. (1964) *Law and Politics on the Supreme Court*, New York: Free Press.

——(1981) *Courts: A Comparative and Political Analysis*, Chicago: University of Chicago Press.

Silbey, S. (1997) "'Let Them Eat Cake': Globalization, Postmodern Colonialism, and the Possibilities of Justice," *Law and Society Review*, 31: 207–35.

Silverstein, G. (2003) "Globalization and the Rule of Law: A Machine that Runs of Itself?" *I·CON: International Journal of Constitutional Law*, 1(3): 427–45.
——(2008) "Singapore: The Exception that Proves Rules Matter," in T. Ginsburg and T. Moustafa (eds) *Rule by Law: The Politics of Courts in Authoritarian Regimes*, New York: Cambridge University Press.
Simon, H.A. (1947) *Administrative Behavior*, New York: Macmillan.
Sklar, J. (1987) "Political Theory and the Rule of Law," in A.C. Hutcheson and P. Monahan (eds) *The Rule of Law: Ideal or Ideology*, Toronto: Carswell.
Smillie, I., Gberie, L., and Hazleton, R. (2000) *The Heart of the Matter: Sierra Leone, Diamonds, and Human Security*, Ontario: Partnership Africa Canada. Online. Available HTTP: http://pacweb.org/e/index.php?option=content&task=view&id=42&Itemid=65 (accessed 23 November 2008).
Smith, A. (1976) *The Theory of Moral Sentiments*, Oxford: Clarendon Press.
——(1978) *Lectures on Jurisprudence*, ed. R.L. Meek, D.D. Raphael, and P.G. Stein, Oxford: Clarendon Press; reprinted (1982) Indianapolis: Liberty Press.
Smulovitz, C. (2003) "How Can the Rule of Law Rule? Cost Imposition through Decentralized Mechanisms," in A. Przeworski and J.M. Maravall (eds) *Democracy and the Rule of Law*, New York: Cambridge University Press.
Solomon, P. (1996) *Soviet Criminal Justice under Stalin*, New York: Cambridge University Press.
Statistics Canada (2008) "Canada's Population Estimates," *The Daily*, 29 September. Online. Available HTTP: http://www.statcan.ca/Daily/English/080929/d080929b.htm (accessed 14 November 2008).
Steensgaard, N. (1977) "Dutch East India Company as an Institutional Innovation," in M. Aymard (ed.) *Dutch Capitalism and World Capitalism*, Cambridge: Cambridge University Press.
Steinberg, G. (2005) "The Wahhabi Ulama and the Saudi State: 1745 to the Present," in P. Aarts and G. Nonneman (eds) *Saudi Arabia in the Balance: Political Economy, Society, Foreign Affairs*, New York: New York University Press.
Supreme Court of Canada (1988) *Reference re the Secession of Quebec*, 2 SCR 217.
Supreme Court of India (1985) *Shah Banu*, 2 Sup. Ct. Cases 556.
Sussman, N. and Yafeh, Y. (2006) "Institutional Reforms, Financial Development and Sovereign Debt: Britain 1690–1790," *Journal of Economic History*, 66: 906–35.
't Hart, M.C. (1993) *Making of a Bourgeois State: War, Politics and Finance during the Dutch Revolt*, Manchester: Manchester University Press.
Tamanaha, B.Z. (1993) "The Folly of the 'Social Scientific' Concept of Legal Pluralism," *Journal of Law and Society*, 20: 192–217.
——(1995) "The Lessons of Law-and-Development Studies," *American Journal of International Law*, 89: 470–86.
——(2004) *On the Rule of Law: History, Politics, Theory*, Cambridge: Cambridge University Press.
Taylor, C. (1994) "The Politics of Recognition," in A. Gutman (ed.) *Multiculturalism: Examining the Politics of Recognition*, Princeton: Princeton University Press.
Thomas, M. (2007) "What Do the Worldwide Governance Indicators Measure?" working paper. Online. Available HTTP: http://papers.ssrn.com/sol3/papers.cfm?abstract_id = 1007527 (accessed 13 November 2008).
Tracy, J.D. (1985) *A Financial Revolution in the Habsburg Netherlands: Renten and Renteniers in the County of Holland, 1515–1565*, Berkeley: University of California Press.

Transparency International (2006) *World Corruption Perceptions Index*. Online. Available HTTP: http://www.transparency.org/policy_research/surveys_indices/cpi/2006 (accessed 15 October 2008).

Trochev, A. (2004) "Less Democracy, More Courts: A Puzzle of Judicial Review in Russia," *Law and Society Review*, 38(3): 513–48.

Trubek, D.M. and Galanter, M. (1974) "Scholars in Self-Estrangement: Some Reflections on the Crisis in Law and Development Studies in the United States," *Wisconsin Law Review*, 1062–1102.

Tully, J. (1995) *Strange Multiplicity: Constitutionalism in an Age of Diversity*, Cambridge: Cambridge University Press.

Tully, J. and Chambers, S. (1998) "Contract or Conversation? Theoretical Lessons from the Canadian Constitutional Crisis," *Politics and Society*, 26: 143–72.

Tyan, E. (1960) *Histoire de l'Organisation Judiciaire en Pays d'Islam*, second edn, Leiden: E.J. Brill.

Tyler, T.R. (1990) *Why People Obey the Law*, New Haven, CT: Yale University Press.

——(2006) "Psychological Perspectives on Legitimacy and Legitimation," *Annual Review of Psychology*, 57: 375–400.

Udovitch, A.L. (1985) "Islamic Law and the Social Context of Exchange in the Medieval Middle East," *History and Anthropology*, 1: 445–65.

United Nations, Office on Drugs and Crime (2002) *Eighth United Nations Survey of Crime Trends and Operations of Criminal Justice Systems, covering the period 2001 – 2002*. Online. Available HTTP: http://www.unodc.org/pdf/crime/eighthsurvey/8pv.pdf (accessed 14 November 2008).

United Nations Development Program (2005) *Human Development Report 2005: International Cooperation at a Crossroads: Aid, Trade and Security in an Unequal World*, New York: United Nations Development Program.

United States, Government of (2003) *Check Clearing for the 21st Century Act*, Washington, DC: Government Publishing.

Upham, F. (2002) "Mythmaking in the Rule of Law Orthodoxy," working paper, Democracy and Rule of Law Project, Washington, DC: Carnegie Endowment for International Peace.

van Dillen, J.G. (1935) "Isaac Le Maire and the Early Trading in Dutch East India Company Shares," in G. Poitras (ed.) *Pioneers of Financial Economics*, Volume I, Northampton, VT: Edward Elgar.

——(1958) *Het oudste aandeelhoudersregister van de Kamer Amsterdam der Oost-Indische Compagnie*, The Hague: Martinus Nijhoff.

Vasudev, S. and Renuka, M. (2002) "Rape," *India Today* (9 September).

Vikør, K.S. (2005) *Between God and Sultan: A History of Islamic Law*, Oxford: Oxford University Press.

VOC Charter (1602) reprinted in E. Gepken-Jager, G. Can Solinge, and L. Timmerman (eds) (2005) *VOC 1602–2002 – 400 Years of Company Law*, Deventer, Netherlands: Kluwer Legal Publishers.

Vogel, F.E. (2000) *Islamic Law and Legal System: Studies of Saudi Arabia*, Leiden: E.J. Brill.

Voigt, S. (2008) *How (Not) to Measure Institutions*, Washington, DC: World Bank.

Volcansek, M. (1994) "Political Power and Judicial Review in Italy," *Comparative Political Studies*, 4: 492–509.

Ward, P.M. (1995) "Policymaking and Policy Implementation among Non-PRI Governments: The PAN in Ciudad Juarez and in Chihuahua," in V.E. Rodriguez and

P.M. Ward (eds) *Opposition Government in Mexico*, Albuquerque: University of New Mexico Press.
Weber, M. (1968) "Bureaucracy," in G. Roth and C. Wittich (eds) *Economy and Society*, New York: Bedminister Press.
——(1980) *Wirtschaft und Gesellschaft*, Tuebingen: J.C.B. Mohr (Paul Siebeck).
Weingast, B. (1995) "The Economic Role of Political Institutions," *Journal of Law, Economics, and Organization*, 7: 1–31.
——(1997) "The Political Foundations of Democracy and the Rule of Law," *American Political Science Review*, 91: 245–63.
——(2004) "Constructing Self-Enforcing Democracy in Spain," in I.L. Morris, J.A. Oppenheimer, and K. Soltan (eds) *Politics from Anarchy to Democracy: Rational Choice in Political Science*, Stanford: Stanford University Press.
——(2006) "Self-Enforcing Constitutions: With an Application to Democratic Stability in America's First Century," working paper, Hoover Institution.
Weiss, B.G. (1998) *The Spirit of Islamic Law*, Athens, GA: University of Georgia Press.
Wheeler, J.S. (1996) "Navy Finance, 1649–60," *Historical Journal*, 39: 457–66.
Widner, J.A. (2001) *Building the Rule of Law*, New York: W.W. Norton.
——(2008) "Building Judicial Independence in Semi-Democracies: Uganda and Tanzania," in T. Ginsburg and T. Moustafa (eds) *Rule by Law: The Politics of Courts in Authoritarian Regimes*, New York: Cambridge University Press.
Williams, R. (Archbishop of Canterbury) (2008) *Archbishop's Lecture – Civil and Religious Law in England: A Religious Perspective*. Online. Available HTTP: http://www.archbishopofcanterbury.org/1575 (accessed 19 October 2008).
Winn, B. and Davis, E. (2004) "Arbitration of Reinsurance Disputes: Is There a Better Way?" *Dispute Resolution Journal*, 59: 22–5.
World Bank (2005) *Economic Growth in the 1990s: Learning from a Decade of Reform*, Washington, DC: World Bank.
——(2006) *Doing Business 2007: How to Reform*, Washington DC: World Bank.
World Bank Institute (WBI) (2008) *Governance and Anti-Corruption*, Washington, DC: World Bank Group. Online. Available HTTP: www.worldbank.org/wbi/governance (accessed 14 November 2008).
World Justice Project (2007) *What Is the Rule of Law?* Washington, DC: American Bar Association. Online. Available HTTP: http://www.worldjusticeproject.org/ (accessed 14 November 2008).
Zakaria, F. (2003) *The Future of Freedom: Illiberal Democracy at Home and Abroad*, New York: Norton.
Zald, M.N. (1970) *Organizational Change*, Chicago: University of Chicago Press.
Zaman, M.Q. (2002) *The Ulama in Contemporary Islam: Custodians of Change*, Princeton: Princeton University Press.
Zilfi, M.C. (1988) *The Politics of Piety: The Ottoman Ulema in the Postclassical Age (1600–1800)*, Minneapolis: Bibliotheca Islamica.
Zubaida, S. (2003) *Law and Power in the Islamic World*, London: I.B. Tauris.

Index